Peter Finch

Trader Faulkner was born in Sydney, Australia. His father, John Faulkner, was a silent screen star and his mother, Sheila Whytock, a ballerina who toured with Pavlova. He began his theatre career in Sydney radio, and trained at the Mercury Theatre under Peter Finch. In 1950 he moved to London and was signed up immediately to replace Richard Burton in John Gielgud's New York production of *The Lady's Not For Burning*. On his return to London he was launched on a successful career in the theatre which included such parts as: Romeo; Henry V; the Moon in Peter Hall's London production of Lorca's *Blood Wedding*; and the juvenile Gaston, in Hall's production of *The Waltz of the Toreadors*. In 1955 at Stratford on Avon, he played Malcolm to Olivier's Macbeth, and Sebastian to Vivien Leigh's Viola in *Twelfth Night*. While under contract to the RSC back at Stratford in 1970 he devised and directed a programme on Garcia Lorca which was subsequently broadcast by BBC Radio 3, with the musical collaboration of Paco Peña. His films include: *Mr Denning Drives North*; *A Killer Walks*; *24 Hours in the Life of a Woman*; *A High Wind in Jamaica*; and *Murder Game*. He studied flamenco in Spain with Antonio Gades, and danced as guest artist with the famous Antonio in London at the Coliseum and Royalty theatres. Besides being an actor, director, and broadcaster, Trader Faulkner is a freelance writer, and translator from the Spanish, and has contributed short stories, articles and reviews to the *Guardian*, the *Observer*, and the *Financial Times*.

Trader Faulkner

Peter Finch

A biography

Pan Books London and Sydney

First published 1979 by Angus & Robertson (UK) Ltd
This edition published 1980 by Pan Books Ltd,
Cavaye Place, London SW10 9PG
© Trader Faulkner 1979
ISBN 0 330 26120 7
Typeset, printed and bound in Great Britain by
Hazell Watson & Viney Ltd, Aylesbury, Bucks

for **Sasha,** that she may grow up to understand human nature, but not judge it, and for **Anna Romana**

Contents

Worthy And pray, what induced you to turn soldier?
Serjeant Kite Hunger and ambition.

The Recruiting Officer,
by George Farquhar. Act III, Scene I

Acknowledgements

I undertook to write this book because I was promised and given very generous help from many people living all over the world who provided photos, letters and vivid memories and recollections that led to unexpected sources of information. The original manuscript turned out to be in the region of 200,000 words and had to be greatly reduced. It is hardly surprising that when I told the Hollywood film director, Robert Aldrich, what I was doing he exclaimed: 'Finch! You could write twenty books on Peter and you wouldn't have covered him.' This helped me realize that information was available and that the problem would be a matter of selection.

For curbing my literary self-indulgence, typing, cutting and correcting the manuscript, my gratitude and thanks to Kitty Black. For typing the manuscript in its various stages, my sincere thanks to Claire Harman, Rosemary Henning, Wendy Jones, Gina Martin and Denise Elman; to Barry Watts and Zeny Edwards (Angus & Robertson, Sydney), and Graham Shirley, for their untiring efforts and enthusiasm; Ian Dear and Jane Freebury (Angus & Robertson, Brighton) for their patience and Herculean labours.

T.F.

Australia : Ted Ardini; Queenie Ashton; Allan Ashbolt; Hugh Atkinson; The Australian Broadcasting Commission Archives; the *ABC Weekly*; Ray Barrett; Ray Bathgate; Ron Beck; Kenn Brodziak (J. C. Williamson Productions Pty Ltd); Sheila Brown; Central army records (Australian Army); Elsa Chauvel; Chris Collier; William Constable; Frank Curtain; Colonel & Mrs Jim Davidson; Elsie Dayne; Robin Down; Ray Edmondson; Alex Ezard; Bobo Faulkner (Mrs R. Rosenblum); Bertha (Betty) Finch; Doris Fitton, CBE; Karen Foley; Lynn Foster; Modesta Gentilé; Dennis Glenny; Ken G. Hall, OBE; Margaret Hayter (Mrs M. George); Cecil Holmes; Edward Howell; Lionel V. (Bill) Hudson; Lois Kay; Patricia Kelly; Rosalind Kennerdale (Mrs R. Cecil); Tom Lake; Ethel Lang (Mrs E.

Brunton Gibb); Hal Lashwood; Jack Lee; Enid Lorimer; Suzanne Loveday Lucas; Nigel Lovell; Cynthia Loxton (Finch); Marjorie Mant (Mrs B. Johnstone); Laurel Martyn (Mrs L. Lawton); Kate McLoughlin; Marian Morphee; Mel Nichols; Ena Noel; National Library of Australia, National Film Archive, Canberra; Max Osbiston; Fred Parsons; Ralph Peterson; Pauline Phillips; Redmond Phillips; Gwen Plumb; Bruce Powell; Susan Powell (Mrs Law-Smith); Leslie Rees; Rosa Ribush; Peter Richards; Elizabeth (Escolme) Schmidt; Dinah Shearing (Mrs Milgate); Thelma Scott; Anthony Scott-Veitch; *Smith's Weekly*; The Theosophical Society, Sydney; Al Thomas; Margot Thomas; Patricia Thompson; Peter Thompson; Charles (Bud) Tingwell; Dr C. C. Wark & Mrs Wark (Marcia Finch); Bruce Webber; Zel Wilkinson; Keith Wood.

Europe: Roger Barry; Jules Dassin; Yolande Turner Finch; Sophia Loren (Mrs C. Ponti); James Mason; George More O'Ferrall; Tom Rothfield; Liv Ullmann; A. van der Stok; Mr & Mrs Bertie Whiting (Bertie for the English translation of Hadrian's *Epitaph*).

India: Captain Dick Balfour Clarke; Rukmini Devi Arundale; The Theosophical Society, Madras.

Indonesia (Bali): Donald Friend.

Jamaica: Bertha (Mrs Barrett); Noel A. Black; Jennifer Daly; Norris Daly; Alistair Dougal; Merlyn Douglas; O. Maffessanti; The Honourable Beverly Manley; John E. McDowell; Sue McManus; Joe ('Blues') Morris; Lesley Nathan; Rex Nettleford; Mr & Mrs Ken Ross; Hope Sealy (Assistant Director of Tourism); The Jamaican Tourist Board (London); Eran Spiro; Robin Sweeney; Wilton Worms ('Carpie').

Republic of South Africa: Antoine Konstant.

United Kingdom: Barry Aingworth; Dorothy Alison; Irving Allen; Anita Appel; Dame Peggy Ashcroft, DBE; Sir Richard Attenborough, CBE; Maxine Audley; Sir Felix Aylmer, OBE; Alan Bates; Geoffrey Bayldon; Mr & Mrs Dick Bentley; Ian Bevan; Roy Boulting; Jeremy Boulton; Muriel Box (Lady Gardiner); Larry Boys; Mr & Mrs Kevin Brennan; Joyce Briggs; British Film Institute; Mr & Mrs Tony Britton; Jenny Bunce; Dennis Carey; James Cellan Jones; Diane Cilento;

Jack Clayton; Contemporary Films Ltd. (Mrs Steinhart); Yvonne Coulette (Mrs D. Carey); Rosalie Crutchley; Cyril Cusack; Nigel Davenport; Ed Devereaux; Bette Dickson (Mrs W. Thomas); Peter Duffell; Robin Eakin (Mrs R. Dalton); Sydney Edwards; Cary Ellison; EMI Films Ltd.; Alan Frank; Anita Finch; Michael Ingle Finch, DFC and Bar; Prince George Galitzine; Royal Geographical Society (Map Room); Sir John Gielgud; Penelope Gilliatt; Olive Harding; Ann Henning; Peter Hiley; Sir Harold Hobson; Ianthe Hoskins; Bill Humphreys; Hugh Hunt; Joseph Janni; Philip Jenkinson; Edward Judd; Arthur Kananack; Bill Kerr; Michael Klinger Ltd; Elizabeth Lambert (Mrs Ortiz); Lloyd Lamble; Mr & Mrs Jesse Lasky; Tom Lester; Patricia Lewis Plummer; Yvonne Littlewood; Jack Lynn; Iain Mackie; Flavia Magwood; Garth Magwood; Wolf Mankowitz; Andrew Mann; Laurene Marriott-Brittan; George Marshall; Sue Mason; Angus McBean; Peter McEnery; Virginia McKenna; C. J. Middleton; Yvonne Mitchell; Barry Morse; George Murcell; National Film Theatre; Peter Noble; Leslie Norman; Lord Olivier; Peter O'Toole; Ivan Page; Laurence Payne; Axel Poignant; Alan Poolman; Dilys Powell, CBE; Michael Powell; Elise Probert; Rank Film Library – Rank Audio Visual; Anthony Raymond; Vanessa Redgrave; Chris Rees; Madge Ryan; Dr & Mrs R. Scott-Russell; John Schlesinger; Peter Seward; R. H. Sharp; David Simeon; Jeanie Sims; Paul Sinclair; Sheila Smart; R. D. Smith; Michele Snapes; Julian Spiro; Betty Stavely-Hill; Robert Sterne; Melissa Stribling (Mrs B. Dearden); Harry Tatlock Miller; The Theosophical Society, London; Ralph Thomas; Wilfred Thomas; Rita Tushingham; Jennifer Unitt; Gudrun Ure; Alexander Walker; Warner Bros; Harry Watt; Dorothy Welford; Alan White; Billie Whitelaw; Trafford Whitelock; June Wimble (Mrs D. Pollard); Carla Worth; Fred Zinnemann.

United States of America: Dana Andrews; Ken Annakin; Irving Asher; Lloyd Backhouse; James Bacon; Hermione Baddeley; Bill Barron; Joe Bleeden; Ray Bradbury; Johnny Carson; Charles Champlin; John Chancellor; Gillian Clements; James Coburn; Joan Cohen (Los Angeles County Museum of Art); Joel Coler; Judith Crist; Walter Cronkite; Bosley Crowther; Michael Doherty; Joanne Dru (Mrs C. V. Wood); Jerry Dunphy;

Eletha Finch; Sherry Fleiner; Sam Gill (Margaret Herrick Library of the Academy of Motion Picture Arts and Sciences, Beverly Hills); Howard Gottfried; Hank Grant (for Miss Ullmann's Oscar presentation speech); Richard Greene (UCLA Medical Centre, LA); Merv Griffin; Radie Harris; J. Hartney Arthur; Anthony Harvey; William Holden; Ross Hunter; Ken Hughes; Pauline Kael; Ben Kamsler; Hal Kanter (for Miss Ullmann's Oscar presentation speech); Andrea Kaufman; Irvin Kershner; John Kaufman; Irving Klaw; Eric Knight; Paul Kohner; Barry Krost; Joyce Lambert; Betty Lasky (US researcher); Henry Levin; Ben Lyon; the *Los Angeles Herald Examiner*; the *Los Angeles Times*; Mr & Mrs Alexander MacKendrick; Patrick Mahony; Henry Manasero; Daniel Mann; Ben Mantz; Michael Maslansky; Paul Maslansky; Murray Matheson; John Means; Paul Myers; The Memory Shop (New York); *New York* Magazine; Chuck Panama; Barbara Pascin (BBC television, Los Angeles); Arthur Penn; Charles Pomerantz; Julian Portman; the Paramedics at No. 3 Station, Doheny Drive, LA; Shirley Ann Richards (Mrs E. Angelo); Tony Richardson; George Rose; Marion Rosenberg; Paul Ryan; Frank Schaap; Edgar J. Scherick; Richard Schickel; Dinah Shore; Howard K. Smith; Mr & Mrs Robert Stevenson; James Stewart; Andrew Stone; Larry Strawther; Kay Swift; David W. Tebet; the US television networks: ABC, CBS, NBC; India van Vorhees; Arnold Weissberger; Elmo Williams; Michael York; Gus A. Zelnick.

Foreword
by Liv Ullmann

Any meeting – any kind of collaboration in life – is truly real only in moments when you find somebody who is willing to communicate as a reachable and touchable human being. Somebody who dares to give of himself, to show himself.

Peter Finch was such a man – and this gave colour and substance to all his acting. What you saw on the screen was always true, because the person you were looking at was not only a figure in a film but a living man called Peter. Someone whose pride in his craft was such that he gave of his own dignity – through the instrument of his body and soul – to be as real as possible.

I worked with Peter in two films: *Lost Horizon* and *The Abdication*, movies as different from each other as winter in Norway and the sun of California. But whatever he might have felt in his heart about being in a musical that made very small demands on his acting ability – in *Lost Horizon* I never saw him share less of himself, or cheat in the work that was perhaps more unreal and strange to him than that required by *The Abdication*, a picture he loved making and which turned out to be one of his very last movies.

You can never act or give more than the material allows you. I had the great privilege of watching Peter give of himself as honestly to the one film as to the other.

There are many memories: his moods, his happiness when he was surrounded by his beloved family, meeting him daily for several months on the set, laughing with him, striving to achieve something together, and understanding and being understood without too many words. They all belong to one of the most human and fulfilling artistic contacts of my life.

Peter had so much to give. I believe that few people who came close to him will stop wondering why he is no longer here with us, because he was so much alive.

No one who experienced moments of self-recognition when Peter was working can say they are untouched by him today. So maybe, in a strange way he who gave so much in life, was so alive, makes our loss easier to bear. Because he left behind him so many paths.

July 1978

Author's note

Peter Finch was a household name as an actor in Australia and a legend in his own lunchtime among his friends and colleagues, when I first met him early in 1946. He had known of my father, then forgotten, who had been a silent screen star in the Australian film industry during the 1920s. My father died when I was seven during the Depression, but Peter had seen and admired what was considered at the time to have been his best film, *Blue Mountains Mystery*, made in 1921, and another, *Tanami*, made in 1928 – both are now lost. Peter was curious to know more about Dad and in 1946 was working with many of my father's friends and contemporaries, still alive and active in the profession. Peter's wife, Tamara, had come to Australia with the de Basil Monte Carlo Ballets-Russes Company in 1939, and knew my mother who was also a ballerina, so mutual interests and curiosity began my friendship with Finchie, as he affectionately became known to many – a friendship that was to last until his death thirty years later.

Through a chance encounter with Peter Finch in a crowded theatre, the course of my life was altered. It caused me to abandon my original idea of going to university to study for the diplomatic service, and to choose the acting career which Peter urged me to take up. Indirectly this has led to my writing this book.

Sydney theatregoers had been turning out *en masse* to the old Theatre Royal to see the first London-style production to reach Australia since before the war. It was Noel Coward's *Tonight at 8.30*, starring the Australian husband and wife team Cyril Ritchard and Madge Elliott. A packed house had once again wildly applauded and was wending its way out of the theatre to the strains of the orchestra playing *We're Regency Rakes*, when my companion tapped me on the arm, saying 'Come and meet Peter Finch.' A few days before, this same person had held me spellbound with a performance he had given on radio as the mad Russian Czar Paul the First, in a play by Ashley Dukes called *Such Men Are Dangerous*.

My first and lasting impression of Finchie was of a withdrawn man, with a quiet assurance in his own ability as a remarkable actor which belied his vulnerability. He was extremely thin and not very tall, with brown wavy hair long at the back, fine prominent cheek bones, a high intelligent forehead, and wonderful magnetic eyes that seemed to change constantly from hazel to greenish-blue. He was round-shouldered which made him appear hollow-chested and look as though he had a slight hump. But the feature that I suppose made me realize he'd have enormous appeal for women, was the full sensual mouth like a tulip. I remember thinking 'you look like one of those timeless characters from the eastern region of the Mediterranean'.

Little was said at that first introduction but he invited me to meet him a few days later in Repin's coffee house in King Street, in the city. I arrived at Repin's at the appointed time to see seated in one of the booths, a wild, flamboyant character (all I could see was an untidy shock of hair) who was waving a pair of very expressive hands at his audience, who were all helpless with laughter. The voice was unmistakable. Finchie was doing his impersonation of the perpetual 'whinge'. A 'whinge' is Australian slang for a moaning, complaining pessimist, who never knows when he is lucky. It was an impersonation I was often to hear subsequently, and I never tired of seeing the new, additional inventive touches. It was a piece which Finch rendered inimitable through his timing and miming.

I was embraced, caught up in the hilarity, and I joined in the laughter as Finchie gave his impression of a randy homosexual camel searching desperately among the desert sand-dunes for a mate with similar inclinations. The whole of Repin's, customers and staff, were by this time paralytic with laughter. This irresistible clown, who never realized the comic aspect of his many selves on film, then began to discuss the theatre and what he felt about acting and the cinema.

Acting, according to Finchie, was the art of saying a thing on the stage or screen, with the conviction that what you speak is as true as the eternal truths of mankind. But it must come absolutely spontaneously. No actor rates as an actor until he has the technique to conceal from an audience his own personal manipulation of the scene and circumstances. The greatest actor is a kind of puppeteer, who makes **you** laugh and cry.

We sat in Repin's regardless of time, hour after hour, while he held us enthralled. As far as I was concerned, it was a case of the ancient mariner riveting the attention of the young wedding guest and leading him off into a world of greater awareness and a realm of fantasy. He described a well-written play as a musical score. The same applied concentration and preparation was as necessary for the actor as for the musician.

He said that he wanted to take on the challenge of playing Molière's *Don Juan* in repertoire with a good adaptation of Tirso de Molina's original seventeenth-century Spanish classic. Finchie felt it was impossible to find a definitive way of interpreting the man. Don Juan was to him an archetype, a symbol, which was best portrayed by the French and Spanish playwrights, who could ring the changes between the mental, physical and spiritual in such a way that all the conflict that makes a character interesting was there, with detached, satirical humour. Above all, there was no sentimentality in their works.

His conversation then turned to Annie Besant, the head of the Theosophical Movement, who had taught him the secret of concentration in India. He said he was reading Ouspensky. Finchie, a theatrical jackdaw *par excellence*, had just discovered the bestseller *Tertium Organum*, and was giving us the Finchie treatise on the content of the book, which dealt with subjects ranging from yoga to Einstein's theory of relativity. Finchie, mouthing Ouspensky's ideas, informed us, all now sitting in dumb amazement, that we went through our lives sound asleep. Our states of consciousness, awake or asleep, were pretty much the same. By now he was sitting cross-legged on the inglenook bench, looking rather like a young Buddha. Most of the talk was way above my head and, I suspect, over the heads of all his listeners – we were all very young, certainly a good ten years younger than Finchie. It was like listening to someone speaking in a foreign language, of which you have a smattering and feel intense relief at being able to understand the occasional word. I remember him saying: 'Your "I" doesn't exist. There are a thousand different "I"s, and a good actor or actress can reveal thousands of truthfully observed "I"s.'

I noticed that this dazzling chameleon was left-handed, as the little pile of cigarette butts (invariably other people's, which in a moment of inspired oratory he would take out of the smoker's mouth and finish off himself) rose to a pyramid on his Repin's saucer.

Suddenly he got tired of talking endlessly about the theatre and began to discuss the spirit of Anzac, the impulse that had driven him to have a stiff whisky and go down to Martin Place in Sydney with a mate, Buddy Morley, and join the Australian Army. He talked too about the First World War, and what the sweet sickly smell of mustard gas must have been like. Had we noticed how many of the Sydney tram and bus conductors were First World War veterans? The nervous tic from shell-shock, the hacking, retching cough that always identified the middle-aged or elderly man who had been in the trenches in France.

In his teens he had rubbed shoulders and drunk with many of the old Anzacs with their crutches, wooden legs, missing ears and noses. He told us that during the Depression in Australia the Defence Department had opened up the warehouses and taken out of mothballs and distributed Army surplus greatcoats. Finchie had managed, he said, to get hold of one, about two sizes too large, to keep him warm. 'They got out of storage all over the country,' he said, 'bits and pieces of uniforms left over from 1918, dyed them a dull black, and handed them out.'

Finchie wasn't moved by any feelings of patriotic fervour, but he was deeply imbued with the spirit of Anzac. To him Gallipoli meant the bawdy, irreverent, slouch-hatted hobo, the larrikin; the man able to persevere against heavy odds, the Australian bushman turned soldier, the Rabelaisian vandal with the capacity to live or die in the instant; a comrade in arms yet never an intimate friend. He said that in the Anzac he could identify with the violence he felt when he was acting or drinking.

According to Australian Central Army Records, NX26035 Peter George Finch served on continuous full time service for a total effective period of 1,494 days which included 1,178 days active service in Australia and 265 days active service overseas. In 1942, my mother was in Martin Place, Sydney, when Peter gave an address in front of several thousand people to encourage the war effort. His appeal however didn't impress one woman who stepped forward from the crowd and pressed something into his hand. He held it up to see what it was: 'I found myself holding up a white feather in front of several thousand people!'

I'd gone in to have a cup of coffee about four o'clock. By nine, we were discussing films.

Finchie was tremendously influenced at this time by the great French screen actors of the 1930s and 1940s, and his great ambition was to go to France and work with Louis Jouvet.

Having spoken French all through his early childhood, he felt he would have little difficulty in getting back into the swing of the language. What he admired was the total professionalism the French actors brought to their craft, crystallized for him in the two great films, *La Kermesse Heroique* and *Les Enfants du Paradis*. Subsequently he took me to see both films at a remote cinema in Narrabeen, and I realized at once the style and standard for which he as an actor and potential director was aiming. This was a form of expression and a working way of life which I wished to follow. I abandoned all thoughts of the diplomatic service and the Royal Australian Navy and joined Finchie's gypsy caravan into the no-man's-land of the actor's world.

In those days I was naïve, very idealistic. Peter widened my artistic horizon, and became a mentor and elder brother figure. He told me much later, 'You needed toughening up and like all actors you lacked self-discipline.' I accepted his harsh attitude because I respected him as an artist who was an even better doer than he was a talker.

I saw a great deal of Peter during 1946, 1947 and 1948, and as a serious-minded student I used to jot down notes of a great deal of what he said. In later years he mellowed and the camaraderie which grew out of the Mercury Theatre days remained. In London he would often ring up or arrive unexpectedly at the houseboat *Stella Maris* – where I lived in the 1950s and 1960s on the Thames at Chelsea – and we'd open a bottle of wine and talk for hours, and sometimes days.

But Peter was very much a myth even to himself. So much of his reality was fantasy. He was a child-man who never grew up but remained an incomparable actor. What I have tried to do is to give a feeling of the quintessential Peter who started me off in the theatre, who remained a friend and influence, and about whom I often had ambivalent feelings. Through the many people to whom I have spoken about Peter, whose opinions and recollections add up to what I feel is an accurate impression, I have tried to weave personal experiences of the Finchie I knew.

A great deal of Peter's life and his secret self must remain secret, and conflicting opinions in the memories of those who remember and want to talk about him. One professional researcher whom I approached to verify my facts assured me that, in twenty years of biographical research, she had never encountered anything so baffling, contradictory or bizarre as Peter

Finch's background: 'The stories of the family all conflict, and a great number of Peter's statements to the press seem now to be totally unreliable.' I could only reply that any actor as good as Peter, with his imagination, would hardly be reliable when it came to anecdotes and recollections of his extraordinary life. Peter himself always believed in exaggeration: 'All actors exaggerate,' he said, 'and as a philosopher, Marcus Aurelius had the answer: "All things in moderation, including moderation".'

As for the reliability of statements made about Peter by various members of his family who had completely lost touch with him for thirty years – who would expect them to tally? The man Peter allowed us to know was very much a creature of fantasy, but what redeemed all his bullshit and nonsense was his great intelligence, his humour and charm, and his professional ability, where few could match him. He was certainly one of the most interesting and complex men I ever knew, and a man of enormous internal conflict. He once told me in an unguarded moment that his inclination to be high on alcohol was to deaden the feeling of the incomprehensible sterility of our everyday existence, sold to us for money; this showed his deep rooted feeling of spiritual isolation. His isolation condemned him to self inquiry which released itself through the characters he portrayed which were unerringly true. More often than not he couldn't separate himself inwardly from his own gallery of characters, all an extension of Peter because they were an expression of his isolation. Like the onion, Peter could shed many skins, but Peter the man behind the protean mask never surrendered to total possession by any woman. Peter the aspiring writer, natural painter, and marvellous actor, belonged nowhere, and always speaking other people's ideas was almost more than a soul of Peter's awareness could endure.

Wherever possible I have tried to let Peter speak for himself, as I vividly remember him doing through to the early hours of many mornings over the years. The phone would ring at three in the morning: 'G'day you bludger (Australian slang for sponging loafer), how's the tide? I'm on my way round, go down into your bilges and get some wine and have it ready.' Like the English sunshine he'd appear when least expected at rare intervals but always welcome. The last time I ever spoke to him, on the phone, he told me he had thought out a private code word Jax.

'What the hell are you talking about Finchie?' I said. Things were going really well for him and he sounded on top of the world. 'If you get a note from me or a call saying there's plenty of Jax around, you'll know there's a fiesta brewing. So get out the castanets and we'll dance and drink, or I might say no Jax.' 'Yes Finchie,' I said, 'that'll mean you've quarrelled with your love and you'll be in for a drop of consolation and a long talk until you're ready to face the day.' 'I'm learning to be a Jax alchemist,' he told me, 'I think I've found the elixir of a little peace of mind. It comes with getting old, accepting it and not being on your own.'

'I've buggered up my own career,' he once told me, 'by going off all over the world, but I feel the urge to live my way as greatly as I feel the need to act. It depends how important money and fame are to you. It's a question sometimes of whether you want to be a really good artist or to create that myth they call success – the two don't necessarily go together.'

1 Finch among the foxes

Peter's birth and early childhood have been a rich seam for mining out myths, conjecture and some very funny anecdotes by many good raconteurs and not least by Finchie himself. A great deal of what Peter told me during our years of friendship turned out to be very like the history we were subjected to at school: the facts pretty dull and difficult to remember, the legends fascinating, memorable and the inspiration for many subsequent works of art.

When I spoke to Peter's agent, Olive Harding of MCA, who nursed him financially and professionally through the first twenty-two years of his English career, I was told: '... You know you'll have to talk to Mum.' Thanks to Olive's tact and diplomacy, Peter's mother, now aged eighty-four and known to a number of her friends as Betty, agreed to see me. I had been warned by several people that she was fed up with the incessant attempts made by people wanting the historical facts and a good story, to rake up a past from which she had suffered and which she wanted to forget. I had seen her, supported by her other two children, Michael and Flavia, at Peter's memorial service at St Paul's Church, Covent Garden, looking pretty dazed and shattered. As I stood at her glass-fronted door in Chelsea, watching a blurred figure slowly advancing, I regretted I hadn't gone up to her then and offered my sympathy.

A small, elderly lady, with very beautiful thick grey hair and a guarded expression in her hazel eyes opened the door – how often I'd seen that look in Finchie's – bade me a polite good-afternoon and asked me in.

She gave me a very liberal whisky and we sat for a while in complete silence. Suddenly she smiled and with devastating charm informed me that she remembered nothing. Her mind was a complete blank, as far as Peter was concerned, until he had rung her up in 1948 and said: 'I'm your son Peter. Would it embarrass you if I came back into your life again?'

There was a long silence.

'We loved each other – my mind is a complete blank!'

'Well, that's a good start,' I said, and I started laughing.

Betty must have been a very beautiful young woman, who, like Finchie, had a fatal fascination for the opposite sex. She has been loved by many men. Mother and son both understood instinctively how best they could survive and get what they wanted from life, with self-assurance and beguiling charm.

'Have another whisky,' she said. 'You know Peter was a breech birth? He landed feet first.'

I said: 'That would explain a lot. The splayed-in pigeon-toed walk. Probably you were the first woman he ran away from when he realized just what a world you'd dropped him into.'

She told me Finchie made his first appearance at two in the afternoon of 28 September 1916, in a nursing home in Courtfield Gardens, South Kensington, a few doors down from where my former wife, Bobo, and I were living when we first married in 1963. In the many subsequent meetings I had with Betty Finch and members of Peter's family on both sides, the following pattern has emerged:

Captain George Ingle Finch, serving with the Royal Field Artillery, had married Alicia Gladys Fisher (no relation, in spite of what has been quoted in the press, of Admiral 'Jackie' Fisher), on 16 June 1915, in the Registry Office in Portsmouth. Betty maintains that it is very difficult for anyone who hadn't grown up as a young, upper middle-class girl before 1914 to understand what many people did when the First World War broke out.

'I was living on the Isle of Wight. I was at the age when you go to a lot of dances. Suddenly the war came and everything changed radically for ever. At first we thought it would all be over by Christmas but, by 1915, men were dying by the thousand. You do mad things, and my first marriage was the sort of thing a young girl of my background and temperament did. No one knew what was going to happen and we all went mad. Boys were going off to the front and they were dead within a week. George was a remarkably handsome man, brilliant, tough and exceptionally brave. But he seemed indifferent to comfort and to the social swing in which I was involved. There was that feeling of euphoria and living in the moment, the gaiety before the international storm which was to sweep over Europe and alter the course of our lives.

'I had lived a sheltered life, and had no idea or thought about anything outside my limited, shallow circle. George went out to

Salonika and I met Jock Campbell at a dance. He was a Major in the Black Watch. Jock was a darling and I fell madly in love with him, but he was far too gentle and kind to me. I treated him very badly but for a time we were very happy. I needed a stronger, less kind man. George was certainly that, but my marriage to George was a terrible mistake. We were just temperamentally unsuited.'

Betty's father, Frederick William Fisher, a barrister, had died when she was nine. Her mother had remarried. She seldom saw her mother, but remembers an Uncle Bill, who had married one of her aunts, as being the really kind and gentle influence in her life. She was an only child and spent her early years living with relatives in Kent. She was sent to finishing school in Paris and was one of the 'Gay Young Things' by the summer of 1914.

George Ingle Finch was born in Orange, New South Wales, in 1888, the eldest son of Charles E. Finch, who was chairman of the Land Court of New South Wales and an internationally known authority on land law. George had his early primary education in Australia, but received his secondary education under private tutors in Europe. The interest in mountaineering for which he became famous began in Paris when, having escaped his tutor, he made an attempt, with his brother Max, to scale the walls of Notre Dame. He studied medicine in Paris, but soon switched to physical sciences, and graduated in Zurich with a gold medal for his diploma course. He became an eminent scientist, and Zurich also afforded him the opportunity to develop his outstanding skill as a mountaineer. By 1913 he had become demonstrator as a research chemist in the Department of Chemical Technology of Imperial College, London. He fought at Mons, was mentioned in dispatches and awarded the MBE. He was a fighting soldier *par excellence* and despised his fellow officers who 'lived soft'. (I got the impression from Finchie and Betty that George took himself very seriously.) He was one of thousands of officers constantly on the move in the early years of the First World War, as units were formed and reformed to go to the front, so that it is impossible to pinpoint where he actually was at any given time during this period.

According to George's side of the family, he took his marriage very seriously, and decided at first to overlook Betty's infatuation with Jock Campbell (Major Wentworth Edward Dallas Campbell first served in the Black Watch Regiment, then transferred to the

Poona Horse Regiment of the Indian Army), but Betty was deeply in love with him and although living with George for appearances' sake, disenchantment with her marriage had already set in. They had nothing in common, but for two years after Peter was born, they continued to live together as man and wife. Betty affirms she had given up Jock to try and salvage the marriage, but the Finch family say that when she carried on her love affair with Jock a second time, George's patience gave out and he decided to take action. What still amazes Betty after sixty years, is the manner in which baby Peter, aged two, vanished from the garden of their home in Lewes, Sussex. Having consulted his solicitors, George had been advised to remove the child from its mother's care and assume custody of him to strengthen his divorce case. In 1918 the harsh Victorian laws deprived an adulterous mother of the custody of her children even if they were young, and especially if they were male; and the child was his in law, unless Betty could stand up in court and prove categorically that he was not.

To be fair to George, who can never give his side of the story (nor would he, I am told, talk about it when he was alive), Uncle Antoine, with whom Peter subsequently lived in Paris, was given to understand that George, and his sister Dorothy who was working in a London hospital, rescued little Peter from his mother in Folkestone where he was being fed champagne by a roomful of very inebriated officers. All three departed for Paris where Peter was left with George's mother, Laura Finch and her son Antoine, as Dorothy, much as she would have liked to, could not look after the boy because of her work as a VAD. Whatever the hard facts, Finchie never remembered how he got to Paris and Betty assures me she last saw him in the garden at Lewes.

Finchie told me that when he first came to London he had gone to see George. The old man, then president of the Alpine Club, had given him a very cool reception.

'I'm sorry to disappoint you, young man,' he said, 'but you're not really my son.'

Finchie tacitly agreed to let that one go. He felt he was really in no position to argue.

'Whose am I then?'

'Better ask your mother.'

The subject then turned to the war and George, apparently,

had no time for soldiers who spent their time dressing up and shirking the issue by joining a concert party and entertaining the troops. Peter, the soldier-actor, obviously stuck in George's gullet. As George had decided to run this encounter with Peter on a collision course, Finchie decided on evasion tactics and let George vent his spleen on Betty, the past, and Peter to his heart's content. Finchie didn't mention his early war career begun the day he volunteered for the Australian Imperial Forces as a gunner in 1941. (George and Peter both served in their respective wars as gunners: George as an officer, and Peter as an ordinary soldier who rose to the rank of sergeant.) George either remained in ignorance of Peter's service in Syria, Palestine, and the defence of Darwin, or chose to ignore it.

Peter respected George's achievements as a scientist and mountaineer – George had attempted Everest with Mallory and Bruce, and in 1922 he and Captain Bruce reached the height of 27,300 feet before having to turn back, and pioneered the use of oxygen for climbing purposes – but felt that he 'must have burnt up a lot of his valuable energy putting the knife into my mother'. George, according to Finchie, had little interest in the man he claimed was not his son and they went their separate ways.

Betty knows that many people cannot accept that an intelligent and respected man like George Ingle Finch would take a child from his mother that was not his own. Why should he bother? Betty affirms she moved heaven and earth to get Peter back later, but was told by the lawyers she had no case against George who, as the wronged man, was in an impregnable position.

Years later Peter saw the funny side of it when he said to me: 'Was it a dog-in-the-manger attitude on George's part, or were they all really convinced I was a little black Campbell? I was passed along the line of Finches like a football through a rugby team. From two to fourteen I changed hands faster than a dud pound note.'

Peter loved his mother but he had those ambivalent moments of love-hate which most of us feel towards our parents. He once said to her: 'Mum, you've been a bit of a bitch to me, letting me go like that.' To which Mother replied: 'When you're as old as I am, my boy, you may have learned to understand.'

He told me repeatedly, usually when he'd had a lot to drink, that his feelings of having been abandoned when he was young had had their effect on him. I reminded him that his abandoning of his own daughter Anita had certainly had its effect on her, and would be bound to have its effect on his other children, Samantha and Charles. That if he really felt he had been abandoned, he had evened up the score pretty substantially with Tamara and Yolande, and his children by them. Mother and son were obviously very alike.

Finchie went to see Jock Campbell in London in the 1950s and felt that he **must** be Dad. He had a great sense of humour, didn't take himself very seriously, was a fine horseman and didn't criticize Peter for his choice of profession or way of life. Mother and Jock both assured Peter that he was theirs, so he decided he'd have two fathers as publicity and the occasion demanded. In Jamaica he claimed he was a Campbell, as Jock's predecessors had plantation estates in Jamaica. Finchie often used to joke about his possible black Jamaican relations! Preparing the speech he had to make at a Government reception in Kingston for Sir Clifford Campbell, the first Jamaican Governor General, he asked his friend Ken Ross to hear him through it.

'The opening of my speech to His Excellency shall be as follows: "You are a Campbell. I too am part of your clan, but you, sir, are quite the blackest Campbell I have ever set eyes upon ...", ' and Flavia, Peter's half-sister, asked me point blank if I had ever noticed that the palms of Peter's hands and the soles of his feet were pink! Flavia is convinced there was a touch of the tar brush in Peter and she always gives her mother, who can't abide being reminded of who Jock's ancestors might have been, an unmerciful teasing about it.

On the other hand he was quite happy to be George's son when the occasion demanded. Crossing over from Dover to Calais with his second wife Yo and the children in the 1960s, an elderly lady, wife of a great mountaineer, saw a man whose appearance seemed very familiar. He was alone at the taffrail, looking across as the ship approached France.

'Excuse me, but you remind me of a man whose father I know very well.'

'Oh yes,' said Peter, 'Who?'

'George Ingle Finch. You remind me of Peter Finch.'

'I am Peter Finch.'

'I thought you must be.'

'Do you like him?' asked Peter.

'Well . . . I like you much better.'

Finchie was amused and delighted and carried her heavy suitcase until he found her a porter.

Jock, with the Poona Horse Regiment of the Indian Army, married Betty in the Register Office at Weymouth, Dorset, in 1922. Once married, Betty had a stronger case for getting Peter back, but Jock was recalled suddenly to India. They had to leave England at once, for the province of Jumkundi, south of Delhi, as the Maharajah of Jumkundi had been rolled on by an elephant and hadn't survived the experience. His heir was still too young to rule, so Jock was appointed Regent. For two years Betty had a delirious time as the First Lady of Jumkundi.

Meanwhile, in Paris, Finchie was adapting happily to his new surroundings at Grandmother Laura's. It was a free and easy, very *avant-garde* little French community and Peter later considered himself very lucky, as an artist, not to have had the traditional English prep and public school background, but to have spent his childhood among all sorts of weird and exciting people who played games with him and treated him as an equal. They lived in a little villa and he remembers Isadora Duncan, with very little on, doing a sort of free Egyptian dance to music played on the harp by his grandmother, who sat dressed in a Grecian tunic with a gold bandeau round her head. He'd remembered the tune, and years later found out that it was Debussy's *Danse Sacrée et Danse Profane*. 'It was *profane* all right,' said Finchie, 'though at the time I didn't realize just how profane and marvellous she was.'

One night a shy little man came to the house. A lot of strange and exciting music was played and Peter, never a child who was put to bed before all the fun began, watched this character, who reminded him of an amazing bird, leap about the room like a grasshopper. Finchie remembered him as being terribly withdrawn. He didn't talk much to anyone, and seemed like an animal they'd brought into the room who didn't belong there. He had a very soft voice. It was Nijinsky.

Next door to Laura Finch there was an eccentric animal painter, who painted tigers like Douanier Rousseau, and he kept one in the studio. 'It stank the place out,' Peter said, 'enough to make you a vegetarian for life,' and he was absolutely terrified of it, for whenever the tiger saw him, it rushed to the window (barred, of course) and roared at him like the MGM lion.

Finchie would grab Argos, Antoine's dog who was his constant companion, and scuttle up into his howdah among the trees.

Peter adored both Uncle Antoine and his grandmother. 'My grandmother was a great Bohemian in her time,' he told me once, 'she wore the equivalent of those gold-looking coats that some of the glamorous pop singers wear today which, along with the gold bandeau and the lamé dresses, made her for me the most exotic, marvellous woman I can ever remember.'

Laura Finch had a tremendous zest for life. She had married Charles Finch in Australia, given him three children, George, Max and Dorothy, and then found life in Sydney too provincial and narrow for her *avant-garde*, Bohemian way of life and had taken the three children to Europe. She sang beautifully, and was a very lovely, statuesque, uninhibited woman, according to Peter, rather unconventional, like Vanessa Redgrave and Jane Fonda, whom he also admired in their way. Certainly, Laura Finch would join in any procession that went by with a banner.

It was in Paris that Laura became imbued with Spiritualism, and Finchie joined in the fun. 'I pretended that I saw spirits, and I used to create these imaginary characters and rush into the house and tell her I saw a grey man standing under the trees in the garden. I'd wait till it was dusk and in that eerie light, I'd play these tricks on her. She believed me and whenever I saw these strange characters of my fancy, I'd describe them to her in detail: a French soldier I'd seen in a book in the uniform of Napoleon's time; or a cowled monk; or some beautiful, medieval French lady in a wimple. Grandmother would reward me and, later, she began to write stories about me and my fairy characters, but that was in India.'

One day, around 1925, Finchie recalled that one of her spirits had advised her to commit suicide. She found a revolver, belonging to her illegitimate son, went upstairs, and pointed it at her temple. Finchie peeped through the keyhole to see how she was going to make her exit. He saw her point the gun through the window and fire.

'I put my hands over my ears as I could never stand loud noises (that's why my army record was never as good as George's). I rushed in and she swore to me that the spirit that had ordered her to shoot herself came and guided her hand away from her temple and actually pointed the gun through the window. The spirit must have had a great sense of humour because the bullet narrowly missed the postman who was not only supposed to be her lover but was arriving with some very important mail from India which was soon to alter the course of my life still further. There was a hell of a scandal because the postman was convinced she was trying to kill him. It was pure Jacques Tati.

'I was lucky because I was never close enough to Laura to be tied to her apron strings. She was even more of an eccentric egoist than I am, and I suppose I must have learned a great deal from her subconsciously as an actor. I'm very grateful to George for sending me to her and that I lived with her as long as I did. Of course, I never ever got in her line of fire. She finally died in Darjeeling, writing pamphlets for Gandhi.'

I confirmed as much as I could of Finchie's reminiscent anecdotes of his Paris days with Uncle Antoine, who vividly remembers his half-sister Dorothy arriving with Peter. 'Neither Nijinsky nor Isadora visited us at Vaucresson,' says Antoine, but, having left home early in Peter's sojourn with Granny, it is possible that Vaslav and Isadora did come and perform at *soirées chez Laura* at a later date. However Antoine is sure Peter met them, 'at a house we visited at Garches, a few miles on the Paris side of Vaucresson, belonging to Jan Styka, a Polish painter, whose enormous canvases (mainly of Polish battle scenes) covered acres of wall in his house. Jan had two sons – Tadé famed for his portraits, and Adam, also a painter who did mainly landscapes. Visiting Jan Styka's house may have remained in Peter's mind as happening in our modest villa at Vaucresson, and given him the impression it was *avant-garde*. Styka kept open house, and particularly on Sundays we would all meet there, singers, musicians, writers . . .'

In 1925 Laura, her daughter Dorothy, and Peter, went to India, via Colombo. Laura had an enthusiastic interest in Theosophy and Buddhism and planned to attend the Fiftieth International Convention of Theosophists in Adyar, Madras. Peter stayed with her at Adyar but Dorothy went on to Australia.

2 Young Bhikkhu

Finchie claimed that his grandmother sold him to a Buddhist monk in Madras. Like Granny's harp, which she was supposed to take to parties, it made a good anecdote and got plenty of laughs, but according to a ninety-three year old eye-witness who, at Grandmother Laura's insistence, tried to assume some responsibility for Peter at that time, it doesn't tally with the facts.

Laura Finch was very anxious that Peter, a gregarious mischievous little boy who was getting bored playing under the giant banyan tree at Adyar, should be kept amused. Totally uninhibited, he would just go up to anybody and start talking to them. When he made friends one day in the crowded compound with a benign Buddhist monk, who was among the 3,000 delegates of religious sects from all over the world who had gathered for the fiftieth annual convention of the Theosophical Society (presided over by Mrs Annie Besant, Bishop Leadbeater and Krishnamurti), Laura was delighted and encouraged the friendship. She had no idea he'd suddenly just go walkabout with his new-found friend and vanish.

Finchie's account of India, one night over dinner when he had limited himself to one glass of wine, was more in keeping with what has subsequently come to light from Madras.

'My grandmother was very much interested in Theosophy and Buddhism and when I was nine we went first to Colombo to this Mahabodhi Buddhist Society, set up by a Colonel Alcot who was a Theosophist and friend of my grandmother. Her daughter, my Aunt Dorothy, had gone with us to Colombo from Paris, but she went on to Australia to carry on with her nursing career. All I remember of that was being told that King Asoka, a follower of the great Buddha, took a branch of the great Bodhi tree from Northern India and planted it in Ceylon. Very soon after that we went across on a boat and then a long very hot train journey up to Madras for this big Theosophical gathering where thousands of people had come from everywhere.

'My grandmother was caught up with her Theosophy and

found me more than a handful at nine years of age, so, left to amuse myself, I made friends with this shaven-headed monk. He invited me to go with him into the city and he and I wandered through the streets of Madras begging for food, mainly rice and oil. The mendicant priests weren't allowed to beg for money – only the barest necessities. What an education! If you want to see real poverty, go to India, where people are born, live out their lives and die on the pavement. We slept on boards on the floor of this little house and spent a great deal of time in meditation. I remember it was a very hard floor and I found it hard to sit still and meditate. Although this man was only a teacher and friend for about ten days, a lot of what he, and later Mrs Besant, taught me stayed in my mind.

'In France I had been vaguely aware of all that strict French Catholic church-going, the everlasting *Ave Marias*, and hell if you weren't a good boy. I was never a good boy, so hell was the prospect I'd come to terms with.'

Then at Adyar he learned from the monk the story of this Buddha. 'It was explained to me very simply. A lot of it I didn't understand at the time, but I did understand that sickness and old age were pain, and that pain could be caused by wanting to possess things. I understood that we may have all had previous lives, that the things that happen to us are possibly a result, for good or bad, of something we have done before. I could accept that what you do you have to pay for, you have to expiate.' He was told his Karma was all his past lives and actions. 'I began to think of myself sometimes as a cat, with nine or many more lives. A cat, like Kipling's cat in *The Just So Stories*, that could go off alone and discover the marvellous places and people of my imagination, of my secret world, I knew that Nirvana was where this cat had to get to in the end. I have always hated violence and I suppose it was because I instinctively believed what I was taught in Madras: that it is wrong to take life; that we all begin in a very humble way; we may have many, many lives, perhaps as an insect, a bird, or an animal.' He could accept and believe, not so much in a God, but that a man could reach Nirvana by his own use of reason and wisdom. 'They had shaved my head by this time, and I had my uniform, a robe which they called saffron, a yellow-orange colour. I didn't have to wear shoes, and I felt wonderfully free and cool. I had my begging-bowl for oil or corn or any food I could con people into giving me. I used to love to go into the temple where it was dark and shadowy, where there was a big statue of this calm, cross-legged Buddha with the long ears, and talk to him and ask him all sorts of questions. You become very attached to certain symbols, if they are part of your life at an early age. I mean, look at the cross and the effect it has on people.'

Finchie also told me about a huge colourful religious procession at Adyar in which he and Laura took part. When Krishnamurti was pointed out to him, he said he didn't realize the solemnity of the occasion and raced out and asked 'The World Teacher' for his autograph, that Krishnamurti gave it, and that later Krishnamurti gave him a stamp album.

The story of the *churel* which Finchie heard in India haunted him for the rest of his life. The *churel* was a peculiarly malignant ghost of a woman who had died in childbirth. She would wait for the passing traveller on lonely roads with her feet turned back to front on her ankles, and she would lead naughty boys into a place of terrible torment (Finchie must have been giving the Theosophists hell with his antics and they were probably trying to put a rein on him).

He was amazingly articulate about India and remembered one experience that was so beautiful and so sensual that it remained with him always. A line of young girls was moving through a narrow defile in a high bank and down towards the river. He described in detail how they walked as all Indian women do, with such aristocratic movements, such measureless tradition, such control of every muscle and yet so supple, so flexible. Under their flowing saris, they wore a tight-fitting short-sleeved bodice, dotted with small pieces of mirror, that glinted in the setting sun. Each one carried on her head one of those jars, exquisitely balanced, with the sort of decorations he saw later in Rhodes. Their beautiful bare arms were hung with several bangles above the wrist, and round their ankles what he remembered as large silver hoops. They had such poise, they moved slowly and their feet seemed to spread as they walked. There was a silence, the kind of silence you get in the Australian bush that is deafening. Each one came to the stream, removed the jar from her head, filled it, stood up, placed the jar on the top of her head and glided off into the dusk. 'I must have been about nine, but I shall never forget it. I've always loved women who can move well. It may have had a lot to do with why I first fell in love with and married a dancer. It certainly aroused in me a feeling of wanting to touch and caress a woman's limbs. It was one of those hot, airless afternoons. I can remember I was terribly excited by it.

'In those market places you'll see the people of India, every caste, every shade of brown and olive skin, idling, meditating, chattering, begging, rescuing their kids, and always those liquid brown eyes, millions of them. They gaze at you. They didn't stare – I remember they gazed in India and their gaze is the only static element in a cauldron of activity.'

Peter on India, when he'd had just enough wine to set him talking and not enough to make him give a performance, was mesmeric. His characterization of a dwarf he'd seen in Adyar performing to a crowd was sheer comic brilliance: 'A pug-nosed, bearded Hindu xit (or he might have said git!) hung round with wooden beads like rosaries, whirling like a dervish on podgy legs like you see on some Chippendale chairs, to the clashing of those tiny finger cymbals.'

Finchie used to watch and imitate the Sadhus begging. 'Serious acting for your living at a really degrading level. Whining for the spare anna and waving the mutilated stump of a missing arm or leg to soften you up for "the moment of charity".' Finchie told me the religious instinct of India was like Europe in the Middle Ages, and that India and Buddhism had bred in him a loathing of everything to do with war and physical violence. 'Go to one of those great pilgrimages they hold at the famous religious centres and you'd see the spontaneity and devotion of the Indian masses and those electric spiritual subforces that underlie the will and psyche of every one of us. If you can harness them, they can be a tremendous asset to any artist. They give you depth and an added dimension.'

So much of what he absorbed he remembered later when he became interested in painting. He said that in India it is almost impossible to paint between about eleven o'clock and half-past three in the afternoon as the shadows were destroyed by the light refracted from the ground. He had found this often in parts of Australia. He said if you look at pictures of Indian buildings the great mass is never used in the way European architects do to get their effects. The Indian architect, according to Finchie, incorporates millions of small shadows in an intricate play of light and shade but always to a disciplined form of structural patterns.

India, to Peter, was as distinct from the rest of the world as Australia, but vastly different. Its intense spirituality had given its peoples an individual quest for awareness and reality, a profound conviction of human inequality, which bred an innate sense of propriety, decorum and the acceptance of status.

On the advice of the Sydney actress Enid Lorimer I contacted the President of the Theosophical Society in London to find out if they had any record of a Captain Dick Balfour-Clarke. To my great delight I discovered that he was still alive, now aged ninety-three and still living at Adyar. Dick Clarke, a practising Theosophist, remembers certain aspects of the nine-year-old Peter vividly.

Peter disappeared one morning and was lost for three days. 'The grandmother came to see me, quite distraught, and said, "I've lost Peter!" I hardly knew the boy, but I started to search for him immediately, all through the Adyar estate and finally found him in a little house with this Buddhist monk. Now Peter, who looked just like that painting of the boy with the clay pipe by Millais, called "Bubbles" (the one used as an advertisement for Pears' soap), was quite beautiful. He had lovely hands and feet. When I finally found him in this dimly lit room (the old house is still there), the golden halo of curls was gone. His head was shaved, he wore a yellow robe with one shoulder bare, and he held a grass fan in one hand. I said: "Peter!" and he said "Halloo!" I told him how distressed his grandmother was. He said: "I'm a chela now." I saluted a harmless-looking Buddhist monk, who smiled and raised no objection when I took Peter's hand and led him out of the room and delivered him to his grandmother. The Buddhist monk was a temporary visitor to the 50th annual Convention, and I never saw him again.

'At that time, I was on a visit to Adyar with Bishop C. W. Leadbeater from Australia. Peter's grandmother asked if Mr Leadbeater and I would take him back to Australia with us. She felt he was getting too much for her. She could no longer control him and feared he might run off again and never be found.' (I said it seemed very odd that Peter had been missing for three days before Granny had worried, but Captain Clarke was quite emphatic that she had searched for the child everywhere before he got word of Peter's disappearance.)

Leadbeater went to Annie Besant, who had replaced Helena Blavatsky as the most important figure in the Theosophical Society, and asked her advice. The idea was that Peter should live with a group of Theosophists, then resident at The Manor House, Mosman, in Sydney. Mrs Besant said that on no account should Peter go to Australia with Mr Leadbeater, as Peter might well be described by the Australian yellow press as 'the Bishop's new boy'. She was adamant. But Peter nevertheless sailed on the SS Otranto for Sydney.

Years later, Peter told me he felt that Australia had been unnecessarily harsh with old Leadbeater in 'drumming him out of the country for fancying the young boys in his care. I was in his care and he never made a pass at me. He reminded me of Moses, with a shock of white hair and a huge white beard, a tall, gentle, patriarchal figure, who kept patting me on the top of the head.' Finchie believed there were trumped-up charges against the old man which the press were using to vilify him. 'All I remember now is that we all had to wear blue socks and tell the Bishop our dreams every morning before breakfast.' As Finchie was too young to have any erotic dreams, he used to make up fantastic stories which made the old boy laugh and kept him happy.

Finchie remembered first seeing Mrs Besant at Adyar 'in a large hall with a polished tiled floor, full of what looked like symbolic signs'. He said there were sort of niches all round the walls, with symbols of different world religions. Mrs Besant wore what looked to Peter like priestly vestments, and her eyes seemed at moments to flame – the most amazing unforgettable human eyes he had ever seen.

'She was formidable and probably a very good actress. I seem to remember she liked dressing up and she struck me as being terribly clever. I do remember she spoke to me as an equal – which is probably why I thought she was clever – and she was motherly in a very positive, down-to-earth sort of way, but I think I was a little bit frightened of her. I was playing around on my own one day, in that big hall at Adyar, which had a polished tiled floor and niches in the walls with round intaglios above. I was getting up to all sorts of mischief when this elderly

37

woman came in and said: "I'm going to give you a game to play. You can play it by yourself." So I said, "Fine. What do I have to do?" She made me sit with my legs crossed, my ankles up in my groin, in the lotus position. "If you can practise it, and keep your back straight and relax, it is the most comfortable way to sit. The Orientals aren't fools! Now," she said. "Look at any one of those round drawings above the niches." I asked her what they were, and she said, "Symbols that have a hidden meaning." She tried to explain but I don't remember what she said.

'Anyway, I was intrigued by one particular religious design. I think she said they were symbols of religions that existed in India and the eastern part of the world. She said: "Are you interested in what you are looking at? That is very important because I want you to play this game often, and you must like what you are looking at." "Yes, I do," I said. "Very well," she said, "keep looking at the round symbol above that niche and when you have looked at it for a while, you will find that other thoughts start coming into your mind. Your mind is like a great banqueting hall and the thoughts that come crowding in to that huge hall are the guests of your imagination and they all want to feast with you. Do you understand me?" "Yes, of course I understand." She made it very simple for a nine year old. "When they start coming in quicker and quicker, don't take your mind off the first guest, that symbol you are looking at. The one you first looked at. He is the chief guest, your guest of honour and he is important to you. One day he may be able to work miracles for you. The others are uninvited. Now," she said, "the difficult part of your game is to keep your invited guest in the banqueting hall and not let him go away, because all the other guests will tend to make him disappear and you won't notice he's going, or perhaps even that he has gone, and you'll have lost a very good friend. But the secret is not to push the other guests out, but to try and keep him in and let as many guests in as you can and keep him as the most important guest of honour".' Peter started to roar with laughter. 'I sat there mesmerized for half an hour, looking boss-eyed at this bloody thing. I was unaware of anything around me. The old woman came back and said: "Well, what's happened?" and I said, "Well, all the other guests got bored and went away. They must have had enough to eat. Maybe the food didn't agree with them!" She

laughed at me and said, "You're learning to concentrate, Peter."
So perhaps I owe a lot in my acting to that legacy from Annie
Besant. She made me play the game each day until I could do it
without any effort.'

Peter found other friends at Adyar who were to have a benign
influence during a formative period. Mrs Rukmini Devi Arundale,
a great dancer in India and a very active force in the Theosophical
Society, told me in London recently that she remembers distinctly
seeing Peter alone in the crowd at the golden jubilee convention
of the Theosophical Society not long before Christmas 1925.
'Who are you?' she asked the very thin attractive child with the
shaven head whom she'd seen wandering on his own among the
vast crowds for several days. 'I have come here to India, from
Ceylon and Paris, with my grandmother, who has left me here
saying many here will look after me. I am a Buddhist Bhikkhu
that is why my hair is shaved off.' 'Have you no guardian or
someone here to take care of you?' she asked. 'I have no one,'
he replied, but was obviously looking for someone who would
be his mother, so she invited him to stay with her for a while.

Rukmini's sister, a practising doctor, was living at home with
Rukmini and their mother, on the Adyar Estate. The three
women doted on Peter. He had another little friend, named
Arthur van der Stok and the two kids were nicknamed 'Rukmini's
chelas'. Rukmini, her mother and sister, found him enchanting
and were very happy to do what they could for him. Both
Captain Clarke and Mrs Rukmini Arundale remember him as
great fun to be with, even at the age of nine.

Rukmini Devi distinctly remembers that Bishop Leadbeater,
hearing of Peter having been abandoned by his grandmother,
was concerned that he should not be left alone at Adyar. 'After
the convention was over, about eighty of us sailed from Colombo
on the Orient liner SS Otranto for Sydney early in 1926.
Balfour-Clarke and I had discussed this with Leadbeater, and it
was arranged we would all put in and pay for his passage, and so
with our group, sailed Peter.'

Rukmini Devi met George Ingle Finch in Poona. 'An
extremely handsome man,' she recalls. 'He knew who I was,
but I was careful never to mention Peter.' George, very active
in India at one stage, seems from all reports, to have been
extremely reluctant ever to mention Peter's name or to want to
have anything to do with him once he had removed him from

his mother and made sure she would not be able to gain access to him.

Dick Clarke clearly recollects that Peter spoke English and French, and was certainly a clairvoyant in a natural, child-like way. 'To our delight, he didn't realize that he could see things that most of us could not. He was delightful, full of fun, and very, very bright. He said he used to talk to the little fairy people who used to come and keep him company and play games with him. They were very clear in his mind and he could describe them vividly. One day he was up on the table. His grandmother wanted to know what he was doing there, and Peter said, "Well, the fairy wants me to be with him up here on the table".'

There is a manuscript, still in existence, containing stories about his invisible friends, made up by Peter, typed out by Laura. The paper is dry and yellow and the first page is missing, but here is a paragraph from one of the stories, carefully kept for the last fifty years by Captain Clarke.

'... So up I jumped and stood on the table too. Then such a queer thing happened: these little men began dancing on my feet, dancing, dancing, dancing, and as they danced, I grew smaller, smaller, smaller, until, lo and behold! I found myself the same size as my little friends!

'And now they set to work, oh! ever so quickly! and dressed me like themselves. They put a lovely bright green jacket on me and a red belt, and tight green trousers, right down to my ankles, and they put on my feet such wonderful green boots, fitting tightly over my trousers and curling up at the toes, nearly reaching up to my knees.'

Dick Balfour-Clarke, who took charge of little Peter during the voyage to Sydney from Colombo where they had picked up the *Otranto*, doesn't remember Peter having any passport or identification papers 'only a cheque for £12, and a letter from his grandmother saying "If my daughter Dorothy won't look after him then please will you take Peter?" The £12 was a first payment to be continued monthly at the rate of £10, which, by the way, never came. The grandmother said that from the outset she was unable to control Peter, and that he had asked to be allowed to travel with us and either stay with us or his aunt Dorothy in Sydney. There was a letter from Dorothy when we arrived in Sydney, in which she explained the impossibility of accepting her nephew and asked us to take him and look after him for a while. So Peter arrived with his little suitcase at the Manor House in Mosman, where about eighty of us were living, and Leadbeater said, "Well, there you are! You see, he was destined to come with us. It was his Karma to come here, for a time, anyway." '

The Manor House at Mosman overlooks the harbour, near Clifton Gardens and Peter, on his first arrival there in the summer of 1926, lived with the sons and daughters of Theosophists in an atmosphere which was supposed to be an attempt at a Theosophical Christian way of life. He came into line at once, very happy in his role of acolyte, and immediately took his place as a happy, integrated member of a community.

'I remember there was a Mrs van der Stok,' Clarke told me, 'with two daughters and a little son, Arthur, and she was supposed to be in charge of Peter as he needed motherly influence. But she didn't like Peter associating with her boy. Peter was far too advanced in his ideas, and his jokes. They were quite naughty! I remember this lady coming to see me and saying: "I will not have my son's mind contaminated by this boy from the Continent". '

Arthur van der Stok, who now lives in Switzerland, remembers meeting Peter. 'I was six at the time, three years younger than Peter, and though I remember little of that time now, I do remember this boy telling me a quite unbelievable story of how he had been sold as a slave by his grandmother in an Arab slave market, and had escaped to Adyar.'

Arthur van der Stok remembers Peter as being rather bullying, as the older boy, and full of extraordinary stories about himself which he had made up and with which he amused everyone, stories which had become totally real to himself.

'He seemed to live in a world of his amazing child's imagination. I remember he came with us on the *Otranto* to Sydney, and we were at the Garden School and the Manor House together for about six or seven months, and he seemed very happy and free . . . Then one day some relatives suddenly turned up and he was gone. I remember a few months later I met him on the Sydney ferry, and he had altered completely. With us he was very *avant-garde* and uninhibited. At the Manor House we were not conventional people and restricted in the bourgeois sense, we didn't dress like the average Australian. The Peter I saw on the ferry had been put into a suit, collar and tie, had had his hair cut short back and sides, was very bourgeois looking, and seemed very uncomfortable and very unhappy. His look didn't seem to fit him. He didn't want to know me or the people of our world at the Manor House anymore. He had become someone else and was not at all friendly. I think now he was disorientated and unable to adapt to an entirely different way of life.'

Although, according to Arthur van der Stok, Peter seemed to be happy at the Manor House, he believes he must have felt some loneliness as there was nobody really to take care of him. Everyone was nice to him, but very preoccupied and with a lot of work to do, so he was left largely to his own resources. He was the odd boy out, and too young to be any constructive part of the movement. Dick Balfour-Clarke did all he could and, luckily, Peter was for a short time under the aegis of Enid Lorimer, a friend of Clarke's at that time. Peter always maintained that Enid was a great, detached maternal influence in his life. She used to pull him up over his sloppy speaking, reading and writing, and made him aware of the need for self-discipline.

Leadbeater was preparing a tour through Java and Dick Clarke was to accompany him. Both felt Peter was just too young at nine to be anything but a burden, so Dick Clarke put him into the Children's Garden School in Stanton Road, Mosman, run by two old Theosophical members, the Misses Arnold and McDonald. 'Peter liked the school,' Clarke told me, 'and we left him happy there. On my return from Indonesia three months later I went to the school to ask Peter if he wanted to come back to us, and check what progress he had made. The poor old ladies said they were sorry, but an old man, Charles Finch, had turned up, claimed he was a baptised Christian, presented papers to prove he was the little boy's paternal grandfather, and had removed him, lock, stock and barrel, from the school. The old man had spoken rather bitterly of the foolishness of his wife, Laura Ingle Finch, in losing custody of Peter. I wrote to the grandfather, and asked if I could call and meet Peter, who was now attending a government school. I told his grandfather: "You don't like me, you don't like Leadbeater, you think we are of the devil, but I did look after your little grandson at your wife's request. She sent me £12 and I spent about £50 on him, which I am only too pleased to have done, but please, might I see him?" When I met Peter, I got the shock of my life. He spoke with a broad Australian accent and said: "Oi down't have to keep me nyles clean now," and I was so amazed to see the transformation into this grubby little fellow, all I could think of to say was: "Are you happy, Peter?" "Oi'm alroight," he said. "Oi'm an Australian schoolboy now! Give me best wishes to Mr Leadbeater." I left, and I never saw him again.'

Dick Clarke summed up: '. . . First his mother seems to have lost him, then his father didn't want him, then his grandmother couldn't cope and had to get rid of him, then Leadbeater and I had to put him into the Garden School, which he accepted willingly and liked very much, and for the first time had little friends of his own age. Suddenly he was removed from that environment too. It all represented a series of unpleasant shocks and changes that must have made little Peter feel he belonged to nobody.'

Rukmini recollects, 'One day Peter came to me crying and said I have to leave you, because my grandfather does not want me to stay here.' To Charles Finch, they were part of Laura's world, which he detested.

Rukmini Devi, on a visit to London in 1949, was taken one night to the theatre by a friend Peter Hoffman to see *Daphne Laureola*. When the leading young actor came on to the stage his lips and the gestures of his hands and certain mannerisms seemed somehow familiar to her. She turned to Peter Hoffman in the interval. 'I'm sure I've seen that man somewhere years ago. We looked at the programme and when I saw the name Peter Finch I asked Peter Hoffman if he'd go to the dressing room and ask Mr Finch if he remembered an Indian lady in Australia when he was a little boy.' Peter Hoffman went backstage to meet him and Finchie jumped up out of his chair saying, 'It must be Rukmini. I want to see her immediately,' and so she went. 'He seemed so thrilled to see me and put his arms around me. He said nothing but would not let me go for some time. I think he was very moved, and so was I. The next day he took me to lunch with his wife who was a dancer. "Let's not lose sight of each other again Rukmini," he said and gave me his address, but unfortunately when I wrote to him I never received a reply and I never saw him again.'

Peter was very much Kipling's Cat, who, through the circumstances of his formative life, would always go back through the Wet Wild Woods, 'waving his wild tail, and walking by his wild lone'. He asked unashamedly through life for what he needed and was not concerned with the account. He had learnt, he once told me, through the brief influence of India: 'to think upon the Cause of things', and was aware of the three great evils that beset the human soul in its Karma: The Hog; The Serpent; and The Dove; Ignorance, Anger and Lust. He remained a seeker all his life, and it was the seeker with his Buddhist indifference to money and material values that we sometimes glimpsed in Peter's acting at its deepest and truest. When he was little he said he often used to repeat his name over and over to himself and let his mind go unbridled, searching for what his real identity was. He felt when he was very young that he was on the threshold of a greater awareness; that his body, so a Buddhist monk had told him, was a little-understood earthbound creature posing as his soul, and that it could, if his will were not strong, lead him into much evil and misfortune; and then after the influence of India receded and he went to live with the Finchs in Greenwich, the curtains of awareness seemed to close on him. His subsequent environment was restricting in every sense and he felt enslaved. As he became more aware of the conflict within him he found the requisite outlet in alcohol, women and revolt.

3 Going walkabout

Peter's grandfather Charles Edward Finch, a retired Chairman of The Land Court of New South Wales then in his eighty-third year and living with his sister, Peter's great-aunt Kate, felt too old to look after Peter. So he was sent to live with Charles' brother, great-uncle Edward Henry Finch, a retired banker aged seventy-three, who had a spinster daughter Bertha, then in her forties. She was remembered by Peter as Betty who should not be confused with his mother Betty in England, whom he hadn't seen since he was two.

Peter's cousin Betty had a bachelor brother Jack who was blind in one eye and worked all his life as an auditor in the Bank of New South Wales. The three of them lived in a bungalow on the corner of Wallace and Mitchell Streets, about two miles up the harbour, at Greenwich Point, and to this home came Finchie for a period of seven years.

Peter used to refer to his days at Greenwich as the Dark Ages. Great-uncle Edward, a kindly soft man who stood apart and who, like Peter, hated rows, let Betty bring up Peter, and Jack supported them all on very little money. Betty, her own life disrupted by Peter (who was quick to sense any resentment or martyrdom in her), tolerated the situation. She had no option, as there was no one who could or would take him on. At least concern was shown for Peter's well being, and though he was craving affection and not getting the amount he needed, he was being disciplined. He had led a very undisciplined life with grandmother Laura in India and now felt he'd been thrust into a household that didn't want him.

According to Betty, Peter was not only untruthful, after his catch-as-catch-can life with Laura, but also had some 'dreadful habits' that were a great embarrassment to Betty in front of her friends. He wet the bed and to antagonize Betty, whose draconian discipline maddened him, he did pee-pees on her flower beds just as guests invited for tea arrived at the front gate – and not only pee-pees and not only on the flower beds according to Finchie! Peter exasperated Betty. He was always playing practical jokes on Jack, and at fifteen used to nick Jack's telescopes and hock them over at Hunters Hill.

Betty used to give Peter a good hiding, which Finchie later, to get attention, sympathy or above all a captive audience, called cruel floggings. Betty, according to Peter, was tyrannical and the sexual drive frustrated in spinsterhood found its outlet in trying to handle and discipline what proved to be the maverick-spirited Peter. But Betty was also kind to him in her way and he once grudgingly admitted that there was the very occasional reward for any good deed done unsolicited. Peter is alleged to have said – it was printed recently in a London newspaper – that to punish him Betty made him eat his own excrement but the facts are that Betty, at the end of her tether on fireworks night, 24 May 1927, when Finchie had bought a basket bomb and put it in Betty's letter box blowing it over the roof and down into Mitchell Street, wanted to rub his nose in it, and that's as far as it went. Finchie told me something of his childhood: that he'd often starved and once ate turnips from a farmer's field in Queensland, just dug them up and devoured them on the spot; that he'd even been reduced to eating the goldfish he'd pinched from the marble pool in the vestibule of the Prince Edward Cinema. But he was neither a masochist nor a pervert. When he spoke of Betty to me, he said she used to make him mow the lawn 'and trim the bloody edges, on a Saturday arvo' when all the other kids had gone to the flicks, or were playing cricket or footie (football) in the spare paddock opposite, that his only mate in that house was the dog, Patsy, and that he did have to collect the horse manure from the street. (Milk, bread and ice were delivered by horse and cart in Sydney right up until the war and in some cases later.) He used to have to dig the manure into Betty's lupins, stocks and marigolds, flowers he always loathed as a consequence, and whenever there was a tea party he piddled on them in front of Betty's guests to get his revenge.

Finchie felt so disorientated and restricted during the Wallace Street era, after Paris and India, that most of it subsequently faded from his mind, but from Betty, he told me once, 'I learned passive resistance and the secret of how to evade.'

He didn't come through the ordeal unbruised, and attended the local Greenwich 'public' school ('public' is the name given to all government schools and they were institutions for the survival of the fittest) and by the time he left in 1929 he had learnt how to survive against the other boys and bullies. By the time Finchie got to the North Sydney Intermediate High School, although never a kid who wanted to get involved in fist-fights, he'd had a brush with the local Greenwich roughs who formed into gangs and he had also learned to run, dodge, keep out of trouble, and win respect by being good with the marbles. He became deft in flicking cigarette cards or pennies against the wall, and playing two-up behind the school 'dunny' (lavatory). He used to love to go rowing with Jack, and the boys down at the local boat shed even made Finchie a little boat. There were some great times but they never made very interesting anecdotes, and basically he felt homeless and rebellious.

He often played truant from school, got on a ferry, and went down to watch the big cranes moving up the two cantilever arcs as the Sydney Harbour Bridge slowly took shape in the late 1920s. He reckoned he just did what any other Aussie kid did in those days except that he was a loner and he preferred to be out on the streets, anywhere rather than in Betty's meticulous 'Victorian Presbytery', as he described the house in Greenwich. When he did finally decide to escape and go for the life of penury and adventure, he teamed up at one stage later on with Donald Friend, the painter, among others. Many people in Australia were virtually starving in the Depression and Finchie and Donald, without two ha'pennies between them, unable to get any work in Sydney, 'jumped the rattler', which meant riding free on the goods trains up into Northern Queensland. They arrived in Cairns posing as two Russians from Omsk, and trudged through the countryside, spouting what they hoped sounded like Russian, round Cairns and Townsville. Donald did lightning sketches of the drinkers in the local bars, and made the odd few bob, while Finchie provided instant cabaret by singing Russian songs and dancing the *gopak*. Afterwards he took the hat round. Both spoke only Russian and never a word of English, with mime added if the natives proved a bit thick between the ears. Though Peter claimed he was absolutely tone-deaf and croaked like a frog, he looked so like a starving Russian that the Cockies (farmers), station owners and the Queenslanders on whose mercy he and Donald fell, usually took pity on them and gave them something to eat and a place to doss down. 'We'd sleep anywhere, under the open sky, in a cane field, or if it was raining we'd sleep under a bridge.' One day they were both questioned by a policeman and gaoled for vagrancy. 'Thank God!' they thought as they settled in comfortably in a Queensland police cell, 'free bed and board'. Next day their gaoler came in and said: 'Me wife's been taken crook. Here's two bob each for your tucker, but promise to come back.' They did and found themselves locked out!

Back in Sydney, Peter made contact with one woman, Enid Lorimer, whom he knew he could trust and who became if not his best, certainly his oldest, woman friend. 'The only woman I always ran to and never away from.'

Enid Lorimer, now over ninety years of age, remembers – when she went out to India in 1925 for the Theosophical Convention – Peter very clearly as a little boy of about nine with his head completely shaven, befriended by the Buddhist monk with whom Captain Clarke found him.

'I remember seeing him, just before he left for Australia, in a little white drill suit which had been cut down for him and a large solar topee sitting like a pudding bowl on his small shaven head. He looked pitifully thin and the hat, far too large for him, came down over his eyes. That impression, after fifty years, is still vivid. When I first knew him, Peter was a pathetic little figure. The problem was that he really belonged nowhere, and nobody really wanted him. Then I talked a lot in Sydney to Jimmy Raglan about Peter. Jimmy's dead now, but he was an ex-naval officer who became an actor and a producer. We both felt very strongly that Peter seemed to be too much for the elderly women who fussed over him but who never really gave him the sort of affection and feeling of well, home! – that he needed. We felt that he needed to be with men. Later Jimmy Raglan became interested in Peter, and put him under contract as a radio actor. That was before the war, about 1936.

'I believe this gave him some purpose and direction, as well as the company of men that he needed. I suppose now, apart from his mother and Dick Clarke, I must be about the oldest person who remembers him. I have always felt very strongly that parents who could allow a little boy of that age to go his own way, and especially in the light of his life in Australia during the Depression, were parents I really didn't want to know. I know, in Peter's case, that for all he may have done to hurt those he loved, those who loved him, many friends and acquaintances, allowance must be made for the absolutely appalling start he had to his life.

'I know Peter knew after a while that he was possibly illegitimate, had a deep-rooted fear of not knowing who he was, of belonging nowhere, always in transit, rootless, defending himself by attitudinizing and with the romantic fantasy of acting every second of his life. At twenty he wanted and needed few of the things most of us want and feel we need, because life had conditioned him differently. He was so emotionally unstable, but there wasn't an ounce of harm in him. I never heard him say an unkind word about anybody. He was generous, agreeable, he was a dear child, and, let me tell you, as bright as a button, so articulate, lucid and naturally intelligent. I taught him to read and write when he first came to the Garden School. He was exceptional. But from the very beginning he was unstable. I feel, having taught in schools, having lived a very long time and understanding a little now about human nature, that Peter's life is a lesson and a great deal can be learned from it. I have also felt, because I saw him in England latterly, that one great tragedy was that through his own fault, through attaining the success he did, he hadn't the discipline to exploit his own great gifts to true advantage, and he lost someone who gave him spiritual balance, his first wife Tamara, whom he loved so much at the beginning, but felt he'd outgrown when he became successful in England.

'I saw all that. I knew Peter and he loved her. She was what Turgenev described so superbly as a woman of "one love". To understand this you must understand the Russian temperament. It's all very well to talk of gloom, depression and melancholy, that is a typical glib and superficial assessment. It was dreadful from Peter's point of view, because for all that might have been difficult, she was a stabilizing influence and he badly needed that always. But he needed a woman who knew how to let go and let him have his head, even when he seemed unreasonable.

'Peter's relatives were rather dull for a small boy who wanted excitement. I felt very sorry for them, mind you, because Peter really didn't belong there, he'd been absolutely foisted on them, and he felt the oppression of this rigid, bourgeois respectability. Those Australian families, in the 1920s and 1930s going back generations but with deep English roots, 12,000 miles from "home", perhaps missing and craving for all the refinement of English middle-class life could be really oppressive. That was certainly part of the grit in Peter's oyster. How could they be expected to cope with a very young, very high spirited, very difficult lad? They took him over after his great-uncle at Greenwich died, and did their level best to give him a home but by the time I came back to Australia again, after 1932, he had managed to get away from them. He desperately needed to escape from an environment that was antipathetic to his very artistic and imaginative nature. It wasn't home. He felt no security, love, understanding or even a sense of communication and he just fled from Greenwich. They came to see me to try and find out where he was.

'He had previously been to see me and told me all about it, and he said: "Please don't let them know where I am," and I said, "Well, dear, I don't know where you are, so don't tell me," and thirty years later, when I last saw him in London, we were both doing Russian plays, and he did as he always did, way back from that time, he threw his arms around my shoulders and said, "Ah, my deliverer from my aunts!" He always called me that, because when the aunts came, I never knew anything, and therefore I couldn't tell them anything.'

A relation of Peter's, Marcia Finch Wark, two and a half years older than Peter, remembers Peter leaving Greenwich because Jack and his father had no job contacts for him, except in the banks. So Peter left and, according to Marcia, spent five months at Wanna Wanna, a 3,662 acre property belonging to his Uncle Alec, not far from Canberra.

'Uncle Alec never raised his voice,' said Marcia. 'He was a kind quiet man, who suffered from asthma and was a good bit older than my aunt Florrie. Like Betty, she had a temper that would flare up and five minutes later, everything was forgotten, but all of us, including Peter, learned not to answer back and Florrie's was always a generous open house. Uncle Alec would harness up the horses to the buckboard, Florrie would drive and off we'd all go for a picnic to the old apple orchard to gather the windfall apples. Some of us would go with her, and Pete would always try to go with Alec on one of the horses. Alec taught us all to be good riders. We had daily chores before we were allowed to play. My twin sister and I had to look after the house and the two rebels, Cynthia and Peter, had to gather the eggs, clean up the chicken yard and gather up sticks and twigs for the bath heater. Then with a cut lunch, off we'd all go down to the creek to climb the trees, dam up the creek, make bush houses ... We were young for our ages, but we had to make our own fun in those days. Riding with Uncle Alec was always exciting, especially when we went rabbit hunting on horse back. It was hilly stony country, and the horses would take us over the logs at a gallop, and we'd eventually find some poor rabbit hidden in the old dead logs. We'd come home with the rabbits hanging by their feet, attached to the saddle. All these things we used to do with young Peter.'

Marcia's sister, Mrs Cynthia Loxton, got on well with Peter but, unluckily for Peter, when Marcia senior in 1926 was asked to have him live with her in Queensland, with her husband and three daughters, she declined. Mrs Loxton used to go south every two years or so and saw Peter whom she feels, in retrospect, '... must have suffered a great shock as a young boy having to live with an unknown family. It would have taken a lot of adjusting to fit into a Victorian household after the life he'd led with Grandmother Laura, because the Finchs were Victorian: gentlemen of the old school, right was right and wrong was wrong, and children were seen and not heard. I know, because I was brought up like that too. It must also have been hard on Betty, going on forty years old, a spinster, to have this little undisciplined boy thrust upon her and told to bring him up. Laura never returned to Charles in Australia. She left him, taking the three children away with her, when George Finch was about fourteen, to Europe, supposedly to have her voice trained. Charles never mentioned her name again after he had made a trip to try and get her back. But he sent money to Laura all his life while he and this maiden sister, Kate, lived in very poor circumstances.'

By 1925, when Charles was still sending half of his income to ex-wife Laura – then living in Paris with Peter and a son, Antoine, by a Monsieur Konstant – Charles' sister Kate was too old to go to the Post Office to send off the money. Betty used to go, so she knew it was financially impossible, apart from anything else, for the old man to support Peter when he arrived from India. (Laura and her Parisian family, it appears, used the money sent from Greenwich to holiday in Switzerland every year. Peter, when he did visit grandfather Charles living two streets away, found him overbearing although he admired and respected the old man and in later years praised him publicly in the press.)

Great Uncle Edward, in whose house Peter was living, died in 1928 but Charles Finch lived on until the age of ninety. Unluckily for Peter, he was just reaching the age at which he could appreciate and benefit from the old man when he lost him. The death of Charles finally severed any family ties Finchie felt towards his Greenwich home.

Betty's reminiscences are now fragmentary, but at times she is very lucid and she affirms that Peter always had the right instincts in that he wrote her a long letter when he left her and put it on the kitchen table. In it he thanked her for all she had done for him but told her he needed to leave and go his way, why and where he was going. She repeated on several occasions: 'Poor Peter did not have a fair upbringing.' Looking back now she wishes she had those years again. Now her financial situation has much improved, but Peter was with her before and during the Depression. Peter often asked Betty: 'Why doesn't my mother want me?' and she'd always answer: 'When you go to England one day you'll be able to see her.'

Betty says that she and Jack went to collect Peter from the Garden School, where he had been with the Theosophists for six months. He had long hair and was very reluctant to leave. 'I don't want to go with you, I don't know you,' was his instant reaction when they arrived. Betty remembers Peter talking to Dorothy in French, which upset Uncle Charlie, as both Dorothy and Peter were fluent. Dorothy came out, according to Betty, to care for the old people, her father Charles and her Aunt Kate, but soon moved to Glen Innes to go into partnership with a friend at a private hospital, when the money was short. Dorothy was very fond of her cats but one sat on a baby in her care and smothered it. Dorothy is then said to have taken poison. Betty and Jack went to Inverell and brought back Dorothy's remains, which were buried in the war cemetery.

Betty remembers Peter having a fight with a boy in the vacant allotment across from the house. He came home bleeding. Betty wept, and Jack just said: 'Leave well alone, boys are boys.' Peter used to walk the two miles to his Greenwich state school with his two mates Paul Brickhill (the author) and Colin Anderson, now a Sydney doctor. When he went to North Sydney Inter he was given a bike. He was just a very average student, not interested in the lessons, and he never got a prize, spent a lot of time looking out the window, his mind on other things and longing for the bell to go. He left school at sixteen. Betty and a friend had gone to the pictures, came home and found the letter saying he'd left home.

Betty now feels that perhaps if she'd given him pocket money, like the children today, he might not have stolen things. Betty wept the day Peter arrived in his ill-fitting uniform to tell her he'd joined up and was off to fight in the Middle East. Apparently he often used to turn up at Greenwich with girl friends and always a different one and sometimes with several. Old Great Aunt Kate thought the girls were fun as they used to act for her, and then Peter and his girls would drive off from the house in some old open jalopy with the young people hanging on everywhere. Betty was present at Peter and Tamara's wedding in 1943.

Jack Kendall, a neighbour who lived across the road from Betty beyond the vacant allotment where the kids played cricket and 'footie', remembered Peter as a likable boy who often used to bring his bike over to be mended, if Jack was away from home. Kendall used to see Peter, Brickhill and Anderson playing football in the paddock – Colin Anderson had a habit of breaking Betty's windows. Kendall's wife Kitty said she was always entertained when Peter did acts on his own for them in the Wallace Street house; he loved dressing up and pretending. He had a little billy cart and he often took luggage down to the ferry for the neighbours, and if Betty was late coming home, Kitty Kendall often found him on the doorstep crying – he was missing her.

In those days messages were tied to their dog Patsy and in this way the two houses were in constant quick communication with each other. When Great Uncle Charles died, Aunt Kate sent a message with Patsy saying: 'Charles does not look well' – Charles had been dead for a couple of hours.

Cynthia Loxton remembers Peter bringing his fiancée, Sheila Smart, to Greenwich in 1940 where she was staying at the time. 'Peter wanted Great Aunt Kate's approval. He loved the old lady and he had grown to love his grandfather, who died in 1933. Great Aunt Kate lived with Betty after Charles died. Just before Peter left for the Middle East in 1941, he went to say good-bye to Great Aunt Kate and Betty, and made fun of his army uniform which didn't fit him. His legendary employment as a sheep shearer was, in fact, holidays spent at Wanna Wanna. Peter was always reticent about his spell at secondary school, North Sydney Inter-High at the height of the Depression, which he left in 1932. He said the day he'd been enrolled there he became the third of a trio of kids, Partridge, Sparrow and Finch. He loathed the school and what he called 'the whole Fascist mentality behind the Aussie educational system'.

'We were physically punished,' he said, 'for not paying attention to lessons that were so dull and sterile that my mind seemed to erase the details as fast as they were forcibly administered.'

The three things that Finchie did acquire at North Sydney were a love of Australian poets like Henry Lawson and 'Banjo' Paterson, an ability to swim faster than the other kids, and a passionate interest in acting, and it was in the school plays that Finchie's star really glittered. (Though it must be said he also had a talent for writing original graffiti on the lavatory walls; the oft quoted piece that goes,

There was a man from Bulli Pass
Who stood in water up to his ankles.
This doesn't rhyme
But it will when the tide comes in

he always claimed was his.) Anybody watching the film, *Windom's Way*, can see Peter doing a little quite stylish swimming in the 1930s Aussie style.

When Peter first left school Jack made plans for him to start work in the bank, but he flatly refused and that was what made him decide to go it alone. He then took his five month spell at Wanna Wanna, reading poetry under the trees, riding round the station with Uncle Alec, who was more anxious to keep him out of mischief than worried that he wasn't pulling his weight. Finchie was sorting himself out and making his decision to leave home and pack up and move on once and for all.

Mac (Max) Corbett, Lionel V. (Bill) Hudson, Paul Brickhill, Alan Reid, the doyen of Australian political journalists, were all copy-boys along with Peter Finch at the *Sun* newspaper in Sydney, when Finchie eventually decided to get a job. Brickhill, also an inmate at North Sydney Inter and living round the corner from Finchie at Greenwich, took a job as a copy-boy on the *Sun* because Peter, already serving there as a 'printer's devil', persuaded him it was worth giving it a whirl. Finchie had got his job on the *Sun* through Norman K. Johnson, a Sydney journalist who was a neighbour of Aunt Betty's. Peter, once he had got into and understood the structured ambience of the newspaper office, loathed every second of it. 'But it was the first time,' said Finchie, 'I found myself in the world of people and not isolated from them.' He dressed as untidily as he could, and desperately sought some way to quit the newspaper.

Most of the copy-boys hoped to attract a favourable response from the editor in order to become cadet journalists. The *Sun Junior* was a house journal sold to the staff for 1d a copy, and wholly created by the copy-boys to demonstrate their increasing journalistic abilities. The *Sun*'s theatre critic, and author, Mary Marlowe, who also worked in the library, encouraged the boys in the production of the *Sun Junior*. L. V. (Bill) Hudson, was the first editor of the journal and the theory of catching the boss's eye must have worked, as he was given a cadetship, and Finchie was extremely envious. Under Mary Marlowe's direction, the money raised by the boys from the sale of their paper went towards an annual party. This was held in the company cafeteria, where the government insurance office now stands.

Mary had been encouraging Peter to do impersonations and give recitations on the occasion of the first copy-boys' party. Finchie agreed to do a piece called *The Hunchback of Notre Dame*. According to Bill Hudson it was Peter's first public indication of his enormous talent. 'There was Peter with eyebrow pencil, make-up and a cloak over his bent shoulders, giving a commanding performance amid the lemonade and sandwiches. We were all stunned. It was the most incredible reaction of any group of people I've ever seen in my life.' (This comment is from a man in journalism for over forty years.) 'I remember it quite clearly, even today. Peter Finch owed me two shillings in those days, and it became a standing joke between us for the next thirty-odd years. I remember bumping into him and his wife, Tamara, at the Australia Hotel after the war and both of us laughed at this unpaid debt. In 1966 I was in Los Angeles. I knew Peter was in Hollywood making some film or other, and I tried to contact him, but his agent would only relay messages. It looked as though I wasn't even going to speak to him. "Tell him I need that two bob he owes me," I reminded the agent. Peter phoned me up two days later, asking me to go to Palm Springs with him, but I was leaving LA the next day, so I couldn't go. It was a great pity. I never saw or heard from him again.'

Finchie says he spent about two years on the *Sun*. He used to be sent off to cover the wool sales. 'If anything was guaranteed to put me into an early grave, it was trying to keep awake during that unforgettably boring ritual. Then I had the luck to become personal copy-boy to George "Doggie" Marks, who used to cover the Supreme Court for the paper. He used to ape W. C. Fields and turn up rain or shine in a straw boater and elastic-sided boots that you could hear squeaking down the corridor before the "Doggie" ever made his entrance.'

Finchie, an inveterate smoker by the age of sixteen, rather than put his fag out when he went into court would hide it in his hat. As he left the court room one day, unwittingly leaving a smoke screen behind him, he heard what sounded like the bronchial cough of a brontosaurus from the Bench. 'I turned round to see Justice Boyce who, like the crocodile on his log, had seemed asleep all through the proceedings, now red-faced, perspiring, wide-awake, his wig pushed back, wiping his face with a large polka dotted handkerchief, beckoning me over: "Young man, next time you enter this court room representing the press, would you kindly extinguish your hat".'

One day in 1934, in a state of utter despair after his appearance as *The Hunchback of Notre Dame*, Peter decided to end his career as a journalist. When he went in to see editor Frank Ashton there was a large jug of water on the desk. They had a violent argument and Peter simply took the jug and emptied it over Frank Ashton. His burning ambition was achieved – Ashton had no alternative but to sack him.

With no money for lodgings he lived, ate and slept where he could, in what was to become Finchie's stamping ground until he left Australia in 1948: Kings Cross, Darlinghurst and the area round Macleay Street and McElhone Stairs, which lead up from that meadow of wharves called Woolloomooloo, to Victoria Street. Palmer Street, Woolloomooloo, was the street where all the prostitutes lived and Finchie often found refuge there. Tilly Devine, who ran the girls, used to live around Palmer

Street and there was a pub called The Macquarie Hotel near the waterfront where, according to Finchie, they used to hold a raffle and the one who got the lucky ticket could take his pick of the available talent and, if it was a nice summer evening, could go and 'knock 'er off in the Domain'. If he wasn't shacking up and being cared for by one of the girls he could easily be found sharing with a mate in Victoria Street.

One evening Finchie met the Captain of the Norddeutscher-Lloyd freighter *Hamburg*, berthed at Woolloomooloo Docks, and over a couple of schooners persuaded the skipper to take him on as a deck-hand for the return voyage to Germany. He was actually on board and the ship due to cast off when the dock police found out, demanded to see his 'seaman's ticket', '. . . and with no time to beg, borrow or steal the bloody thing they had me off that ship and down on the jetty neck and crop . . .'

Running up or down McElhone Stairs, Finchie claimed he often used to meet Rosaline Norton, nicknamed 'The Witch of the Cross' – an exotic larger-than-life creature who plucked out her eyebrows and painted in new ones that curled up at the corners. She used to work part time at the Arabia coffee lounge in Macleay Street, and was eventually put in the 'giggle house' (Callan Park Lunatic Asylum), where she produced a coffee table book of hilariously erotic drawings that enjoyed a tremendous success among the elite. Finchie always maintained Rosaline Norton's treatment by the prudish hypocritical Australian establishment was a ludicrous attempt by the zealots of rectitude to deal with a sane rich individual personality who was proving an embarrassment to too many important people. 'In Paris they'd have understood her,' Finchie said to me 'because the French aren't cursed with our false modesty.' She had earlier posed for a series of 'fabulously erotic and very pornographic nude stills', one set of which was discovered in Eugene Goossens' baggage when the conductor visited Australia. The authorities very promptly 'drummed him out of the country' – what Finchie referred to as 'everyone's chance to put the knife in to the boy who was found out' – he greatly admired Goossens as a musician. Goossens didn't get over the scandal and died soon afterwards.

Another of Finchie's friends was Bee Miles who, while attending Sydney University as a girl, had a brainstorm, and ended up as one of the local eccentrics. In recent years much has been researched and written on the life of Bee Miles and the brainstorm theory has now been written off as a tactic of Bee's wealthy father after she had rejected his incestuous advances. She would rush on and off trams, stop taxis and order the drivers to take her to some impossible destination, and if they refused she'd wrench the door off. She always wore her hair cut very short, a green tennis eye-shade and sand-shoes. Once she hailed a taxi in George Street and demanded to be taken to Kalgoorlie, in Western Australia, to see some friends. (That's about the distance from London to Istanbul.) The driver demanded to see the colour of her money and, when she produced a wad of notes, he was obliged to take her 'all the way there across the Nullarbor Plain, and all the way back again'. Bee, like Finchie, often used to sleep in church doorways or, if she needed a bath, as she was scrupulous about her personal cleanliness, she'd shack up for a night at the Salvation Army's People's Palace in Elizabeth Street.

One of the very early Sydney press reports on Peter relates: 'The Cross and Potts Point district certainly provide some interesting sidelights. Last night we had the pleasure of watching a man, slightly undressed in a towel and bathrobe, climb a rickety ladder to his third-floor flat. Apparently he'd left his key inside when he went to the local communal bath, thereby setting himself a nice little climb after his ablutions, and was that Peter Finch trying desperately to keep the ladder steady?' The keyless ladder-climber was another legendary character (who became a derelict and died of drink) and a bosom companion of Peter's at this time: the actor, Cecil Perry.

Peter and Errol Flynn, filming together in *The Dark Avenger* at MGM's Elstree studios in 1954, were reminiscing one night about their days spent round 'the dirty half-mile that lay between Kings Cross and Darlinghurst': Flynn in the late 1920s before he went to New Guinea as a district officer; and Finchie in the early 1930s, when he was on the bread line. According to Flynn, there were a bunch of toughs who used to give any 'nong' stupid enough to resist handing over his wallet, an x-mark across the face – an oblique mark laying the cheek open first on one side and then on the other. Peter said he was more or less safe as he didn't have any money, let alone a wallet, and always looked as though he was starving. Flynn, more of an obvious target, only lasted a week, until his mate Thomson was picked up in the gutter with his throat cut and both cheeks slit wide open.

Finchie claimed he was always terrified of that area – though a lot of his acquaintances lived there, and he could sometimes scrounge a bed – and lived in terror that he might be thought to be horning in on someone else's girl. He felt safer sleeping in the Sydney Domain, the big park overlooking the harbour. The park was open at night, and there were plenty of down-and-outs around for company and Finchie would often hole up in one of the caves where a crowd of Domain dossers set up house for the night. They'd build a little fire and put newspaper inside their shirts and trousers to keep out the cold. Both Finchie and Flynn maintained that the pangs of real hunger will turn a man 'as cunning as a shit-house rat'. Both had seen themselves in exactly the same Sydney scene within five years of each other, a pair of down-and-outs, François Villon characters who, when they finally did meet in the 1950s, claimed, 'We were the last ones in London who could draw a sword and cut up a dark alley.'

4 Flotsam and jetsam

Sixteen years of age, out of work after getting the sack for baptizing news editor Frank Ashton, determined never to return to Greenwich, with thirty shillings, the suit he stood up in, two shirts, no socks and an edition of *Don Quixote*, Finchie made up his mind he'd join the mile long dole queues and scan the advertisement section of the *Sydney Morning Herald* posted up round the Salvation Army shelters. He joined in with the hundreds of boys of his age, all hoping to get at least a day's work, but at first Finchie was not lucky. From those months of near starvation he learned of the generosity of the very poor, and the humanity that can exist between people when their backs are really to the wall. Once he got himself a job with an advertising firm selling space for a magazine, but one day the manager disappeared and the business folded. He got a room for a week by Sydney's central railway station for five shillings, and then an old actress with a heart of gold, Nan Taylor, who had a boarding house for actors in Sir John Young Crescent, Woolloomooloo, took him in for a while and fed him. Then there was another landlady 'mum' who cared for the destitute Finchie, an Irish lady Mrs O'Halloran 'who used to share her one luxury with me,' said Peter, 'a bottle of stout every Saturday morning. Mrs O'Halloran knew I was absolutely skint but, like Nan Taylor, she fed me, mended the frayed cuffs, the holes in my pockets and would darn my socks until it was a case of all darn and no sock.'

Those were kaleidoscopic flotsam-and-jetsam years for Finchie, of intermittent work as an amateur, semi-professional and professional actor, delivery boy, tout, waiter, and once he borrowed an old rattle-trap bike and got a job as a taxi hailer in Taylor Square; he did anything to bring in a few bob. His very athletic hand-to-mouth existence made him ideal material for a very hard-up Italian artist who had got a small commission to do some portraits of St Sebastian receiving his arrows, St Lawrence being devilled on his Roman grid iron, a very hungry looking John the Baptist without his head. 'My skinny body and prominent rib cage earned me no pay on that assignment,' said Finchie, 'but while it lasted I was given a place to sleep, fed on really good Italian spaghetti, copious glasses of claret, and he taught me to fence in the Italian manner! – and for a long time the passers-by could look at me in the window of Pellegrini's, Sydney's Catholic book-sellers, looking rather like an Italian's idea of El Greco.'

He once borrowed a waiter's suit from a sick friend and talked himself into being taken on at the Astra Hotel, in Bondi. 'I had to get up at five in the morning to polish acres of bloody brass work and sweat it out until seven thirty at night.' He was sacked at the end of a fortnight for uncorking a bottle of champagne and showering the contents on a dinner party which included a woman in a very elegant Parisienne evening gown.

He then started making artificial flowers, mixing them with wild Australian bush flowers, like boronia, and small painted fir cones, the odd bit of wattle and any dried flowers he could work in, and hawked his posies from door to door in Darlinghurst.

From the time he started with the *Sun* newspaper and into his career as an actor, Finchie found that he was tolerated by the moneyed establishment because he amused them. He felt that what was considered the higher echelon of Sydney society found him good value, but he was never really accepted. He'd sometimes go into a tirade about the pomposity and the patronizing attitude of so many 'politically fascist-minded, socially and financially ambitious products of the system ... respectability at all costs, a moribund, Victorian colonialism with its own Aussie identity.' He saw himself as the court jester of old, necessary at times to provide amusement and laughter, but he belonged nowhere. He would drink with them, accept their hospitality, make love to their women, but it was all a game. Take what you need and give what pleases. But he'd have no true allegiance because he had no port. He knew very early on that his flag was the skull and crossbones.

Ian Bevan, now a successful theatrical agent in London, started out as a cadet on the Sydney *Sun* five years after Peter left. Peter told him that some time after he left the *Sun*, one job that did keep him financially stable for a few weeks was being the spruiker outside Sharman's boxing tent at the Sydney Royal Easter Show. Peter was the man in the crowd who, when Jimmy

Sharman banged the drum and said, 'Who will fight the champion five rounds for five bob', had to stand up and offer to take on the champ. Peter used a multiplicity of disguises: a drunken sailor, a hick down from the bush, a commercial traveller, a barman, a navvy, changing his personality throughout the day and in a series of carefully worked out fight routines, completely taking the public in. He told me he'd also been a barker outside the tent that housed 'Ubangi', the Pygmy Lady from the Jungle. He had them queueing up right round the tent with an amazing spiel about the origins of Ubangi. One day on the advice of a friend he'd made in the dole queue who had said to him, 'With that toffee bloody voice of yours, you ought to try and get a job with Coady up at the Maccabean', he went up and saw Joe Coady and asked him for a job in his vaudeville show at the Maccabean Hall, near Kings Cross. He spun him a yarn that he'd worked in London, showed him an improvisation he'd worked out about a multiple amputee trying to hail a taxi, and got a job with Coady's vaudeville. He started as a chorus boy. 'I was a buck and wing hoofer. Most of the audience were Depression characters with the arses out of their pants. As the curtain rose there were twelve of us in crumpled pink dinner suits covered in stains stinking of moth balls with those patent leather pumps that have never seen shoe trees and curl up at the toes like Sultans' slippers. There we were, dancing like six ungainly cherry coloured galahs, bawling out our song, the Depression theme song "We're in the money, Let's spend it, Lend it, send it, Rolling around!", while the poverty stricken audience sat glumly huddled together with their coat collars turned up.'

Peter got his first professional break in this vaudeville with the American comic Bert La Blance, who had come out to Australia during the First World War. In those days, you could be booked as a straight man without ever having met the comedian before, and you'd work with him that night. According to Peter, Bert was suddenly short of a straight man. Finchie offered his services and Bert said, 'Do you know, "My father and my father and my father and my son?" ' 'Yes,' said Finchie. 'Right my son. You'll get ten bob extra if you're any good tonight and get me my laughs. I'll wink with my upstage eye when I've finished speaking, and it's time for you to give me the feed lines.' They did the whole sketch unrehearsed, with Finchie improvising desperately. Of course he didn't know the sketch, but he wasn't going to admit he didn't: he got La Blance his laughs and he was in.

He was a pro. There were a limited number of sketches that the comedian and his stooge would know as a matter of course, but Finchie very soon knew every vaudeville gag in the book. He was also the occasional feed to a comic named Mugsy Desmond. He watched and slavishly copied Roy Rene with his lisp, dead-white face and six o'clock shadow, known to millions of Australians as Mo, who topped the bill on the Tivoli Circuit for years. Mo did a sketch called Flo's Letter and Finchie, doing a take-off of Mo, did one called Floth's Lettah! (I saw both doing that sketch.) It was just one of many instances that showed Peter had more mimetic prowess than any actor in Australia when he reached his Australian flowering at the Mercury Theatre twelve years later. Finchie, in his teens, at ten bob a night if he was lucky, was on, improvising and learning the technique of vaudeville comedy, in front of a live audience at the Maccabean Hall in Darlinghurst.

From his early vaudeville experiences with comics like La Blance Peter evolved many of his famous party pieces, one of which I saw him do one night in a crowded pub in the Kings Road, Chelsea. He called it his 'one-armed flute player routine'. He took off his jacket, put one arm down the front of his trousers, and then put his jacket back on again. A piece of curtain rod served as a flute, and he put on one of the ladies' hats. After playing a tune on the flute, he attempted to pass round the hat, but in order to do this with his only free hand, the flute had to be grasped by a forefinger emerging from his fly!

His stage appearances in 1934 were infrequent but telling: a one-night stand at the Chatswood Town Hall in *Journey's End*; and then later in the year he went to work for Doris Fitton, then running Sydney's leading amateur theatre, the Independent. 'I remember him coming to me one day,' she said, 'to ask me if I thought he could be a straight actor. We were about to rehearse *Counsellor at Law* by Elmer Rice and I said to Peter, "There's only one part left, about three lines, but you can have it if you want," and he said, "I'll take it." It was the part of the boot-black: the Counsellor was too busy to go out, so the boot-black came to him and polished his shoes. "Yes boss. No boss", but you felt what a nice little fellow he was, and off he went. He was only on stage three minutes, but I thought, well there is a talent. The next thing I gave him was a pirate in *Peter Pan*. He didn't have any lines, except among the general chorus. He decided he'd be a one-legged pirate and trussed up one leg; Peter always had imagination. Nobody gave him any direction, but there he was hopping around, and I thought this boy is really going places.'

Patricia Thompson had one of the two leading roles in *Counsellor at Law*, and she remembers Peter in 'a tiny cameo part as an Italian boot-black. We both got the best actor nominations at the end of the year (not that that meant anything, it was a newspaper critic only). I seem to remember that Peter was a bit of a cut-up and used to upset Doris' sense of correct behaviour, and there was a rumour around at the time that he pinched fellow actor John Alden's cigarette case; that was the sort of reputation he had. He was a bit younger than me and I quite liked him but, more than that, was immensely impressed with his acting talent . . .'

Doris invited the eminent actor Frank Harvey along to her theatre to comment upon the performance of a leading man of whom she expected great things. Frank, when asked to pass judgement had said: 'Yes, he's fair to middling but who's the young man who plays the guard in Scene One? Now, he really is an actor.' Pat Thompson saw Peter '. . . always doing bit parts and making them shine out from the general Independent level of refined amateurism.'

After *Peter Pan* Finchie was cast by Doris as the Fair Page Maudelyn in Gordon Daviot's *Richard of Bordeaux* (1935). Later Finchie, when at the Mercury, described his stint at the Independent as mostly trying to build live characters out of virtually non existent parts – batting on a lousy wicket against the leading actors, most of whom he knew he could outplay, and not even being paid a penny for it. But Doris was trying to keep the legitimate theatre alive on a shoe-string, and didn't always have the money to pay. She paid her actors when she could but, in Finchie's day, she had to forsake the Savoy Theatre for an alternative location because she couldn't meet her overheads.

Edward Howell who, during the golden years of radio in Australia, wrote, produced and played in the very popular situation comedy series, *Fred and Maggie Everybody*, gave Peter his first substantial break in the legitimate theatre – a week's work for £3 in 1935 – as a young reporter in the play *Interference* by Roland Pertwee and Harold Dearden. In a press review of the show, the leading actors were praised, with reservations, but 'Peter Finch made his young reporter, Douglas Helder, an engaging personality'. He got the part through Claude Fleming, who had directed my father in his first Australian film, *£500 Reward*, in 1918. Finchie was a non-fee paying student at Claude's academy for a very short time, after which Claude had put him on the books of his casting agency. Claude with the wisdom to see that Peter at eighteen would be infinitely better exploited than mistaught, cast and directed him soon after in Finchie's very first film, *The Magic Shoes*, nicknamed *The Tragic Blues* by the entire unit involved in its shooting.

The Magic Shoes was based on the 'Cinderella' story. Peter played the beautiful young prince; Norman ('Foggy') French, who was to work with Finchie on the George Sorlie tour, played the court jester, and Helen Hughes (daughter of Billy Hughes, the Australian Prime Minister) played one of the ugly sisters. The film was shot at the then brand-new National studios complex at Pagewood, near Botany Bay. The two-reeler, never exhibited, was basically made to test the new studio facilities, but it is believed that the subsequent failure of the film was due to Fleming's inexperience as a film director. Having failed to find a distributor, the film was re-edited with the intention of making it into a promotional piece for a shoe manufacturer, but, even when the recut was finished, Finchie's first picture failed to find a buyer.

Consistent work as an actor was proving elusive and, by the end of 1935, Peter had found work as an odd-job man in a boarding house in Challis Avenue, Potts Point. He wasn't paid anything but was given his board and lodging. He slept in an old Packard car parked in the grounds. Margaret Hayter, then aged fifteen, lived in one of the stately old Sydney homes opposite. She had been a boarder at the Theosophical Garden School, which must have been one of the very first coeducational boarding schools in Australia, starting there in 1930, four years after Peter had left. At the time she met Peter, Margaret was attending commercial art classes three times a week and was supposed to work at her drawing at home the rest of the time. Finchie would pop over to visit her when he had finished his chores and share a can of baked beans and cigarettes they made out of toilet paper and Mr Hayter's pipe tobacco. Finchie used to do his comic turns and make Margaret shriek with laughter.

The Hayters rented the top half of the house, and downstairs lived a mean-spirited old hag whom Finchie nicknamed 'Gagool' after the old crone who guarded King Solomon's Mines. She told Margaret's papa that 'that perfectly frightful young man, who works in the boarding-house opposite, is never out of the house', so Hayter forbade Margaret to have Peter there again. Much to Margaret's delight, the following morning the Hayter laundry was delivered by a Chinese laundryman, who charged up the stairs with a pile of the hotel laundry on his head. When 'Gagool' heard Margaret and allee-same-Chinese-Flinch falling about with laughter, she went hot foot back to Margaret's papa.

A few days later, a pair of skinny legs were seen coming up the front path beneath a mound of vegetables. From among the pumpkins and 'chokos' the croak of a pubic baritone could be heard singing 'Parla mi d'amore, Mariu', probably better known to an Anglo-Saxon audience as 'Love's last word is spoken, cherie'. When Finchie eventually left the boarding house, he moved into a basement flat in Macleay Street, which he shared with the actor Cec Perry. He was just beginning to break into radio and invited Margaret to a party one night. 'Peter kept saying the food was coming,' said Margaret. 'At last his friend arrived, in the early hours of the morning, with the most gorgeous goodies. His friend had a part-time job as a butler and had to wait till the guests left before he could carry home the left-overs.'

When Pete got his first big break in *So This is Hollywood* at the Apollo Theatre, in Melbourne, he rushed round to find Margaret. 'He arrived looking so smart, in a suit someone had lent him. He'd managed to buy a shirt, but he couldn't run to a tie, so we cut up my best red velvet slacks and made one. I think it was after making that big sacrifice I realized I loved him.'

It was Robert Capron, the American comedian, who played the lead in *So This is Hollywood*, who first gave Peter serious advice and guidance with his acting. Capron, who saw at once that 'The Juvenile' had the makings of an exceptional actor, would often take him aside and coach him in the elements of practical stage technique. He made Peter realize that ability and potential will get an actor with good looks so far, and from then on it's an endless slog and repetition until the scene is polished and becomes second nature to play. 'Capron,' said Finchie, 'used to wander round his hotel room in Melbourne, a glass of whisky in his hand, moving the furniture and turning the place into roughly what our set looked like at the theatre. He was a brilliant comedian and a wonderful friend. He'd show me how to open a door and close it, how to walk across a stage, how to turn, and the technique of how to use a telephone on stage and how to read a paper; all the things an actor has to learn how to do and then forget so that the audience take them for granted.'

During the run of the show Bobby Capron was drowned in the Yarra River. In the press cuttings in Margaret Hayter's scrapbook it says that Capron's fox terrier pup Noni fell into the Yarra, where it flows through the Warrandyte Tunnel. Capron dived in and both man and dog were swept 130 yards through the tunnel, and Capron was drowned. The press reports go on to say that Finchie ran round to the other end of the tunnel and saw Capron emerge with the pup still clinging to its master's back.

'Running along the bank, Finch lost sight of Capron when a clump of bushes obscured his view. On reaching the other side of the bushes he saw only the dog in the water, and jumping in, brought it out. The Royal Humane Society will ask for a report of the action of Mr Peter Finch, 21, with a view to recognition of his attempt to save Mr Capron's life.'

The story that Finchie jumped in and saved the dog is accurate, and the Royal Humane Society did file their report. But a local resident, living thirty years of his life near the Warrandyte Tunnel says (a) the Yarra doesn't pass through it, and (b) the tunnel is a mile long, and part of an adjacent aquaduct system, and (c) the road connecting one end of the tunnel to the other is two and a half miles long. So, either Finchie had his seven-league boots on, or someone on the paper was already busy on the Finch legend.

According to Thelma Scott, who was playing the ingenue in *So This is Hollywood*, they had all gone off on a picnic. When the little dog fell in the water, Capron jumped in after it, caught it and threw it back to Finchie. The next moment, Robert disappeared. He'd gone over a weir and broken his neck. 'Peter dived for him – he dived until very late at night. I was rung up and told what had happened, and I went to the flat where Capron had been staying and found Peter. He was shivering and obviously suffering from shock. They didn't find the body until long after. That was on the Sunday, and on the Monday night, at the theatre, I said to Peter: "I think you'll get a big ovation, so if you do, when you come on stage, don't say your opening lines, but come straight over to me and just stand perfectly still and wait." Well, he got the ovation, and what an ovation! I'll never forget it! They rose to their feet and clapped and clapped. He kept very calm, very quiet, and just went on with the show.'

Thelma, who later starred with Peter in his Macquarie award winning radio play, *The Laughing Woman* (1946), described him in *So This is Hollywood* as 'a little stiff and a little wooden, because it was one of the first things he had ever done. But he did it well and he improved and relaxed, but this was really his first important commercial role in the theatre, and the beautiful cheek bones and those wonderful eyes helped him a great deal. He was so untidy and actually arrived in Melbourne with two shillings in his pocket. Eventually we got the management to give him his first week's salary, because in those days you didn't get paid for rehearsals. The company did a whip-round, bought him some fresh clothes, a toothbrush and soap, and generally smartened him up. And then of course he was very well dressed in the show because Ernest Rolls always insisted that everybody should be dressed immaculately. He looked very handsome in his dinner jacket when he made his first entrance – but one evening, no Peter. He had missed his entrance because he was upstairs chatting in the dressing-room. When he realized he'd missed his cue we could hear him coming down those stairs four-at-a-time. Ernest Rolls really tore a strip off him and he got such a roaring-up from everybody that he never did it again.' Finchie described Ernest C. Rolls as, 'the most violent man I've ever known. He gave the stage manager such a hammering at one rehearsal that the poor bugger turned up next day in a full suit of armour.'

When Margaret Hayter's family eventually left Challis Avenue, Potts Point, and moved back to their old home in Coronation Avenue, Mosman, Margaret's father relented a little and Peter became a more frequent visitor. Margaret believes the reason he came so often was mainly for a decent meal. 'He was always so hungry after dinner, he'd rush out to do the washing-up so he could eat what was left in the saucepans.

He seldom had his tram fare unless he'd managed to pinch someone's milk money, so he usually had to walk that marathon from Kings Cross. Sometimes Mother would give him his fare home.'

One day, Peter hired a rowing-boat at Clifton Gardens, and he and Margaret set out on a picnic for Clark Island. Half-way across, a squall blew up and lashed the harbour into a very choppy swell. Finchie lost an oar and round they went in circles as the sea got nastier by the minute. Margaret sat in the stern, terrified, while Finchie, a very good swimmer with no thought of the many sharks that cruise about those waters, suddenly pretended he was Grace Darling, punting out furiously to rescue the survivors from the *Forfarshire*. Margaret, caught between seasickness and stark terror, used her skirt to try and bail out the water, while Finchie turned a menacing situation into phantasy and hysterical laughter. Eventually, the *SS Dee Why*, rounding Bradleys Head, had to stop and pick them up – though the *Dee Why*, a ferry of some 800 tons that used to ply between Circular Quay and Manly, eleven miles away, never stopped for anything! They were put down in the boiler room until they dried out, where Finchie confessed he was very disappointed they'd been rescued so quickly as he had really intended to elope with her to Shanghai.

The Hayter family were all very involved with the Australian theatre and cinema, and Papa, Clive Hayter, supported Doris Fitton when she started The Independent Theatre. His sister, Meta, had started Shirley Ann Richards (now Mrs Edmund Angelo) on her acting career and Shirley, in turn, was indirectly instrumental in Peter's testing for, and getting the part of, the boy next door in his second film, *Dad and Dave Come to Town*. So Peter was a member of Shirley and Margaret's Mosman set, and when the Hayters gave their 'at home' parties everyone was expected to get up and do their party piece. Margaret had wanted to invite Peter to one particular party, but Dad, remembering the *Dee Why* escapade, had said, 'No way!' Finchie, however, knew Clive Hayter was a keen fan of Australia's great musical comedy star Gladys Moncrieff, and said he would bring her if he were asked. So on that occasion he was allowed to come. He arrived in borrowed tails too long for him and a disposable cardboard shirt, but without 'our Glad' which was a bad start. When the time came for Finchie's act, he did a recitation called: 'I Like To See A Murder When I'm Out', a very dramatic piece in which two men fight to the death with a dagger. Finchie held them transfixed, but finished up on the floor with a dagger through his heart in a pool of IXL tomato sauce, concealed in his inside pocket. Even Margaret felt he'd gone too far. In the heat of the action the paper shirt had melted, and lay like confetti all over the floor. There was a stunned silence until Clive Hayter boomed: 'Get that ham out of my house!' Before he made his final exit from the house, still tailed but now shirtless, he secretly gave Margaret a ring he'd bought at Woolworths, '. . . which he wisely suggested I wear on a ribbon round my neck and under my blouse, and we were secretly engaged. I can't remember much of what happened to our romance after that. I suppose my father's attitude and those long walks over the Sydney Bridge eventually wore us down, and we drifted apart.' When Margaret Hayter's daughter went to England in 1961, she rang Peter up and he invited her to tea at Mill Hill. His greeting to her was: 'Your mother was the first woman I ever loved.'

5 Under the big top

The two leading players, Rosalind Kennerdale and Murray Matheson, and Ted Ardini, the acrobat-turned-theatre-technician during the tour, all knew and worked with Peter in the 1930s when George Sorlie, the black impresario, used to take variety and then legitimate theatre out into the far reaches of New South Wales and Queensland under the 'big top'. Roz Kennerdale – 'my first leading lady', to quote Finchie – remembered Peter as a pimply, thin kid of nineteen, suffering from malnutrition and pyorrhoea.

'I don't think he ever had enough to eat. On one occasion Horey Thomas, a New Zealander half Maori, a singer who played opposite me in one of the plays, came into the compartment on the train and found young Pete sound asleep with his head on my shoulder. I'd felt a bit lonely in another compartment on my own and had gone in to join the crowd who were all laughing. Peter, who had been sitting in the corner, came over, sat next to me, and just suddenly fell asleep. He'd probably been working very hard the previous night. Horey said: "I can't have that dirty little boy leaning on you," and he woke him up and put him over on another seat. But Pete did scrub up well eventually when he started to make the grade, and sometimes it was obvious he took a great pride in his appearance and looked really well groomed. He grew into a very handsome-looking young man, but in those days he was really down on his luck and got about £2.10 a week as a prop boy and scene shifter, with the occasional small part.'

Twenty years later, when Finchie went out to Australia to make *The Shiralee*, he phoned Roz from Sydney's Wentworth Hotel. 'Guess who I saw on the next sound stage while I was working in Hollywood?' Finchie said to her. 'Your leading man in *While Parents Sleep,* Murray Matheson, looking very *distingué* with grey temples. The memory of the Sorlie days brought us together like two old campaigners falling about with laughter at the recollection of an amazingly funny battle.'

Roz remembered Finchie had been given the part of Hunter

in *Ten Minute Alibi*, and he was also cast in *Laughter of Fools*, *Married by Proxy* and *Fair and Warmer*. 'He had very little experience, if any, and was absolutely brilliant, just a natural. William McGowan, the director, guided him, but it wasn't training. He just had it in him. He was born a great actor. Peter never ceased to remind me in later years of a seduction scene I had in *While Parents Sleep* with Murray. Finchie was supposed to help me take my dress off. He would unzip it down the back and I would step out with only a long slip on as in those days one didn't wear a bra. Well, one night he pulled down my zip and out I stepped quickly. But trust Finchie! He had taken my slip off as well. On I went and there was a hell of a gasp from a packed audience. Murray stood there, really looking as though he had seen a naked female for the very first time in his life. Poor Murray! He was rooted to the spot, absolutely transfixed. He hadn't the experience at that time to realize he must try and screen me. Finchie and the rest of the cast were hysterical with laughter in the wings. In '36 that was considered a really hot scene! Years later Finchie gave it out to the press abroad that the incident happened to him playing Jerry opposite me, his leading lady. But Finchie was never in *While Parents Sleep*, it was Murray, but it made a good story.'

When Finchie had approached Sorlie, the offer was: seven weeks to rehearse the repertoire without pay, then seven pounds a week to play as cast, and be useful. When Finchie got this chance to get a wealth of experience for a weekly pittance, he had been hoping to make a start in radio and had gone to see Lou Vernon, an older very experienced pro doing well in radio. 'Should I take this on, Lou?' he asked.

'Do you want to be an actor or a good script reader?' was his answer. One of Peter's lasting memories was one night with Sorlie, in Cairns, when the curtain came down on *Ten Minute Alibi*. When he came on to take his bow with the others, 1,100 hard bitten cane-cutters rose to their feet in a body and started whistling and shouting their approval.

'Finchie was so good in the parts he did with Sorlie,' Roz added, 'that when I got back to Sydney, I suggested him to Lawrie (Lawrence H. Cecil was married to Roz) who was then head of drama at the ABC (Australian Broadcasting Commission) and he cast Peter without an audition. He gave him a small part as an RAAF officer and Peter was brilliant in that too.'

Finchie told me he owed so much to Lawrie who used to keep him back after rehearsals to go over whatever part he was playing, line by line, and Lawrie directed him in *The Laughing Woman*. Lawrence Cecil and Finchie had an enormous mutual admiration for each other. Lawrie, speaking of Finchie after he had left for England in 1948, told me, 'I remember the day that kid came into the ABC in 1936, when Roz had recommended him. I took him up to the mike, showed him where to stand and gave him one or two tips and went into the control booth. I switched on. What a quality! It was extraordinary. The impact was colossal, a vibrant, emotional warmth in just a few lines. I came out and said, "You've got the part, Pete." It was a hot day and he had his coat collar turned up. "Take your coat off, boy," I said. "You must be cooked to a turn in that." "It's all right, Mr Cecil." "Go on," I said, "take it off". He took it off. I realized my mistake. He hadn't the money to buy a shirt.'

Peter described Sorlie's Big Top as a bell tent, a self-contained theatre which held about 1,100 people. To beat the opposition, a vaudeville company known as The Vanities, there'd be a train call after the show and their waggons would be coupled up. The 'get outs' on which Finchie worked had to be quick. 'We all worked like hell and everyone glad of a job, no union rules in those days. There was so little work you were lucky to get it.'

Sorlie had a regular circuit going from Sydney up to Cairns. He used to play the show dates: agricultural shows, and each one would follow in rotation, right the way up the coast, and all the carnival people would go. They were a part of Sorlie's vaudeville circus circuit. He used to have barkers going outside: 'Come inside and see the greatest collection of metropolitan talent ever collected together under one canvas.'

'We used to meet up with various side shows,' Murray Matheson recalled those days when I met him in Los Angeles in 1978, 'you know, the Tattooed Woman, the Ardinis with their Flying Trapeze act, and there were various animal acts, a lion act, and during our drama you could hear the lions roaring from the circus next door. Sometimes we were all in together like a sort of Fred Karno show. We all travelled by a very second class train. Mrs Sorlie used to sit there, outside the tent, with her stubby fingers weighed down by very dirty diamonds. The Sorlies really cleaned up on these shows. They had toured them for years. We played the Queensland dates like Toowoomba, Townsville, Cairns, Mackay, Rockhampton, all big time for us, but we set up in some very strange places. We played in an old cemetery, where they had removed all the tombstones but not the bodies. Another night we set up on a gigantic anthill. The ants didn't appear until the half (the half-hour call before curtain up), and the Musical Macs struck up "I'm in the Mood for Love" frantically. Sometimes we'd see a snake or two crawling about, or you'd open your mouth to speak and in would fly a large insect. But Finchie was never thrown by any of it. He had amazing poise, even at that age. For me, acting was always an effort, but never for Peter. He moved beautifully and was amazingly coordinated. He never had any real training but I wasn't surprised when Olivier took him up and put him under contract. I saw Peter in London after he had opened in *Daphne Laureola*. Whenever we met, we just collapsed with laughter over Sorlie and his tent shows: jet black, fuzzy hair, lots of diamonds, dirty nails, a half caste and what a fascinating man, a great larger-than-life character to whom both of us owed a great deal – a rare personality in any age. At the mention of Sorlie, Finchie and I would suddenly both become terribly common and Peter, despite the fact that he was English, would become absolutely Australian and talk in "Strine". He was often more Australian in his outlook than I ever was. But it was a *persona* he could assume or discard absolutely as he chose.'

Ted Ardini and his wife Jean had their trapeze act called 'The Flying Ardinis'. They first met Finchie in 1935 during the Australian Depression era. Things were very bad for everybody at that time. 'We met Finchie at Balmain. We used to call him Peter the Hound in those days, because he was so thin. He always looked like a sad little dog that needed a good feed. The Sorlie Legit Theatre Tent Show opened in Balmain, a suburb of Sydney, on Saturday, 8 February 1936 with *Ten Minute Alibi* and a repertoire of six plays. We did, I think, a fortnight in Balmain, then off we went, from Katoomba right up to Cairns. Pete, as I remember him, played the leads in most of the shows. He was a terrific actor, very young, great ambition. You could see, even in those days, that he had what it took for stardom. He was always very sure of himself. We tried to persuade him to become an acrobat. He used to practise with us on the mats. We taught him handstands, catherine wheels, and he started to learn the back somersault, the flip-flap. He was pretty good and could have made a very good circus acrobat, but he said he was an actor and we were performers and there was a difference, and he was determined to become a great actor.

'I remember we used to ask him what was the secret of his acting success, and he'd say, "Well, it's like your practice. You keep on and on at it. To be an actor," he'd say, "you must actually be the character." He'd imitate Jack the Ripper, "Now I'm feeling I am Jack the Ripper," and suddenly looked really sinister.

'One of the other actors in the company was supposed to have a broken leg. Peter didn't approve of what he did at all. No way! The actor, according to the script, fell off a horse and he had to keep his leg very stiff all the time. But this character bound it up and went around all day with two splints on it. Peter shook his head and said to me, "If you've got a broken leg, then you've got to have it mentally. You have to feel the pain in your head, nobody needs to hobble about in splints. Who's he fooling? If you feel the pain of that broken leg in your mind, the audience will feel it too." He knew, even in those days. He always became what he was playing. If it was a playboy or a detective, Peter became a playboy or a detective, and always went into tremendous detail. Everything those people would do, how they'd think, and he remained that person until he stepped off the stage.'

Ardini went on to describe 'poverty point', where Finchie and all the vaudeville and variety artists, all the actors, everyone in the entertainment world in Sydney, gathered to try and get work. This was the world on whose fringe Finchie at eighteen was already known and liked among all the old pros, and rated as an exceptionally promising youngster.

' "Poverty point" was the corner of Pitt and Park Streets, Sydney, and the old sign is up there to this day. There was the Criterion Theatre on the corner and Lew Dunn's Dance Studio at the back of that. On the other corner there was a chemist's shop and above that, Percy Lodge, who was the biggest theatrical agent in Sydney at that time, had his office. We knew Percy, of course, and all the other agents around there, because we were the performers, booked for the big vaudeville shows, George Sorlie, all the night clubs, that sort of thing, and everything went through those agents. A great deal of the booking was actually done on the corner of the street. That was our office.

Stanley MacKay, Cole's Varieties, Barton's Follies, Les Ship with his Suburban Circuit, George Drew, all the performers were booked on that corner. The business was actually done with a notebook out in the street. The other corner, on the Castlereagh Street end, was the actors' corner. They were a mile apart, a different race of people. We didn't like each other at all. But, of course, there were a few exceptions such as Peter Finch, Murray Matheson, and Bill Kerr who were always very friendly, and we got on very well together.

'Finchie's mate in those days, the actor Bill Kerr, and Finchie used to stand on the corner at "poverty point". There'd be a whole crowd of actors down on the pavement hoping for a job. Perce Lodge would stick his hand out with the index finger up, meaning there's a one quid job going, and if the actor to whom he pointed accepted he'd give Perce the thumbs up and the job would be his. Thumb and index finger from the actor, in reply to Perce's index finger, meant "I want one and a half a week" – one pound and ten bob. Back would come the quick index and middle finger up, "fuck you" from Perce, and he'd point at the next starving actor with his index finger.'

Ted Ardini can remember one occasion vividly, 'when the only man who had money between the three or four of us was Peter, who had about three shillings. We were all so hungry we were nearly rattling, and we decided to go down to Coles. So we went down to Coles and had a doughnut and a cup of coffee, which used to cost 2d each. Peter, being the flush one, stood us all that round and then back we went to "poverty point". Peter was there for a few minutes and then he said, "I won't be a tick. I'm just going to slip up to the Cross (Sydney's Kings Cross)," so he jumped into a tram and he was gone for about an hour and a half. When he came back, somebody said, "Well, come on, Peter. What about it?" "What about what?" " 'Bout time we had another cup of coffee." He said: "What with?" We said: "Well, you've got money." "Nah!" said Peter. "Not any more, I haven't." "Well, hell, what have you done with it?" "Well, it cost me tuppence to get up to the Cross by tram." That left him with 1/6d. "What did you do with the other 1/6?" He said: "What about my manicure?" And spread out ten unbelievably groomed nails. His last 1/6d, and he'd spent it on a bloody manicure! Oh, Finchie could always surprise you!'

That was typical Finchie. The arse could be coming out of his trousers and off he'd go with his last 1/6d to get himself a manicure.

The Sorlie contract tour under the big top doing straight theatre meant, hopefully, at least six months steady if gruelling employment for the Ardinis and Finchie. Ted reminded me of Finchie's extravagance when he felt really flush. 'One night, up in Queensland, Cairns I think it was, we were sitting in the dressing room about half-past seven, and in came Pete in a beautiful new shirt. "Like the shirt? Nice bit of hessian!" "Yes, Peter, and a hanky in the pocket too, a nice blue hanky and a tie to match. You've smartened yourself up. A bit of a swell all of a sudden! Where did you get it?" "Oh, Coles. Two-and-six." "What!" I said. I hopped up out of my chair and had a look. Other friends came in and had a look. Everybody had a look. We decided we'd all go down and get one of those tomorrow. So Peter turned round, took his coat off and hung it up on the hook. We suddenly saw that the entire back was cut right out of his shirt. A piece of string had been tied across the shoulders and a piece tied across the tail. He had sliced the back out and cut himself a tie and handkerchief to match!'

Ardini felt that Peter had learned a tremendous amount from his months with the Sorlie outfit. A totally different audience every night, one night rural, the next miners, the next cane-cutters, the next an industrial town, and they weren't playing to theatre-going audiences. Every night a different play with no chance of becoming set.

'The experience must have stood Peter in good stead and given him a lot of ideas for his Mercury Theatre. After that, Jean and I met Peter now and then. We'd have a drink and a yarn and talk about old times, but we all went our separate ways and then the war came. Then Peter hit the big time. But I feel now, thinking back on the young Peter the Hound I knew forty years ago, that his absorption in his roles, the fact that he would *become* the particular part he was playing, probably hastened his death. I mean, he played that alcoholic man under terrible stress and strain and died of a heart attack. Every part he played, he not only told me himself but proved it night after night, he actually became the character to the best of his ability. He also had that knack of being able to wipe everything else from his mind during that time. He would get into conversation with anyone who was a model for a part he might one day play. He'd buy him a drink, laugh and talk and find out how that person thought and what made him tick, and, when you wound him up, how the springs turned. That's why to me, in those Sorlie days, he was such a great actor. He said to us, "The secret of acting is to **be** the person. The secret of **your** success is practice".'

When I decided to throw in my lot to train as an actor with Finchie at the Mercury Theatre, and we'd had a fortnight's classes of Finchie's theories on acting as adapted from Louis Jouvet and Stanislavsky, he took me aside and asked me if I'd be game to be used in an experiment. He wanted me to take an eighteen month course with a friend of his, two nights a week, and get a thorough basic training as an acrobat. 'You're young enough, just, you're slight, with enough stamina and agility to make a stab at it.'

A physical coward by nature, the prospect appalled me, but to please Pete I agreed to go with him to the gymnasium where I was literally put through the hoops. Exactly where the place of torture was I don't remember, but I was introduced to Ted and Jean Ardini, The Flying Ardinis, as they were called. For Finchie and the Ardinis it was a great reunion. They hadn't actually met up since 1936 when the season collapsed in Tamworth and the George Sorlie Players had headed back to 'poverty point'. Ted and Jean were told they were to try and knock Finchie's young and aspiring student into physical shape as a acrobat. The bait, of course, was that if I could do a back flip-flap, which Ted had been planning to teach Finchie twelve years earlier, plus a back somersault, flying dives over chairs and tables, and so forth, he would then consider directing either *A Midsummer Night's Dream* or *Romeo and Juliet* so I could be an acrobatic Puck, or a Romeo who could leap up very spectacularly over the wall and out of sight into Juliet's garden. Finchie's idea had been inspired by seeing Olivier, as Hamlet on the screen, leap down from the rostrum on to Basil Sidney's (as Claudius) double's chest in that memorable final acrobatic encounter.

Ted Ardini, one of the gentlest and most patient teachers in the world, went through four months of unmitigated boredom, pulling my spine and trying to get my body into the relaxed condition whereby I could defy the laws of gravity. The dreadful moment of truth came six weeks later when I had to leap into the air as high as I could, upwards and backwards, turn a somersault, land on the palms of my hands and then spring back on to my feet. What in acrobatic terms is known as the flip-flap. Finchie had agreed to stay away during the agonizing weeks when the beginner, attached to a harness, and a pulley attached to the ceiling, is turned upside down and over hundreds of times until the bodily reflexes begin to respond. Finally you find yourself going through the motions of the flip-flap and back somersault in the safety of the harness, with Ted or Jean Ardini's hand firmly placed in the small of your back to make sure you don't land with skull first on the concrete. In retrospect I can only say I've never known such physical terror as those long tram rides to the acrobatic torture chamber where I felt at any second I would be crippled for life. I never seemed to have the physical strength to get myself high enough off the ground to make the back spin. Finchie treated it all as a great joke but he did agree that he would put on a play in which it could be used. So came the day when the harness was removed and Peter arrived. I took up my position on the foam rubber mat on the concrete floor and Ardini shouted, 'Hu-up!' I bent my knees, threw my arms down, preparatory to making the desperate leap and suddenly remained rooted to the spot through sheer funk. Ardini assured me that for four weeks I had been doing the routine without his using the pulley at all, but with that belt round my waist I had felt safe. Without it I felt naked and incapable of doing the trick without landing on my spine or skull. Finchie as an actor could see the agony of the situation, but Ted Ardini was absolutely convinced I could and would do it. The hall was packed with kids ranging from five to fifteen years of age, who could and were doing flip-flaps, one and a half's, the splits, backbends, catherine wheels and making the whole thing look like a piece of cake. Finchie and Ardini cajoled, coaxed, wheedled, bullied, shouted. Finchie promised the earth: *The Tempest* with this Ariel flying around on invisible wires and spiralling up into a tree, an effect that would blow the Mercury audiences right out of their minds. But the subject of their threats, promises, and Finchie's experiment, stood nailed to the earth in stark terror, knowing at any moment he would have to take off backwards into space, and knowing he would kill himself if he tried. Finally, cringing with fear and shame, while the entire class of thirty-odd mini-acrobats had gathered round to try and goad me into orbit with taunts or yells of encouragement, I promised to have a go if Ted would put me once more into the harness. He did and I managed to do the flip-flap, followed by a clean back somersault with no problem at all.

Finchie got angry. 'You expect me to rig up a mobile pulley and jerk the fucking strings every time you make an entrance on the stage?' I said: 'You try, Finchie, and I'll pull the strings!' I was beginning to feel like a circus animal that refuses to go through the fiery hoop. They took off the harness and again, with that umbilical cord gone, useless as it was, I couldn't get off the ground. Finally, Finchie went off and came back a little later with something behind his back. He whispered to Ted, who came over to me and said, 'Peter and I are going to stand on either side of you and when I say go, give it all you've got. Swing yourself up as high as you can and we'll catch you, whatever happens.'

Finchie had started to break out in a sweat, but Ardini was very cool and ambled up slowly and stood on one side while Peter stood on the other. 'Now shut your eyes, and . . . go!' I felt a pain across the calves of my legs as though they had been flicked with a hot iron. Up I went what seemed like three times my own height and I saw them both on the floor, upside down, landed backwards on the palms of my hands and on to my feet. I never knew who had given me a whack across the legs and I never saw what it was. It stung like hell for a few hours but the freedom, the exhilaration, the sudden surge of power, at having accomplished what I believed was impossible was thanks to Finchie and Ted Ardini. From then on, week after week, Ardini's acrobatic lessons for the actor were the most thrilling classes I ever had in my life. It was the element of risk, and the exhilaration of being able to fly through the air that released so many fears. Peter understood this, and in this he was a great, though I thought at the time, a cruel inspiration.

I said: 'Come on, Peter, I've done your bloody flip-flap, now you get in the fucking harness and let's see you go over.' Finchie, with his hump, his pigeon-toed walk, and his round shouldered body, got in and had a go. He had forgotten to take his coat off and his shirt was hanging down in front. He flung himself up, Ted pulled the rope and swoosh! over went Finchie. 'Look at him!' said a very small acrobat, standing beside me. 'It's grandpa, all over the floor, like a mad woman's shit.' He'd come down, albeit very gently, on the crown of his head. Ted had pulled hard on the pulleys and the whole place exploded with laughter.

'Bravo, Finchie!' He had proved he was game to have a go. He left, pale and shaken, to down a large scotch in the nearest pub. He was about to start me off on a course of juggling when I was rescued by Olivier who advised Peter to go to England.

6 Beginners please

Before the war, Peter's closest rival was probably Lloyd Lamble who, by 1936, was already a star having made an overnight success as Danny in Emlyn Williams' *Night Must Fall*, for the J. C. Williamson Management at the Comedy Theatre in Melbourne. Lloyd actually opened during Peter's second week at Balmain with George Sorlie. He had trained as a concert pianist and switched to acting in Melbourne radio. After *Night Must Fall*, he became a young leading man for J. C. Williamson Theatres when the standard of the legitimate theatre was very high. The reason for this was that many leading artists from abroad were touring Australia in the 1930s. Lloyd was getting the leading roles but Peter soon got into films and, although still at the beginning of his Australian career, was very highly regarded. By March 1939, when Cecil B. De Mille inaugurated the first Lux Radio Theatre programme by trans-Pacific telephone, both young actors had become widely known on Australian radio.

The first play presented by Lux was *Interference* on 19 March, and a press headline on 29 March read 'Finch stole show in new Lux play ... In that quiet, disillusioned voice, he somehow expressed all the resignation, the irony, the savage despair of the man who has been sentenced to die.' Peter had got his first real break in radio with the BSA Players at Pagewood Studios (later called the Macquarie Players) through James Raglan, the actor and producer friend of Enid Lorimer, to whom she had introduced Peter. Raglan had spent four years in Australia, working for Williamson, as well as producing and playing in radio. He was a professional father-figure to Peter until he returned to England in 1938.

Ethel Lang, working at that time with the BSA Players, or accompanying her two children to the studios where they were contracted to appear in children's serials in which Peter Finch usually played the leading part, remembers Peter as an incorrigible prankster. 'I can still see him, around 1936 it must have been, climbing monkey-wise up the curtains of the old 2 GB Studios in Bligh St.'

Ethel developed a maternal concern for Peter and, seeing one day that he was in dire need, bought him a shirt. She was always scolding him for his dirty shoes. 'He never cleaned them and, having a husband who was a meticulous dresser, Peter's shoes were a constant offence to me. But my scolding had little effect. When my youngest son, David, played the small boy in Peter's production of *French Without Tears* I was there with him at each performance. Peter also played the Commander and what an elegant, romantic figure he was until I looked at his shoes – they were still uncleaned. I remonstrated, but to no effect.'

When Peter turned twenty-one in 1937, dead broke and sharing a room with a mate, he came into a very small inheritance from his grandfather – about £300. In those days it would have been enough to take him to England and sustain him for a couple of months till he got started on what everyone knew, even at that time, must eventually be a distinguished career. Did he go? 'Not on your life,' said Ethel. 'He threw this enormous party for all his mates – actors, wrestlers, gangsters, layabouts, people from every strata of Sydney's society. When I got my invitation, I said, "O Peter, why don't you use that money to get to England?" He replied, very pleased with himself, "Oh, it's all right, Mummy Gib, I've got money in the bank." "Have you," I said. "How much?" "Oh," replied Pete. "I'm fine. I've got eleven quid." I didn't see much of him after he went in the army, except for a show we did at the ABC when he was in uniform, and then he appeared remote and strange, as if our relationship had faded away.'

Like the Spanish who have very protracted fiestas to commemorate anniversaries and saints' days, Finchie celebrated his coming-of-age over a period of several days. Mario, who ran the Florentino restaurant in the basement of a building opposite *The Sun* newspaper office in Elizabeth Street, gave Peter a gala lunch for all his friends. Peter maintains that he and a party of mates broke into an old Sydney mansion, then empty and boarded up, and danced and caroused there all night. Ian Bevan remembers a party given with elegance and taste at Marian Morphee's home down at Collaroy. It was Ian who introduced Peter to Sydney society hostess Rada Penfold Hyland, whose Bacchanalian revels at 'Toftmonks' Peter later attended with his current fiancée, Sheila Smart. By 1937, although he would never really believe it himself, many remember Peter as very much *persona grata* among some of Sydney's wealthy set. It was through Margaret Hayter that Peter met Marian Morphee, who first really took him in hand and knocked off some of the rough edges. His relationship with her lasted on and off from 1937 until 1942. Marian, older than Peter, was travelled, sophisticated and very attractive. Finchie admitted that she and her mother (it was her mother who forgave him his lapses and treated him as a very lovable rogue) made him aware of the need to look his best sometimes, even if he only regarded it as yet another performance for the benefit of his public. At 'Shipmates', their ultra modern beach home with swimming-pool, they kept open house with endless parties, and Peter was always welcome. Finchie once claimed that he first went to 'Shipmates' as a butler for a party to earn a few bob. When he really misbehaved, got very tight and very ill, Marian who felt she had made some progress in grooming the slothful Peter – 'totally lacking in any social grace, untidy and frequently going for several days without soap and water' – banished him from their home and told him never to return. Finchie had disappeared into the house and gone on one of his exasperating benders, which were subsequently to cause such havoc and unhappiness in his marriages. Marian had become really fond of a Peter who could always make her laugh, but violating the home in a sick and drunken state was not on, and out he went neck and crop. The prodigal son bided his time. The next day when Marian returned home she heard peals of gay laughter coming from mama's room above. On entering she found Finchie and the old lady helpless with laughter at one of his outrageous impersonations.

Marian was fiercely protective towards Peter and he often had to use the evasive tactics learned during his sojourn with Betty at Greenwich. Sometimes Marian found it difficult to understand and forgive his many infidelities with other women, and his hurtful behaviour, as when she lent him a gold signet ring keepsake which had belonged to her father, and Finchie promptly went out and pawned it. But Peter needed Marian because she was the first person in his life who made him feel he wasn't rejected. She may have tried to dominate him, but she also made him feel he was a man. In her own way she tried to adjust to the younger, unpredictable Bohemian with the wandering eye. During their time together he had once tried to telephone George Finch in England but his reputed father refused to speak to him, which upset Peter for a long time afterwards.

Peter got a terrible rocket one morning at 'Shipmates' for not cleaning his teeth. When asked how long it was since they'd last been brushed, he answered, 'This morning.' 'That's a lie,' was the reply, 'you don't even possess a toothbrush. Borrow one and clean them at once!' Finchie proceeded very sheepishly to the bathroom, selected a toothbrush, emptied a liberal dollop of powder on to it, and scrubbed away. Unfortunately, he used the powder for holding dentures in place, and emerged from the bathroom 'frothing at the mouth' with what everyone thought at first must be lockjaw. Peter with a mouth full of denture powder had the entire family falling about with laughter, and it was laughter that always brought Finchie back to Marian who, with difficulty, would forgive him.

When Marian was living up at Challis Avenue in Kings Cross, she had a friend staying, and Finchie used to bring up his washing. One day the friend rushed into the kitchen to Marian and said: 'I've just washed Finchie's socks, and when I put them in the water they fizzled!'

One afternoon Marian and her sister, Cicely Stewart, went to the Prince Edward Cinema to see *Hellzapoppin'*, in the course of which a funny little comic crosses the screen, carrying a potted plant, calling 'A plant for Mr Jones, a plant for Mr Jones', a piece of inconsequential business that had the audience in fits of laughter. In the interval, as they were sitting happily, eating their ice-cream buckets with their little wooden spades, they heard a familiar voice behind them calling, 'A plant for Mrs Stewart, a plant for Mrs Stewart,' and there was Finchie, walking up and down the aisle, with a large potted palm, removed from the floral display in the foyer. Needless to say he was soon thrown out.

In a very old copy of the *Week-end Book* still in Marian's possession, there is a table in the back pages of a game they used to play at Collaroy which listed qualities: Peter on Marian, Marian on Peter, and Peter on Peter. Out of a possible twenty points, Finchie at twenty-one years marked himself:

Beauty	11	Willpower	1
Brains	12	Sense of humour	20
Charm	2	Tact	0
Taste	20	Sincerity	0
Tolerance	15	Humility	0
Discretion	1		

Marian had a son by her first marriage, and Finchie knew the lad quite well. In 1952 this son, aged twenty-two, was involved in a collision between his motor cycle and a taxi. In spite of two emergency operations, he died two days after the accident. Peter only heard the news in England four years later, but he immediately wrote to Marian:

'Dearest,
I have only just heard of the tragic news about Peter. What can I say? You must know I feel it deeply for you. I still have the small Bible you gave me in '41. I often thank the 'bon Dieu' for the days we had together. I hope to be in Sydney in May or June. Hope I may see you. Love, Peter F.'

Some time after, Peter arrived in Sydney to make a film and contacted Marian, asking her to join him for dinner. She agreed, but only on condition that the two of them would be alone, as she had been upset by the way many of his old friends had commented on how lucky Finchie had been to make the big time, and she wanted to talk to him quietly. Peter assured her that they would be à deux, but she arrived to find an ever-swelling crowd of old mates, all fawning over him. She left immediately after the meal, having only had a word or two with Peter.

Soon after they first met, Marian asked Peter what his main ambition was and he said there was only one thing he really wanted, that when he died, they would put on his tombstone, 'He was a good actor'. On learning of his death, Marian wrote immediately to Eletha, Peter's third wife, telling her this story. When I saw Eletha on the screen accepting Peter's posthumous Academy Award, I wondered if she remembered the story and realized how in a different way his wish had come exactly true.

In 1938 things began to move for Peter, as he appeared at the Theatre Royal in Sydney as Clyde Pelton in *Personal Appearance* by Laurence Riley, starring Betty Balfour, and he also did a special Sunday invitation performance at the Theatre Royal in April of Leon Gordon's *White Cargo*.

Having actually got (thanks to James Raglan) his first break in radio in the serial *Khyber* in November 1935, by 1938, between his theatre work and filming, he was making a modest living in radio, doing serials like *We Await your Verdict* and *Into the Light*. But it was Ken G. Hall, the Australian film director at Cinesound studios in Sydney (who ended up with eighteen Australian feature films to his credit), who gave Peter his first successful part into pictures, casting him as Bill Ryan (the boy next door) in *Dad and Dave Come to Town*, (released in the UK as *The Rudd Family Goes to Town*). Hall was the most financially durable producer/director in Australia during the 1930s at a time when the American distribution monopolies had a firm grip on the entire industry in Australia. Ken Hall, and Charles Chauvel who directed Peter in *Rats of Tobruk*, gave most of the exploitable acting and technical cinema talent in Australia what opportunities there were in the 1930s and 40s to learn and develop in motion pictures. Shirley Ann Richards told Peter about the auditioning, and he went along to Cinesound to see casting director George Cross, and Ken Hall. Hall needed a young man to play the ingenue Sally's boy friend, a gangling youth, not only very young but able to stand up to a solo scene with Bert Bailey, the star, whom Hall knew would demolish any youngster who couldn't really act.

'I auditioned young Peter, then twenty-one, and although he'd only had radio experience, that tour with Sorlie and the odd theatre part, he was dead right for the juvenile. He was half-starved, long, cadaverous, and looked like a country yokel. He lived mostly on his wits, and occasionally on his talent when he could get work. Peter was just a nobody, and I think he got three days work on that film, one on location in Camden, and two in the studio with Bailey. To get a scene with Bailey in any picture was something, because he could really hold an audience, but Peter Finch stood up to him as I sensed he might. In terms of the scene they played he lay down to him as the script required, but as an actor of quality, he stood up to him all right, giving Bailey back all he was getting. The part required Peter to be terrified of the old man. Everyone was supposed to be. Peter came out of that film magnificently and in the cinema he got tremendous laughs. When I saw the film, twenty-six years later, Peter was still getting his visual comedy laughs. He had a very funny scene of total misunderstanding with Bailey. He comes to see him to ask if he can marry his daughter, Sally. As a typical Aussie, Peter refers to her as "Sal", which happens to be the name of Bailey's dog. The old man thinks the lad has come to buy his dog and shakes Finchie to the depths of his hobnails when he replies: "Well, you'll have to watch her. She's a nice little bitch, but greedy, mind you." '

In the film, viewed forty years after it was made, Finchie, even in his first appearance on screen, is very relaxed and very real, a typical young Aussie, with his felt hat, thin bony face, a tooth already missing, showing the gap on the upper left-hand side when he smiled, a real goof and very slow. His is the visual comedy of naïvety and his training in vaudeville gave him that natural split-second timing for the knockabout slap-stick farce situations in the film that enabled him to match the rhythm and style of Bert Bailey, and get his laughs. He had that open-mouthed gormless adenoidy look of a boy in the last stages of adolescence who 'pulls his pud a bit' and longs 'to root a sheila' but is far too shy to make anything but a very timid overture. The biggest Adam's apple in the business certainly helps, but everything is suggested through his imagination and nothing is ever overstated.

So Peter established himself with Hall at Cinesound as an actor who could play rather weak, gangling young men and when casting his next feature, *Mr Chedworth Steps Out*, starring Cecil Kellaway, his immediate choice for Arthur, the eldest weakling son of the family, was Peter.

'I said, "Get young Finch," and he had a good part, also against a strong actor, which is always helpful for any beginner, even if it's only one scene. But Peter had several good scenes with Kellaway. This was his second picture. Finch did very well out of it and he was excellent as the weakling son because in many respects he was a weakling himself.'

Finchie himself remembered two things about *Mr Chedworth Steps Out*. He had to escape from some crooks and gained perspiring realism and loss of breath by running round the four walls of Cinesound studios before the take. On a very humid Sydney day the result was that . . . 'I was absolutely knackered when I rushed through the front door to telephone the Police and had to rest for a few minutes before the actual shot.' In escaping from the crooks, he had had to punch one of them. But carried away again by his own realism, he forgot to pull his punch and one crook, Leslie Victor, who happened to be a good mate in real life, lost a front tooth.

Alex Ezard was working as a make-up artist at Cinesound when Peter tested for Ken Hall to play the love scenes with Valerie Scanlon (Sally), in *Dad and Dave Come to Town*. Alex first met Peter in 1937, and remembers him playing a lot of foreign parts, Russians, Germans, Frenchmen, Poles, etc., on radio. Finchie was so conscientious about his work that if he had a Russian character to play, he'd go and find a Russian cook in a restaurant somewhere and work as his assistant for two or three weeks, to get right under the skin of the part. Peter would meet Alex for a drink smelling of cooking fat and absolutely into the role he was contracted to play, and he'd practise his accent and physical mannerisms on Alex, even though it was only for a radio show. Alex really had to study Finchie's face as a make-up artist for the camera and feels that in those days his high cheek-bones, like a Red Indian, and his gauntness, went against him. When Peter did the make-up test for *Dad and Dave Come to Town*, he wasn't too keen on having 'poufterish make-up all over his face'. Peter was very unhappy about it. Most of the parts he played were in natural, straight make-up. He just played Peter Finch. 'I recall at one stage out here,' Alex said, 'we had an English cameraman who wanted to use filters on the camera, a red filter to bring out the clouds in the background. So to counteract this, we made a test and put red greasepaint on Peter's face. Boy, didn't he go berserk about that! He said, "How can you act when you look like a Red Indian?" '

Though Hall was very much in charge as the director, Peter learned to trust Alex's judgment, and after each take he'd go up to Ezard informally and say, 'What d'you think?' and Alex would say. 'I think you might have overplayed a little. You might have been a little heavy. Keep it down.' 'I shudder to think now,' Alex said, 'in retrospect, considering what he became as an actor, giving him advice like that, but he always took it, thought about it, made his own decisions and went on getting better and better all the time.'

Even in those days Peter not only analysed his own performances but he wanted to know about the techniques of filming. He was always asking about dolly shots when the camera tracks, high angle shots, and told Alex he was interested in directing, and Alex felt he had the intelligence and potential to be a really

89

good film director. He had an infectious enthusiasm and people were keen to help him.

According to Alex, the actor from whom Peter learned a great deal about the actual technique of film acting was Cecil Kellaway. He can remember Cecil taking young Peter aside during *Mr Chedworth Steps Out* and showing him the importance of how to position himself for the lighting, hitting his chalk marks so as to find his right pattern of back and side lights. 'In those days we didn't have the number of grips, gaffers and technicians to carry the equipment, nor the stringent union rules that operate now. Peter would pick up a tripod or help adjust a reflector. The young actors at that time were expected to hoe in and do their bit all round, and Peter was always more than willing to do his share of the chores.'

From March 1939 until June 1941, Peter was under contract to the Australian Broadcasting Commission, the ABC, with options every six months, and in 1940 was released to make a film in which he played an English-educated German spy who joins the RAAF to advance fifth column sabotage activities in war-time Australia. The film, called *The Power and the Glory*, was written, produced and directed by Noel Monkman and released in April, 1941, three months before Finchie embarked as a soldier on the *Queen Mary* for the Middle East. Finchie regarded *The Power and the Glory* as a war-time quickie, made on the cheap with cheap effects, but again, like a number of his films that as films don't stand up to much in retrospect, many of the excerpts are interesting as regards the now maturing Peter. *The Power and the Glory* began shooting in June, 1940 at Pagewood, and Figtree Studios just round the corner from where I went to school. It is melodramatic and there is some hefty overacting, though not from Peter, but it has always been underrated. Some of the photography and technical skill are every bit as good as the Hollywood low budget films of that time. Peter, as Frank Miller the traitor, doesn't have great opportunity in a mainly action film to show much subtlety or richly observed characterisation, but he has unmistakable screen presence. Here, two years after *Chedworth*, he has really begun to mature. He is relaxed and assured. In one scene, when he is slapped across the face for bungling a sabotage job on a squadron of aircraft, he has to launch forth into a diatribe against England and lauding the Fatherland, a scene which is an absolute melodramatic pitfall for any but an experienced, natural actor, but he skates over the wafer-thin-ice-of-a-speech that is pure bathos, and you believe him. The intensity and stillness are compelling and it shows the beginnings of an actor able to master a pedestrian piece of writing and make an audience aware only of the passionate belief of the character.

Leslie Rees, the author of a standard work on the Australian theatre, was federal drama script editor at the ABC before the war, F. D. Clewlow was federal controller of productions, and Lawrence H. Cecil was the chief Sydney drama producer. According to Finchie, Lawrie Cecil and old Frank Clewlow absolutely detested each other, but with Peter they did agree on one thing – he must be put under contract. Finchie, cast in everything from Shakespeare to Shaw, was expanding vocally and getting a thorough grounding in radio acting, working under directors like Clewlow, who was English, Cecil who had played on Broadway with John Barrymore, and Charles Wheeler, whom I remember as an elderly man when I was breaking into radio, who could generate enthusiasm and get remarkable performances from his casts with scripts that seemed at first reading to be very pedestrian.

Thanks to Rees, Finchie was even able to tackle some of the Greek tragedies, as part of the enormous variety of roles he was playing twice a week. At one stage, Rees became concerned and told Clewlow that if they weren't careful Finch would wear out his welcome and become over-exposed. Clewlow, always on the look-out for a bit of denigration, used to talk about 'Finch's moon wobble'. He used the phrase meaning a sort of falsely facile romantic tone.

When Lawrie Cecil fell ill, Leslie Rees took over the production of Robert Sherwood's *Abe Lincoln in Illinois* which Rees had adapted for radio, with Peter playing the young Lincoln. 'Peter seemed to be in complete control. He knew exactly what variety and nuance to give the character. We had an American in the cast and Peter worked and worked and got his Southern American accent to perfection. He always took infinite pains, no matter how much work we gave him.'

Jean Robertson and Neva Carr-Glyn both working with Peter in *Mr Wu* at the ABC in 1941 told me that once he got to the microphone, the Chinese character seemed to permeate him. It was not just a Chinese voice, the man playing the part became

Oriental and to anyone who has worked in radio, that kind of transformation is extremely rare. They both remarked that Peter's face, through sheer concentration and imagination, began to acquire an oriental look and you forgot completely that you were in an antiquated recording studio. Neva used to say she was always at Peter to clean his nails, and for a while his hands were really beautiful, but that in many respects Finchie was like a young horse that no one would ever really be able to manage. He'd be docile and amenable for a while, but with a genius for slipping the halter and with a constant need to romanticize in order to gain some form of identity and equilibrium for everyday living.

7 One of the boys?

Harry, a young actor and close friend of Finchie, always wondered about the contradictory variations in his childhood stories. The facts about Paris and Madras would vary radically according to the enthusiasm and credulity of Finchie's audience, and depending on how the alcohol intake inspired his story-telling muse. Harry knew Bert La Blance who used to relate with great pride to anyone who would listen how Finchie, working as a stage hand with Stanley MacKay's Gaieties, a vaudeville touring show, was on hand to take over one night when Bert La Blance's straight man became too drunk to stand up, let alone appear. Many of the Sydney actors, Finchie and Harry among them, used to frequent three well-known underworld night spots, the Fifty-fifty Club, the 400 Club, and the Palms. These were night clubs operated on the sly grog circuit and were brothels as well. Finchie was usually part of a trio with Harry and a fellow entertainer, Buddy Morley, and at the end of the day's work, if all three had been lucky enough to get any (or even only one had been), and as long as there was enough brass to buy a drink, they'd start the evening at the Fifty-fifty, move on to the 400, and end up at the Palms around two in the morning.

The clubs varied in quality. The 400 had a certain amount of 1930s style, the Fifty-fifty was further down the scale, and when you entered the Palms you'd hit the bottom rung. Actors were especially popular at these nocturnal havens of delight and iniquity and the other clientele would frequently give the actors drinks and encourage them to stand up and perform. Finchie was quite likely to recite anything, from pornographic Byron, or 'The Joys of Masturbation', to 'The Song of Solomon', but his favourite choices were Walt Whitman and Shakespeare. Buddy Morley was, according to Harry, a 'bloody brilliant entertainer, a near genius'. He was a script writer, song writer, comedian and dramatic actor especially adept at character parts. Harry recalls that Morley had a standard repertoire of around seven characters; and one of his routines was 'The Pigtail of Lee Fang Fu'. A more serious item was a monologue about a man wrongly accused of murder. Before he had finished, even the hoodlums and prostitutes were in tears. Other entertainers would be cheered, clapped, and called up to 'give us a song, blue', 'Come on, shorty', 'Hoofaway, twinkletoes – give us a tap dance'. The sport would often last until dawn. The Fifty-fifty and the 400 were run by the same patron and Finchie gained a great deal of his cabaret experience and acquired his lust for the night-life there. The Fifty-fifty and the Palms had steel front doors as a safety precaution against criminal gangs and police raids. The Palms was really rough, attracting a greater share of gangsters than the other clubs. One night, word came through that a gang was invading up the stairs, their object a rival gang whom Harry and Finchie were in the midst of entertaining. As the first shots rang out, the big steel door at the top of the stairs clanged shut. Finchie and Harry swallow-dived for cover under a large table and the siege of the Palms continued until the arrival of the cops.

Another working friend of Finchie's was Nigel Lovell who had come into radio in 1938 from Sydney University's dramatic society, where he had been the secretary. He and Finchie had both started with James Raglan and when they were working on Saturday mornings at the Columbia studios out at Homebush, getting paid ten bob for the morning's work, they'd spend it at Sid Godfrey's pub. Sid had been a champion boxer, owned the pub, and had a daughter called Phyllis. When the customers got obstreperous, Phyllis would reach under the bar, produce a thick wet bathtowel, screw it up into a club, and wallop anyone within reach. If that didn't work, she'd call Dad and the offenders would be out on the pavement before they knew it. One day Nigel went in with Peter, who was always practising his accents. 'There was this little box on the counter inscribed "Could you spare a coin for the crippled children?" Peter picked it up and said, "Hey, Phyl, this is empty. D'you want it filled?" So she said, "Well yes, sure." So Peter said, "Watch this." I went round with him. He said, in his best American accent, which was pretty good even in those days, "Say I'm from the States and I'm just having a drink here, and I find that this box for the crippled kiddies is empty. Don't you think you folks could put in something?" And they'd put something in, a bob or a coin, and he was going from group to group, around the bar, with this box. He tapped a fellow on the shoulder, who happens to be an American and went into his routine. The American said, "You from the States, are you, buddy?" And Finchie said, "Yeah." "Well, what part do you come from?" asked the Yank, and Finchie said Kentucky, and then realizing he wasn't using a Kentucky accent, "Well, that's where I was born, but when I was three we started to move around. My Pa was in Union Finance." Finchie, having blinded him with science, went on to have a long conversation and I do believe, to this day, that guy didn't know Finchie wasn't American. He carried it through and he was full of gags like that, and he ended up with the box full.'

When Finchie and I met up in Rome, he told me of his hell-raising adventure with Big Merv's bird at the Palms, which Nigel confirms as he had actually been with Finchie on this particular night. 'The Palms was down in Rushcutters Bay,' Nigel explained to me. 'A long flight of steps led up to it and it was a real dive. In those days the liquor laws were pretty tough. The whole of the Sydney underworld met there, and Peter knew them all. They used to love him. "Good-day, Pete. What stories you got for us tonight?" Anyway, he met a girl down there one night, he thought her rather attractive. She must have thought he was a bit of all right too, because the next thing anybody knows, they'd both vanished. At this time he was living up at the Cross at Gleneagles which was a rooming house, with Cec Perry, who was another real rascal and a legend. They shared this sort of bedsitter-cum-small-cooking-arrangement-type-place, very barely furnished. I went up there once and the only thing I remember about it was an ancient refrigerator full of booze and a couple of day beds, but on one of them there was an arrow pointing down and it had "casting couch" printed on it. I found out about the sequel to our night at the Palms through being in a radio play with him at the time. We all turned up at rehearsal the next morning but no Peter. Now, he was always pretty punctual. He was professionally very good that way, so we thought, oh, something's happened. Ten minutes, quarter of an hour went by, and then people started looking for him and nobody could find him. We found him later the next day. What had happened was that morning very early, there was a knock on his door. He opened the door and a couple of big bruisers said, "You Peter Finch?" "Yes," he said. They said, "Just come along with us," and they took him downstairs and shoved him into a big black car. There were more fellows in the car and they drove him right out to Long Bay where the rifle range is and the jail. It's just scrub country. They held him down and poured a bottle of castor oil down his throat and said, "You know that bird you rooted? Well, don't ever do that again. That's Big Merv's sheila and your knocking off his sheila's not on with Big Mervyn, so just keep cool tool," and they just drove off and left him. He was so sick he was yellow and green and really white around the gills and it took him several days to get over it.'

Finchie and Harry often used to visit a high-class brothel on Sydney's Bayswater Road to read poetry to the Madam, a tall, gorgeous redhead with a body, according to Finchie, 'like a sexy serpent' and a taste for Walt Whitman's *Leaves of Grass*. Finchie and Harry took it in turns to read her Whitman while she reclined in ecstasy listening to the alternating duo of male voices and both were paid handsomely for their services. Both gave this exclusive performance when they really needed money which meant the glorious redhead was frequently indulged. Their patroness left Australia shortly afterwards and married a very respectable American business executive.

Not long after the castor oil episode at Long Bay, Finchie and Cec Perry, returning home to their respective daybeds at Gleneagles, were weaving their way unsteadily down Victoria Street about five o'clock one morning when a party of very pretty young whores on a verandah (Cecil assured me they were all extremely beautiful, 'otherwise Finchie and I wouldn't have made the ascent') invited the pair up. They forgot to pull down the canvas awning and Finchie ended up on the balcony in *flagrante delicto* with an auburn-haired beauty. Finchie reached his top C to the accompaniment of resounding cheers from the street below. A gang of dockyard mateys on their way to McElhone Stairs and the Loo (short for Woolloomooloo, not the Gents), had stopped to encourage the display of machismo.

At the time Finchie was living with Marian, his sex-life away from "home" was unfailingly vigorous. As an indoor sportsman he could have won the Olympics for Australia. In his choice of woman Peter wasn't particular. He went for extremes. His selection included an amazing assortment of prostitutes. They, and the amateur prostitutes, the courtesans and the as-yet unbroken fillies, came in all shapes and sizes. More than once, Harry was staggered at what Finchie could have seen in a particular woman. He would see Finchie, thin as a Ronald

Searle cartoon, with some female gargantua and wonder 'how'.

But according to Donald Friend, the Australian painter, Peter was not interested only in women. 'I had taken an attic room, in Rockwell Crescent, off Macleay Street up at the Cross in the 1930s, at ten shillings and sixpence a week. Peter and I had met at a mad sleazy Bohemian party, given by a public servant, called Ralph Curnow, where there were a lot of unemployed actors. Poor Peter was broke beyond belief. We had the same sense of humour, great rapport and we became lovers for a while. He became absolutely fascinated by my stories of "jumping the rattler" up in Queensland as a hobo and, as this was the height of the Depression and things were so bad, we decided to give Sydney a miss and head up north, riding free on those goods trains. I showed him the ropes.'

Finchie often spoke of Donald, a year older than he was, who had offered him a refuge when things were desperate but the only allusion he ever made to me of his nights at Ralph's was 'penury, propinquity, a high libido and a sense of life's absurdity at times can breed queer bed-fellows. I had early on acquired a well developed sense of the erotic in all its forms, and in the good old pubic days, I landed up in some pretty queer situations. We all laughed a hell of a lot but as regards men, I was never really interested.' And there's absolutely no evidence that he ever was.

Certainly, every Saturday night, in those Depression years, Ralph Curnow would declare his flat open house to a select and amazing cross section of Sydney's way-out society, and the guests included queers, whores, pimps and squares. Ralph would provide the beer and at midnight would put on a one-man drag show. They were wild nights and, perhaps, Finchie, physically well-endowed but not sexually fastidious, caught up in the euphoria at Ralph's, decided he'd shack up for a while at Donald's. He was virtually starving but Donald was getting the odd quid for his sketches and he took Finchie under his wing and off they'd go to an underworld dive called 'The Mirrors' in William Street where Finchie would be obliged to act for his supper. Sometimes he'd give a command performance at a thug's birthday at the Maccabean Hall and the gangsters would get a double bill with Donald as Peter's comic feed. Peter would convulse his audience with 'The Disenchanted Emu', followed by 'A Chinese Acrobat with the Trots'.

Referring to Peter's love life, Donald seemed to think that at one stage Peter was actually engaged to Marian Morphee when she lived with her mother at 'Manar' in Macleay Street, where Peter often used to stay, accept their hospitality and behave abominably. Then Donald went to London to pursue his career as a painter, but remained in touch with Peter over the years. They met for the last time on the Eamonn Andrews TV show, *This is Your Life*, in 1961.

Certainly in Australia there was a sort of tradition among artists to behave with a kind of riotous high-spirited Bohemianism. This standard may have been set by the well-established Australian artist Norman Lindsay, who was painting what were considered in the 1920s to be rather pornographic orgiastic pictures of bacchanalian fiestas and stark naked ladies with magnificent breasts, urn shaped waists and thighs like Greek discus throwers. The very respectable home of my uncle, J. D. MacDonald, in Moruben Road, Mosman, was a veritable gallery of Lindsay paintings. One day in 1948, I took Finchie there when I knew the entire family would be out. My uncle, a real Victorian puritan, used to bellow at me every time he caught me sneaking a look at the gorgeous Lindsay nudes. I thought I'd never get Finchie away. He wandered round gaping, unable to believe there were so many originals under one roof. Peter was a tremendous admirer of Lindsay's originality – what he referred to after as 'a brilliant artist's impression of cornucopian copulation' not only as a painter but also as a writer (he'd always wanted to adapt and produce Lindsay's *The Magic Pudding*, as a children's radio serial for the ABC), and the Bohemian tradition started by Lindsay was certainly carried on and upheld in Sydney by people like Peter Finch and his circle of friends.

Possessions and money never meant a thing to Peter, though his Sydney friends were always trying to instil in him a sense of the need for security and saving up for the future. 'Why? What future? How can you ever be sure you'll have one, better to invest heavily, if you've got it, in the present.' One day he bought an old delivery truck for £14. He had no licence and couldn't even drive it properly. A mate was teaching him to drive up on a deserted road in French's Forest near the old Manly reservoir. On his second lesson Finchie skidded on a large ant heap and tipped the truck over into a gully. They had a crate of beer in the back. 'For Christ's sake save the fuckin beer,' yelled his mate. Between them they carried off the undamaged crate full of booze. 'For all I know,' said Peter, thirty-five years later, 'the truck is still there.'

Max Osbiston first met Peter in the Depression years when they were doing amateur theatre work. Peter was playing in Edgar Wallace's *The Ringer* in March 1934. The *Sun* wrote: 'There was some clever Cockney characterization from Peter Finch as Samuel Hackett.' Max felt that 'when Peter turned up for rehearsal in those days you'd have voted him the least likely person to succeed in the acting field; a scruffy, hollow-chested, round-shouldered rather insignificant teenager, but once he started rehearsing, the talent that was in him blazed forth to such an extent, even then, you forgot completely about his not very prepossessing appearance.'

Several years later, in March 1939, they were doing *Romeo and Juliet* on the radio at the ABC. Nigel Lovell was Romeo and Peter, Mercutio. Frank Clewlow, Max remembers, kept pulling Finchie up in rehearsal. 'Peter, you must learn to laugh properly. Your laugh is dreadful. It sounds to me like a bad soda syphon going off.'

'Well, twenty-seven years later, I saw Peter in his posthumous award-winning performance in *Network* and he had some Herculean laughing scenes with William Holden and, enthralled as I was by watching Peter and Holden together, I couldn't help thinking back to that time when his laugh was no better than a bad soda syphon.'

One Sydney radio critic, after a performance of Peter's wrote: 'If Mr Finch thinks that breathing asthmatically between sentences is effective, let us recommend him to stop breathing altogether.' This advice was written indelibly on Finchie's heart until such time as he learned to appreciate the humour of being a good actor capable of being a bad one.

Ron Beck, an ex-radio, and now a television, producer, shared the same flat at the Blackstone with Finchie shortly afterwards. Ron maintains he lasted five days with Peter. 'I couldn't stand Finchie in the flat. I must be quite honest. Finchie never hung anything up. He never washed a cup or saucer, never put anything away. Of course he always had birds in to do it, but laundry was an old-fashioned word with Finchie. If a shirt did go to the laundry, it usually fell off him on to the floor first, so we didn't last very long together.'

Queenie Ashton who, up until 1938, had been doing light entertainment shows with Dick Bentley, arrived at the studio for her first radio commercial serial, *Marie Antoinette*. 'Everyone spoke about this wonderful radio bloke, Peter Finch. I was fascinated to meet this actor about whom I had heard so much. He was cast to play one of the leading roles. He'd already become quite a law unto himself. He never turned up. However, everyone sort of said, "God bless him, that's Peter".'

They did eventually do many shows together on radio and one memorable one, live at Macquarie Radio Theatre, in full evening dress, in front of an audience. Queenie had run a needle through her hand on the Saturday and they had bandaged her arm up in a sling, so that it was unusable. She had to stand at the microphone and, unable to turn the pages of her script which had been specially clipped to a music stand, her leading man, Peter, not only gave a stunning performance, but turned every single page for her during the live transmission.

Fred Parsons, a comedy script writer for the Australian variety shows, remembers Peter when he was slogging away in a little office in the old radio 2GB building in Bligh Street. 'I was writing for a show called "Crackerjack" and giving myself a migraine trying to think up those comic gags that would get the laughs. Suddenly I became aware that someone was standing in the doorway, watching me. I looked up and that was the first time I saw Peter, and he said: "Why is it that comedy writers always look as if they're writing a three act Russian tragedy?" '

Fred speaks as he writes and his conversation and memories of Finchie, brilliantly witty and quite unprintable, are coupled with a slight stammer. According to Fred, Lenny Lower, an Australian comedy writer who used to do a column strip in the Sydney papers, and Finchie, had both been celebrating in the Journalists' Club, and were returning home to their rooms in Ithaca Road, about three one morning. J. Albert, the music publisher, had a huge and stately mansion in Ithaca Road, and was giving a very grand party in his garden. The place was festooned with lights, sizzling chickens were revolving on their spits, and the champagne was flowing. Everyone was in evening dress. Finchie and Lenny, passing by, saw this, rushed up to the iron gates, and started rattling them violently, shouting 'Masters, masters! Let us in. The peasants are starving!' Peter then began a voluble spiel in the little bit of Russian he had once had to learn by heart. The guests, absolutely nonplussed by Finchie's life-like Russian desperation, tried to carry on regardless. When they finally realized the party was in danger of being disastrously disrupted, the white tied Cossacks started advancing on all sides. 'Ah, bloody Sunday in St Petersburg,' shouted Finchie, and the two *agents provocateur* continued on their way.

Fred Parsons was working for the ABC when Finchie is supposed to have played his famous game of ABC roulette. 'Sir Charles Moses, head of the ABC at that time, had an office with an entrance and a separate exit. He would go in through the main door to get to his office but he could also sneak out the back way so no one ever knew whether he was in the office or not. Finchie's roulette consisted of flinging open one of the great man's doors and yelling: "Moses is a bastard." '

Peter claimed he even did his stint as a newsreader during his versatile radio career and claimed he was the perpetrator of a gaff that became bar-room legend. Very nervous, he got through the main news items without a fluff. He then had to read a local bulletin, relayed only out to the Riverina district of New South Wales. Now, in Australia, there is a particularly nasty insect called the trapdoor spider, also known as the funnel web, which tends to leap at its victims from its webby orifice, and its bite can be lethal. What Peter reckons listeners in the Murrumbidgee Irrigation Area heard from him on that occasion was, 'This afternoon a farmer's wife, living between Gidginbung and Sproulers Lagoon, was rushed to the Temora District Hospital. She had been bitten on the funnel by a finger-web spider.'

Once Peter joined the army and went to the Middle East in 1941, the era of the hungry, scruffy kid, eating and sleeping where he could, on the fringe of everything, getting himself engaged every other month, ended. His life changed completely, though his character remained the same and the kid in many ways never grew up.

Before he joined up, he got himself engaged in such a way that it hit the society columns of the *Sydney Morning Herald*, and his less respectable mates began to believe he really was going to marry and move into the establishment though all knew, including Finchie in his heart of hearts, that such an event could only end in disaster on both sides. He'd had a very narrow matrimonial escape, some years earlier, having again got himself secretly engaged. This was after Margaret Hayter and during the period he was playing the gypsy prodigal with Marian.

Of his one long engagement, to Sheila Smart, lasting six months and the last before his marriage, there are three versions: Dick and Peta Bentley's, who met Peter before the reception to be given for the engaged couple at the Hotel Australia; Nigel Lovell's, who was working with Peter at the time; and Sheila's, to whom Peter was engaged. Finchie's side of the story became so entangled in bar-room anecdotes that it lost all vestige of credibility. Dick and Peta Bentley's version is that they found Finchie, wild-eyed in Castlereagh Street, saying that a society girl had wanted to marry him, she had been really kind to him, and in a moment of fatal weakness, he proposed and produced a ring. 'But then, without telling me, she had organized a big engagement party at the Australia Hotel and invited all the socialites.' Finchie, in a frenzied state, had downed a few drinks, and knowing, *au fond*, he couldn't face the music, had bailed out. The last Dick and Peta saw of him on that occasion was Finchie going fast in the direction of King Street.

Nigel remembers Finchie becoming engaged to Sheila who lived in Macleay Regis in Macleay Street. That Finchie, of all people, should get himself engaged to a member of a family in society was hilarious to all his friends and colleagues in the Bohemian set. As the nuptials approached, said Nigel, Peter got more and more restless and drank more and more. It was really staring him in the face that he would have to walk up the aisle with this bird and maybe lead a sort of stuffy, society sort of existence – well, stuffy for Finchie. He became more and more irritable and uncomfortable about the whole thing and there were various tea parties, and of course Finchie was the prize exhibit. One day he got absolutely plastered and he went down to the flat, flung open the doors, and there they all were, sipping tea and nibbling cakes, and he said: 'Shit to the lot of you' and banged the doors and went. And that was the end of the engagement. He never did anything by halves.

Peter and Sheila had met in Packey's, one of those sleazy Sydney dives near Hyde Park that the more adventurous frequented after dining out. 'Peter just came over, sat down, and started to talk to me, unbelievably attractive and quite the most amusing and clever man I'd ever met. And what a mimic.'

I asked her what had particularly attracted a girl of her conventional and protected background to the classless unpredictable Finchie? 'Yes, I know for a fact he lived with prostitutes, and his early background was just too terrible, but he got drawn into the sort of society I knew. The war had started and there was that element of uncertainty that makes the wealthy a bit more frivolous and less inhibited. Anyway, we had been dancing – Peter was the most gorgeous dancer – and he said, "We must get married." We were all there, drinking like mad, tipsy of course, as we all were an awful lot during the war, and he was giving one of his wonderful shows – telling these marvellous stories. Everyone was falling about laughing. I never stopped prompting him. I'd heard quite a few of them, but I never tired of hearing them. Most of it was just pure timing but brilliant, and you didn't have to push him much because he simply adored being the actor and he really did act all the time. People used to ask for the same ones, over and over again, because he always managed to make them a bit funnier.

'When we met in London, many many years later, I saw him coming up Kensington High Street and he had his arms out. It was twenty or thirty years since I had set eyes on him. "Darling! Darling! Don't move. I've got to go over here to buy some cigarettes. Don't move. Stay there. I'm going in to see Diana Graves. We're both collaborating on a script, so you and I'll go and see her together. Wait for me. Wait for me." And so in we went to see Diana Graves and we spent the entire afternoon, drinking wine and talking of old times. And he said how wonderful all his lady friends had been, including his wives – the ones he did marry – and how he adored them all. "You were all so nice," he said to me. How many of us, of either sex, can look back and say that?'

In 1940, Peter and Sheila became officially engaged. It was announced in all the Sydney papers and the *Sydney Morning Herald* came to Sheila's mother's flat to take the engagement photos. Sheila's mother had given the engaged couple a lovely little flat, and provided them with the money to buy furniture. Peter had even taken Sheila up to Greenwich to see great-aunt Kate and Betty. He wanted to show her off and to know that old

Kate and his cousin approved of his choice. On the night the engagement was to be announced, a party was being given for them by a society hostess to which fifty guests had been invited. The night before, Sheila had sensed all wasn't well. Peter took her to the St James's Cinema in Elizabeth Street, and he kept wanting to hold her hand and she kept removing it. She was wearing the engagement ring which he had given her and he kept twisting it round and round.

Sheila extended her hand during our conversation. 'Look,' she said. 'I still wear it. This is the ring he kept twisting and twisting on my finger. God knows how he managed to pay for it.' It was set with a sapphire, a ruby and many semi-precious stones. It was beautiful and simple, and showed Finchie's very good taste.

'I remember,' Sheila said, 'that I felt terribly cold. It was one of those moments between two people when nothing is said and volumes are spoken in utter silence. Peter was the sort of character I felt that had to get in first. I was beginning to get cold feet and we both felt, with the big day drawing nearer and nearer, that we were committed. The night of the engagement party, Peter dropped me off there first and went on to the ABC where he was to play the title role in *Richard II*. He was due back at Amy's reception about ten. That was the last I saw of him. He just vanished. I knew where he was the very next day, but could I get to see him? Not on your life! He'd holed up in our new flat. Gone there after the broadcast with some of his mates. I knew a hell of a lot was going on in there but he'd made quite sure I couldn't get in. Can you imagine? Blind drunk, and there I was, round the corner, with Mama, in a flat full of presents that all had to be handed back.'

That must have given Sydney society something to bite on for months.

'My mother was terribly upset. She adored Peter – used to make him mint jelly. Peter had a craving for mint jelly and she'd make jars of it for him. Thought it would be nice to put on his lamb, when he had it, but as he scarcely had enough to eat half the time, he used to have it on his toast for breakfast.'

So Finchie had gone off to the ABC, played *Richard II* and in sheer terror at the prospect of marriage, had rounded up his mates from the Fifty-fifty Club, and spent the next fortnight, horizontal, knocking back the grog from the best china teacups, and blurring the unfaceable reality with the prostitutes from

Victoria Street. When Sheila finally gained access, the revellers had all departed, leaving teacups with the remains of stale beer and whisky, unmade beds and saucers full of cigarette butts. Three months later he called her.

'Well, Peter,' she said. 'Just where are you?'

'Please, will you come and see me?' was the reply. 'I'm down in a street nearby, having a party. I want to see you. I'm leaving and I want to ask your forgiveness.'

'. . . And when I arrived, of course, that actor was down on his knees.'

' "Will you ever forgive me for behaving the way I did?" He was in full uniform, a private. His boots all polished, looking so pathetic. He ripped the AIF insignia off the shoulder of his uniform and handed it to me.

' "I want you to keep this. The *Queen Mary* sails tomorrow. I'll probably never see you again." '

When she did see him again, a quarter of a century later, that afternoon in Kensington High Street, he behaved 'like a child, he very proudly opened his jacket and said, "Look at this!" It was beautifully cut, Savile Row, and lined with silk. How could you be angry with Peter? There he was with money, and the style and taste to go with it. His shoes were immaculate and at last those hands were beautifully kept. I thought of the days I used literally to pull off those revolting socks, force him into the bath and scrub his back. At times he was like someone from a primitive tribe who was totally unaware of the need to bath. But he was never consciously dirty, nor did he ever appear unwashed. It wasn't that he was slovenly. It was an attitude of mind that was different from what is normally acceptable. Peter had different priorities.'

The day he and Sheila met after so many years, like his reunions with Murray Matheson from the Sorlie days, Finchie would start talking with a broad Australian accent and she reminded him of the night the bookie gave the big party at Bondi and took over an entire cinema in Bondi Road. It was black velvet, caviar, the lot. The place was packed and suddenly Finchie decided to go down on the stage and give them all a turn.

'He just stood alone on that stage, improvised and kept us all in fits of laughter. It was like going to the theatre. The book-maker giving the party had no idea that Peter would be there, or would get up and amuse his entire assembly of guests. He would live off prostitutes, take a permanent loan, but to me Peter was never a sponger. When he was with me I had to take his ABC money and keep it for him because he was quite capable of off-loading his entire earnings on some poor wretch without food or a bed. He gave as liberally as he accepted. Dear Peter . . . When you were the focus of his attention you were the most important woman in the world and he could really make you believe he meant it.'

8 The army's worst gunner

Peter once quoted me a passage he was reading from a book by Salvador de Madariaga: 'Only the Spaniards, the Irish and the Poles fight on when they know it is to no purpose. It is the absurd in them that exults in a kind of glory over death.' 'As it's a portrait of Europe, we can forgive him excluding the Aussies,' added Finchie.

By the time war broke out in 1939, Peter had established himself as certainly the best young actor in Australia, although he had done only two films and the occasional play. He had become known and acclaimed through radio and felt he was coming up on the crest of an exciting phase of his life. The war in Europe meant no more to him than grim news bulletins, news reels and announcements on the wireless that Europe was in for one almighty blow-up. He became really aware of the war through the Australian military confrontation with Rommel in the desert. Those of us who lived near the harbour in Sydney became aware of the war by the number of men in khaki, but more by the activities of the Royal Australian Navy when tired old ships that had lain idle at their buoys through the 1930s, suddenly appeared freshly painted and patrolling off the entrance to Sydney Harbour.

The cruiser *Sydney* sunk the Italian cruiser *Bartolomeo Colleoni* in the Mediterranean in 1940 and returned to a triumphant welcome at Circular Quay in early 1941. But then, in May, according to Peter, one of the rusty old grey ladies that had been towed out of mothballs in September 1939 to join the famous Australian 'scrap iron flotilla' was sunk by enemy aircraft on the 'milk run' in Suicide Alley in a desperate bid to get ammunition and food from Alexandria to Tobruk. She was the old V & W class destroyer *Waterhen*, recognizable to Sydney-siders by a large black 'D 22' painted on the hull. Finchie had read of this incident in the paper. The loss of the *Waterhen*, and why she had gone down within an ace of reaching Tobruk harbour, had made Finchie more aware than anything else of the seriousness of the war. This, and the story he had been told of the battle involving

Australian infantry at Amiens in 1918, had stayed in his mind, and on Monday morning, 2 June 1941, he went to Martin Place and volunteered for the army.

Peter told me how the sinking of *HMAS Waterhen* had affected him during a coffee break when he was producing an ABC children's serial in 1947. I checked his story recently and found his version absolutely accurate in every detail, including the fact that they got everybody safely off *Waterhen* before the tired old lady retired to the seabed. Peter lost a month somewhere. 'The old chook', as she was affectionately called, bombed by Italian and German aircraft, went down off Sollum on 30 June 1941. In every other detail Finchie's recollection was accurate. Either he had got the whole story from his friend, now Admiral Sir David Stevenson, ex-Chief of Staff of the RAN, or he was extremely observant and retentive about many things besides acting.

Bette Dickson, who was rehearsing *Meet Mr Disraeli* with Peter on that June weekend in 1941 at the ABC, recalls the whole episode of Peter enlisting. 'We had been rehearsing over the weekend with Peter and we were due to broadcast the show on the Monday night. At ten thirty on the Monday morning we were all called and no Peter, so they got in another actor, James Maxwell, to take his place. Old Charlie Wheeler was producing, and was worried stiff in case Peter had gone on a blind and met with an accident. Of course Finchie knew we'd break for lunch at one, have the afternoon off and do the show live that night at seven. At one o'clock, in walked Finchie with this big thick-set tough character, Buddy Morley, Peter rather unsteady on his feet in a slouch hat and full uniform. He had enrolled in the 2nd AIF, and a month later he was on his way to the Middle East despite the fact he'd been cast to play three leading roles in the next fortnight.'

Incidentally, Bette was one of the gallant army of girl friends who washed Finchie's socks, but she saw a different side of Peter.

'. . . No, he wasn't fun to be with. Too conceited. It certainly mattered to those of us younger than Peter that we pleased him in scenes we played with him. He had an incredibly sharp eye for what was phoney in acting. What he used to call "rubber stamp acting".'

Wilfred Thomas, now married to Bette, used to employ Peter

as one of his regular actors in his radio programmes. Wilf sums up Peter in one word: quality. 'Finchie could smell out inferior material I might have written in a script, perhaps only three or four lines, but he could always nail it to the syllable. He was an instinctive writer himself and he knew at once if a script was unbalanced and exactly where it was weak, and wouldn't work. It was Finchie's taste, judgment and professionalism that made him one of the most stimulating people I've ever worked with.'

Peter was always very reticent about his early spell in the army. He detested sudden noise and although he got used to the sound of the ack-ack guns he manned, he was relieved when they kept finding him unsuitable as a soldier for the tasks he had to do. The transportation of the Australian Division to the Middle East in 1940 and 1941 was referred to as the 'Cook's Tour', and the liner *Queen Mary* left Sydney in June 1941, with Gunner Finch part of Specialist Group 2, attached to the 2/1 Light Anti-Aircraft Regiment. She was bound for Port Tewfik, where she would disembark her troops for the Middle East campaign. When she reached the Red Sea, Finchie had organized the ship's concerts. 'Three shows a night, and we played to capacity in desert heat conditions. It was the toughest work I ever did in the business and certainly my hardest effort of the war.'

His most valuable experience, while serving in the Middle East, was being able to watch the Jewish actors at work in the Habima Theatre in Tel Aviv. He told me that he had seen *Twelfth Night* in Hebrew, which he could follow because he knew the play so well, and that the production, while retaining all the intrinsic values of the play, had had the added dimension of Jewish humour. One of the reasons Finchie admired Olivier's original interpretation of the Jewish Malvolio in the Gielgud 1955 production of *Twelfth Night* at Stratford-on-Avon was his having seen a Jewish actor do it in Tel Aviv. He saw another play in Hebrew, which he didn't understand at all, but met a Russian actor there who had acted in London with Gielgud and had been a pupil of Stanislavsky in Moscow. (Later, when he met the Latvian Jew, Dolia Ribush, in Melbourne, Ribush really stimulated Finchie's interest in Stanislavsky, which formed the basis of what he taught me as his own Stanislavsky/Jouvet method in 1947–8 at the Mercury Theatre.) Paul Muni had often played at the Habima Theatre and Finchie recalls that although he didn't understand one single word of the Hebrew play, *Maturaha* (which means Matriculation), apart from having read a programme synopsis, he sat riveted by the action and unaware that he was on a very hard wooden seat. He was a tremendous admirer of Muni after seeing his films, *Scarface*, *The Good Earth*, and *Juarez*, and felt that the simplicity and quality of the Habima could be nurtured in Australia when the war was over. And he was dead right.

He was always surprised by the fact that the Aussies were the best-liked troops in Palestine. 'We were bloody monsters but when we left we did leave them all our armament.'

One day at Mersa Matruh, he decided to try out his acting ability as a Bedouin Arab, dressed himself up and wandered into the lines of a machine-gun battalion. 'The outraged machine-gunners called me a fucking wog and told me to bugger off and chased me into the sand-dunes with their bloody bayonets and I had a hell of a job to find my way back through the barbed wire to my own gun-pit.'

In the Middle East, he tried out pieces of Shakespeare very informally on his fellow Diggers: Mercutio's death speech, with an introductory lead-in for the benefit of many who had neither read nor seen *Romeo and Juliet*; the seven ages of man, from *As You Like It*, with appropriate vaudeville mime; 'To be or not to be', when he felt safe enough to put in the philosophy of life and death; and, finally, to rouse the spirit of Anzac, the famous battle speech with its climactic cry from Henry V: 'God for Harry, England and St George.' That was the beginning of what was subsequently to become Peter's major contribution to the Australian Army.

By May 1942, after being shipped back to Adelaide in the ammunition ship *Niger Stroom*, he was next manning a Bofors quick firing anti-aircraft gun in Darwin, trying to shoot down Japanese Zeros, and the bombers that were raining their bombs down on the town. The Sydney papers were playing down the seriousness of the Japanese threat to Australia and the bombing raids that were taking place up north, from Darwin to Port Hedland. I learned more from a conversation with Peter about the Japanese bombing of Darwin than I ever read in a Sydney newspaper.

'The first time the Japanese came over, we all dug trenches for people to get into as a sort of hopeful protection from bomb blast. Suddenly the Nips' Nellies and Sallies (bombers) accompanied by their Zekes (fighters) came over and dropped a stick of bombs. One poor cove in a slit trench was covered in earth right up to his chin. When they flew off, a couple of us came out of another trench and went over and started digging this poor bloke out with our hands. Then a second lot of Japs suddenly zoomed in, so we had to bugger off and leave him. But before we left, I put a fag in his mouth and lit it and said, "You'll be jake, sport. Just hang on a while. I'll be right back." So we left him. Impossible for him to move his arms to take the cigarette away. All you could see over the top of the trench was his head, and him puffing away for all he was worth on the fag. Just as well it wasn't a night raid with the black out regulations we had up there.'

At the end of July, 1942, Peter was granted leave from the Army for duty with the Department of Information, and he then made several propaganda films, one called *Another Threshold* which Ken Hall directed, and Charles Chauvel directed him in the War Loan documentary *While There is Still Time,* the DOI's attempt to get people to buy war bonds. In September, F. D. Clewlow, determined that Finchie would do one of the plays he was scheduled to do at the time he enlisted, recast him as Captain Scott in Douglas Stewart's *Fire on the Snow.*

During this period, he was also engaged in producing impromptu shows to entertain the troops. At that time, servicemen played all the women's parts and Finchie and 'Smokey' Aarons, son of the organist at the Sydney State Theatre, wrote musical comedy sketches which Finchie produced. He found a tremendous amount of impromptu talent among the troops, most of whom had never even been on a stage. At one concert, they made a stage of oil drums, covered with tent boards, raided a Chinese shop for their stage curtains and played home-made satires like *The Colonel's Daughter, A Fate Worse Than Death, Naughty Nineties,* to an audience of two thousand troops. The company soon became known up north as Finch's Follies.

'I had people like Freddie Park, a leading aircraftsman, as my leading lady. Bloody good she was, too! Two other aircraftsmen were natural comics. We had an American ex-college band leader, who played the clarinet and Gunner Jim Macfarlane on the mouth-organ.'

By popular demand, Finch's Follies went on every Wednesday night and became such an institution that, when an air raid alert sounded one night in Darwin, and the entire company had to rush out to the gun pits just before curtain up, the audience demanded that the show begin, when the 'all clear' sounded at one in the morning.

The audience always demanded the very highest standard and Peter claimed that his memory of that company was of no hard feelings – never any jealousy and, crude as it may have been, it really was an ensemble theatre. Finchie had incorporated into Finch's Follies a tremendous amount of material he'd learned from the vaudeville and situation comedy on and off stage during the Sorlie era, along with his own abundant natural talent and resourceful ingenuity. This all paved the way for his work as director and actor in the Army Amenities Unit 12 at Pagewood two years later which ultimately led to his participation as director and actor for the Mercury Theatre from 1946.

When Finchie was posted to Sydney, the last words of his commanding officer, Major Mander-Jones to him were: 'I'm sorry you're leaving us, Gunner Finch. You weren't the Army's greatest gunner, but you've been bloody funny.'

9 Pas de deux

When she first met Peter, Tamara wasn't dancing with the Borovansky Ballet but, like most of Sydney's sun-loving population in the hot weather, was spending her time at the beach. Peter, on leave of absence from the army, was appearing at the Regent Cinema during the intervals, campaigning for people to buy war bonds. Not long back from the Middle East, thin as a bamboo cane and enveloped in a large slouch hat, he was doing his eloquent 'help the war effort' spiel for the Department of Information. He made four appearances daily between films and the rest of the time he'd be sunning himself down on Bondi Beach or at Redleaf Pool.

Redleaf Pool was at that time the public pool in Sydney for those without private swimming pools, who lived in the elegant old buildings round Woollahra, Bellevue Hill and Edgecliff. For years Finchie gave the Redleaf kiosk as his address for the frantic phone calls, telegrams, messages and letters that used to pour in from radio producers all offering work. Peter's lackadaisical attitude about accepting work at one stage became legendary among most of us who were very hard pressed to break in to an élite acting circle, and Tamara once told me that Peter's refusal to get up and go out for work was a bone of contention throughout their marriage.

One summer day at the end of 1942, Finchie, looking rather like a copper-coloured Aborigine with skinny but shapely legs, was ambling round Redleaf when he suddenly saw an exotic raven-haired beauty reading Maxim Gorky by the edge of the pool. He decided to make himself known to her, laid out his army towel alongside hers and just gazed at her.

Shortly before, he'd done a 'schmaltzy documentary' for the DOI, an army recruiting short called *A Voice is Heard*, in which he played a young, blind soldier who couldn't read a letter from his sweetheart so someone had to read it to him. He must have been giving a very convincing performance with the gaunt face and the staring eyes that couldn't see because when Tamara looked up from her book, amazed recognition and rapport were immediate. They swam together and Finchie became infatuated and dazzled by the young Russian ballerina, Tamara Rechemcinc Tchinarova from Akkermann, near Odessa.

Finchie's acting friend, Harry, was friendly with Tamara, and was at Redleaf when Finchie suddenly appeared. Harry had no idea Finchie had returned from the Middle East though by then Peter had been back in Australia for over a year. There was a very warm reunion and, according to Harry, he introduced Peter to Tamara. Tamara didn't mean anything to Harry so he had no qualms about leaving them together while he went off to do a matinee at the Minerva Theatre. The next day Finchie phoned Harry to ask if he was going steady with Tamara.

'No, we're just friends,' replied Harry. Finchie then used an expression current at that time. 'I wouldn't go under your neck, sport, if she was your sheila.'

'No, go for your life,' Harry replied. And Finchie did!

When Tamara was born, just after the First World War, the lovable Bessarabian Mamouschka Tchinarova, still alive and much cared for now by Tamara, was married to an officer in the Tsar's Regiment of Death, the Black Guard. In those days Bessarabia was still part of Russia, then in a state of political turmoil. She and Mamma fled to Paris when Tamara was five, and she arrived there about a year before the eight year old Peter left it for Madras. They weren't to meet until eighteen years later, in Sydney, in the early summer of 1942.

During those years of the war in Sydney, Tamara and Mamma were living in a small flat in Phillip Street near Circular Quay. Since Colonel de Basil's Monte Carlo Ballets-Russes Company, or the Ballets-Russes as it was more normally called, had left three years earlier, there had been no ballet, and for Tamara no work. She was absolutely broke, and kept the pair of them going on the occasional money she earned as a photo colourist. As Tamara and Mamma both had Rumanian passports they were both registered as 'enemy aliens', which meant an obligatory stroll a few yards along the road to the Phillip Street police station each month. After one or two visits by the Phillip Street police, an extremely *simpatico* humorous lot (one was a ballet fan with a penchant for Russian borsch *à la* Mamma), the passports were stamped at home, over a bowl of delicious soup, with flowers on the table for Mamma which the inspector brought concealed in a suitcase.

For the infatuated Finchie, the reserved Tamara who had already toured most of the world with the Ballets-Russes by the age of twenty was the personification of all the legendary magic of Diaghilev's Ballets-Russes. Redleaf became Peter's daily and then his hourly oasis. Finally he proposed. They were promised for about a week and married at St Stephen's, Bellevue Hill, on 21 April 1943. Finchie's dowry on their wedding day comprised a dixie, a toothbrush, one enamel army mug, a kitbag, an aluminium spoon, an army shirt, a jersey, a threepenny bar of chocolate, a pair of swimming trunks, a packet of emergency dressings, 3/6 in cash, and an army allowance of 6/- per day.

Dick and Peta Bentley, Trafford Whitelock, then variety producer at the ABC, all three old friends and among those present at Finchie's first wedding reception, remember a demented and utterly besotted Peter. He was passionately in love. Tamara was the only girl in the world he had ever really wanted to marry. There would never be another woman if Tamara turned him down. The only alternative was living death: celibacy, without even the protection of the cloth, or taking up residence at Buggery Barn down the bottom of George Street.

Alex MacDonald was best man at the wedding. There was no money so the bride was dressed not in white but in a dress run up by Mamma Tchinarova, made with more care and pride than any she had ever created for the ballet. There was no honeymoon. Mamma gave them £20 to pay the rent of a flat in Bellevue Hill for a month. After that they moved into humbler dwellings. Peter went back to camp and his work with the sixth division concert party, and was subsequently transferred to the army entertainment unit. Because of Peter's great natural charm and his ability to be completely at ease with anyone, he won Mamma's heart and she spoilt him whenever she could. To Peter, Tamara and Mamma appeared totally Russian, utterly different from anything he had experienced at that time.

At first all seemed well and it was a very happy home. But soon Finchie suddenly took to disappearing, and would go off with the boys to the Journalists' Club, and really go on the bottle.

Once Peter started to play truant, he found himself up against a very formidable Russian twosome. According to Alan White, who was Peter's young protégé from the army days at Pagewood and one of Peter's few intimate friends who, as a man's man, really understood and loved him, maintains 'it was a very good marriage for Peter in so many ways until Tamara gave up dancing and concentrated on her husband. It may have been what Finchie thought he wanted, but it was not what he needed at that time. Tamara was ambitious for Peter and when they first arrived in London and Finchie was out of work for three months, nearly doing his nut, Tamara kept needling him – she kept on at him to ring up this one and that one, and Finchie just used passive resistance and evasion tactics. He wasn't a canvasser for work. It wasn't in his nature to hassle that way and campaign for work. He was an irresponsible natural actor, never a true intellectual. His easy-come, easy-go philosophy absolutely maddened Tamara. Tamara used to get very worked up about Finchie's gypsy ways and in Sydney he'd find it more and more difficult to get away. He had to make more and more excuses. I'd be there and there'd be a terrible row between them, which Finchie would engineer, and he'd get hold of me and we'd be out the door and he'd say, "Where'll we go for the night?" having deliberately blown up the storm first in order to escape. Like so many artists, he had to fly free sometimes and Tamara just couldn't accept him as he was. Women always imagined they could reform Finchie.'

But in the beginning, marriage and the domestic way of life, was a novelty which he found very stimulating. Through Peter, Tamara's English improved because he guided and advised her on her reading. He would bring his film, radio or theatre scripts home and Tamara would be his audience. He could talk out his ideas, and work out his timing on her as he needed someone there to spark him off. Tamara was the ideal foil. Before they met, she had only seen him in *A Voice is Heard* and had had no idea of Peter's status and reputation as her English was so poor she never listened to the radio.

Borovansky had originally formed his company in Melbourne in association with the J. C. Williamson Theatres. He asked Tamara to be *première danseuse* and also to recreate some of the ballets they had both danced in for the Ballets-Russes.

Whenever Finchie had a spare moment he was at these ballet rehearsals. Borovansky put Tamara in charge and she organized and welded the large groupings, drilled individual dancers and took her place at the head of the company. Borovansky was an experienced lighting man and knew a lot about decor. He was a painter as well as a dancer; at the Mercury, Peter told us he had learned a tremendous amount from watching Borovansky and the company.

Peter was insistent that actors, as compared with dancers, have very little discipline. He was always on about the need for self-discipline. His use of me as a guinea pig training as an acrobat with Ardini was an example. Borovansky, although obsessively jealous of Tamara as 'his ballerina', admired Peter very much. Peter loved music and had very good musical taste and Borovansky really took him up. He was welcome at rehearsal and any suggestions Peter made were always accepted and considered. Borovansky regarded Peter as a colleague and treated him with great respect.

It was very difficult to get Peter to talk about his Australian films and he refused even to comment on *Red Sky at Morning*, available for release in 1945, but which was actually shot in mid-1943 while he was on leave without pay from the Army during his term with the sixth division concert party. *Red Sky at Morning* was based on a play by Dymphna Cusack, set in New South Wales in 1812. Finchie, the hero Michael, plays an Irishman who is sent out to the penal colony for causing political trouble in Wexford. It was eventually released in England and then re-released as *Escape at Dawn* after scenes had been removed and a new opening and ending shot. The re-release was aimed at capitalizing on Peter's name but it was never released in Australia in either version. The tiny Fanfare Studios of North Sydney where the film was shot weren't sound proofed and when the girl next door practised her scales they were picked up on the soundtrack of the film.

Jean McAlister, the heroine, tied to a swaggering bully in the New South Wales rum corps, meets the young Irish political prisoner, Finchie, in an inn at Parramatta, and they decide to make their escape together in a storm. Peter nearly lost his life during this scene as he had to plunge into torrential water on horseback. The current was so strong and treacherous that both horse and rider were nearly sucked under and drowned. Finchie never wanted to be reminded of *Red Sky at Morning* but, like a lot of the things he wanted to forget he'd done, he benefited and matured as an actor by the experience. In the same year, 1943, he played a brief scene as an RAAF pilot in a propaganda documentary film *South West Pacific*, about Australia's role as the main Allied base in the South West Pacific. There was a new depth in the voice and an assured lightness of touch.

The second year of his marriage turned out to be Finchie's busiest and most important as an actor and organizer during the entire war. His work that year included *Jungle Patrol*, a twenty-minute documentary film shot in the forward fighting areas of the Ramu Valley and Finisterre Range when the Australians and Japanese were fighting for possession of New Guinea. It gave an insight into the fighting methods of the Australians in jungle warfare at that time. Written and directed by Tom Gurr, its pictorial intensity was quietly enhanced by Peter's commentary. Finchie also wrote and broadcast on the ABC that year a talk on *The Case for a National Theatre in Australia*, in which he urged the need for such a theatre to be established in order to give 'that long-needed and delayed chance to young Australian playwrights, musicians, and choreographers, a national theatre that will inspire our young local painters, actors, singers, dancers, and producers to greater artistic theatrical heights, the presentation of which all may see at a price which the lowest-paid man in the community can afford'.

Later that year, on 19 June 1944, Peter made his first appearance at the Minerva Theatre, Sydney in Ayn Rand's New York courtroom drama, *Night of January 16th*, as District Attorney Flint.

Very unusual for those days, the curtain was already up when the public entered the auditorium and twelve members of the jury were selected from among the audience for each performance, and Finchie and Lawrence Cecil, who played Defence Attorney Stevens, tore each other to shreds in a battle of legal polemics and, of course, each successive evening the ending varied according to the jury's decision.

During the run of *January 16th*, Finchie was also filming during the day on the sand dunes at Cronulla, as Charles Chauvel had cast him in his first starring role. 'When Peter came to us to play the poetic English writer in *Rats of Tobruk* for Charles,' Chauvel's widow, Elsa, told me, 'he was slight, boyish, slim and very sensitive. He always struck me as a retiring character.'

Peter became the self-appointed muleteer during the location shooting as there were four mules who gave extremely aloof but telling performances – if you are quick enough to spot them as the Aussies ransacked Tobruk. They are dressed up in *haute couture*, supposedly looted from the Italians: old straw hats, museum piece neckties, scarves and shirts. Peter remembers a bit of millinery hastily whipped up on the set for the leading mule: a purple snood, with slits for its ears, cut with a bayonet. Peter's chore was to fetch his four performers each morning and return them to their paddock each evening. His devotion to the largest and most glamorous artiste, a white mule, was not requited. 'She kicked the hell out of me but we had an understanding. She was droll.'

Occasionally Peter would wander into the Chauvels' room before they turned in, squat on the floor like Peter Pan with his legs crossed and his eyes alight, and say: 'Mr Chauvel, don't you think if I did so and so in that little scene . . . this is the way I'd like to play it.'

Watching the film after thirty years, Peter, in this first piece of screen acting that shows him beginning to realize his potential, instinctively trusts himself not to 'act' on the screen. He does quite a bit of the narration and with the olive-soaked voice colours it beautifully. In his scene with the very young nurse, Mary Gay, in the hospital, when he has regained consciousness after being wounded, he deliberately avoids any hint of sentimentality.

Elsa wondered how the gentle, sensitive Peter she knew had by the 1950s and early 1960s acquired such a mask. 'What made him so hard later on? He was so intelligent, why couldn't he withstand success? By contrast, Errol Flynn, whom Charles directed in his first film, *In the Wake of the Bounty*, in 1933, remained true to type, right to the end. He never changed in character, even with his success he was the same boy, good, bad or indifferent, but there he was. But Peter changed so terrifically. It seems to me, looking back now, that every part he played he played so intensely that he kept a portion of it, like a mosaic, within himself. Then he'd play another part, and he never completely turned his back on that part and became himself in between. He was always those pieces of himself, scattered about within his character, till in the end I really don't think Peter knew what he wanted to be or what he really was as a person.'

Peter returned to the Minerva Theatre that October to star in Terence Rattigan's *While the Sun Shines*, directed by Frederick J. Blackman, who had a real flair for good casting and turning in a polished production that brought in the public. Roger Barry, an impeccable light comedian, had coached Peter through rehearsals to give him the polish and style he needed as the English aristocrat. Barry had played in most of the Coward and Maugham productions in the 1920s and 30s and had known both writers. Peter used to insist that Roger stand in the wings at the Minerva and check him out on every scene he played. Barry, now retired and living in Portugal, remembers Peter as working to perfect every nuance and subtlety suggested to him right through the run of the play and towards the end had really acquired a very good light comedy technique. According to Barry, 'Peter had a hand complex and, as he was in sailor's uniform, was in a fix as to what to do without pockets. So I told him when I first went on the stage I suffered from the same thing myself, that he must just learn to concentrate and really listen to what was being said to him and gradually he would find that during the run the hands would begin to take care of themselves. Every time I watched him, I could always see the tremendous improvement. He worked meticulously but always using his intelligence.'

The press reviews of *While the Sun Shines* declared it was one of the best evenings in the Australian theatre and predicted that if the standard were maintained, theatre-goers were going to see an upward trend in the style and presentation of commercial theatre.

10 Going troppo

Peter was given leave from the army to do *While the Sun Shines* and one night Dick and Peta Bentley took Peter out to dinner after the show. They were walking along Macleay Street, laughing and joking, when they saw Lieutenant-Colonel Davidson coming towards them. 'Put your hat on, soldier,' was the very curt order Finchie received from his commanding officer as he passed him by.

The last time I spoke to Finchie he told me that with Colonel Davidson he never escaped having a smudge on his boots, his hat incorrectly worn, or a button slightly askew.

The amenity services had originally been founded under the leadership of Jim Gerald, a veteran variety comedian who had formed it to send variety companies of musicians, dancers, acrobats, jugglers, comedians, and just a few actors, to help along with sketches for the troops. The various units under his successor, Lieutenant-Colonel Davidson, were so organized that drama, comedy, music (a symphony orchestra was formed), vaudeville were set up as separate entities to tour for the troops stationed all over the south west Pacific. Davidson had six hundred men and twelve women under his command; Australia's best artists with talents varying from stand-up comedians, circus performers, jazz and long-haired classical musicians, opera stars, crooners and actors, all there, volunteers and conscripts, stationed at the old Pagewood film studios. The newly formed Army Theatre Company, under Peter, included some of the best known actors in the Australian theatre.

Rehearsals began for four plays, but they would be interrupted, much to Finchie's rage and frustration, by orders from the CO to do fatigues, route marches, drill and general military training. Instead of the men having to dress up to play the women's parts, Davidson had commandeered several service-women. The women were not allowed to come to rehearsal in the men's barracks – any scenes involving the women had to be rehearsed in the women's barracks where the company would be heavily supervised by hawk-eyed butch ladies in uniform to see that whatever fun was to be had was good, clean and conforming to the rigid dictates of Aussie morality.

Tom Rothfield, who remained a close friend of Finchie's from the army days until he died, called for a redress of wrongs over Peter. He was the lieutenant-in-charge of Peter's unit number twelve at Pagewood in 1945. As a commissioned officer, he was the go-between directly answerable to Lieutenant-Colonel Davidson. The relationship between officers and men, or between director and actor, is always a difficult one in Australia as the officer or director is seldom one of the boys. Peter was very much one of the boys and when Rothfield arrived he saw that Peter was paying a very stiff price for his lack of soldierly discipline and insubordination, and for using every trick in the book to antagonize his superiors.

But Peter was talented and had made a name for himself. He'd done his bit in his ack-ack unit and was now really difficult to handle, extremely naughty, and broke every rule if he could. He refused army discipline and there's no soldier in the world who can torment an officer by his very existence in quite the same way as the Aussie when he puts his mind and his incomparable wit to it. Finchie would smile and taunt and at times be just bloody impossible. Zel Wilkinson, an actress recruited to unit twelve, said the unit gave Davidson a hell of a time. Whenever they rehearsed in the sand-dunes, that was it. Everyone would disappear for hours and he needed an army of spies with binoculars to keep trace of his scattered forces, most of whom had done a bunk to tank up with a few beers. Davidson knew what was going on but by 1945 he was no longer dealing with soldiers. He had a platoon of actors, many of whom had really done their bit, or at least, as in Finchie's case, had tried to at the beginning.

By this time, the war was nearing its end and the boys wanted to stay in Pagewood, because a trip to New Guinea might well have meant you never came back. While Finchie remained in Sydney he could obtain leave to work as an actor. It paid the army to have Peter appearing in the theatre, on screen or on radio, as his aura created prestige in the amenity unit.

Peter had recently been in hospital, with dengue fever, and then he had really 'gone troppo', playing it up to the hilt as only Finchie could to give Davidson still more trouble. 'Poor bugger, he went troppo,' was a great expression during the Australian military campaign against the Japanese. It was a kind of tropical neurosis, caused by the nervous tension and terror of jungle warfare, but also caused by the isolation, heat and boredom for those stationed in the Australian outback who never reached the fighting zones. Finchie told me, shortly before he died, that one of his greatest performances ever was the role of 'a gibbering troppo sergeant in unit twelve for Davo. That's how I eventually got out of the army. I had to act my way out.'

Zel Wilkinson more than anyone made it possible for Peter to get out of the army. Davidson had apparently not yet discharged Peter, although he was then hospitalized, and neither had he discharged Zel, although she was married. Instead he put her in charge of reception and his two-line switchboard. She used to listen in quite unashamedly to all the conversations which seemed interesting, which of course included any calls about Peter's discharge. She would relay the pertinent points to his friend Sergeant Redmond Phillips who passed them on to Finchie in hospital who was always able to keep one move ahead of Davo and in the end he got his discharge.

Tom Rothfield's dilemma was to ascertain how much of Peter's neurosis and illness was real and how far he could induce Davidson to take a more tactful line with Finchie. The important issue was to get the plays on and touring up to the fighting troops, and somehow keep Finchie and Davidson apart. Peter never once admitted he was ill. What many people never realized was that Finchie was an extremely subtle man, calculating, ruthless, adept at creating political situations favourable to his own personal ambitions.

Peter had first worked for Jim Davidson, then an ABC band leader, in 1939 as compere in what *Smith's Weekly* described as 'one of the many new programme ideas from the ABC which can be placed under the heading of their "showmanship campaign". Jim Davidson's *Colour Canvas*, perhaps the most entertaining show we have heard, is tops in music and rhythm, singing and production, with the addition of a clever commentary which we think will hold its own against some of the shows on the American Blue Network. Young Peter Finch, who does the compere part of the act, is a lad with talent.'

When Peter actually asked to join unit twelve under Davidson's command at Pagewood five years later, Colonel Jim knew what he was taking on, as Finchie had already shown Davidson his political leftish anti-establishment side during *Colour Canvas*. The ABC at that time had a sacred rule demanding that everyone should wear a dinner jacket when broadcasting. If there was no audience, Finchie would refuse to don his black tie and would appear simply in a dickie front and greatcoat. What neither Peter nor anyone else ever knew, except Davidson and his engineers, was that Davidson had a pact with the engineers. 'We used to boost Peter's voice,' said Davidson. 'He was young, enthusiastic and he had to sell the programme, but the voice at twenty-two was still just a shade on the light side, so we put a little more low frequency into it than was in it naturally. I wanted to romanticize Peter for the listeners, and I did. To me on those other radio shows he had done he sounded very light and very youthful. For *Colour Canvas* it wasn't sophistication we gave him but he sounded just that little more experienced through the depth of vocal tone. Furthermore, I don't know of any person in broadcasting at that time who could have brought Colin Will's *Colour Canvas* script to life in the way Finch did. He had an intonation that was different. He could speak Australiana, but the intonation was not native to this country. He had a vocal quality, no vocal affectation whatsoever, and this, plus his spontaneous intelligibility with dialogue as an actor, set him apart from the others.'

'Sergeant Finch was given the job of teaching a bunch of novices the merest rudiments of legitimate acting. I can hear Peter now in his best Shakespearean Aussie accent, the voice I heard him use in *A Town Like Alice*: "I've now got two good actors in the company, one professional and one amateur, but I'd rather have a man to train from scratch than begin with some inexperienced no-hoper who has begun and then left off." Like most of us, Peter found it difficult to knuckle down to army routine, a not unusual trait in any army of Australians. Peter fought hard and long and suffered many discomforts in the army, along with the rest of us. As the CO of this skilful hillbilly circus the ultimate responsibility for staging light entertainment and musical comedy was mine. The unqualified success with which our wartime efforts were received was, to a large extent, due to the untiring efforts of Peter. The last meeting I had with him was at the first night of *Oscar Wilde* in London. From the lean and hungry high-shouldered Australian I once knew, I was not prepared for the roly-poly fattened up Oscar who greeted me with, "Hullo, Colonel. Long way from Pagewood! Come and have a drink". '

Jim Davidson at that time was assistant head of light entertainment at the BBC, a position he held from 1947 until 1963. He was always very aware of Peter's deep sympathy and identity with the underdog and considers of all the roles Peter played, two, Joe Harman in *A Town Like Alice* and Macauley in *The Shiralee*, were the closest Peter ever came to playing himself as Davo knew him.

Davidson and Finchie had met at the Australian Army camp in the Sinai desert at Beitjerja, in 1942. Finchie was a member of a unit that had gone to see Davidson's show, 'All in Fun' and had gone backstage to say hullo. 'Fine bastard you are, Peter,' said Davidson. 'You should be here with us, entertaining.'

'Well, you never know,' said Finchie. 'One day I may be, if you'll have me.' And off he went up to Syria.

Davidson heard a good deal about what followed through officers in the mess at Tel Aviv but Peter, hazy about it himself anyway, was not anxious to say much to Davidson because if he did Davidson might be obliged, as his CO, to court martial him. What he did tell Davidson at Pagewood, and to me much later, does tally. Apparently Finchie had been celebrating with the boys during the Middle East campaign. He was driving a jeep illegally along a desert road, swerved to avoid an oncoming vehicle, and turned the jeep over, seriously injuring himself and the other occupants. They were all in hospital with concussion and Finchie, suffering from amnesia, never remembered the actual crash, but he developed an antipathy to driving and refused ever, with one near-disastrous exception, to take the responsibility at the wheel of a car again. Film directors tried to get him to drive in shots that were needed to show him able to drive, but he was adamant. It took him years to recover psychologically from the accident because he knew he had very nearly killed himself and his passengers.

Colonel Davidson maintains that he had no personal animosity towards Peter as a man. 'Peter was a born actor, and life was his scenario. He enjoyed life to the full and loved to relax because anybody who could read a script twice and say it thereafter perfectly without stumbling once, has a certain type of mind and temperament, but it was very difficult to know Peter Finch the man – very easy to know Peter Finch the actor.'

Finchie regarded himself as the prize lion of ringmaster Davidson's travelling circus. Davidson used to crack his whip at the lion, who certainly would have tried to devour him if he'd turned his back, but the troops loved the performing lion and Davidson had the glory of being able to make the reluctant lion jump through his fiery hoop.

Davidson laughs about that time now. 'I had to close my eyes to a lot that was going on, absence without leave, returning to camp pretty grogged up, leave passes they weren't supposed to have ... I wanted the goods delivered and I knew Peter could and would do it his way, and he did. But I had to run Pagewood, and discipline a tremendously talented but unruly bunch of individuals as best I could. Often I'd see a car drive up at six thirty in the morning, and a bedraggled, familiar figure would stagger into camp to be on the parade ground by seven – Sergeant Peter Finch. But he was only one of many. Sixteen years later in London, Peter said to me, "I didn't know you ever knew." "Nobody ever told me, Peter," I said. "All I had to do was keep my eyes open." With a temperament and innate talent, and a totally uninhibited personality like Peter, I realized that normal army discipline was useless, so I used coercion and camaraderie. Why remind a man like Peter of his indiscretions if you want to get the best out of him?

'Peter's great personal flair as a dramatic actor was never really extended in the army because we weren't there to present that type of show. We were there to relieve the minds of the fighting men, to try and give them back a sense that life was fun. I felt it wasn't quality we were after but to give the troops release from their pent-up feelings, and to make them roar with laughter. We were an emotional safety-valve. Peter was idealistic and saw us in terms of quality rather than in terms of the material we were presenting and we often had strong differences of opinion over this. But he never sulked or gave anything but his very best in what he knew as a poor compromise.'

11 The laughing woman

The closing months of Peter's career in the army were full of frustration and misery. He longed to get back into that beautiful, big, anonymous carefree civilian world again. Apart from having 'gone troppo' and being hospitalized, he had also contracted what Tamara called urethritis and what his Aussie digger mates called a dose of the 'jack'. At one stage, the army had a hospital out at Maroubra, and Whitie, who also knew where Finchie was and what he was up to, when asked by the other inmates at Pagewood 'where's Finchie – haven't seen him around the last few days,' replied, 'He's gone for a rest, up to the house that Jack built.'

What saved Peter's reason at the end of 1945, the only time he was really ill in his life (apart from a bout of hepatitis caught in Spain during the filming of *10.30 p.m. Summer* in 1965), was his marriage to Tamara, his great love of literature, and the prospect of doing something to form a legitimate theatre.

In November, 1945, once he was released from the army, he went to Tasmania to convalesce and to be with Tamara, then on tour with the Borovansky Ballet.

Finchie spent a great deal of his time in the Hobart library, researching a book he was planning to write on the history of the Australian theatre about which he subsequently gave lectures at the Sydney University dramatic society. He assisted Borovansky in any way he could, watched and learned how a ballet company functions, read Confucius, Voltaire, the German philosophers and comparative religion, and pursued his abiding interest in geology.

There is a theory prevalent that Australia once had an inland sea. This fascinated Peter, and he had an almost obsessive interest in the primordial aspect of the Great South Land. When the mood took him, off he'd go on his own, opening up rocks to find trilobites – those extinct, petrified crab-like creatures that existed on the earth in prehistoric times. He was fascinated by those luminous and illuminating sermons in stones, the cockle and mussel-shells petrified in glowing opal in the vast wastes of uninhabited Australia. Almost every known jewel is to be found in some part of the country and Finchie once told me that east of Alice Springs the hills and plains are sparkling with central Australian rubies that just lie about in the desert, richly red, of a deeper fire than the garnet, and that many years ago the miners prospecting out there made money on them until one fool loaded up a camel with them, and carted them off to Melbourne where they sold for a couple of bob a dozen. He reckoned if you gave a lubra (Aboriginal girl) a plug of tobacco, she'd find you a tin-full in an afternoon, with a big chunk of crystal and beryl added if she was feeling generous. He used to go to the museums alone and spend hours familiarizing himself with calcite crystals, chalcedony, the olivine with its liquid green gleam, quartz crystals, sequinned pyrites faintly pink with rust, crysolite, jasper, and the steely ores of antimony. From the bushmen, whenever he was in remote areas of the country, he learned where to look for felspar, with its enamelled texture, and how to recognize the prismatic flash of tourmaline and the midnight blue of radium. It was through the myriad colours of geology, he said, that he became interested in painting. Everything for Peter was interrelated and at this time he was in a ferment to absorb from life in every direction. 'Sudden freedom from the army,' he once said, 'was like coming up again into the light.'

His marriage was in its best phase. The great bond between Tamara and Peter was their mutual love of music, painting and every aspect of the arts, and at that time a deep love, respect and need for each other. Tamara was a marvellous cook but when Finchie had remembered to pick up one of his cheques, they'd go out to dine at one of Sydney's Jewish, Dutch, French, Italian or Chinese restaurants, and when the money ran out, Tamara would reproduce some gastronomic masterpiece out of next-to-nothing.

Eugene Ormandy was at that time conducting the Sydney Symphony Orchestra and in those days, because the Conservatorium had such a small auditorium, many of the music-lovers had to sit outside in the Botanical Gardens and hear the music relayed. Finchie always associated Beethoven's Sixth, the Pastoral, with summer evenings lying on the grass gazing at the skiffs under full sail skimming across the harbour, dodging the ferries, while he made plans for his theatre and the future. Peter's taste and natural selection in literature at that time was extremely good. Neither Peter nor Tamara had had much academic education. Tamara had gone very early to train with Olga Preobrajenska in Paris for the ballet and Peter had left north Sydney intermediate high school at sixteen to try his luck as a journalist. Tamara had been brought up on the French and Russian classics, Balzac, Dumas, Victor Hugo, Tolstoy, Gogol, Turgenev, and, in return for a crash course in English literature ranging from Chaucer to D'Arcy Niland, she was able to introduce Peter to her own favourites, and he carried the works of Chekhov under his arm for the rest of his life.

At that time he was also guiding his young wife's taste in reading to improve her English. He attempted to learn Russian, but found the problems insurmountable and, having forgotten his French, was too restless to apply himself for long periods to what was now a totally unfamiliar language. His interest in writing grew out of the unbearable frustration and futility of army life and his love of poetry came from an instinctive ability to speak verse. He derived tremendous pride and satisfaction from having been published in an Australian anthology of poetry. Kenneth Slessor, the Australian poet, aware of Peter's intelligence and potential as a poet, had approached him with the offer to publish his poem 'Tell Them' in the 1945 anthology, hoping that Peter would continue with his writing and develop his literary gifts. One afternoon he brought his slim little grey volume to a class he was giving at Mercury and showed it to us. No film award, he said later, ever gave him the sense of fulfilment comparable to seeing a poem he'd written and dedicated to Tamara, in print.

Because of his literary aspirations Peter's spiritual home and ultimate escape-hatch from his marriage was the Journalists' Club at Federation House in Phillip Street. To be regarded simply as a remarkably good actor didn't carry any weight among the hard-bitten writing fraternity. Its members then included such literary pundits and eccentrics as King Watson, editor of the *Daily Telegraph*, Sam Finlayson, of the *Sydney Morning Herald*, the critic Lindsey Browne, Alwynn Lee, an Australian newspaper man who could match Finchie on every level as an inspired non-conformist, Jo Jonsen, the mad Swede, Neville Cardus, the music and cricket essayist, 'Unk' White, Brodie Mac, 'Demented' Donaldson, one of the greatest among black and white artists, and a host of others. These people formed Finchie's circle of friends, acquaintances and drinking cronies. Alex Macdonald worked with many of them and through Alex and others, Finchie was accepted and became a favourite in what he called his 'journalistic Shangri-La' where his stimulating and diverse crowd of companions provided him with rich material on which he could draw as an actor. The Journalists' Club was open twenty-four hours a day. There was no sleeping accommodation. It had a billiard room, kitchen-bar and dining room. In Finchie's day, the associate members were musicians and actors. After midnight the kitchen closed and you cooked your own steak and put what you'd had up on a slate. Everything was on trust. It was a closed shop, in the very narrowest sense of the word. Wives would ring up and the barman would look across for his cue. After a negative response from the figure leaning askew against the bar, he'd say 'No, sorry, Mrs So-and-so, your husband doesn't appear to be with us at the moment'.

On 27 April 1946, Peter won the first Macquarie Radio Award for his part as René Latour in *The Laughing Woman*. It was his favourite radio part, and it marked him as the leading Australian actor of his time. Thelma Scott, his leading lady, knew that Peter had originally played it with Neva Carr-Glynn in 1939, with Lawrie Cecil directing. Lawrie would now direct it again and after the first read-through at 2GB on the Friday afternoon he expected Peter to improve on his 1939 performance. Thelma, who knew Peter spent most of his weekends at the Journalists' Club, was quite determined that they would both do justice to two superb parts, and made it her business to pin him down and get him to go through their scenes in minute detail. After rehearsal on the Saturday, Thelma grabbed Peter, took him home, cooked him dinner and they then worked on their scenes until half past three in the morning. Then she sent him off to bed and they met again for a late lunch on the Sunday, discussed the play, rehearsed with Lawrie from three until five, broadcast it that evening to a live audience, and it made Australian radio history. I heard it. Peter was inspired, and from that moment he never looked back.

During the Mercury Theatre days, Peter always said that Tamara had provided him with Russian understanding for three very important parts he played on radio during this time: Czar Paul I in *Such Men are Dangerous*, Fedya Protasov in

Tolstoy's *Redemption*, for which he won his second Macquarie Award in 1947, and Raskolnikov in Dostoevsky's *Crime and Punishment* the same year.

Max Osbiston was in the cast of *Crime and Punishment*, and during the final rehearsal he recalls: 'I had finished my part and went and sat in the auditorium and watched the final scene when Rodya is finally cornered by Petrovitch, the police inspector who has been tracking the murderer down throughout the entire story. I'll never forget Finch's final confession: "I am Raskolnikov and I killed Lisaveta with an axe ...", and I'll never forget either the feeling Peter exuded and the vibrations that came from that gaunt personality. He wore a beard at the time and looked like a half-crazed prophet, straight off an ikon. I think he wore a beard because he was about to work on *Eureka Stockade*. He looked so Russian, with those high cheek-bones and his beard. The spotlight illuminating the microphone area was on him, and the theatre was empty and everything was silent. You forgot it was a radio play or in fact a play of any kind. Here was a cathartic confession coming from a man haunted all these years by this double murder, and you got this feeling of immense relief that, although he was going to the gallows, he was able to let the agony of the past flow out of him. In one line he gave you the whole feeling. I can see him now ... something I'll never forget.'

Peter was not just working for radio. Early in 1946 Ken G. Hall was involved in a decision which might have radically altered Peter's film career, and was certainly an example of Peter being passed over in his quest for major roles, something which was to happen to him throughout his career. Hall was casting *Smithy*, which he was to direct for Columbia Pictures and Peter was up for the much-coveted role of Sir Charles Kingsford-Smith, the Australian aviator. Hall was responsible to Nick Pery, the representative in Australia for Columbia Pictures, and producer of the film. Hall recalls: 'I put up Finch and Ron Randell and tested each separately. I knew Peter was better and the more experienced actor but he was still ever so thin. When we ran the tests I knew what was going to happen. They called in their entire staff, men and women, which is always a wise thing to do, and they all voted for Randell. Ron Randell was cast as Smithy and as soon as the picture was finished, Harry Cohn, the head man at Columbia, put him under contract and he has been there more or less ever since. Peter was very sore about it and I never saw him again.'

Also in 1946, Eric Porter, an independent film producer, cast him as 'Paul Graham', the wastrel husband in *A Son is Born*. The film, made at the Fanfare Films studio in North Sydney, was Peter's sixth and his second starring role. It was rated by the critics as 'a romantic melodrama' and Finchie, as the unsavoury husband, made 'a thoroughly convincing cad'.

In the film Peter gave a very controlled performance as the husband, for he was learning what to throw away as an actor, where and how to create the effect he needed to make in a scene. He was now twenty-nine, and his voice had its full maturity and range, and the character in the film was in many ways a foretaste of what the wives in real life were to know. He was never afraid as an actor to draw on the less flattering aspects of his personality, everything was beautifully and effortlessly realized from within, nothing was ever imposed. His scene, when he uses the baby in its bassinet as a weapon against his wife, his over-generosity towards the small boy on his birthday, when he arrives with an armful of presents for the child and never gives his wife anything, and the final quiet, but tenacious, struggle for custody of the child showed at that early stage Peter's assertive strength when he wanted to use it, and gave a strong indication of the film technique he was to go on mastering through the next decade.

In June 1946, John Thompson's brain-child, a radio feature called 'Quality Street', introduced by its signature tune, Dvorak's *Slavonic Dance No. 5*, second theme, followed by Finchie's whimsical narration, began its twenty-seven year career on the ABC. Every Sunday night at six thirty, listeners could take, for example, a cultural excursion with Peter Finch into the music, writings, poetry, history, to say nothing of the habits and customs, of the eighteenth century. Peter was its first and only compere until May 1947, when he went to film in Arnhem Land. 'Quality Street' was neither pretentious nor academic. One evening, I remember, Peter introduced his audience to some of Mrs Beeton's gargantuan recipes, John Gielgud in dramatic excerpts, Beethoven's popular *Rage Over a Lost Penny*, scenes from Aristophanes' *Lysistrata*, featuring Kevin Brennan and Muriel Steinbeck, and finally read some verse himself.

During this time Lynn Foster secured him a basic weekly salary by writing the part of Stephen Crane, the lawyer, for him in the serial *Crossroads of Life*, through which he became known to millions of Australian housewives; and people like Joyce Lambert, writing for the *Radio Weekly*, were enhancing his public image with a glowing tribute to him, 'for his radio performances which continue to bolster up my personal belief that he is the best young actor in Australia, even when he lacks a stage to work on.'

The lack of a stage was becoming an obsession with Peter. He was getting fed up with what he felt was the commercial radio conveyor belt and he knew he was becoming automatic with the clichés 'sprouting like warts everywhere'. But he would always do any good script by an Australian writer if it came his way, such as Ruth Park's play about Abel Tasman, *Early in the Morning*. Actor Tom Lake can remember Finchie, in a moment of passion, throwing his script on the round table at the ABC and, in order to get the effect of Tasman climbing the rigging of his ship, he clawed his way up one of the studio sound screens and shouted the lines back over his shoulder. 'He was alive every moment and instinctively in character,' said Tom. 'And he drew you in with him.'

Max Afford's twelve-part episode serial, *The Mysterious Mr Lynch*, Sumner Locke Elliott's satire on the Sydney Radio *ménage*, *Invisible Circus*, and Catherine Shepherd's twelve-part serial of Ernestine Hill's bestseller, *My Love Must Wait*, about the cartographer and explorer, Matthew Flinders, were other examples of Peter's interest in being involved with the best native talent. But by May 1947, he had more or less finished with radio.

12 Into the never, never

It was in May 1947, that Peter took on his first technical job in films, as assistant to the director George Heath. He flew to Arnhem Land in Australia's Northern Territory, to film the Aboriginal documentary, *Primitive Peoples*. Producer Ralph Smart commissioned the trip on behalf of Gaumont-British-Instructional Films. Rank Audiovisual still distribute the film all over the world. Made for the school age group of eleven years and upwards, it is a thirty-four-minute film in three parts, an authentic record of the daily life of the Australian Aborigines. It was filmed among the Wungorri and the Iriji tribes, nomadic people who lived in the Paper Bark Swamp, a hundred miles south-east of the mission station at Yirrkala, 400 miles east of Darwin at Cape Arnhem on the western tip of the Gulf of Carpentaria. The Yirrkala Mission collaborated with them and the unit travelled eighty miles to the Cato River, where Bijar-boomba, who 'white man name Slippery', acted as liaison man and brought his people to the place appointed to meet the unit. First, they had to get permission from the administrator of the territory to enter Arnhem Land, an Aboriginal reserve. Having got this, they were passed over to the Native Affairs Department who assigned Patrol Officer Ted Evans to accompany the unit on its trip, both as a guide and also to protect the Aborigines' interests. The nomadic Wungorri move far and fast, hunting to live and, according to Peter, they only stayed with the film unit because the unit fed them. It was an economic arrangement and, by the end of the month's shooting, they had eaten 2,000 lbs of flour, which was made into a paste with water and swallowed raw as 'bubble-bubble'. Finchie and the crew lived more luxuriously, on wallaby, sugar bag honey and echidna. Peter became very friendly with the Iriji people who gave him a two-foot pipe carved from pandanus palm inscribed with the name Iriji.

It was not an easy film to make, because the Aborigines got bored very quickly, but they all cooperated very cheerfully, hunting, cooking, dancing and marching along in front of the camera, but the acting was never sustained. George Heath had to catch them in short snatches. Finchie found that they were very intelligent and caught on to any idea very quickly. A seventeen-year-old Aboriginal boy, Bookra, attached himself to the unit as 'No. 1' cameraboy. During the actual shooting, the Wungorries put on a special corroboree for the camera. Finchie said that he saw one Aborigine, painted with white pipe-clay for a death corroboree, standing absolutely motionless on one leg, looking exactly like a desiccated tree. He was amazed at the almost petrified rock-like immobility with which they could stand for hours, with the spear or woomera poised to kill an unsuspecting bird or animal. He believed they had a knowledge of herbs and because of their very primitive existence, knew many of the secrets of herbal cures for organic bodily diseases. He also said they could smell water miles away.

On one occasion a few of the men were planning a walkabout. Peter, who rated himself as a walker with stamina enough to outwalk anyone, insisted against their advice on accompanying them. 'White fella get sick. Him long way. Too far for white fella.' But Finchie was adamant. Finally they went to one of the elders and the elder told Finchie it was unwise and that he would tire. But Finchie was determined, and went. He had to be carried back to the unit where it took him several days to recover. 'I don't know why. They didn't seem to walk any faster than I did, but by the time we'd covered twenty miles, I was done and I just dropped where I stood.'

Part one of the film, 'The Nomads', showed the clans of the tribe hunting, making fires by friction, cooking, making their shelters of paper bark. Finchie saw one young boy dive from a rock and catch a moving fish in his hands. Part two, 'The Hunt', showed a kangaroo hunt during which the men used primitive magic to exert their power over the pursued animal. There is a ceremony for the eating of the kangaroo, followed by a ritual dance. Part three was a funeral corroboree. During their first eighty mile walk from Yirrkala to the Cato River, a Wungorri baby had died, and that night the tribe, in three groups, had sung the death songs by their fires. Next day they danced their ceremonial funeral corroboree. It took place, according to Peter, on the inter-tribal corroboree grounds in 'neutral Abo territory, and we were able to get some amazing shots of Abo remains on their high burial platforms'. First of all, they wrapped their dead in paper bark, then the bodies were placed on a high platform. Finchie described it graphically. The elaborate ritual for placating the spirits, accompanied by music made from their primitive instruments like the didgeridoo. Once the basso breathing of the didgeridoo begins, the gil-gil sticks take up the theme with a clear high treble, like the sound of a million crickets. Then in a descending, chromatic scale, men, lubras, piccaninnies and elders join in, shoulders swaying to the music, all singing softly at first and then the sound rises to a crescendo. The words seem meaningless. Boomerangs click together. Some old man on the edge of the ring beats two tins together, and in the distance the long howl of a chained-up dog. The singing reaches a frenzied climax, then stops, and, in a pulsating death-like hush, Peter remembers looking up at the tiny dead form, shrouded in paper-bark. When the recording of the John Antill album of the ballet suite, Corroboree, was first made by the Sydney Symphony Orchestra, Peter gave it to me just after he came back from Arnhem Land. I still have it. It gave absolutely, he said, an idealized evocation of the ancient corroboree sound. The Arnhem Land episode made a very deep impact on Peter. He described the corroboree as 'the swan song of a vanishing people ringing out to the stars in the great echo-less emptiness of the spinifex deserts.'

I heard and saw a corroboree subsequently and I understood why he responded to the primordial rhythm that is the very heart-beat of that primitive, lost Australia which he loved so much and understood so well. He knew the Aborigine was doomed. The childlike aspect of Finchie's character responded to those children of sunny skies and a sunny philosophy – and it's a great key to his love for his third wife, Eletha.

After his return from Arnhem Land Peter gave a series of lunch-hour lectures on the history of the Australian theatre to the Sydney University dramatic society. He was over a year into his five-year task of writing his comprehensive history and the lecture I heard him give at the Wallace Theatre indicated that had he ever finished it the book would have been a very valuable contribution to Australian historical literature. Peter held his audience by making his subject interesting, and because he had researched it in such a way that he could really give his lecture off the cuff. He was terrified, as all actors are, when having to speak *ex tempore*, but didn't show it. He began by saying that the popular reason given for the failure of Australian theatre to become part of its people's life is the absence of any tradition. He repudiated this by tracing in detail the origins of the Australian theatre to the exact day, 11 February 1788, a fortnight after Governor Phillips' arrival and the setting up of the penal settlement at Sydney Cove. The play was George Farquhar's *The Recruiting Officer*. The cast were convicts and the performance was given on Wind Hill, in the Governor's mud hut which had just been vacated for another at Circular Quay, on the site accepted as that of the first Government House.

Finchie had done his homework, or Tamara had (which was more likely), in meticulous detail. In this lecture, which was an excerpt from the book, he described the style of acting as he imagined it to have been in the days of lamplight, tapers and whale-oil fuel when the crude lighting must have affected the acting performances in a dimly-lit hut where any fine gestures or slight changes of facial expression would be lost. He went on to say that the convicts in the nineteenth century had constructed a theatre, which was a replica of Drury Lane, and he felt it was significant that Drury Lane was the model for Australia's first theatre and that the two plays of worth produced there, *The School for Scandal* and *Henry IV*, were popular in the London of the late nineteenth century, revealing that 'our Aussie theatre' hadn't changed in a hundred and fifty years from being a distorted reflection of contemporary London. The lecture was a great success and showed the depths of Finchie's interest in the theatrical traditions of his adopted country.

In September 1947, Harry Watt cast Peter as the articulate pacifist miner, John Humffray, in the film *Eureka Stockade* for Ealing Studios and made him responsible for a good deal of the Australian casting. This was to be a £200,000 film, the biggest attempted in Australia up to that time (the equivalent today would probably cost ten times as much). Once the shooting started Peter was also made a second assistant director on location at Blind Creek below towering Mount Dangar sixteen miles north of Singleton in New South Wales. Finchie rounded up every good available Australian artist he could find, and even sent his Mercury Theatre students to Harry Watt and Leslie Norman, associate producer and film editor, for interviews. All Peter's old mates were well to the fore, including myself as assistant to Tom Shenton, the make-up man, a position I shared with Ken Graham, a young character nicknamed 'The Spiv' because of his genius for getting things no one else in the unit could lay hands on. Ken and I used to sit side by side, hour after hour, like the brothers Rumpelstiltskin going cross-eyed weaving handfuls of human hair with a minute hook on to fine mosquito-net-like lace to make wigs, side-burns and moustaches. Between us, we made hundreds. On the first day of shooting, 19 November, three hundred and fifty people lined up at six in the morning in front of Tom Shenton, the Spiv and me, to be fitted out. Finchie was furious because the hair on my creations flew out in all directions and one Irish miner I fitted appeared on the set looking like a mad ginger tomcat. My work was always being sent back to be remade and in the end an exasperated Tom Shenton gave me the job of simply putting on the beards of troopers way out in long shot, the type that just fitted over the ears like spectacles, and I was then demoted to tea-boy. I was also put in full charge of Cecil Perry, Peter's old mate from the pre-war days to see that he neither drank nor misbehaved. 'If he does,' said Peter, 'you're out.'

Al Thomas, who played Scobie, an ebullient, stocky little Aussie, who could make a stone laugh, was on the same comedy wave-length as Finchie, and he and Peter often had to be kept apart when there was serious work to be done because their clowning used to make us all laugh so much. Al and Peter used to go off together to visit the three Aboriginal families we had on loan from the Government reserve, twenty people in all, ranging from little Hedley Docherty, aged four, to Willy Dynever, who was sixty-four, but looked ninety. Then there was a magnificent Aboriginal horseman, Henry Murdoch. He and Peter used to ride round the location together and Henry would teach Peter and Al some of the finer points of Aboriginal horsemanship. 'The Aborigines used to teach us how to throw boomerangs and handle spears, and Finchie and I used to go hunting rabbits with them. They were amazingly agile and their aim deadly. They had a welfare officer who used to come down to see where they were eating and sleeping and make sure they were getting the same as we were. He needn't have bothered. Peter was their self-appointed protector and he protected them wonderfully. They wanted to have everything we had, but asked not to have to live too near us, so they were billeted about four or five huts away, but under exactly the same conditions. Finchie saw to it that they were allowed once a week to go back to being Aborigines. They had little corroborees. Al remembers 'they did a wonderful thing. I'll never forget, the second last night before we packed up everything and finished at Singleton. They mimed us all making the movie. They imitated the reflectors, the cameras, and you could tell when they imitated Finchie. The shoulders well rounded, the little hump at the back, and that pigeon-toed walk. They absolutely had him off to a "t".'

During the shooting of *Eureka*, Peter began to assume the characteristics and appearance of the Aborigines. He could speak and sound exactly like them and he told us a marvellous story about Billy Bargol with one of those Tex Morton-type rodeo shows, a very handsome, Nestlé's milk chocolate-skinned Aborigine, who wore a little clipped moustache, a red satin shirt and white moleskin trousers. He did the whip-cracking, axe-throwing, buck-jumping routines, and when they used to tour all those remote little towns, out would come all the poor Aborigines to see him perform, all of them, jet-black, covered with flies and in a very bad state. 'Now Billy Bargol was a bit of a lair (show-off),' said Peter, 'and up he struts to one of these black, black elderly Abos – "Ho there, midnight," says Billy. "I mebbe bloody midnight," says the black, "you only bloody half-past eleven."'

For Harry Watt, *Eureka Stockade* was one of those disastrous films when everything went wrong and they were held up for months over a taxation problem. 'I was tremendously excited about this film,' says Harry. 'Originally, I'd gone out to Australia, not to make a film at all, but at the invitation of the Australian Government on behalf of the British Ministry of Information. But the outcome of that visit was that we should make *The Overlanders*. I was comparatively inexperienced as a feature director and I wrote the script with Gordon Jackson in mind, and both Charles Chauvel and Ken G. Hall, the two Australian film directors whom I approached, had advised me not to use Finch. This despite the fact he was a big star on radio on Sunday nights for Lux and Macquarie and was, in fact, their brightest star. It is also interesting that neither of them used him in their pictures, *Sons of Matthew* and *Smithy*. This is where I was stupid, and I've regretted it all my life. Finch was also my star for *Eureka Stockade*, but of course I couldn't see it. Well, we finished *The Overlanders* and returned to England to prepare for the next film to be made in Australia, *Eureka Stockade*. As I said, I was tremendously excited about this film, and I felt that it could be my great political picture. Then the British Quota Act came in and we couldn't afford to make it unless we got a British quota. In other words, it had to be a British film, made abroad with British finance, not an Australian film. For months Les Norman, my assistant director, and I, sat on our arses waiting while the Board of Trade read the script from end-to-end and worked out line-by-line, and word-by-word, which lines had to be played by British actors to make its quota. The actor playing Governor Hotham had to make one speech which ran for two pages in the script. I cast a very good Australian actor for that part, Athol Fleming, but because this speech was longer than some of the others, I had to import Ralph Truman from England for one day's work. He had to be flown 12,000 miles for what turned out ultimately to be two days shooting.

When Peter saw the rough-cut he was thrilled as many of his scenes, as one of the miners who believed that rational arguments would win a better case for the miners than violence, were still intact. But then Sir Michael Balcon saw it and said that it was too long, not a subject anyone knew about, and that it was to be cut to 100 minutes, and Finchie's part, good as it reputedly was, ended up on the cutting-room floor.

But Harry Watt felt that in directing Peter, 'you always had a sense that here was a great person on the screen. You might not agree with what he did. In *Eureka* he had a small part but he had this indefinable aura that he gave out on the screen and although perhaps sometimes you could criticize the performance, he was never a star who "stole" scenes. He was a professional. It was that indefinable something that excites a director behind the camera. That little extra, Peter always gave you that.'

13 *The Imaginary Invalid*

I still remember the tremendous sense of excitement at the Sydney Conservatorium of Music on the night of 16 July 1946, when the Mercury Theatre under its directors, Peter Finch, Sydney John Kay, John Wiltshire, Allan Ashbolt and Colin Scrimgeour, went into orbit with a triple bill of one-act plays, *Diamond Cuts Diamond* by Nicolai Gogol, directed by Sydney John Kay, *The Pastrybaker* by Lope de Vega, directed by Peter Finch, and *The Broken Pitcher* by Heinrich von Kleist, directed by John Wiltshire. Peter Finch was to be Ikharev, the card-sharp in the Gogol, direct the Lope de Vega in the traditional Spanish Commedia del Arte style of seventeenth-century Madrid, and play Adam, the lecherous old judge, in the von Kleist.

Peter conceived his production of the Lope de Vega as a period knockabout farce which he'd researched in any books he could lay his hands on at the NSW Public Library. Constable designed a painted market-place representing the traditional Lope de Vega 'Madrid corral' enclosing a crude travelling players stage for the Spanish classic. Several of that Mercury company, looking back now after over thirty years, remember Peter as a very agile young director, with a vivid imagination and a natural facility as a director to demonstrate everything superbly, better than others could hope to do on the spot. Surprisingly, this is not a good trait in a director, as it tends to inhibit an actor during early rehearsals from trying to find his or her way of doing what's required. Peter would become impatient and frustrated when some of his artists couldn't respond exactly as he wanted.

After the season at the Conservatorium, which was launched on a wave of critical acclaim, Mercury Theatres Pty Ltd were unable to purchase a building, as most prominent theatres were leased to the film distributors. They began negotiating for several theatres but all the deals for any reasonable sized premises fell through. John Kay did manage to get a short lease of a very tiny theatre and Mercury established a workshop there, a theatre school to bring in some money, where I was enrolled as one of the first students, and a Mercury Theatre Club of well-wishing subscribers was also launched. According to Finchie and John Kay, the idea for the Mercury Theatre began over a long discussion between five people in a cafe called 'The Green Parrot' in Bligh Street: Kay, a Jew of German/Peruvian extraction, who came to Australia just before Second World War with the Weintraubs; John Wiltshire, who was an experienced actor, producer and script editor working for the ABC; Allan Ashbolt, a writer, actor, publicist and journalist, who has subsequently been responsible for raising the standard of radio and television journalism in Australia; Colin Scrimgeour, 'Scrim', who was on the managerial side of commercial radio; and Finchie. Out of that long discussion at 'The Green Parrot' emerged what its five directors hoped would be the post-war beginnings of a national theatre in Australia.

John Kay and Peter Finch were constantly deploring publicly the lack of any opportunity for the proper development of Australian talent in the theatre. Peter felt that the most capable actors had been absorbed and artistically speaking often either stultified or stunted by doing too much radio. Finchie was not, as has often been claimed, a direct pr›duct of Australian radio. He was always warning us, as Mercury Theatre students, against the dangers of radio technique in the theatre. He was very aware that the standard of radio acting in Australia was very high but that the standard of literacy in Australian radio drama, especially in the commercial studios, was abysmally low.

Kay made his aim clear from the outset. 'The Mercury Theatre intends to begin where Continental and Russian traditions have now arrived, on the basis of a professional repertory company. We also have the example of the Old Vic and the newly formed American Repertory Company before us. If we can achieve that standard, and ultimately we will, the Australian public will welcome us.'

John Kay was the inspiration, catalyst, imagination and driving force behind the Mercury Theatre, while Peter Finch was its director, its front man and its star who drew the public and gave the enterprise the prestige it needed. Through Peter, and the work he did for Mercury in 1946, 1947 and 1948 – the three years he considered the most productive, busy, worthwhile and happy in his professional life – Mercury began with tremendous advantages. It was professional and could call on the resources of the very best Australian artists, designers, directors, actors and technicians available at that time, and it only finally petered out some six years after Peter had left for London. But by the time he left it had played a vital part in his development as an actor and he had realized some of his potential as a director and teacher. Even so he was really too volatile and too much the actor to teach as well as he should have. As one of the group of his first students, I remember he was very impatient, amusing, inspired at times, playing the role of the professor, formulating and expressing his ideas.

I kept an exercise book and wrote down a good deal of what Finchie taught us at that time. One marked: *1946-7 Theory of Acting* contains handwritten notes I made of words that dropped from the maestro's lips on the afternoons Finchie gave his classes.

Finch: Whatever happens on stage must have a purpose. When you are sitting still, and let's hope to God you are listening to the other characters on stage even if he or she is not addressing you, what are you thinking? How are you keeping your character alive? And that golden thread of concentration in existence between you and the audience?

Peter then quoted the great French actor, Coquelin, the original Cyrano de Bergerac, a role he coveted more than any other all his life. 'The actor creates his model in his imagination and then, just as the painter does, he takes every feature and transfers it not on to canvas but on to himself.'

'And write that down as well,' said Peter. So I did.

Finch: The external immobility of a person on stage does not imply passiveness. You may sit perfectly still and at the same time be charged with inner action. Frequently, physical immobility is the direct result of inner intensity and it is these inner activities that are far more important artistically. The essence of art is not in the external forms but in its spiritual content. Therefore it is necessary to act on stage inwardly and you automatically feel and look right outwardly. Imagination and feeling are the key to acting but there must also be 'cerebral activity'. Cerebral activity: that was Finchie's catch-phrase at the time.

Finch: When you are a character speaking dialogue, it is the subtext, what you are thinking not necessarily what you are saying, but how you are feeling and saying what you are thinking

143

that separates the men from the boys and, of course, the women from the trivial, empty-headed 'sheilas' (with a big grin at a very pretty redhead in the class called Adele Romano).

That's a fragment of the written part of the first class I ever had with Peter who already had some twelve years practical experience in every facet of acting. He won our respect because he was a professional actor and he was the best Australia had. Some months later, in another class, he spoke very eloquently in a way he never did or wanted to speak, once he became really caught up in films in the mid-1950s.

'For a man of the theatre, the theatre of the future is the one he's involved in now, the theatre he's aiming at making a reality. His rules, as he goes along, will be his own likings or his own methods of working. The theatre we hope to establish here is part of the tradition evolved from the primitive life of man through ancient Greece, Rome, the Church, the Renaissance, France, England, to our present era. But what we are up against is a self-conscious rejection of the spiritual values, the great catharsis and communion between the actor and audience are threatened by the demands of a materialistic society where those prepared to pay to keep us going want to see the illusion of banal reality. We are not voyeurs who want titillation to enliven sterile, soulless, sad lives. The value of today's theatre is its eternal value, its ability to mirror the eternal human preoccupations which are created among the assembled people, an understanding of them and a common awareness. We have a long way to go in Australia to build up public interest, to see society reflected seriously in terms of great writing, whether it be tragic or funny. But we are beginning, and there's only one great problem: the problem of success. There is no theatre without success. Success is the only constant law of our profession, the public acknowledgment, the applause and patronage are, in the final analysis, the problem of this art which Molière called "the great art", which is the art of pleasing.'

Finchie, as I realized many years later, had read avidly and widely, and like a true theatrical jackdaw had amassed a glittering hoard of literary treasure and was experimenting constantly as an actor as well as clarifying and adapting his ideas as a teacher. With Peter it worked because although no intellectual, he was highly intelligent, intuitive, articulate, and with a burning, inquisitive mind. He contributed very little to Mercury in terms of organization, ideas or the practical drudgery of getting the whole project launched financially: he left that to Kay, Allan and 'Scrim'.

Many people in Australia and in London knew a very different Peter from the one who charmed and won the respect, admiration and love of millions of cinema-goers throughout the world. In America the majority of those I spoke to praised him as an actor and as a man with childlike reverence, but those closely involved with him in the three vital years at Mercury see Peter as someone with whom everything was of the moment, charged with his personal magnetism, a mesmeric personality who caught one up in the magic of his enthusiasm and the dazzling aura of his imagination which all evaporated the moment his audience had gone.

A close friend of Peter's for most of his working life sums him up as an actor like this: 'The irony of Peter's career is that he achieved fame in the medium he used openly to despise and ridicule, namely cinema. He cannot be said to have succeeded to anything like the degree where he had set his heart, in the theatre. *Two for the See-saw*, his return to the London Theatre from the cinema in 1958, saw him outplayed and off balance in every scene with Gerry Jedd, and he admitted this. His second and last theatrical come-back as Trigorin in *The Seagull*, with a cast of formidable names headed by Dame Peggy Ashcroft, showed Peter giving a round-shouldered film performance that might have been magic to his fellow actors but didn't project beyond the first three rows of the stalls, a far cry from the Peter with the dynamic theatre magic of former years. Lighting, good direction, camera work and quick takes revealed at times a brilliant and inspired screen actor, but in the theatre, where the actor has to sustain a performance unaided by any cutting, editing and mechanical device, he simply faded out after 1952. He became a product of the studios.'

One of Peter's enthusiasms resulted in his insistence that all students of the Mercury Theatre School should attend the movement classes of Madame Gertrude Bodenwieser, who held classes in modern dance. The classes were held twice, sometimes three times a week and Peter maintained that every class she gave in movement to actors was an inspiration and that by the end of her classes we all looked, even if we didn't feel, that we knew what we were about. She used a different technique for each student, according to his potential or limitation. Finchie used to come along and sit there, watching us going through the gyrations of modern expressive dance until one day I said, 'Come on, Pete. You obviously love watching these classes. Get in, have a go and show us how.' And he did. Bodenwieser had a spacious mirrored studio in Pitt Street, somewhere above McIlwrath's the grocers; right opposite was Adam's Hotel, now replaced by the Hilton. Her system for us was all based on the figure of eight, not unlike eurythmics. We had to circle round her enormous room, doing what I can best describe as lyrical loops, all variants of the figure eight with our arms and entire bodies. On this particular afternoon, Finchie was leading the circle of rather inhibited muscle-bound Australian men and women of all ages and sizes, and we were all starting to feel really free. Madame Bodenwieser examined our movements through a lorgnette, sitting in the centre of the circle like a mini-guru.

'Gooot – gooooot. But Meester Feench, you must rise ven you move. You are too much on zee heels. You must learn to gliiide on ze balls – on ze balls, Meester Feench.' I could see Finchie's shoulders starting to shake. 'Noah, Meester Feench . . . calm vit ze shoulders and up on ze balls!' The *raffinée* Madame Bodenwieser had no idea why her group was contorted, trying not to laugh. Finchie in desperation rose with a kind of corkscrew movement 'up on ze balls' and looked like an agonized apostle moving gingerly across a hot-plate, his arms circling in eurythmic figures of eight. Suddenly there was a yowling chorus of drunken voices from Adam's Hotel opposite: 'Take a look at those poofters! Hey, that's Finch! Look at him! Thinks he's a fuckin' emu!' Adam's, of course, was a haunt of Peter's. 'Finch, ya great poofter, how's your rotten form?'

There were no curtains in the studio, It was a stifling summer afternoon and the windows were wide open, so there was no defence. Finchie stiffened visibly, but stoically kept up on his balls. The abuse rained down on us from across Pitt Street and the spectators, helpless with laughter, got a free show of Finchie giving one of his rare modern dance recitals while Bodenwieser, quite unperturbed and oblivious to what was being said, took us through her amazingly simple and varied versions of the figure eight.

In 1947, Peter revived his army theatre production of *French Without Tears* for Mercury at the request of the Mercury

Theatre Club with original members of the 12th Detachment AIF Army Theatre, and with guest artists and students from the Mercury Theatre school. We opened at the Sydney Radio Theatre on 24 September after which Peter went away on *Eureka Stockade* until the spring of 1948. The Mercury Theatre Club had been organising club readings in the evenings to keep the enterprise afloat somehow and a notice went out to the press that 'John Kay and Colin Scrimgeour, a director of Sydney's Radio 2UE, unable to buy premises anywhere for the Mercury Theatre and refusing to let their repertory movement lapse, had started making plans for their players to appear in radio plays.' Kay and Scrim always managed to come up with something, as when Kimbal S. Sant arrived from America, writing and producing his own radio material. Kim had worked with Orson Welles, Jack Benny, and many other American stars, and Finchie and I were soon working in his productions. When the Oliviers came to Australia, Kim, who had produced them on radio in America several times, organized an eight o'clock exclusive Sunday night radio show, which was introduced and compered by Peter, with the Oliviers doing excerpts from Shakespearean plays, and films, they had played in together.

It was while the Oliviers were in Australia that plans were laid for the lunch-time performance of a play that was to alter the course of Peter's life: *The Imaginary Invalid* at O'Brien's Glass Factory in the presence of Sir Laurence Olivier and Vivien Leigh who were to be the guests of honour. June Wimble, who was the secretary for Mercury Theatres Pty Ltd, as well as playing Toinette the maid in the play, had the job of organizing the Olivier matinée.

'The place was packed. It was the second time we'd played O'Brien's. We did the play on the floor of a section of the joinery shop which had been cleared. There were chairs, but people sat on the floor everywhere, including right in front of the first row of chairs. John Kay sat on top of a piano, to one side of the proscenium. I think there were about six people on that piano, and an enormous crowd was standing. It was a real crush but nobody minded, and the presence of the Oliviers in that unlikely place, gave the whole atmosphere an electric theatricality.' It was after that performance that Olivier and Vivien Leigh came backstage and Olivier said, 'Peter, you should come to England.'

He was planning to go in any case, and it had been Tamara's

aim for him for some time, and it was Tamara and Mamma who got the money together for their fare. Peter's dream had also included Paris.

'When you come,' said Olivier, 'be sure to contact us. There'll always be a job for you,' and Vivien added her warm congratulations. Had it not been for John Kay, it's very doubtful whether the Oliviers would have seen Peter in action. It was Kay's idea to invite them to a lunch-time performance. When he told Peter he planned to write to Olivier, Finchie tried to dissuade him. He argued that John was crazy and that his production and the whole presentation wasn't anything like good enough to perform in front of the Oliviers. Peter didn't want to be any part of it. John persisted, sat down in his Colgate-Palmolive office, typed the letter himself and received the following reply:

Dear Mr Kay,

Thank you very much for your letter. I am so very sad that we are already booked up for Sunday evening.

We should have liked nothing better than to see Mr Finch and his Molière. If you could let us know where the performances might be on Friday 13th and 20th, we would do all in our power to see whether we could fit it in, but I do feel I must warn you that we are really quite frenzied with obligations as our time is drawing to a close, and we might not be able to take advantage of your kind offer.

Yours sincerely,
Laurence Olivier

Kay wrote again and finally pinned him down for Wednesday, 18 August. Finchie was furious and felt that the tenacious, irrepressible Kay had gone too far and 'would land us all in the shit'. June Wimble maintains that Peter was the perfect figure-head for Kay's brainchild, but was quite incapable of thinking ahead. 'He would never think of putting £20 aside for John Kay, his fellow-director and the real power and drive behind Mercury. Peter was its glamorous show-piece. He'd give twenty quid to a hungry actor or musician, yet Kay might desperately need that twenty quid for electric light, or publicity he'd organized for the theatre, and he'd have to find it somewhere and invariably did – out of his own pocket. Peter was thriftless. Real concern for someone in trouble was often not within Finchie's scope of awareness but we were all, of course, swept along by his glamour. He had an enchanting boyishness and that "don't care" charming attitude so admired and loved by Australians. It was a case of

"Easy come, easy go", but he also had a ruthless side to his character. He was extremely shrewd in some respects, ambitious, tenacious, very sure of himself as an actor, and determined to get to the top.'

Mercury was regarded as 'Peter's theatre' but the irony of it was that as a stage actor after the war Finchie floated on a cushion of prestige, and created a reputation that derived from just three performances: two at the Conservatorium in the triple bill on 16 and 17 July 1946 and the performance of *The Imaginary Invalid* which Olivier saw at O'Brien's Glass Factory on 18 August 1948. Finchie, during 1946, 1947 and 1948, was only intermittently at Mercury as it wasn't providing him with a living wage. Instead, he was filming *A Son is Born, Eureka Stockade*, playing in radio, producing for the ABC Children's Session, and making *Primitive Peoples* in Arnhem Land. Mercury at the time was as necessary to the ambitious, egotistical, very theatrically idealist Peter as he was to Mercury as a prestige figurehead to launch it successfully. It was a perfectly timed marriage of convenience. Kay worked himself into the ground and spent all his money on the Mercury Theatre but for Peter it was just a lucky stepping stone. After Peter left Australia, in 1948, the Mercury Theatre was a means by which many people saw a repertoire of classical and modern plays with the best available talent in Sydney, but its initial glamour was Peter Finch. Peter's own opinion was that 'Mercury was the dead-end of an evolutionary process.'

14 End of the Australian episode

On New Year's Eve, 1947, the Mercury Company did a performance at Killara on Sydney's North Shore. Afterwards, we all wanted to see the New Year in together, so I organized a party at my home. The family were away, so the house was ours. There were about thirty people and the old home, now demolished, had an L-shaped sitting-room at one end of which was an open fire-place with a large chintz-covered sofa, on which Finchie was sitting, framed in my grandmother's Victorian sampler. He was sporting the *Eureka* Messianic beard and was in a frivolous and rather daemonic mood. Tamara was touring with Borovansky in New Zealand so Peter was his own master. He was regaling us with a favourite story that illustrated his basic philosophy, an anecdote about a cane-cutter who works solidly for ten years in the cane fields of Queensland, comes to Sydney to spend his money and enjoy life, meets a prostitute, they shack up together, and while he's asleep she goes through his pockets and skins him – all his savings gone in an evening. The moral of the story: 'easy come, easy go'. He'd told the story many times before, but he always made it fresh with new bits and that evening it ended as a brilliant monologue. Among those present was a red-headed woman, a friend of Finchie's, who ran a chiropody business, who I'll call Rhona, though that was not her real name. She was about forty-five years old, with a body like a boy's, bald as a bandicoot, for her cluster of red curls was a wig. At the end of 'easy come, easy go', Finchie suddenly went over to Rhona and whispered something to her. He then drew me aside and asked if we could go somewhere quiet for a chat. I took Peter into the front bedroom. I remember it was one of those brilliant, moonlit nights, when everything is bathed in a silvery light, and Peter's eyes had a really wicked glint.

'You'll never make an actor,' he said, 'until you get rid of that bloody awful pure look. Time you were initiated into the rites of love, and Rhona's the ideal woman for you.'

In those days, I was extremely shy, very puritanical and held Finchie in the highest regard. I'd already proved I was ready to break my neck for him as an actor through my tuition with Ardini as an acrobat. In this particular bedroom was an ample feather bed, with a deep hollow mattress that you could have sailed boats in if you'd filled it with water, and a very hard iron frame. Not even for Finchie was I going into amorous combat in that feathered hollow with Rhona who, I suspected, would take off the wig and hang it on one of the brass bobbles of the bedstead. The prospect absolutely appalled and terrified me. I pleaded with Peter, and told him if he wanted to wipe the puritanical expression off my face, he was going the wrong way about it.

At that moment Rhona came in and Peter made a very swift exit, taking the very large key out of the very old lock, and locking the bedroom door from the outside. Rhona went over and quietly sat on the edge of the bed. Granny's bed! I thought, this just isn't happening. I went over to the window, which looked out on a wide expanse of orange, lemon and mandarine trees, and there was that wretch, with several of his hangers-on, leaping about like priapus plucking silver oranges from the fruit trees. I knew the only answer was to sit it out.

Rhona and I sat perched for about an hour, like a couple of owls on a bough, on the sharp narrow edge of the bed, a yawning feathered chasm behind us. The most disconcerting aspect of the whole incident was that she never said a word, only smiled at me and held my hand. The hand, lightly clasping mine, was hot, dry and bony. Rhona had been primed to make the plunge but was tacitly waiting for me to take the initiative. I sat in silence, trying to think of something to say so as not to let her think I didn't fancy her, but not wanting to encourage her. It was a hot night anyway, and I began to perspire. Every now and again, Finchie's grinning face would appear at the window to demand a progress report. In the end, Rhona, who was a really good sport, called out to Finchie and told him to let me off the hook.

By September 1948, the press throughout Australia had printed their stories of Peter Finch's intended departure for England.

For the very last broadcast he did in Sydney, he gave his fee to the United Nations Children's Appeal. He collected his cheque, paid it over and then went off for his taxation clearance. The tax inspector then informed him that the United Nations Children's Appeal was not a recognized Australian charity, so he had to pay up and was taxed on the fee he had given away. But he found compensation from an unexpected quarter. A taxi driver, who'd picked Peter up with Wilf Thomas at the Cross and driven them to the ABC, refused to accept Peter's money when he tried to pay the fare. 'Have it on us, Mr Finch, and good luck in England!' Chips and Quentin Rafferty gave Peter and Tamara a farewell fiesta on the eve of their departure. Wilf Thomas describes it '. . . do you remember those drawings in old-time illustrated magazines of assemblies of roistering Bohemians, each one numbered with a table of names below? That's how it was.'

I'd never seen a room so absolutely jam-packed with poets, actresses, musicians, beautiful models, film technicians, artists, journalists. If the borer (Australian woodworm) had really done their job and 249 had crumbled beneath the weight of the dancing and revelling, half Sydney's newspapers, radio stations, theatres and night-clubs would have been out of business. Peter received from all of us what must have been the longest cigar ever made. There were no tears, but endless ribald laughter. Everyone was genuinely pleased that Peter had decided to go for the big time in England, and Finchie rose to the occasion, mounted a step-ladder heroically and declaimed, 'It is a far, far better thing I do than I have ever done before.'

Shortly after Finchie's departure for London a story appeared in a Sydney newspaper that the ball-cock balancing arm had given way in his lavatory system. Someone had climbed up to adjust it and found he had used his 1947 Macquarie award for *Redemption* to support the mechanism. Macquarie took an extremely dim view of this and the actor Alan White, who had inherited Finchie and Tamara's eyrie at 249 William Street, had to go down and try to appease Reg Lane, who was running Macquarie. In the end Chips Rafferty was asked to take the award to England officially and restore it to its owner. He gave it to Peter who roared with laughter. The only thing he had left behind he wanted Chips to bring was his Italian bayonet which he had found in the desert during the war and used as an ice pick. It was one of the few possessions for which Peter had any regard because it was supposed to be an exact replica of a weapon used in the Roman army in Caesar's time. He had found it lying beside a deserted Italian gun-emplacement.

Tom Lake travelled across to England in the *Esperance Bay*

with Peter and Tamara. Originally they had been booked to sail in the *Moreton Bay*, which I was to take seventeen months later, when I too left Australia to try my luck in England.

Thanks to Tamara and Mamma's thrift, the Finchs had the nearest the *Esperance Bay* provided in the way of a stateroom. Lake, a shy, retiring man, remembers that as soon as it was known that Mr and Mrs Finch were on board, an invitation was issued to join the Captain's table. Peter and Tamara said they would be delighted but had a friend travelling with them, so a place was made for Tom as well.

It was during the voyage to England that Peter met John Rogers who encouraged and started Peter off as a painter. Rogers was a painter himself and, with time on his hands, Peter became really interested in using water-colours. He had always sketched spasmodically and as early as 1937 was doing very good charcoal sketches of his friends Cecil Perry and old Nan Taylor his landlady. But Rogers gave him a few lessons and taught him the importance of drawing an object such as a tree or a church, a figure in the distance, bushes, flowers, and trying to master the form and, having achieved some mastery of detail, to try and paint an impression, 'Peter's own impression', of what he was seeing. Luckily he had a good visual memory which stimulated his imagination. Peter was very anxious, as his flair for painting developed, to express with it something of what he felt as an actor. Tamara always used to say, 'I had to take Peter's paintings away from him to stop him ruining them. As an actor he was always so careful never to put on too much paint, but with a paint-brush he never knew when to stop.' She'd hide the canvas and Finchie, dissatisfied, would ferret it out and slap a bit more on – just that little bit Peter knew it needed and Tamara knew would spoil it.

What Peter claimed he admired about Augustus John was his power to express experiences of wide human application, without being limited to one place, time or person. Peter felt this tremendous urge for liberty as an individual and, for Finchie, John realized it in his painting. Finchie felt an affinity with John's ability to capture the isolation of primitive peoples, like his gypsies. In his own painting, Peter felt he had achieved a mild success. More important, he had pleased himself. He knew he was about fifty years out of date but always tried to convey an impression, a spirit, rather than go into the realms of pure abstraction. He gave a lot of his paintings away and sold a few to admiring friends (Peter O'Toole once paid him £20 for a picture).

Between Malta and Gibraltar, there was always a party organized on board ship when everyone was expected to get up and do a turn. Tom was hoping that Finchie would convulse the men and really make the women blush with some bawdy sketches from the past, but Finchie was playing a very conservative role on board. He had his eye on the future and wasn't going to step out of line just to please a few new-found friends on a sea voyage. No, there would be no low comedy! He would read them poetry, so Tom had to go down into the hold and root around in his trunk for a large compendium of the *World's Great Poets*. At the end of the evening, Peter threw a little champagne party for a few select friends and before producing the champagne, made it quite clear to everyone that it was going to be best vintage Aussie champagne – none of your French vinegar.

When they arrived at Waterloo, Mitchell Hill, a girl from the Mercury Theatre who was working for a London theatrical agency, had come to the station to try and persuade Peter to sign up with her firm. Peter was very affable, very surprised and flattered at her eagerness in coming to the station to meet him, but didn't feel he could commit himself until he had seen Olivier and got his advice. For, of course, it was Olivier who had prompted Finchie to leave Australia.

15 *Daphne Laureola*

At a big cocktail party in Sydney, Olivier, with his arm round Peter's shoulder, had said, 'Now, don't forget, Peter, if you do come to London one day, you must promise to get in touch with me. You're a damn good actor,' and Tamara, with £1,000 saved, had said, 'Let's go', and that was it. But when they arrived on 17 November, 1948, London was shrouded in fog, cheerless and damp and, for an unknown actor, seemed a pretty unpromising city. When Peter rang Durham Cottage, the Oliviers' home in Chelsea, he was told they were in America and not expected back until the following day. Tamara found a cheap, depressing rather grubby flat in Powys Square, Notting Hill Gate, and Peter rang round to his friends, film producer Ralph Smart, director Harry Watt, and Geoffrey Bridson, who was producing radio features at the BBC and who had admired Peter tremendously in Australia. This resulted in his first job in England which was reading an early morning meat report from Smithfield Market for the BBC Home Service, six in the morning, on 14 December. His second job was also for the Home Service, the New Year's Eve programme, on 31 December 1948.

In the interim a bunch of flowers and a card had come from Larry and Vivien, back from America, and an invitation to Chelsea for drinks. They talked for half an hour over sherry and biscuits before the Oliviers had to dash off to a dinner engagement. But Peter had been recommended to go at once to see Larry's agent, Cecil Tennant at MCA. 'You're all right, aren't you?' Larry had said. 'Good luck and keep in touch.'

Before that evening Olivier had already read James Bridie's play, *Daphne Laureola*, and decided he must present it as his second venture into independent management. Garson Kanin's *Born Yesterday* had been his first. He also realized that Peter would be ideal for the part of the Polish student, Ernest Piaste. However, he said nothing about it to Peter over the sherry and biscuits.

Peter felt the need to be working rather than sitting meditating and staring into the gas fire, wondering if he could afford another shilling in the meter, until money came through from a Sydney radio station for whom he'd been doing interviews of 'Aspects of London Life'. (He created chaos in a street market on one occasion by plugging his recording machine into their lighting system instead of using batteries. There was an almighty bang, the whole fuse box blew, and the area was plunged into darkness. The distraught Finchie, embarrassed out of his mind, started frantically passing round the little money he had. 'No, guv'nor,' said the Cockneys. 'We don't want yer money. All we want's a bit of light.')

Harry Watt quickly came good. When Basil Dearden, the director of an episode of the next Ealing film, *Train of Events*, was reluctant to cast the unknown Peter, Harry went straight to Michael Balcon. 'Ealing was like a family, and the final decision always rested with its head.' Harry won the day, and Peter was cast as Philip Mason, the small part actor and murderer, opposite Mary Morris.

MCA, now handling Peter as a client, were already negotiating very effectively to their client's advantage. For his first BBC play engagement they had doubled the basic fee given to other actors in a similar situation. 'He may be a star in Australia, but we don't know him over here, do we?' was the radio drama booking office's argument. Peter was told by MCA not to leave his flat until they'd got him the money they were asking. Olivier's name was mentioned in connection with Peter Finch, and he left the flat half an hour before the first rehearsal.

The second round fought and won by MCA on Peter's behalf was on the sensitive subject of his film billing. Peter was determined from the beginning that his name should always appear above the title or with requisite prominence when the part merited star or feature billing. He told a friend who asked why he was so insistent: 'If you start your career in an important part with poor billing you can remain a supporting player for all time. A lot of English actors have made that mistake and lost their rightful status as leading actors. I don't intend to.'

When Ealing Studios agreed Peter's money with MCA they said to Peter, 'For God's sake don't tell them in Australia what we're paying you.' (Ealing then had plans to make more films in Australia. Peter replied, 'You don't know the Aussies. If I don't tell them, they'll imagine I'm getting twice as much as I am!')

When shooting began, the already despondent Peter had also to contend with a bout of gastric flu. Luckily the sensitive, introverted and vulnerable character Philip Mason was ideal casting for him making his screen debut in England. His scenes as the frustrated second-rate actor who murders his wife in a fit of passionate jealousy and stuffs her body into his theatrical skip make the most memorable sequence in the film. C. A. Lejeune, writing in the *Observer* on 21 August 1949, described him as, 'a young actor called Peter Finch who adds good cheek-bones to a quick intelligence and is likely to become a cult I fear.'

During the last week of filming at Ealing, Peter received a telephone call on the set from Olivier. He told Peter that the script of a new play would be delivered to his flat that night and that he'd very much like Peter to read it. Cecil Tennant, head of MCA and managing director of Laurence Olivier Productions, brought the script himself. Peter was told to be at Wyndham's Theatre on the following Tuesday to give an audition.

Peter arrived at the theatre on a freezing December day, along with other actors, ready for the part. Diana Graves, who was understudying Edith Evans, read in for her. Finchie had studied the script non-stop since he'd received it, but, on seeing the other actors waiting nervously in an empty theatre with a harsh naked working light on the bare stage, he felt he knew nothing about the character at all. This kind of audition is the most intimidating, paralysing experience an actor can be subjected to. The stalls were pitch black. Peter could see no one, only hear voices. He knew that somewhere down there were Sir Laurence Olivier, Dame Edith Evans, Vivien Leigh, James Bridie, and the play's director, Murray MacDonald.

Two bentwood chairs were set on the bare stage, one for Diana Graves, one for Peter. 'When you're ready,' called a voice from the darkness. They started reading. Peter was a brilliant sight reader and, aware of the waves of encouragement and admiration from Diana Graves, at once forgot his terror and began to get the rhythm and momentum of the scene.

Diana Graves had already read with a number of the actors auditioning. Years later she recalled, 'As soon as Peter walked from the shadows on to the stage I thought "here is someone different". One line and I knew he was Ernest Piaste. It was simply extraordinary. He sounded absolutely Polish to me, but there was something else too . . . something compelling. I thought,

"My God, here is a talent." It was unlike any audition I've ever known.'

After some time Olivier's voice cut in very politely: 'Thank you, Diana, thank you, Peter. Just wait a minute.'

Finchie sat with that hideous feeling of stark, lit exposure, gazing into the pitch blackness of the orchestra stalls, with the sibilant sounds of a decisive conversation going on some twenty feet away. Diana, unable to bear the tension for Peter, took his hand and squeezed it, and Peter suddenly turned away. This warm impulsive gesture from a stranger was too much for him and he started to cry. He put his head down on the back of the chair trying to pretend he was deep in thought. The voices continued to whisper, papers to rustle. Then, in Peter's own words, 'Suddenly I heard a rich, bell-like, rather mannered but arrestingly beautiful English voice calling me from the darkness. I turned around to see a woman leaning on that balustrade by the orchestra pit at Wyndham's. "My name is Edith Evans and I shall look forward to seeing you at rehearsal on Tuesday." '

Olivier had already left the theatre, but he rang Peter later to tell him he'd be under contract to LOP, and then said, 'I'm so glad you came along and read for us, and that you're going to join us for a while as a contract artist, because this is the kind of thing I had in mind for you when I was in Australia.'

There was no question in anyone's mind once they'd auditioned Peter that he was perfect casting. But it was generally agreed later that he would never have been cast initially in anything but a foreign role such as Ernest Piaste, because of the Australian vowels which kept seeping through in unguarded moments, and his unmistakable intonation. Knowing this did a lot to rob him of confidence in the beginning. In those days BBC English was the accepted norm, and people were very quick to pick up discrepancies in an actor's speech. So Peter had to be extra careful lest his character sound like a Polish Australian.

Later Peter told me of his nervous apprehension of these unconscious overtones of Australian accent during his first days of shooting on *Train of Events* and during the rehearsals for *Daphne Laureola* with his nerves already wracked at the looming prospect of a West End première. During rehearsals Murray MacDonald had just been letting Peter go on without giving him any notes. Peter was feeling more and more unsure, worried about his voice against the perfection of Edith's. He felt he

158

badly needed direction, and did not realize that Murray was letting him have his head because he was building the part instinctively, and his director did not want to pressure him. Halfway through his long speech in Act Two Peter suddenly broke off and said, 'I can't go on. I've lost my nerve,' and dashed into the wings. Edith Evans rushed after the absolutely shaking Peter, caught him, and brought him straight back to the side of the stage. 'Young man, come on now, settle down,' she said. 'Take control of yourself, go back on that stage and do your scene. When this play opens next week you are going to be a star. There's nobody else in this country who can play the part as you are doing. So back you go and do it.' And he did. He told me that Dame Edith's words put him back on his feet and enabled him to build up the character confidently from that moment. Her reaction had been instant, and it touched Peter deeply that she cared enough actually to run really fast after him and catch him.

On the opening night, Wednesday 23 March 1949, the curtain was to go up at seven. This London first night would be the grandest and most elegant in the legitimate theatre since before the war. When the half-hour to curtain call came Peter was in a dressing room absolutely papered with good luck telegrams, staring into his mirror, putting on a simple five and nine Leichner make up, adding a little olive to give a sallow effect, a black pencil line to bring up the eyelashes, and powder to take out the shine and absorb some of the sweat. He knew out front was a house packed to suffocation. Coming down into the wings just before the curtain rose he heard on the other side that muffled roar of an excited audience, waiting for an Olivier first night, and to see Edith Evans in a modern play.

The house lights went down and the audience sat silent, and for Peter came that moment when every actor goes through an excruciating, seeming hundred years of agony. Curtain up, and that vacuum in time before one's first entrance, on a first night, before a now silent, expectant and critical London audience.

Lynn Foster, sitting towards the back of the theatre, was on the edge of her seat for Finchie, fully aware of what was at stake for him. It was his first stage appearance since September the previous year, when, in very different circumstance, he had played Argan in *The Imaginary Invalid* at the Sydney Town Hall.

Peter described that first moment of trial and confrontation, before an audience, with a *non-pareil* like Edith, as having a sensation of being disembodied with sheer terror before actually speaking, a taste of salt in the mouth, and the first few minutes of dialogue like a fledgling bird suddenly forced to fly from the nest at a great height, into the dark, with unfamiliar flashes of light, and a terrifying, invisible live presence watching, judging and waiting.

Lynn said: 'During the first act he didn't have much to do, and the audience were just dazzled by Edith Evans. What an actress and what devastating charm! She was incomparable. Came Act Two and Finchie's big scene, and I could see he was absolutely grey with nerves. For the first two minutes he wasn't actually giving a very good performance, then suddenly he got the better of his nerves and just took off and had the audience right where he wanted it. In his first declaration of love to his "Gloriosa Donna", Lady Pitts, both Peter and Edith Evans sparked each other off and an absolute magic was created between them, enthralling the audience.

'His scenes with Evans and Felix Aylmer were charged with an undercurrent of nerves, that suggestion of risk, fiery, passionate, everything at stake as a character on stage, and as an actor in real life as well. Everything was truly in the balance. When the final curtain fell after Ernest asks for a double brandy there was that few seconds of absolute silence, and then thunderous applause, an absolute triumph for Edith Evans. When Peter came on to take his bow the audience suddenly exploded emotionally and for a second it was unbearable, as I remembered Peter's career over so many years. He obviously didn't realize the impact he'd made. The audience started to whistle, stamp, and shout bravo! At the end I was crying unashamedly. Peter's wife Tamara turned to me and said in a small voice, "Are they really applauding him?" It was incredibly difficult for Peter to play a poetic young man of twenty. He was so much older in every way than Ernest. It could have been such a disaster.'

At dawn the press representative, David Fairweather, phoned him from Knightsbridge tube station, where he was reading Finchie's reviews in his pyjamas. Peter took a taxi and joined him on the corner, where they roared with laughter and approval at the press notices by the light of the street lamps.

He made headlines in the papers. It was a triumph for Bridie, Olivier, Edith Evans, the company, its director, and a unique

London press for an unknown actor. The *Evening Standard* rated Pitts as the best acting Edith Evans had ever done, but her triumph was aided by a young Australian actor, Peter Finch, who played Apollo. 'Lyrical idealism beautifully expressed by Peter Finch as the student,' wrote the *Star*. 'Peter Finch as the Pole makes a name in a night,' was W. A. Darlington's view in the *Daily Telegraph*. 'Finch's performance is sensitivity at its greatest, and the whole evening is the wittiest, most hilarious, with often the most tender acting seen on the stage for years,' from Paul Boyle in the *Daily Graphic*.

Peter's friendship with Edith Evans developed as the play ran on. He respected and worshipped her as an artist and was always grateful for the famous tip she gave him about playing comedy. During the run they were beginning to lose laughs and Peter, although he tried not to, was forcing a laugh line on his audience and was losing them. Edith called him aside one night and said, 'As I see it, Peter, the art of light comedy is to fire powder puffs out of a cannon. You, dear boy, are firing cannon balls.'

Peter was always grateful to his director, Murray MacDonald, for teaching him one very important lesson, never to make a distracting movement away from the central action on stage when not speaking, but rather how to make the slightest head or hand movement that could enhance what was going on. 'It's amazing how much Murray knew. He and Edith were very subtle, and luckily some of their experience washed off on me.'

The novelist Charmian Clift, who knew Peter when he and Tamara were living in Dolphin Square during the run of *Daphne Laureola*, remembered him as a man always needing assurance that he was good, never quite able to believe it had all happened to him, and that people really meant it when they wrote or told him of his unique ability as an actor.

On Olivier's advice Peter turned down Alexander Korda's offer of a leading role in *Angel with a Trumpet*. Olivier knew that by filming from dawn to dusk and playing at night in the theatre his performance as Ernest Piaste was bound to suffer. Peter realized the folly of suddenly trying to start what might be a promising film career at the expense of what he already had in the way of secure success, and only accepted two very small, but extremely effective, one scene film parts. He did the RAAF officer in the prisoner-of-war hospital in *The Wooden Horse* for

Jack Lee, which was a one shot scene added when the film had already been completed. In *The Miniver Story*, he did another one shot scene as the Polish officer. Sidney Franklin, who was producing the film for MGM in England, went to see Peter as Ernest Piaste, and was tremendously impressed by his performance as the Pole, and asked him if he'd like to do a short day's filming in the film H. C. Potter was directing at Elstree with Greer Garson and Walter Pidgeon. After the day's shooting the elated Franklin arrived home to tell his wife Ruth that he'd had a unique and wonderful experience. 'This morning a young man arrived on the set ready to discuss three different ways of interpreting the character he was about to play in a very brief scene. Working with him was the greatest pleasure I've had in this country. He was magnificent.'

Finchie had been giving a lot of thought to his character, who had one long speech. He was in a state of great excitement anyway, as Tamara had presented him that week with a six-and-a-half-pound baby girl: Anita.

In *The Miniver Story* he played a young, debonair Polish officer who bursts into a pub and makes a speech congratulating the allies on VE night in 1945. When he says, 'Very soon I return to my dear wife in Cernitzin,' you feel that Poland was in his blood and that he did long to go back. He captures in a few seconds all the Polish *élan* and dash. Here, you felt, was a man who was gallant, courageous, and bred from the best of the Polish bourgeoisie, or perhaps the aristocracy. He had that ebullient, unselfconscious Polish passion and gaiety which, like the Irish at their best, has a dash of madness in it. His brief, flamboyant cameo has no hint of the romanticism of the disillusioned youth of his Ernest Piaste, but it shows a facet of Peter, the sort of quick-fire, off the cuff, imaginative acting he sometimes gave so unexpectedly on Sydney radio.

After Anita was born, Peter and Tamara moved from their little attic flat in Burleigh Mansions, St Martins Lane, to a top floor flat in Grenville House, Dolphin Square. He acted in BBC radio plays and features, and painted on the roof of Dolphin Square.

16 Olivier and Orson

There was no play immediately available for Peter after *Daphne Laureola* closed, so, on Olivier's recommendation he accepted an offer from Stanley French, to direct *The White Falcon*, a romantic play about Henry VIII by Neilson Gattey and Jordan Lawrence. Basil Radford was to play Henry, and Sheila Burrell, who had made such a success in Peter Brook's production of *Dark of the Moon* the previous year, was cast as Anne Boleyn.

Sheila remembers Finch as 'a very volatile director, full of ideas all pouring out of the top of his head, quite mad, but lovely to work with because here was this marvellous actor to whom the structure of a play mattered, who was amazingly articulate, could be sympathetically subjective to us actors, and knew every problem and hangup we had because he had been through the hoops himself so many times, but who could also switch off and be a ruthless, objective, but never repressive or paranoic, director. He was very articulate, and quite frankly we were all a bit in the dark about that play and I think Peter was too, but he had this natural instinct and intelligence of a man capable of taking an overall view of a play and making it come alive. His rehearsals were crazy and exhilarating.'

Peter was working with a strong, experienced cast which included people like Hugh Griffith, Alan Wheatley, and Joan Haythorne. The play opened in Blackpool, toured for six weeks and petered out in Nottingham. The production had pace, but showed he needed to work as a director on all the technical details and subtleties that come through years of experience. Where, of course, he did score was in his handling of the actors, but he himself at that time felt he needed to sit and watch someone like Olivier set up and direct a production.

While *The White Falcon* was on the road, Barry Morse, launching his first production as a West End manager, decided to present an absolute rarity in the London theatre, a comedy about Australians with a part Australian cast, *Pommie*, by W. P. Lipscomb and John Watson. Barry was searching for a director who was either Australian or knew the scene. Stanley French, whose partner Barry had been the year before, immediately suggested Peter.

Lipscomb had been in Australia three years earlier in connection with *Eureka Stockade* and had written a play about a 'pommie', an Englishman, to be played by Leslie Howard's son Ronald, a suave rascal who comes to Australia to find a wealthy wife. Peter met Barry Morse for lunch and admitted he didn't know a great deal about life on a Queensland sheep station, but read the play and agreed to do it. However, at the same time Olivier cast him as Henry Adams the communist agent, opposite John Mills in Bridget Boland's *The Damascus Blade*, which was to open on a pre-London tour at Newcastle on 13 March 1950. As *Pommie* was scheduled to open on 20 March at the Grand Theatre, Blackpool, it was agreed that Peter should simply advise on the casting of the Australian parts, and on the overall production.

Ivor Brown, the dramatic critic of the *Observer*, writing of the new names of rising importance in British acting, mentioned Anthony Quayle for his work at Stratford-on-Avon; Paul Scofield for his acting at Stratford under Sir Barry Jackson during 1946 to 1948, and for his performances as Konstantin in *The Seagull*; Denholm Elliott for his appearances at the Malvern Festival, and as the poet Keats; and Peter Finch for *Daphne Laureola*. But in a press interview in late 1950 Finchie stated that he looked upon his work in England as a preparation for his return to Australia to work for an authentic Australian theatre, and he still had ideas about a 'group theatre movement' like the Mercury Theatre. However, his enthusiasm to return to Australia soon dwindled as he became absorbed in the challenge of playing the variety of parts offered him, which included playing Professor Winke in Olivier's production of *Captain Carvallo* and an unexpected chance to do an Anouilh play with Mai Zetterling. Finchie told me how this came about over a drink one day in 'the Salisbury', the actors' pub. He was convinced he was the only actor ever to be solicited in the gents' lavatory and beseeched not to show his parts but to play one, the part of Orpheus. I didn't believe him until Kitty Black, who translated the play from the French, and Peter Ashmore who directed it, assured me that Peter had been seen going in to 'splash his boots' as Kitty and Tony Forwood, a friend of Dirk Bogarde's, entered the bar at a moment of appalling crisis. Tennent Productions had waited a long time until Mai Zetterling and Dirk Bogarde were free to star in Anouilh's *Point of Departure*. On this particular Friday, Kitty, working for H. M. Tennent, arrived at the Duke of York's Theatre to be met by Tony Forwood with a face as long as a wet Monday. Disaster had struck: Dirk had been to see his doctor in the afternoon, and the doctor had ordered Dirk to leave after that evening's performance.

Everyone had known that Dirk hadn't been particularly well, but this crisis was worse than anyone had expected, and Mai then stated that she wouldn't play opposite another, available, actor because 'I get nothing from his eyes!'

So Kitty and Tony decided to take Tony's car and scour London for an Orpheus who could not only 'return Mai's service', but 'turn her on as well'. They went from the Duke of York's to 'the Salisbury' for a stiff gin before undertaking the quest for Orpheus, when who should be disappearing into the gents but Finchie. 'After him!' Kitty yelled to Tony. Finchie turned, and, not realizing the situation, fled into the tiled underworld of 'the Salisbury' and slotted up the 'engaged' sign in one of the cubicles. Tony pleaded with him to come out, that he had a desperate proposition to make and Tony, in due course, returned with the dumbfounded Peter who was thrown into the role on the spot. He'd signed a contract that afternoon with Walt Disney to play the Sheriff of Nottingham in *The Story of Robin Hood and His Merrie Men* to be directed by Ken Annakin, but he did have six weeks before he started filming. He said he'd open on the Monday, but Mai wasn't ready suddenly to spring into action with somebody completely new and unknown to her, so Peter opened on the Monday week, 12 March 1951.

For Peter, Orpheus was the only other character he played in the English theatre comparable as a romantic part to his Ernest Piaste in *Daphne Laureola*. He seemed by this time to have become very polished, but he lacked the naïve spontaneity of Dirk Bogarde. The true sensitivity and warmth of his René Latour in *The Laughing Woman* had gone. There was less feeling in Orpheus than there should have been. The compassion and sweetness which Peter was perfectly capable of conveying were lacking. He never, he believed, got into the feeling of the role as he had in *Daphne Laureola*. Yet the role of Orpheus, though different in concept to Ernest Piaste, made similar demands of emotion and youth on him.

Dirk had planned to wear the traditional French blues: very dark blue shirt and trousers, a gold medal hanging around his neck, and navy blue espadrilles. Finchie had very pale green-blue eyes, so Kitty Black told the wardrobe mistress to throw the lot into a bucket of bleach and bleach the dark blue into a pale washed-out blue, which absolutely transformed the clothes and the part for Peter. In those days he wore his hair longish with a side parting. It was very wavy and had a heavy untidy look. When Kitty saw him on Sunday afternoon at the dress rehearsal she said, 'Stick your head in a bucket of water and comb your hair straight back and I think you'll look like a lion.' He did. Quite soon afterwards he had his hair cut short at the back, and he wore it like that for the rest of his life.

The interesting aspect of Orpheus in *Point of Departure* is that the girl leads the play. Every single scene is started by her. This is Kitty's comment as translator; and when I spoke to Peter about it he admitted it was Mai's play. But, he said, 'It never worried me that Orpheus was really a passive character almost dominated by the girl. In the context it seemed so natural. Maybe I learned that almost feminine acceptance in the East!'

As soon as Peter had finished his six week contract in *Point of Departure* he went straight on to *The Story of Robin Hood and His Merrie Men* at Denham Studios. The Americans were very anxious to make an authentic, accurate film on the Robin Hood legend and Carmen Dillon, who had done memorable artistic work on Olivier's film of *Henry V*, and who subsequently designed *Richard III*, was sent to Nottingham to do detailed research. They were also very keen, says director Ken Annakin now, to get 'what we'd now call National Theatre actors, which surprised everybody, because they never did manage to get any'.

Richard Todd, a contract artist, had already been cast as Robin Hood, and Disney were determined to test everybody for the Sheriff of Nottingham. All the best available actors were tested. Peter had only done *Train of Events*, for Ealing, and he didn't regard himself as a costume actor. But 'Peter's test,' says Annakin, 'was simply great and everyone agreed he should play the Sheriff. He brought a sincerity to the part with a lot of bite, and I would say it was rather like the casting of Guinness in *Star Wars*. He gave the whole of *Robin Hood* a lift with consummate acting. He had some marvellous scenes with Hubert Gregg as King John, another very good English actor. Of course he had to do a lot of action stuff as well.

'I remember one Saturday afternoon we had him on one of the typically untrained horses that England produced at the time. We had to do seventeen takes to get a close-up of him on the horse, and it took us the whole afternoon. Every time we turned over, the horse seemed to understand at once, and played up. Peter showed great patience. In fact, he was one of the most professional actors I've ever worked with. He was a sympathetic person and very responsive to direction. In his later life we all know he had a period when he started hitting the bottle. I never saw a sign of this when we were making *Robin Hood*, but clearly his life was not satisfying him entirely.

'He was a marvellous actor, but if one had asked him in the old days whether being an actor was the sort of thing he really should be doing, I suspect his answer would have been that he needed more out of life than just that. I think he found himself forced into a shoe, a shape, which for a long time he didn't accept.

'He had the intelligence to be a director. I don't know whether he had the patience to apply himself constantly. I always feel that direction is about forty per cent obstinacy and forty per cent patience.'

To Ken Annakin, Peter at that time was deep down a very typical Australian, an outdoor man who loved the country and riding, and did not have a great deal of patience for the meticulous details and hours of drudgery that are part of a director's lot.

With the Sheriff of Nottingham Peter began to be accepted in England as an important actor in terms of screen potential. Ken Annakin maintains that what Peter Finch did with his role was the best that an actor had done in that kind of film until that time, and that people in the film industry began to take serious notice of him because of this. It gave a tremendous boost to his confidence, and the possibility of a substantial film career really fired his enthusiasm.

The 'Once a Jolly Swagman' image he often projected among colleagues like Ken Annakin, Basil Dearden, Sidney Gilliat, and the other directors with whom he was working when his film career in England was starting, gave him distinction, a strong individuality among those with whom he was feeling his way professionally and off the set.

Another chance encounter with Peter in 'the Salisbury' is described by actress Maxine Audley.

'I won't say how old I was,' mused the beautiful and sphinx-like Maxine. 'Let's say I was young, but experienced! I went into "the Salisbury" with two friends. There were these huge mirrors along the wall and you could see all the faces of the people standing at the bar, and there was this ravishing young man, beautiful – well, to my eyes he was – and to lots of other ladies obviously! Very thin, a slightly battered face with marvellous cheekbones, and although still young he already had two straight lines down the cheeks.

'I think he brought out the mother in a lot of us, as well as being a very attractive fellow in other respects. He was leaning on the bar drinking by himself, and I gazed at him in the mirror, and I suddenly became aware that he was looking back at me. I was determined to meet him and somebody finally introduced us. He was playing in *Daphne Laureola* at the time. As far as I remember I went backstage that evening. There was Diana Graves, who was playing the bored lady in *Daphne Laureola*, and several other people, and then we went home and Peter stayed the night. I've never been so determined. I mean, it wasn't determination so much as sheer attraction at first sight. Peter just loved all women, it was part of his nature. We had an affair for a few weeks, and then I went off to Stratford and we didn't meet until *Othello* in 1951, in which Peter played Iago.'

Welles had just made his film of *Othello* with Michael Mac-Liammóir as Iago in Venice and Mogador. He was still in love with the character and, under the aegis of Laurence Olivier Productions (he was very friendly with Larry and Vivien), he mounted his production at the St James's Theatre in October, 1951 and brought with him the music he'd used in the film for the stage production.

Maxine believed that Orson, a giant of a man physically, stout even then, had such determined ideas about how he wanted the play done, and how he wanted to play Othello, that he surrounded himself with actors of the smallest stature he could find. Peter was very skinny and 5 foot 10 inches tall, Maxine, 5 foot 4, Gudrun Ure, 5 foot, and Orson, 6 foot plus, wearing gigantic lifts, lumbered about like a dinosaur among pygmies. Everything about him was enlarged and padded! Rehearsals were a kind of nightmare, but great fun according to Maxine.

Half the rehearsal time was taken up by Orson telling anecdotes, at which he was brilliant. Peter, being a great raconteur himself, would cap these stories, and they'd go on and on; and, according to Maxine, very little work was done.

They all stayed at the Turk's Head in Newcastle and every night after the performance there were terrible inquests in Orson's suite. They were noisy sessions with a great deal of eating and drinking. Peter and Maxine, man and wife on stage, clung to each other for comfort in their terror during that pre-London tryout. Peter, despite his state of nervous tension and blind panic, seemed able to outlast Orson, and kept them all in hysterics with his Australian anecdotes, while Orson slept soundly in an armchair.

Halfway through the week Peter and Maxine were making such a row in one of the rooms that the night porter appeared and told them they'd have to leave the hotel as they were disturbing all the other guests. So, with bottles and baggage, out they had to go in the early hours of the morning to wander the streets of Newcastle. The first place they saw where there was a possibility to lay their heads was a temperance hotel, and there they were welcomed with open arms. Neither had ever realized before that you can go to a temperance hotel and drink with your own bottle. They just don't serve liquor on the premises.

The upshot of their eviction from the Turk's Head was that the following week Gladys Cooper arrived with a very respectable company and they were all turned away. Theatre casts were not allowed admission to the Turk's Head for a very long time.

They played a nine-week season at the St James's Theatre in London. Kenneth Tynan, writing for the *Observer*, felt that Orson Welles had the 'courage of his restrictions' and the performance English audiences had seen him give as Citizen Kane had been transformed that evening to 'Citizen Coon'! Peter was dismissed as puny, humourless, charmless, and a bantam weight.

Finchie, like Maxine, spoke in retrospect in nothing but the most affectionate terms of Welles. He had the deepest respect for his achievements, and that tenacity to rise above every obstacle, which made the moments spent in his company magical if hair-raising at the time. Finchie maintained the *Othello* production was a traumatic crash course in an amazing larger-than-life experience. First of all Olivier came to see the production before it opened in London, and ticked off Peter for the dying inflectional fall at the end of every line that was taking all the meaning out of Shakespeare's poetry. 'You've got a good diaphragm,' Larry told him. 'Learn to use it like an opera singer when you play Shakespeare, or else the poetry starts to sag with a lot of unnecessary pauses for breath.' Finchie was urged to go and take lessons from Cicely Berry who could get him to breathe properly. Off went Finchie, and a week later his voice was rising beautifully like a castrato's at the end of every line of the bard's iambic pentameters. However, one night Noël Coward, by then a friend of Peter's, arrived at the dressing room after the performance and told Finchie's dresser, 'Pour the master a VERY large gin because I'm going to be naughty.' As Finchie entered he was greeted by Noël. 'It's an impeccable performance, Finchetta, dear boy,' and then after an immaculately timed pause, 'but why are we playing Iago in Welsh?'

The night I went to see Finchie as Iago was the only time I ever saw him totally distraught. Welles had certainly been the focus of our entire attention and Peter had been quite out-gunned. He was shaking with rage and out came a torrent of broad Australian. 'Playing Iago, to him, is like trying to act against a warm rainstorm. Last night he spat so much in one scene a bloke in the front row of the stalls actually put his umbrella up!'

I could never think what it was about Finchie's Iago that looked somehow wrong. It wasn't in the acting, but his appearance was almost comic, and was completely at odds with what he was doing as a character.

Both Peter and Gudrun Ure, who played Desdemona, were utterly perplexed by the solitary, larger than life genius with boundless charm, who was always, Finchie said, trying to work out who he really was. To Maxine, Gudrun and Peter, Orson Welles was a loved and hated almost paternal figure. They'd leave the stage ready to cut his throat, then a message would come recalling them to the stage. Back they'd go, and there would be Orson in a red dressing gown, sitting centre stage, holding a balloon of brandy. He would then tell his 'family' about *Othello* and regale them with anecdotes about the old Hollywood days, and they'd all fall under his spell again.

Gudrun Ure was always amazed at the internal violence that Orson's handling of Peter as Iago stirred up in him. In private the venom poured out in four-letter-word invectives. Gudrun and Peter, feeling like two hostages, were drawn together in a close platonic friendship, always trying to bolster each other's confidence, and she was able to observe him very carefully and quite dispassionately. 'He was in a new environment and very much swimming with the stream at that time. He was going places and he knew it; he was mixing with the top people and the right people and he was very aware who they were, but he was extremely subtle about it, and his great natural charm stood him in very good stead. He was always very sweet to me and tried to give me confidence without any flattery. He never exploded and said what he really felt to Orson when the whole production started to sour on us because Peter, as an old hand at the game, always knew exactly what was going on, and was always very careful what he said. People say now he never cared what he said. Well, he was extremely careful in the time we worked closely together. He minded his Ps and Qs when it was a question of his getting ahead in our precarious business, and he watched exactly where he was going to put his foot down next. Peter did unquestionably have a very rough deal in *Othello* and suffered both physically and mentally, as did Orson, who also suffered great and unmerited indignities. We all did.'

What always fascinated Gudrun Ure were Peter's hands. 'Very mobile, beautiful, but in a kind of disturbed way. They were almost too supple, as though he had no joints, with those flattish finger tips. I kept saying to him he should do more painting because I felt that whatever was disturbed within him, he might have got rid of through painting. His hands at times used to worry me. Peter often seemed to be crying inside, not in any obvious way, but being in a state of terror your awareness and perception often become heightened and you observe more deeply. With Pete there were these self-protective layers of apparent indifference, but he was always looking for comfort really and he'd often come to me in that way that people gravitate to one another when they have feelings of inadequacy. "I haven't a light," he'd say. "Got a cigarette?" He'd be writing or sketching, "Got a rubber you can lend me?" He was a little boy looking for protection. He didn't really need it by that time, but it was touching. I'd see him put up a façade with someone who'd joined us, almost immediately. Then he'd be big and confident and sometimes rather brash, almost worldly, but in fact he wasn't any of those things.'

Peter's last play for Laurence Olivier opened at the Lyceum in Edinburgh for one week, and then went into the St James on the 30 January 1952. *The Happy Time* is a domestic comedy by the American dramatist Samuel Butler, set in the 1920s, about a French Canadian family in Ottawa, whose sentimental theme is love and desire, a little light philosophy and tenderness. The play revolves round the young son of the family, Bibi, played in that production by the twelve-year-old Andrew Ray, son of the comedian Ted Ray. Bibi is struggling with the birth of desire and puberty, and to understand the meaning of love and truth. Rachel Kempson was the Scots Maman married to Peter, playing Papa the musician with the light hearted philosophical tolerance of a *demodé* Frenchman that he might have created from reading *The Beloved Vagabond* by the Victorian novelist W. J. Locke. Peter had to chat to his young Bibi and try to make him see that desire must be accompanied by love, and that sexual curiosity and desire unaccompanied by love leads to the greatest spiritual desolation, and the ruin of mankind. The *Daily Telegraph* critic spotted Peter's genuine French speaking English and even Kenneth Tynan found him well cast, for once, and a warm quizzical father. Peter's press notices were consistently good, and discerning of his depth and sensitivity and the gentle humour of his characterization, and it was felt that in the scene with his son a vital truth between the boy and his father on the facts of life was touchingly expressed with subtle delicacy and understanding. The *Sunday Times* critic, Harold Hobson, wrote of Peter: 'Mr Peter Finch plays Papa quite enchantingly with the most delicate discretion and there are echoes in his voice that take the ear like divine music.'

Finchie had been working on his voice. The gallery first nighters, however, were against American plays, and they decided to kill it if they could. When young Andrew Ray, who had had the onerous task of helping to carry a West End comedy with masters of comedy like Ronald Squire, stepped forward to take a well deserved bow and make a little speech, the gallery yelled: 'Shoot the author', and tried to shout him down.

The Happy Time, which had been a Broadway success with an American cast, was an unlucky production. I'd seen both productions and, although the New York company enjoyed themselves more, the English company were subtler, more Gallic, and had the play run they would have got every ounce out of it as they had more depth and quality than the New York cast.

After *The Happy Time* closed Peter suddenly found himself out of work though still under contract to Larry. Alexander Korda, about to put *The Story of Gilbert and Sullivan* into production with Sidney Gilliat directing, stepped into the breach and signed Peter up for the part of Rupert D'Oyly Carte, manager of the Royalty Theatre in Soho and the impresario who presented the Gilbert and Sullivan successes in the 1880s and 1890s. In this Peter plays an elegant Victorian Englishman 'to the manner born'. His timing was impeccable, he has wit, style, *élan*, and polish, and the scene where he announces to seventeen members of the D'Oyly Carte Company that he is going to build a new theatre, the Savoy, is Finchie at his most debonair and devastating on the screen. The magic of which Fred Zinnemann speaks is very much in evidence when Pete plays D'Oyly Carte, and there is tremendous variety of mood in what has been a very underrated performance by Peter. In his scenes with Eileen Herlie, as Mrs D'Oyly Carte, there is a tremendous warmth and charm which can change instantly to the smooth indifference with which he treats Gilbert. The film, in Technicolor, was Korda's twenty-fifth anniversary production for London Films, and their Coronation Year presentation. The only moment in the entire picture when Finchie wasn't his convincing self was when he was dying, when he had a surprisingly youthful look and an unmistakable agility of body, a trap into which he very uncharacteristically fell.

Hugh Hunt, brother of Sir John Hunt, mountaineer of the 1953 Mount Everest climb and colleague and friend of George Ingle Finch, was artistic director of the Old Vic Theatre when Peter was approached to join his company. In the summer of 1952, the Old Vic was in a crucial situation. In 1951 the triumvirate of Michael St Denis, George Devine and Glen Byam Shaw had resigned as artistic directors in circumstances that had shaken professional confidence in the management. An attempt to revive the theatre's prestige with the engagement of Tyrone Guthrie as artistic director had proved financially disastrous and had added little to the theatre's artistic credit. By the end of the 1952 season the Arts Council was threatening to withdraw its subsidy.

'It was in these circumstances,' said Hugh Hunt, 'that I approached the new season with the difficult task of recruiting a company of players willing to risk their reputations for the meagre salaries we were able to afford. The stage artist, be he player, director or designer, needs to be hedged around with confidence, to feel that however much the outside world may doubt him, he has the trust of all who work with him. It must have been some particular providence that led me to engage Claire Bloom, Athene Seyler, Alan Badel, William Devlin, Lewis Casson and Peter Finch for the opening play of the 1952-3 season, *Romeo and Juliet*. Peter was to play Mercutio, his second classical part in London. He must have needed confidence as much as I did, and there grew between us a mutual understanding that needed no words, each realizing how important this production was to the other. Mercutio is, of course, a part that can easily steal the limelight from Romeo. Peter never attempted to do so; his whole efforts were bent on the success of the play as the work of a team. His example of dedicated hard work inspired us all with the feeling of confidence and success that we badly needed.'

But the press on Peter's Mercutio was mixed. There seemed to be no question that Alan Badel could handle the verse infinitely better than Peter, who tended to break up the Queen Mab speech into uninspiring lumps of prose because he was trying to make it a purple passage. But T. C. Worsley, the London critic, felt – and this was the general opinion – that Peter could not speak the verse with the obvious appreciation of its richness, but that he was in control of affectation in his delivery, and wrote that he believed him to be the coming actor of that time. As Ernest Piaste, Professor Winke, and Iago, Worsley felt that Peter had brought an uncommon ability to communicate to the audience the vital elements behind each character. The public queued right round the entire Old Vic building to see the production, which was packed out at every performance.

Denis Carey directed Peter in his next play at the Old Vic, *A Italian Straw Hat*, in November 1952; and Yvonne Coulette, his wife, who had seen Peter as Ernest Piaste in *Daphne Laureola* and played with him in *Romeo and Juliet*, was struck by the sadness in the portrayal. Denis Carey, thirty-five years after the production of *An Italian Straw Hat*, said what remains in his memory now is Peter was not English as 'Beaujolais'. 'With certain actors, you get the feeling that they are the archetypes of more than just one culture. With Peter, I always felt many cultures had formed him – England, France, the East, and Australia – a certain distillation came through in this actor and that is what I remember most now. He was just different from the ordinary run of English actors.'

As Monsieur Beaujolais, the press said, Peter boomed and blustered, and the production generally was criticized as lacking in the necessary lightness, deftness and speed of good French farce. The cast seemed to attack the piece with desperate gaiety and coyness.

I saw the production and I remember Paul Rogers, brilliant as the reedy-voiced, poignant, moist-eyed and very pathetic Tardiveau, and John Warner, outrageously camp as Achille de Rosalba, the ridiculous lover singing an absurd song, called 'Gentle Zephyrs', to his beloved. Rogers was memorable, and Warner had the audience hysterical with laughter. Along with Rogers' and Warner's, Peter's performance stays in the memory as he sat moustached and choleric, with his feet in a hot mustard bath, absolutely immobile, glaring at the audience for fully three minutes. Annie Besant's lessons on stillness and concentration at Adyar were paying their comic dividends as the audience started to get the giggles while Finchie's Monsieur Beaujolais glared his disapproval.

He told me at the time, he was going to play Mark Antony in Hugh Hunt's production of *Julius Caesar*. But an offer came which seemed crazy to turn down and he went to Hugh Hunt and asked if, after *An Italian Straw Hat* ended, he could be released to make *Elephant Walk* for Paramount Pictures. Irving Asher offered him a Hollywood contract for the picture to star opposite Vivien Leigh. That moment was the watershed in Peter's domestic and professional life which led to the break-up of his marriage seven years later, and took him out of the theatre. Once he left the Old Vic, less than half way through the season, he set his sights on films, and the theatre became a secondary consideration to which he was only to return during the next eleven years for two productions.

17 Elephant Walk

Everything was going beautifully in Peter's career before he left for location work on *Elephant Walk* in Ceylon in early 1953. George More O'Ferrall, directing Graham Greene's *The Heart of the Matter* for British Lion Films, thought Peter would be ideal for the very difficult small part of Father Rank, the missionary priest. Peter had problems with the character as he wasn't in sympathy with the priest when he first read the screenplay, and knew he wouldn't be convincing. He found the solution during an encounter with a drunken priest (who had temporarily given up his vocation) in the King's Head pub in Chelsea. Roger Ramsdell and Finchie got into conversation with this character who had rationalized himself out of his ability 'to take all Catholic mumbo jumbo seriously' and was in the process of deadening his ability to rationalize about anything at all.

'Is it only the mumbo jumbo you object to?' asked Finchie, 'or is it Christianity in general?'

'No! No!' said the man, 'it's the Pope and his bloody infallibility and this demand for implicit obedience I find I can't stomach.' The perpetual celibacy was also getting him down.

'No problem then,' replied Finchie. 'Opt out and be a good Protestant.'

'Christ!' replied the indignant cleric. 'I may have lost my faith, but I haven't lost my self respect.'

'In an instant,' Peter said, 'Father Rank clicked into place.'

The thread that would give Father Rank conviction was an inner spiritual conviction, an intuitive faith of which the outward form of the religion was purely technique, and Finchie decided he'd play the part off the cuff on that premise.

The character, though very briefly on the screen, is subtly observed. The little touch of vanity, running his hand through his hair before he knocks at Scobie's door knowing there may be a woman there, and the delayed pouring of the drink, so uncharacteristic of Peter, but aptly characterizing a temperate celibate twelve years without leave in Sierra Leone. Finchie portrays an utterly sincere priest who seems to understand he ought to avoid theological argument, realizing he would be wasting his time using church logic on Scobie. He is detached, and, without any sentimentality, makes several subtle attempts to bridge the gap between them to give Scobie peace of mind, and leave it at that.

George More O'Ferrall, now retired and living in Spain, remembers Trevor Howard, who starred in the film as Scobie, Peter and himself 'putting a great deal of work into those scenes between Scobie and Father Rank. Before we shot the film I said to Graham Greene that I thought the priest would have attempted to produce a reason that would enable him to give Scobie absolution, to which Greene replied: "Then you have been bloody lucky." We both laughed at this, so I felt free to go ahead, and with the help of a Jesuit theologian made the scene a little longer. When Graham Greene saw the rough cut of the film, he said that, because of this, the credit must read "Based on a story by . . ." instead of Graham Greene's *The Heart of the Matter*. So O'Ferrall re-shot the scene after the film was finished, exactly as Grahame Greene wished, except for a few words, which were no part of the argument. Months later the Irish film censor, who in those days thought it part of his job to make a cut in any film of Greene's, cut out those very words, which were not, in fact, written by Greene.'

The film script of *Elephant Walk* was sent to Olivier by Paramount with the idea that he and Vivien should star in it. Olivier felt it was a bad script, and would turn out to be a pedestrian film, and advised Vivien not to touch it. She insisted that it had merit. Olivier still refused to do it but when Irving Asher, the film's producer, asked his advice about a suitable British actor, Olivier took him to an Old Vic matinée to see Peter's Monsieur Beaujolais in *An Italian Straw Hat*. 'I went backstage after the show,' said Asher, 'and signed him up for the picture on the spot without having much idea as to how good he would be as a film actor. I was a little worried about some aspects of his face but I liked the fact that he wasn't a pretty guy. I trusted Larry's judgment and he looked like a man. I sent some film on him to Paramount in Hollywood and they agreed to go along with me and accepted the agreement I had drawn up with Finch. Peter's break was entirely due to Olivier. I would never have heard of him if it hadn't been for Larry.'

By accepting the offer Peter might well have realized the risk of becoming involved with Vivien, whom he'd always found immensely attractive, but decided he would play the situation by ear. He knew this was his chance to become known in Hollywood. He had no idea that Vivien was ill, in fact, or that he would be caught up in a relationship that would radically alter his career and his personal life.

Irving Asher and Dana Andrews who played Dick Carver the manager of the tea plantation, both remember Peter as the easiest, most professional person to work with on what turned out to be a film that was jinxed in its making from the very start. Even the Comet which took the company to Colombo crashed from metal fatigue with a total loss of life two flights later, having a devastating effect on the morale of the unit. Finchie provided what comic relief he could, despite the fact that he was deeply involved in a very uncomic relationship with Vivien Leigh.

When the unit were on location in Ceylon, Dana Andrews sensed, very soon after they started shooting, that something was wrong with Vivien. 'She was very anxious always to just go, go, go, and she and Peter would try to get me to go off at two in the morning to some place where there was a celebration. I said I had to work early in the morning and just couldn't take being up all night and filming all day. "Oh, stick-in-the-mud," she'd say, and off they'd go.'

Peter, utterly infatuated and like a child enjoying a fabulous adventure, went along with Vivien all the way. Both were drinking heavily but, according to producer Irving Asher, nothing affected either Peter's performance or his appearance when the rushes were shown.

Among diverse aspects of Peter that intrigued Dana Andrews in Ceylon was his feeling for mysticism. When Dana could be persuaded to go with Peter and Vivien (who both had childhood backgrounds in India) to watch the Sinhalese folklore rituals, Peter would explain the mystic symbolism of a certain dance and Dana was amazed to see in Peter in that environment signs of extra-sensory perception which were never apparent later. It was as if Peter drew into himself aspects of the environment of his early childhood. Dana also told me that there seemed to be a tremendously strong rapport between Peter and Vivien.

But on location in Ceylon, Vivien's health was right on a razor's edge, and, with his own marriage to Tamara disintegrating,

Peter couldn't cope with what developed. Olivier, who knew the symptoms of Vivien's illness to which was now added a recurrence of tuberculosis, had done all he could to stop her making the film, but she was adamant. She wanted to be with Peter, had never worked with him before, and was determined that the outcome would be memorable.

During the last week on location Vivien had one of her attacks and began having hallucinations. She followed Peter everywhere he went and began calling him 'Larry'. Finchie suddenly found himself in the situation which all his life he tried to avoid – that of taking the responsibility for another human being who had become dependent on him. He admitted later he was at a loss as to what to do. Vivien would recite her lines as Blanche DuBois from *A Streetcar Named Desire*, always go to Peter, who had become 'Larry', for protection, and burst into fits of uncontrollable sobbing. Peter tried to keep outwardly calm, but inwardly began to panic as he knew, with Vivien in that state, filming could not continue much longer.

The seventy-two hour flight to California was the nearest thing to hell on earth for Finchie. Just as the plane started to take off Vivien had an outbreak of hysteria, and they had to sedate her during the flight. When they reached Los Angeles, Peter, joined by Tamara, took her to the house they had rented. 'When we started shooting on the set at Paramount,' Peter told me, 'poor Vivien had lost her memory. I tried to help her, go over and over her lines with her, but it was no good, she needed to be right out of the whole set-up. She was in no state to work, and hadn't been from the beginning. She wouldn't allow me or anyone else to help her. David Niven was a tower of strength. He was an old friend and seemed to be the only person who knew how to handle her.'

For Irving Asher *Elephant Walk* was a producer's nightmare from start to finish, a film of compromises in which Peter and Elizabeth Taylor, who took over Vivien's role when she collapsed after four weeks' filming, became the victims of circumstance. In Hollywood, with all the exteriors in Ceylon shot and Vivien too ill to continue, Asher didn't see much hope of salvaging the picture. Elizabeth Taylor was under contract to Metro-Goldwyn-Mayer at the time, and Paramount were horrified by the price Metro wanted to loan her out at, but decided to engage her. At first Peter was utterly despondent, because he knew the age balance had gone, and, to quote Asher, 'was really aware of my problem as producer on the picture, faced with an almost impossible situation because in the original story there was a shrew who really created problems for her tea-planter husband. He would rather stay downstairs and play childish games with the boys, like riding around on bicycles, than face the scorpion Vivien waiting for him to go up to bed with her. You will understand that Vivien was absolutely perfectly cast. She just had to stand there and tacitly demand his presence. The camera did the rest. But Elizabeth, extremely young then, and simply magnificent to look at, coming down in a negligee, trying to get Peter to come up with her, just didn't ring true. There isn't a man on earth who wouldn't have raced up those stairs!'

Once it was decided to salvage what had been shot of *Elephant Walk*, Peter, Dana and Liz – 'we unholy three', as Dana described them – in desperation, and with the need to create some sanity and levity, formed the Fongu Club. The Club went to lunch every day at Lucey's, across from Paramount Studios, and made it their business to prime themselves for the terror of working on such an important film about which none of them felt confident. 'Fongu' was a more acceptable way of giving the world the 'Wednesday finger sign' (up you!). Finchie had a hand sculpted on a base as the club emblem. It was presented to the other two at a party to remind them of the need to band together. With the whole original concept of the film now drastically altered, they desperately needed the camaraderie of frivolity. Finchie always believed that the elephants hired for the film had formed their own Fongu Club. In the final climax of the picture the elephants, determined to get to their accustomed drinking place, are supposed to stampede through the plantation house, leaving a trail of destruction behind them. When they came to shoot the scene, circus elephants were brought in, lined up in a semi-circle and ordered by the mahout to destroy the house. Everything in the set had been partially sawn away in advance: tables, chairs, banisters, staircases, window frames – all were prepared to collapse at the merest touch. But the wretched elephants had had a lifetime of training never, ever to touch anything. The cameras rolled, the clapper boy marked the scene, and called out 'Take One'. 'Action,' shouted the director. 'Charge!' shouted the mahout – and up went their tails, and 'Fongu' went the elephants. The mahout whacked them and pushed them, but they had been trained like well-brought up elephants to step over matchboxes. The beasts were terrified and confused, and it took them several hours to make them relax and enjoy themselves sufficiently to complete the work of destruction.

Because the film didn't turn out as it was conceived was perhaps one reason why Hollywood didn't pick Peter up then and there. Asher was absolutely certain that Finchie was going to have a fabulous career, 'because he got good notices, and everyone I talked to in Hollywood at the time thought he was just great as an actor and great as a man. I cannot think why it took so long for Hollywood to use him again, but I do know that he received great recognition for some of the films he made in England and, when he finally achieved recognition in America, Hollywood really took him to its heart as an actor and as a person. Had he lived, he would undoubtedly have gone on to far greater things. He was one of the very top actors in films today. I don't think he was the strongest character who ever lived. I think Finchie was the sort of man who did what he wanted to do on impulse, more or less. But to me he was a good friend when he realized we were in trouble on that picture, and a delightful human being.'

But by the time the cast reached Hollywood, the love affair which was so radically to alter his domestic and professional life, had become a nightmare for Peter. Neither Peter nor Tamara had been to California together before and Tamara realized she was fighting to keep her husband on unfamiliar and alien ground. Before her final collapse, Vivien had arranged a big reception party for Peter at a rented apartment on Wilshire Boulevard so that Peter could meet the celebrities of the Hollywood firmament. According to Peter, Vivien went for Tamara with a pair of scissors and had to be forcibly restrained. She then couldn't face the ordeal of the party and left Tamara to get on with it alone. Olivier was sent for and he flew out to Hollywood; Vivien was put under sedation and taken home to England.

As Peter said: 'Of all the women I loved, Vivien had the mind, intelligence, style and wit to match her beauty. If ever there was a flawed masterpiece it was Vivien,' and years later, in Rome in 1969, he told me that he had felt her brief entry into his life had stretched him to the very limit, and that she had left him 'confused, and it took me many years to readjust.'

18 The watershed

The decisive break in Peter's life, when he began to alter course domestically and professionally, was after *Elephant Walk*. Although Peter told me that he had tried to reason with Vivien that the affair had to end, Vivien was quite determined to take Peter from Tamara. 'I didn't realize the tenacity and determination of the woman I'd fallen for,' he confessed and he tended to go with whomever tugged hardest, and so began a great internal conflict within him which, at that time when he was in the ascendant professionally, he didn't want to resolve. Vivien saw in Peter the full measure of his capabilities and, of all his women, she was the only one with whom he had mental rapport. Vivien could outdistance him intellectually, and there was no question as to who was dominant. I saw a good deal of Peter at this time. He loved the glamour and the ambience that Vivien could create but he found the demands she made on him physically, socially, and on his liberty, insufferable. The relationship for Finchie was for a long time very ambivalent and he admitted much later that she had forced the pace and made so many of his relationships with other women seem unsatisfactory. He resented her baiting Tamara and demanding he leave Tamara's bed for hers with her tongue-in-cheek, Scarlet Woman tactics aimed at shaking what she considered was Tamara's bourgeois sense of propriety to its foundations. One night when they were in Hollywood she lay in the corridor outside Peter's door and created merry hell as only Vivien could. She was like a woman possessed, and using every demonic wile she knew to create trouble for Tamara. The really wicked thing about Vivien was her incomparable sense of humour, which many people just didn't understand. Once Tamara went up to see her while she was having a bath, and much to Peter's amusement, she tried to seduce Tamara, or truer to say, she tried to shock her. She knew Peter's character and that he was contemptuous of the decorum and respectability which formed Tamara's background. There were times when Peter was bored with Vivien and wanted to get away from her, but she had beauty, intelligence, allure and a certain amount of power and influence where Peter's career was concerned.

For Tamara, it was a cruel and unfair game, and Vivien was ruthless. She wanted Peter and she got him as she had wanted Olivier, and got him away from his first wife, Jill Esmond. Vivien was outrageous. She reaped what she sowed, however, and when Peter dithered, unable to make any decisive stand, Olivier made the decision for all three. In the end he showed who could best handle the situation. Peter was not strong enough to handle Vivien or man enough to stand up to Olivier. He took evasive action and the two people who suffered most in that *débâcle* were Tamara and Anita. Vivien's mental and physical illness; the position the Oliviers occupied at that time; Peter's ability and ambition; these and many other factors caught Peter up in a protracted situation which was disastrous for him both as an actor and as a man. He always had a bad guilt complex about Tamara and Anita, and they found him difficult to endure. Finchie could always make a tragic story from the wrongs he suffered from his first two wives but they claimed he could, at times, be a monster. Yet Vivien Leigh did not finish his marriage any more than Shirley Bassey finished his marriage with Yolande. Peter's first two marriages were flawed from the very beginning – Peter was not the conventional marrying kind. His beliefs, background and temperament were such that the average woman could not accept him. He always went for strong women. He adored women but was utterly selfish, irresponsible and too much the genuine child for most women to handle for very long. It was his half-sister Flavia who occupied a unique position in his life and who could handle him and who came to his rescue when he finally walked out on Tamara.

Olivier did not, as has been suggested, stand back and just let things happen between Peter and Vivien, but both of them told me that their relationship was on a sublime level, and nothing could have stopped it. They were very important to one another and neither was self-seeking in the material sense. It seemed to bring meaning to both their lives, while it lasted, and afterwards.

It was a dynamic union in which, according to Peter, Vivien became very possessive and tiresome but, out of physical attraction, a real friendship and rapport developed at a much higher level than the purely sexual aspect which adverse publicity so magnified and distorted. What they had in common, apart from the physical attraction, their careers and a great sense of humour, was an Oriental background which gave them a deep understanding of one another. Vivien, born in Darjeeling, often used to speak of her sense of belonging to both the East and the West. She was very drawn to Peter's outlook on life, and to Vivien he spoke more intimately of what he really thought and believed than he did to any other woman. Vivien was both supremely intelligent and intuitive. She sparked Peter off, but there were severe ego conflicts.

Vivien told me she would never have broken her marriage for Peter. She understood him, but the problem at the beginning of their affair, apart from her illness which was a major factor in its disruption, was that she was accustomed to having her own way, and Peter, being a past master at evading any issue, very often avoided a confrontation by simply opting out. There was certainly a power struggle between Peter and Vivien and the competition between them was destructive to both. For Vivien it was a tragic situation because her illness aggravated feelings of tremendous emotional and sexual frustration.

Vivien knew what was best for Peter as regards his career as an actor, and one night over dinner she really berated him for not being man enough to make his own decisions and determine his own course as Larry had done. Nevertheless, there was always great respect between Vivien and Peter, and Peter knew that Vivien had his interests at heart. Peter confessed he knew he had come to England too late to realize his true ambition, and that he didn't really belong in England or anywhere, and that he felt he had to take what he could get. 'But you **don't** take what you can get,' Vivien said to him. 'You let people persuade you as to what they think is best for you and throw dust in your eyes. You're a good enough actor to stand alone as someone quite different and still do what you really want as an actor, but you have no follow-through. You play at life, play with women, and you dissipate your God-given talents because you don't believe in your own wonderful star.'

It was a lucid analysis and he simply answered by asking: 'Why didn't Hamlet put his sword between his uncle's shoulder-blades when he had a God-given opportunity?'

Sublime, romantic and adorable as Peter may have seemed to Vivien, he was absolutely crucifying Olivier and he knew it. After a considerable absence, he had reappeared on the domestic

Major Edward Dallas (Jock) Campbell

below right George Ingle Finch on the 1922 Mount Everest Expedition

below Peter's mother Betty and brother Michael

With fiancée Sheila Smart.
Sydney, 1940

With Tamara on their wedding day.
Sydney, April 1940

With Flavia at a Flamenco Fiesta

left to right Sydney John Kay, Vivien Leigh, Kimbal S. Sant (producer), Peter Finch, Colin Scrimgeour, Sir Laurence Olivier rehearsing for the interstate network Australian broadcast, September 1948

With Grant Taylor (left) and Chips Rafferty (right) in *Rats of Tobruk*. Australia, 1944

Peter with his favourite leading lady in *Simon and Laura*

With Vivien Leigh and Abraham Sofaer in *Elephant Walk*, 1953

As Flambeau, disguised as a gormless beggar, outside the Paris Catacombes in *Father Brown*, 1953

With Yolande and the children, 1962
Aged forty

With Glenda Jackson and Murray Head in *Sunday Bloody Sunday*,
for which he won his fourth British Film Academy Award for Best Actor, 1971

As Air Force General Umberto Nobile in *The Red Tent*

As Oscar Wilde in *The Trials of Oscar Wilde*, 1960, for which he won his second British Film Academy Award for Best Actor (1960) and the Moscow Film Festival Award for Best Actor (1961)

With Alan Bates in *Far From the Madding Crowd*, 1966

With his wife
Eletha on their
wedding day in Rome,
November 1973

On Johnny Carson's NF
Tonight show the night
before he died, Thursda
13 January 1977

scene when the Oliviers were in the middle of the 1955 Shakespeare season at Stratford-on-Avon. This period of his life is something Olivier really wants to forget. I was in the company at the time and saw a great deal of the agony. One afternoon, Larry and I had sat in deckchairs in the garden at Avoncliff, where the Oliviers were staying (and where Finchie would make his unexpected appearances and disappearances from time to time). Peter Brook's production of *Titus Andronicus* was due to open that night and I was hearing Larry in his part. He was word-perfect. He never seemed to show the company the tension and strain under which he was living at that time. However, at a reception that evening, I saw him sitting in a corner, talking to Angela Baddeley, propping one eye open with an index finger. It was one of those elegant first-night parties impeccably arranged by Vivien, glittering with celebrities. Finchie, doing one of his improvisations had a group of ladies, among them Vivien, in fits of laughter with an astounding pantomime rendering of erotic wallpaper in an old spinster's bedroom; randy centaurs streaking after dryads, floral patterns of forget-me-nots, pussy-willow and acorns; gum trees and kissing koala bears – bawdy beyond belief and side-splitting. He **was** obscene wallpaper.

'Summoned to Stratford by Vivien,' as Finchie put it, the cast would see him either at the theatre, at dinners after the evening performance at Avoncliff, or at Larry and Vivien's weekend retreat, the beautifully restored thirteenth century Notley Abbey, at Thame, near Oxford.

Not being a member of the company made Finchie feel more of a loner among his fellow actors than ever before. He knew he was damaging not only his own public image, but Vivien's as well. He had cut himself off from Tamara and Anita and had taken refuge with his mother and Flavia. He needed money, so he had put his head into the noose of a contract with Rank, exchanging freedom for financial security. He resented Vivien's authoritarian attitude and the lack of freedom the situation imposed on him. The conflict of selfishness and shame in Finchie at that time was giving him a very rough ride. The social tensions beneath the surface during the 1955 season at Stratford were as dramatic and traumatic as anything the general public were queuing all night to see in the theatre.

Vivien was at times deliberately indiscreet about Peter, and what many of us dreaded was to be drawn into the crossfire. It was impossible to take sides. It was their personal business. But one day Vivien told me how warm, sweet and thoughtful Peter was, 'like a wild, sensual Pan!', and that Larry could think of nothing but his career. Larry, with the responsibility of leading one of the world's most distinguished companies, was battling for survival. He was exhausted, nearly demented with worry, and this was one of the most important seasons of his career.

Twelfth Night, the opening production of the season, on 23 April, Shakespeare's birthday, was probably the most eagerly awaited first night in the history of the Shakespeare Memorial Theatre. Larry was playing Malvolio, with Vivien as Viola, and Sir John Gielgud directing. Everyone was sure it would be the definitive triumphant success of the season, but the play opened to a very lukewarm press. Vivien's notices in particular were very poor. Olivier's interpretation of Malvolio as a lisping Cockney Jew with straw-coloured fuzzy hair was original and his comic inventiveness absolutely inspired until one day Gielgud in rehearsal said: 'Larry, it's all so vulgar!' The remark, in no way meant to hurt him, caught Olivier at a vulnerable moment. He didn't recover until the opening night of *Macbeth* when he took off like a dark thunderous rocket, and the performance went down in the annals of history as one of his greatest.

Vivien, as Lady Macbeth, giving a performance of compelling realism in her moments of madness, once again did not receive a unanimously good press. The manic depressive symptoms were flaring up intermittently as the domestic tension mounted. 'How well I remember!' Larry remarked with a smile. 'Peter would scuttle off down his burrow faster than any rabbit when there was any likelihood of a confrontation, a crisis or mutiny in the camp!'

I, too, remember the tension at that time well. One Saturday evening during that season several of us had been invited to spend the weekend at Notley after an evening performance of *Twelfth Night*. I had driven down alone with Vivien, while Larry and Peter were following ten minutes behind in another car. Vivien was on edge as we sat alone in the drawing room, drinking gin and discussing reincarnation. She was convinced Peter was 'an old soul,' full of timeless wisdom, tenderness, understanding – all the qualities that every woman looks for in every man. Larry was 'a brand new soul with a plastic Karma and a marital deficit balance'. From where I was sitting, I was suddenly horrified to see Larry's familiar shadow outside the door silhouetted against the wall, listening. Finchie, sensing a confrontation, had gone for a walk in the garden. Realizing that Larry was being subjected to his routine humiliating *auto-da-fé*, I suggested that, for a first innings as a reincarnated soul, Larry was, to use a cricketing term, scoring an easy century. This was not the reply Vivien wanted and she rounded on me with a scathing riposte to the effect that I would always manage to say the right thing at the right time. Just as reluctant as Finchie to find myself 'between the fell incensed point of mighty opposites', like a character in Hamlet, I pretended I had been taken short suddenly and made off in search of Finchie. I found him in the walled garden by the dovecote trying to make conversation with a very reluctant flock of white doves. Cooing ineffectively, he was trying to lure out the sleeping inmates.

'Prrr-prr, come out, you bastards, oh shit!' he moaned, as the horror of his situation alternated with his attempts at pigeon seduction. 'I'm being manipulated,' he said. 'It's my own bloody fault! I've been drawn into this bloody circle because there's a grotesque Mr Hyde in my Jekyll that lives for the moment, and gets a sort of perverse enjoyment out of the dramatic situation. I hate myself for being fascinated. I'm a selfish bastard. I want to be quit of all this and make a clean break! I can't drive a car, so I can't leave. I need a stiff whisky and I can't face Larry and the battle of Agincourt down there,' and he pointed to the lighted mullioned windows and Gothic silhouette of Notley.

I felt for Finchie. He really was writhing about like a damned soul, but at that precise moment, one of the doves flew out of the cote and landed on his shoulder. I burst out laughing. 'The dove of peace,' I said. 'Even the birds fancy you. Stop trying to play Pierrot and Don Juan and stick to your pen and ink sketches of this place. Come on. We'll have to go back.' The gregarious Finchie, torn between his need to be part of the farcical tragi-comedy that was being played out and his inability to cope when the heat was on, had turned into a sad puppet-like figure of fun.

During my interviews with him, Larry was emphatic about that time: 'The little I want to remember of all that now is highly comical and eminently forgettable . . .' But he does not blame Peter for the break up of his marriage, though he did ask him to give up the affair with Vivien, and told her to be reasonable and try to make the marriage work. Peter himself told me of the confrontation which took place between Larry and himself as to whether Vivien was to become Mrs Peter Finch or remain Lady Olivier. He was invited to Notley where dinner for three was served with impeccable elegance. Vivien departed with the coffee and Larry summoned Peter to the library to chat over the port. Finchie suddenly got the giggles at the idea of being interviewed among the calf leather and the moroccos. Once in the library with the door shut, neither actor knew how to begin the scene, so there was a very long pause. Eventually Larry, the most resourceful and ingenious of men, began to play the rather idiotic lord-of-the-manor, realizing the need to stop embarrassing Peter and put him at his ease. Peter, taking his cue instantly, was transformed into Sir Laurence's elderly, rather seedy butler, who had served his lordship from his youth. They continued in this fashion and gradually built up a scene. Both ended up hysterical with laughter at their own wit. Suddenly the door burst open and there stood Lady Macbeth. At her most imperious she demanded, 'Will one of you come to bed with me now?'

To set the record right, Peter Finch was well aware of what Olivier had done for him as an actor, and although he was crazy about Vivien, he did agree, finally, out of feeling for both Larry and Vivien, not to see her any more. Peter, Vivien and Larry all confirmed this. Larry, to whom I have spoken on several occasions, does not wish to be quoted, or for the subject to be raised further. Vivien Leigh was very ill. Olivier realized how ill she was and how devastating the symptoms could be. Vivien was appalled, she told me, by what friends told her she had done during her attacks. Peter was not aware, at the time, of how ill Vivien was and his wanting to leave her and end their love affair has been totally misinterpreted. He wanted to end the relationship out of respect for Larry and Vivien. Olivier had a position to uphold, and Peter and Vivien were liable to bring him into the limelight of the press in a way that could only be detrimental to all three. Peter told me in Rome that his second marriage was really undertaken on the rebound from the feeling of desolation at being cut off from Vivien and estranged from Larry who had shown him nothing but kindness. Larry, he said, was the fairest, kindest friend to him and the most generous employer he had ever worked for in the business. For his part Larry spoke of his protégé with genuine affection. 'Finchie!' he said. 'Brilliant! The first second I saw him as Argan in *The Imaginary Invalid* at that glass factory in Sydney in 1948, I realized he had that very, very rare quality that made you watch him. He was absolute magic! He was a natural clown. The inventive bits of comic business woven into the performance of the youngish-looking hypochondriac had the whole lot of us rocking with laughter. Peter didn't attempt to make him look too old. That was where he was clever! He had imagination, an innate sense of comedy, and was able to weave his own original brilliance into Molière's masterpiece. Stunning!

'We all sat on what I remember as very hard benches with a packed audience of workers, trying to eat sandwiches and drink Tooth's KB Lager. The whole production, props, costumes, scenery (very little of it), Molière superbly boiled down to fifty minutes for a lunch-time audience, was an original and inspired concept. Finch was unforgettable. He got us from the very first moment with his wonderfully funny and inventive stage business.'

Larry admired the enterprise of the Mercury Theatre in giving the public something which no one had ever thought of at that time: a lunch-time theatre presenting first class modern and classical plays that would reach everybody in versions not longer than fifty minutes. 'It was a magnificent idea. It really was theatre for the people, to think of taking it to their place of work. That's going right back to the beginnings of theatre. Instead of having people come to a particular theatre, what an audience you can reach, and without their having to sit through long plays. To that audience in 1948, unused to it, what a marvellous way to acclimatize them to concentrating on a good play . . .' When he met Peter afterwards, Larry was so impressed with the whole achievement which Sydney John Kay had engineered, and which Peter and Kay had produced, that he offered to put Peter under contract for three years, if Peter got himself to England. 'I agreed to pay him an increasing amount each year, and we'd split fifty-fifty over and above his weekly salary if he was contracted during his free time to anyone else. I had three artists under contract at that time in London, and though no Sam Goldwyn, no Louis B. Mayer, I like to think that perhaps I was the last of the old fashioned actor-managers and not too mean as regards my contract artists getting a fair deal. When Peter arrived in London from Australia I had nothing for him at the time and he had to go off and find work as best he could. But when James Bridie's *Daphne Laureola* was due to go into production, he came and auditioned, got the part and got his contract, Edith Evans adored him and he was magic. I knew from the moment I saw him in Sydney that he could become one of the truly gifted actors of our time. I do remember Peter was worried about his Australian accent, and before *Daphne Laureola* opened he came to me and said: "Tell me honestly, is there anything wrong with the way I speak English? I want the truth." "Nothing dear boy," I replied. "No trace of the Aussie in you at all, except for the vowels: A,E,I,O,U." '

Not long before the play was due to close in London, Olivier decided to put Peter straight into another play to cash in on his initial success, and at Anita's christening, with the Oliviers as godparents, Larry appeared rather surreptitiously at the church door of St Martin's in the Fields with a script under his arm. 'Let's go down into the crypt, I want to talk to you quietly for a moment,' he said, and the godfather ushered the new father down into the musty depths of the old church to brief him quickly on a possible new play, *The Damascus Blade*.

Peter was excellent as the seedy but respectable agent, Henry Adams, in *The Damascus Blade* and Larry had an ideal theatre, the St Martin's, for the play. But John Mills – playing the lead as Daniel Bonaught, a modern Irish soldier of fortune, demobbed from the British Army, who advertises for adventure in a newspaper, finds it, and ends up dead in his own backyard – got cold feet and implored Larry not to bring the play into the West End. Olivier was very reluctant to agree to this despite his third production as actor-manager, *Fading Mansion*, not having been the success he had hoped. For he had got Peter ready to go into London in a very good part. He had also invested his money in, and had directed, this play with a cast whose potential he was prepared to back. But John Mills had been a friend since the very early days, so, against his better judgement, Larry took *The Damascus Blade* off in April 1950, after a five week pre-London tour.

Christopher Fry's *Venus Observed* had, in January 1950, been Olivier's first production at the St James Theatre, London, as artistic director. Now, his next production to come to London, and in which he had also found a suitable part for Peter, was Dennis Cannan's *Captain Carvallo*. 'Peter was very keen to play a comedy character, so, remembering his performance as Argan at the Glass Factory, I cast him as Professor Winke, a middle-aged atheist celibate professor of biology, who turns anarchist seducer, and his farce scenes with Dickie Goolden as the lay preacher/farmer were beautifully played. His timing was very precise. He had great wit, and made his character rather desiccated...'

The play opened at the 1950 Edinburgh Festival and on the first night at the St James's there were clusters of Aussies, Finch supporters, scattered all over the theatre. During an early scene Professor Winke had to fumble through his pockets for a cigarette knowing full well he had none and would be offered one. This, of course, was absolutely true to life to the many in the audience who knew Peter – Finchie never had a cigarette to offer and he was well-known as 'the most famous fumbler in Australia'. So, during *Captain Carvallo* when he started to fumble, the scattered Aussie patrons started to giggle. We knew it was coming, and did he time that one magnificently! 'Anybody – (It's a wonder he didn't get a chorus from the audience!) – got a cigarette?' A hundred or more people in that audience fell about laughing, and the rest couldn't understand why. Finchie had played his joke to the 'private gallery' to the hilt.

Later, when Larry went to see him as Orpheus with Mai Zetterling in Anouilh's *Point of Departure*, Larry commented that 'he was absolutely different again, lyrical, romantic, and his performance was spot on. In Orson Welles' stage production of *Othello* he came unstuck with Iago because of Orson who paid too much attention to his own role of Othello. You just can't do that when you're directing and playing a leading part. I know, I've tried it. What's more, Orson was neither vocally nor physically in condition. You need the English background, training, and tremendous physical stamina to tackle those Shakespearean heavies. Peter was terribly mishandled.'

I asked Larry how he felt about the moments of Peter Finch's Iago that he had glimpsed when Peter had managed to get himself out of the shadow into which Orson seemed to have so carefully placed him. His reply was surprisingly honest and very disarming: 'It's terribly difficult for me to judge him as Iago and Mercutio. Basically he was excellent but, quite frankly,

I was jealous. I'm always jealous watching any actor who is any good playing a part I have played myself. My judgement becomes subjective because I immediately begin to play that character, especially if I remember it and know the character really well. I'm still unhappy with the way I played Mercutio and Iago in those early days. Perhaps because in retrospect I felt I didn't play them as well as I knew I could have done at the time.'

He started chuckling and remembered the financial disaster during his tenure of the St James's Theatre: '. . . *Top of the Ladder*, Tony Guthrie's play, which I invited him to produce as well, with John Mills playing the lead; *The Happy Time*, Peter's last play under contract to me; and Orson Welles' *Othello*, all left the financial coffers rather like Mother Hubbard's cupboard – not a brass razoo. *The Happy Time*, which had turned out to be the unhappy time, ran a month and died with King George VI. I was cleaned out and had to start again'. At the end of *The Happy Time*, Peter had been under contract to Larry for three years and had done five plays. He went to Olivier and said he felt he ought to try his luck in other directions. Olivier said that Peter should feel absolutely free to do as he chose. 'If the right parts had come up, I would always have been delighted to use him. Peter was one hundred per cent reliable and we parted the best of friends. He went to the Old Vic which I felt was a very good and important move for him. I would always have employed Peter in any theatre of mine. He was an original and unique actor.'

19 *Make Me An Offer*

After *Elephant Walk* was completed Peter and Tamara took a slow boat back to London through the Panama Canal. *Elephant Walk* hadn't impressed the big Hollywood executives and the only film he was offered, *French Line*, he felt would have been a retrograde step. He thought it better to go home with Tamara and Anita and take the whole family, including Mamma, for a holiday in San Sebastian before starting work again in England.

On his return from Spain, Peter began work for Ealing on *Father Brown*, as Flambeau, the master of disguises, with Alec Guinness in the title role. Based on the book by G. K. Chesterton, it was directed by Robert Hamer. This was one of Peter's favourite roles as it gave him a chance to play a diversity of character parts in the many disguises Flambeau adopts attempting to elude the tenacious Father Brown. As the half-witted beggar outside the Parisian catacombs, and as the old man with the chess set in the auction rooms, Peter is only glimpsed for a few seconds but reveals his ability as a great character actor. Finchie as Flambeau, undisguised, elegant, secretive, cynical and smooth, the man who stole to decorate his lonely world, is Finchie at his most attractive to women. But once filming on *Father Brown* was over, no new projects appeared on the horizon and by mid-1954 he had been out of work for a considerable time. Life at home in Dolphin Square, where they were now living, was a series of arguments over Peter's apparent inertia about going out to look for work, no money coming in and Peter out on the loose, coming home at all hours of the night and often not at all. (He'd go off and stay with Betty at Bury Walk if he found the pressures at home with Tamara, backed by Mamma, were becoming too much.)

Then, at last, he was approached by Wolf Mankowitz who was setting up a film with a small company called Group Three, to film his short autobiographical novel, for which he had written the screenplay, *Make Me An Offer*, about a Jewish antique dealer with a passion for Wedgwood. Here, Peter felt, he had a chance to play light comedy, his favourite genre. As

Charlie, the charming young Jew devoted to but always quarrelling with his wife, the part would provide him with an opportunity to ring the changes as an actor only cast so far in romantic, character or melodramatic roles on the screen. He could also draw on the experiences of his shaky marriage with Tamara and his relationship with Anita.

The filming of the Wolf Mankowitz story, with Cyril Frankel directing, filled all the requirements Finchie needed at that moment, plus the added challenge of being a convincing Jew. Wolf felt at once that although he wasn't Jewish, he had absolutely the right appearance and style to play the character. He and Peter spent a good deal of time together, because Peter wanted to go round 'the trade', meet various antique dealers and see how it all happened. He really soaked himself in the atmosphere. They drank together. He was funny, easy-going, but a very difficult fellow to really get to know. Wolf found him 'very secretive about his philosophical background which certainly didn't show at an intellectual level. He wasn't a conscious intellectual and he didn't show the control or training that often goes with philosophical awareness.

'He wasn't a drinker at that point, not as far as I could see. I saw him all through the making of the picture and when the performance began to take shape on the screen, I suddenly realized what a cleverly observant man he was. I thought he'd been taking in all these characters you meet in the trade, but what he'd really been observing closely was me. He knew that Charlie, the lead character, was largely autobiographical. I was a dealer at that time and what I had written about was the persona that I'd assume when dealing in business. He developed Charlie through awareness of my attitudes, mannerisms, and style. He did this quite deliberately. So I rate him as an exceptionally skilled observer. It didn't worry him that it was a small film and not paying either of us very much money. He put everything into getting it right.

'When I first met Peter, I felt he was highly organized. He seemed to become more unstable as he became more successful. Not with any ideas of self-importance, just in his ability to cope with his own nature in terms of everyday life.'

In *Make Me An Offer*, Peter's use of his hands is truly Jewish. His vaudeville training was very useful for the moment when he discovers the Wedgwood panels are fakes. Then his handling of a cigar, his timing watching the slumping Ernest Thesiger in the chair, conveying everything by the slight raising of his eyebrow, show how every minute detail of Peter's characterizations were always meticulously thought out. He keeps his performance alive every second he's on the screen and his description of the green Wedgwood vase he treasures is sheer magic and if you look for it you can see in Peter's performance the influence of India, for there is a gentle depth in it. His tenderness with Rosalie Crutchley is a quality that made Peter so loved and which women found irresistible. This little comedy cameo reveals a side of an earlier Peter on the screen that the public seldom saw.

After *Make Me An Offer*, Peter was approached by Warner Brothers to play in what the American director, Henry Levin, described as a 'western in armour', *Dark Avenger* (retitled *The Warriors* in the US), which starred Errol Flynn. Though Flynn, a fellow Australian, had befriended Peter while he was making *Elephant Walk* in Hollywood, Peter, according to Levin, had refused to go along with Errol's unprofessionalism while they were on the set, but did his very best on an impossible film with a screenplay that was virtually nothing but action. Peter told me that he drank far too much with Flynn, and he was really ashamed of the performance he turned in on the film.

Levin said that Warner Brothers originally planned to get a young American star for the leading role, but the deal fell through. Peter had been listed for the supporting role as the heavy, but Levin urged Warner Brothers, as Leslie Norman had urged Harry Watt years before, to give Peter a break, because Levin felt that Peter would turn in a performance in the leading part that would give an unpromising film dimension and depth. But the producer wouldn't accept Finchie so Levin went off to Rome while they decided on a leading man and finally settled for Errol Flynn. After the first day's shooting Errol took Peter aside and said, 'Cut it out sport, you're violating the code.' Peter asked him what he meant. 'What you were doing in that scene was real acting.' 'Well?' said Peter. 'Well, you'll show me up!'

Filming was chaotic and Errol used to come clanking on to the set at Elstree surrounded by little poodles, which were quite undisciplined and peed all over everybody. As the days wore on it was proving more and more difficult to get a shot, and once Peter saw the situation was hopeless, and Errol was well away and starting to sing, Peter would just join in and off they'd go, arm in arm, and work ceased for the day, usually about eleven in the morning. 'Errol was a wild man but very sweet to me,' Joanne Dru, the leading lady in the film said. 'He went shooting in Scotland and returned to the Connaught Hotel in London where I was staying, knocked on my door and presented me with a very bloody grouse. I sent it back by the waiter. Flynn was mortified. I told Peter about it the next day and he said, "Oh my darling, throw it out the window, flush it down the lav, or give it to me, but never return grouse!" '

Dark Avenger was followed in October 1954 with another film Peter felt was best forgotten. The Rank Organization assembled a cast for *Passage Home* full of Rank stars and starlets – Bryan Forbes, Gordon Jackson, Patrick McGoohan, Michael Bryant, Anthony Steel and Diane Cilento – but it did the film no good. Peter was 'Lucky' Ryland, Captain of the *Bolinge*, who in the Depression year 1931, sets up a deal in a South American port, Vilamonte, to carry a cargo of pedigree bulls home to England.

Peter at this stage was very anxious to cultivate the right sort of film image, and when he got the script he rang up Alan White, not long over from Australia, and said: 'Your father's a sea captain. Quick! Write him a letter. Ask him to describe exactly what it is like during the times he's at sea, every detail of his everyday life and so on.' White wrote to his father and Peter subsequently got a detailed letter back from Captain White. 'He just completely absorbed everything my father had written,' said White, 'until he was completely coloured by the character of Lucky Ryland.'

Diane told me that to relieve the boredom, and banality, of what, in its making, was proving to be an 'assembly line picture' she, Peter and the cast used to perform the 'sandfly' dance in the bar at Pinewood, a sort of tribal corroboree dance, where they all went berserk to let off steam at the end of an endless day's shooting, turning the studio bar into a compound, and the furniture into totems. Peter and Diane shared the same chauffeur, Paddy, and they met every day going to and from the studio, and she found Peter enormously sympathetic and protective. He treated her as a much younger sister. She was feeling very homesick for the warm tropical sunshine of her part of Australia, and Pete, being very much an Aussie at heart, sensed this and used to tell her stories about his adventures in the outback of Queensland, when he was younger than she was, and how he had knocked about as a swagman in his early years. There was a marvellous affinity, and a platonic rapport between these two rebels at heart.

Diane always found Peter as an actor incredibly in control of the situation, both of himself, and of other actors with whom he was playing any scene. She remembered him as Iago and couldn't stop laughing because Orson Welles was wearing a false chest. She felt that it was a marvellous 'hand to hand' combat between the toreros Welles and Finch, those two, so ill-matched in weight, battling it out. She found him a cunning actor and very innovative in his own way. 'He could always turn a moment of his acting into something exciting. He was a good-looking man, and he knew that. He was aware he had a very sensitive face, and he had a sort of way of presenting himself. Until he started really drinking, he always looked to be in wonderful trim. We always had fun, and he was fun to be with. I'll always remember him as so protective. Unlike other actors, I felt at home with him, totally at ease. In private life, he was someone you thought, "Oh good! He's here! I'm all right!" There are some people you recognize deeply immediately. I sort of knew him. You know what I mean? And it wasn't just that we came from the same background and environment. I just never felt worried with him, but there are some actors you have to play intimate scenes with, and you just feel you are walking around on hot tiny needles. Peter loved bar room company, talk, gaiety, the sense of fiesta, but I noticed a tremendous change in him during the last seven years. He got drunk much more easily, very quickly, on very little. He always seemed to be in a frightful hassle with the ladies. He certainly didn't seem to be happy in himself, he longed to spark off!'

He'd always hinted to Diane about a lot of strange incidents in his background. She always felt that his extraordinary early background and his awareness gave him an unusual depth, and knowledge of 'other places' at times. She was struck by his overwhelming nostalgia for the Never-Never, for going out and away into the primitive solitude. 'He was interested that I grew coffee and pepper, and that I have a school up there in the Australian outback in a latitude almost identical climate-wise to his plantation in Jamaica. We used to exchange views on that geological part of the earth, that is so hot and tropical, and which holds such a fascination for me, and did for him. From time to time I met him again and he seemed to be running away. I sensed that he was desperate. I remember seeing him in the last performance he gave in the theatre, as Trigorin in *The Seagull*. I saw in his face that he really had that terrible malaise, and Trigorin, I think, has that. Trigorin is someone who could have been someone tremendous in life. He keeps saying things like, "When I die they'll put on my plaque, 'A very nice writer, but not as good as Turgenev.' " In a funny way, Peter himself had that aspect of Trigorin! "I'm a very good actor but not as good as . . ."

'You always knew there was a defensiveness in Peter but he also had an extraordinary strength. I was just a kid when I first met him and I didn't know anything about anything. I knew nothing about the film industry, about people or the exploitation of people and he was extraordinarily nice and showed me the ropes and tried to show me how I could play a scene to the best advantage. Luckily for me, I was much too ingenuous to be attractive to him, so I could get very close to him, and be really friendly. He was always involved with the ladies and he used to tell me about them because, I suppose, with me it went in one ear and out the other.'

Indeed, the ladies were not Finchie's only troubles for, though his film career was now beginning to develop, Roy Boulting, one of the major influences in British films, who invited Peter to play in *Josephine and Men* (February 1955), saw early on how Peter's drinking habits could affect his professionalism. 'We were making *Josephine and Men*. Glynis Johns was in it, Donald Sinden, Jack Buchanan, giving his last performance on the screen, and Peter. Now Peter was getting pissed rather too often. One morning, I arrived at Shepperton Studios early just as a car was pulling up outside Stage E, and out stepped dear old Peter, who should have been in make-up at least an hour before. He then proceeded to weave his way, unaware that I was just behind him, from the car to the studio block and disappeared inside. I knew he was stoned out of his mind, so I went on to the set, found the assistant and told him to go up quickly and give me a report on Peter's condition.

'We both loved Peter, but nevertheless it was now after eight and we were shooting at nine on the dot, and that sort of thing cannot and must not happen when you're making a film on schedule and on a budget. The assistant came back a few minutes later and said: "Oh my God! I've sent up black coffee, and he's looking quite terrible." Peter was in the first shot, so I had plenty of black coffee standing by when he came on to the set. He was still stoned, but it wasn't just that he was stoned. We couldn't shoot on him because his eyes were totally bloodshot. He was playing a romantic scene with Glynis Johns and those great round greyish-green eyes were like two enormous red marbles swimming in pools of blood. I said to my cameraman: "What do you think, is it going to register?" "What the hell can I do about it?" was the reply. "No filter on earth and no amount of careful lighting will ever disguise the fact that Finchie has had more than a bootful!" So we couldn't shoot on him until after lunch. I was furious. I don't believe one has a right to give in to unprofessional behaviour. Being paid more, I felt he owed more. Some poor electrician who made a real boob, someone on the side lines caught loafing, or smoking when it was strictly forbidden, could at that time have been sacked, but someone being paid thousands of pounds for their services behaving badly and getting away with it, was just not on. So at the end of the day, I took Peter aside and simply said: "Peter, no go! This is not going to work, and we're just not going to have this. You have a contract." He didn't attempt to argue, and this to me is what made him a personality very hard to resist.

'My brother John was producing and I was directing and we felt we had to make a stand, we had to indicate to the rest of our floor crew, and those who were working for and with us, that whether they were stars or clapper boys, no one was going to get away with it. So we just put it to him straight. "Peter, your inability to perform today has cost this production a great deal of money. As one of the stars we don't expect less from you, we expect more. So we propose to impose a penalty. We can't recoup our losses but at least it will remind you that you are a professional. So this morning will cost you £500 of your salary." Peter looked at me, and then he smiled and said, "Jesus man! You are absolutely right! I was bloody awful, a disgrace! I should never have appeared on your set in that state. For Christ's sake, please forgive me!" I said: "Forget it." So how can you feel anything but deep affection for a man who has the humility and sincerity not to try and bluff it out. Peter knew that if the standby carpenter had turned up on the set in that state he'd have been out and I knew that as far as we were concerned it would never happen again.'

One of Peter's great qualities was his sublime sense of the ridiculous, with no sense of his own dramatic importance. Drinking in a bar he could lose in a second that dark brown voice and become utterly unpretentious and untheatrical.

In these years the 1950s when his career was building no one casting ever gave Peter the opportunity to make fun of his own persona. Few realized what a master of self mockery he was. Peter when young, constantly cast in the unlikely role of semi matinée idol, could have gone to the verge of caricature and have been loved and understood, because he had that unique chemistry and did it incomparably in life with his hilarious improvisations. Nobody at this time would take that risk in films, yet he had shown in the theatre under Olivier and later at the Old Vic, that he was a marvellous comic. From a career point of view, it was felt his chances of being the big romantic leading man would have been spoilt. A sense of humour which Finchie certainly showed in some of his roles, is not a sense of one's own absurdity. A sense of one's own absurdity is of course not a healthy attribute in any aspiring romantic leading man, and yet Peter was capable of bridging that seeming contradiction. Women adored him. He could make them feel they were women and he could make them laugh. Peter was not only romantic, he had that extra dimension, he was ironic.

20 Contretemps and *The Shiralee*

In November 1954, during the making of *Passage Home* for the J. Arthur Rank Organization, Peter was offered a contract by Rank which was quoted variously at £45,000 for five years and £70,000 for seven years. Earl St John, the Rank production chief, announced: 'We are going to build Finch into a major British star.' This indeed proved to be the case to a certain extent for Finchie made nine films while under contract to the Rank Organization and three of them won him British Film Awards for the best actor of the year.

But Finchie was miserable from the outset. By signing a contract he believed he'd lost his liberty and freedom of choice but his living style was rising with his income and the security offered by Rank provided an adequate means of supporting his family. Nevertheless, he regarded most of the scripts sent him as rubbish, and found the whole atmosphere at Rank 'very British stiff upper lip, unimaginative and pandering to popular taste at an unnecessarily low level'.

Certainly things got off to a very bad start on his first picture for Rank. Muriel Box had cast him as Simon in the screenplay of Alan Melville's West End stage hit, *Simon and Laura*, and a team of writers including Peter Blackmore, Frank Muir and Denis Norden, had done the adaptation. This was Finchie's first big chance as a light comedian in an important feature film playing opposite Kay Kendall whom everyone remembers as the hilarious scatty star of *Genevieve*. Muriel Box had won a running battle with her executive producer to allow an untried comedian in the cinema, Ian Carmichael, who had played the part of the TV director to perfection in the theatre, to repeat his performance on film; Muriel Pavlov was cast as the secondary love interest; and the supporting cast included such comedy veterans as Thora Hird and Maurice Denham. Peter was being launched into orbit against some pretty stiff competition, and he found himself anything but happy working with a director whose methods he doubted suited his particular style of acting, and Muriel Box, already having trouble with Kay Kendall, was faced with two sensitive and nervous stars, so agitated that all her efforts to put them at their ease and get the film off the ground failed miserably. 'Kay had recently been involved with Sid Field in a musical film which had been a resounding flop and she felt she had to work doubly hard to prove herself and score the kind of success she had had in *Genevieve*. She had a curious inability at times to pronounce certain words in dialogue, like a sort of vocal dyslexia. Nothing I said could reassure her, and on the first morning of shooting, she was in a state of absolute panic. I went to the dressing room on the second morning to calm her down but she had convinced herself that I had come to say she was not strong enough for the part. She refused to believe me when I said I had cast her because I thought she was ideal for it, and was certain to make a big hit. Kay's nerves naturally affected Peter's and put him in a similar trembling state of fear. They just reacted on each other, so it was only to be expected that when Peter made his entrance during the first take of the picture, he registered all the terror of a man making his first appearance in a West End stage play that could make or break him.

'Next day, they both asked me if they could see the first lot of rushes prior to them being shown to the film crew. I agreed, and they joined me for the viewing. The only other person present was my editor, Jean Barker. There were only a couple of establishing shots, since the first day's shooting on most films is inevitably of a preparatory nature and rather short while the cameraman explores and lights the set. Kay and Peter sat in front on their own and in a few minutes the rushes were over. They rose and left the theatre together without a word, which seemed rather odd behaviour since they had been given the privilege of seeing the rushes before anyone else on the unit. I went back on the set to line up for a close shot on Peter. Eventually he was called and I waited but there was no sign of him anywhere. The next thing I heard was that he and Kay had gone to see the executive producer, Earl St John. On their way they had roped in the producer of the picture, Teddy Baird, who gave me to understand they didn't like the rushes or the way they were being directed. Neither Teddy nor I had encountered this sort of situation before nor could we envisage at this point how to handle it. Earl St John was responsible for setting *Simon and Laura* in motion as a film and for persuading me to direct it. I realized Peter and Kay had gone right to the fountainhead of power to lodge their complaints.

'I rang Earl who said: "Come straight up," and I found Peter and Kay a few minutes later sitting glumly in his office. Earl said: "The position is, they've seen the rushes and are very unhappy with them." I said: "I can't understand why. They both play ideally together and I'm delighted with the little I've seen so far."

'Faced with this conflict of opinion on their merit, Earl decided the only way out of the problem was for him to see the rushes alone that evening and give his opinion in the morning, and we all agreed to abide by it. Peter was persuaded to go back on the floor so that we could do his close-up. We did very little work that afternoon, since it was quite useless to go on with Peter in that mood. Next morning I rang Earl and he said: "I don't know what they're complaining about. The rushes look fine to me and their acting is first class." As nothing had been said explicitly and nerves were really taut, it was decided to have it out with Peter and Kay who had obviously put their heads together on the issue. We had a round table conference on the third day at eleven o'clock in the morning. Earl St John, Teddy Baird, the first assistant director, Kay, Peter and myself, all gathered in my office. We agreed there was nothing wrong with the rushes, so Peter was asked to voice his grievances. Whereupon, with arms waving emotionally, he told us reluctantly that he felt he was boxed in by the camera. He wasn't used to being so confined and having to do everything so precisely. "I like to be more free and easy during rehearsals, to find my own way about the set," he said, "I feel all these camera angles cramping my style. I can't move my hand a fraction of an inch this way or that, and I become totally strained and awkward."

'I realized he hadn't the experience of this sort of comedy on film where the slightest movement of one's head can alter the whole tone of a scene or the point of a joke. It was explained to him that the film had to be visualized by the director in terms of shots and angles unlike a stage comedy and these had to marry precisely in cutting and editing to ensure pace and successful flow.'

Director Muriel Box was principally concerned that *Simon and Laura*, as characters, should sparkle and feel completely relaxed, and free and happy on the set where so many scenes had to be shot, so she felt the only thing was to let Finchie have his head for the time being and rehearse scenes in the way he felt happy and confident. 'Although I had mapped out Peter's and Kay's moves to help them and give them a sense of direction, I now felt if he improvised, the spontaneous approach might be caught and repeated in successive takes and achieve the results we were after.'

But though Muriel was trying every way she knew to give Finchie and Kay confidence, it was to no avail. Both finally admitted they couldn't work in what they felt was such a constricted atmosphere, where so many technical demands seemed to be being imposed on them. Reminding them that Frank Muir and Denis Norden had greatly improved their roles with their satirical brand of humour failed to cheer them up, and Muriel's assurance that they played well and instinctively together as a team was met with sceptical gloom.

'We had a sort of armed neutrality for the rest of the film. The following week we shot the sequence where Peter comes down the staircase and crosses over to Kay sitting on the settee. It was an enormously long sequence, with the rest of the cast coming in and out of the set from all angles. It lasted about six pages. We started to rehearse and I gave Peter his cue to start the action and go wherever his instinct led him. After about two or three pages of dialogue, while he wandered about, the scene slowly ground to a halt. I looked up and said: "Right. Where do you feel you want to move next?" I had been making notes on his movements and waited. He looked puzzled. "Well! I don't know." "Okay," I said, "let's start again." We went through the same routine again and reached the identical spot where he had "dried" before. Again it was chaos. I said: "Peter, we've got to plot the scene meticulously with the other artists and in considerable detail, don't you agree?" He nodded. I think the finished take finally convinced him that we really did have to work on the scene this way to get the results we wanted. As he and Kay were hypersensitive artists and acted superbly together, we eventually managed to make the chemistry work between us to the end of the film.'

'Initial lack of confidence,' to quote Peter, 'can be the most destructive element in an actor's work, if it isn't somehow rectified. It's usually some small and sometimes very insignificant happening that can put your dislocated self back into joint. Lack of confidence, if you can't regain it, spreads like a bush-fire until there's nothing left but the charred remains. It's a meta-phorical reverse. The spark goes out and all the audience sees is a rather wooden, boring performer.'

When Peter was discussing the difficulty he had in playing that comedy on the screen, he said he used to try and devise, 'what I hoped were legitimate technical ways of stopping myself from becoming static in what I felt was a static scene, and I had to be still for a very long time. I would just start pulling the lobe of my ear. In other words, trying to stay alive inside, but not in such a way as to distract from the people whose important moment that might be. Edith Evans taught me the importance of that.'

For Finchie, Kay Kendall had a mad magic. He said that she turned him on, both as a clown and as a stunning woman. *Simon and Laura* brought them very close physically like a man and woman sharing danger, in this sense the risk of failure. Eventually, when the film was ready for the press show, Peter asked Larry Olivier to come and have a look at it. Muriel Box remembers her surprise at turning round in the theatre before the lights dimmed and seeing Peter and Kay sitting isolated with Larry in the middle of the front row. 'I got the shock of my life when I knew the film was being vetted by a master. I didn't see Larry when it was over, but when I came into the foyer both Peter and Kay rushed over and flung their arms round me. Peter had Larry's delighted approval and he had said Kay had all the sparkle of good champagne. We all three became the best of friends and Peter and Kay received wonderful notices.

'Finchie was mad about Kay and would certainly have married her, but he wistfully commented that "she opted for Rex Harrison, a steadier and more stable man, and let's face it, a much better comedian than I am. Kay was crazy, and I loved her, and that was our magic for the little time we were together."'

Film scripts began arriving more and more frequently and Peter rejected them all. With his knowledge of writing he was able to assess the value of a screenplay at sight, and he realized that the material he was being offered wasn't going to do anything for him as an actor or advance his career in any way. 'I'm on a merry-go-round of unparalleled mediocrity, getting paid to churn out movie fodder for the moronic masses,' he told me once, and he was drinking and getting himself very unfavourable publicity in the press, posing as a hell raiser. It was Olive Harding, his agent, who persuaded him when the part of the Australian soldier, Joe Harman, in *A Town Like Alice* was offered him – and subsequently Captain Langsdorff of the *Graf Spee* in *The Battle of the River Plate* – that although neither parts carried the picture, both could gain him enormous prestige and that he'd be a bloody fool not to accept. Peter always wanted a leading part, not necessarily the longest, as long as it showed him off to advantage.

He didn't want to do *A Town Like Alice* and Olive asked him into the office and they talked for a very long time, then she eventually found herself in tears. 'What's wrong?' asked Peter. 'I can't get your career to move,' Olive told him. 'It won't budge, and I thought that this short part would do it. That part can't fail.' It wasn't that he didn't want to be cast as an Australian, it simply took him a long time to see that a part which involved so few days filming could give him the opportunity on the screen for which he'd been waiting seven years.

Olive read through his scenes with him to show him just how effective they were, and how well they served him in relation to the other characters. The most astute actor can sometimes fail to see, when first reading a script, what the finished product is going to be like. 'But once Peter became absorbed in a part,' said Olive, 'he'd play it day and night and it consumed his entire personality.'

The second role Olive had to persuade Peter to take was in the Powell and Pressburger film, *Battle of the River Plate*, which, in her opinion, should have been the film that marked for Finchie a definite step towards international stardom. It was one of Sir Winston Churchill's favourite films and the librarian at Rank Audio Visual, who hold the print, told me he used to send for it again and again. Frau Langsdorff, after seeing the film, sent Rank a letter saying how magnificently he had recreated her late husband.

Michael Powell who directed him in the film said: 'Oh Peter! Ask him to do something, as I did with Langsdorff, and he'll give you back all you've asked for and more – "Don't forget, Peter," I said before we shot one particular scene, "by the time you're driven into Montevideo, there's pressure from Hitler as well as those cruisers just over the horizon waiting for you." We shot the scene and, if you look at it again, he suggests a whole background, the breeding of a German officer of the old school, disciplined but with always that touch of compassion. A gentleman playing at war when war was no longer a gentleman's game. He gave me, as a director, not only what I asked but so much more, a performance with that dimension and imagination no director can implant in a great actor. It was there in Peter, and when the camera turned on him as Langsdorff, he had this subtle, sincere magic.' John Schlesinger said: 'I used to watch him, fascinated. He was Langsdorff. Unostentatious and so moving because you saw the vulnerability of the German involved in a war, serving a Nazi party in which he didn't believe.'

Peter was actually filming *A Town Like Alice* and *The Battle of the River Plate* at the same time for Rank, during the autumn of 1955. When I saw him just before Christmas 1955, professionally he was happier than he had been for a long time. He had been approached by H.M. Tennent to star with Vivien Leigh as Hali Alani in Noel Coward's play *South Sea Bubble*, about which I remember Vivien telling me she was very excited. The play eventually came into the Lyric Theatre, Shaftesbury Avenue, in April 1956, with Ronald Lewis replacing Peter who had been offered a part in the film *The Shiralee*.

He was really enjoying the work with director Jack Lee on *A Town Like Alice*, and Michael Powell on *The Battle of the River Plate*. Towards the end of filming, he told me he had really grown to understand the character of the Captain of the German pocket battleship: 'I think he was a great man, and the sad thing about playing Langsdorff is that I feel very deeply the loss of this man dying alone in his hotel room.' Finchie always believed that if an actor is strong-minded enough he can think himself into a shape and size and assume absolutely the point of view of the character he is portraying. 'If you're old you develop "old habits", after a while you ease yourself out of a chair instead of getting straight up, or you develop little idiosyncrasies like ... I somehow developed a slight stoop for Langsdorff, he walks like a sad slow greyhound. Don't ask me why! He just grew in me physically. I became devoted to him and understand completely his point of view.'

In June 1956, Peter sailed for Australia in the *Port Hardy* to make *The Shiralee*. The ship ran into a hurricane off the coast of South Africa and had to seek shelter in Durban. In a letter dated 9 July, written on board, to his half-sister Flavia before the ship berthed at Port Adelaide, Finchie makes his first mention of the girl he was to marry almost exactly three years later:

Durban was quite fun – but the underlying hatred and fear is terrible to behold. I met a fairly nice character on the beach called Yolande Turnbull with the best legs I have ever seen in my life. She is coming to London and is going to ring you up and join the gang. I'm getting off the ship at Adelaide and flying to Sydney as there are dock strikes all over the country and we wouldn't get there till 1958 . . . The Australians on board are the narrowest minded, most insular and aggressive characters I've ever met. The Count of Monte Cristo can't wait to get back to the nest, homesick already. Practise up the dancing. Love Peter.

He didn't fly but went by train to be met at Central Station, Sydney, by crowds of reporters and, recognizing an old friend among the crowd, said: 'What do you do round here for a bit of crumpet?' The reporter for one prominent Sydney newspaper was a dear little girl who solemnly reported on the front page next day that Mr Finch had expressed a fondness for crumpets!

He met up with a lot of the old mates in Sydney after seven years away. There were parties and reunions, including one with Marian Morphy and all the hangers-on and, as Finchie said, it was marvellous as long as you didn't overstay your welcome. But when one character asked him, 'How long you stayin' mate?' and another said: 'Finch, ya rat bag, ya'd shag anything with hair on it from a barber's floor upwards,' he realized that the world of his struggling years was no longer his world, and he was soon restless to get up-country and start work on the film. But there were several life-long friends he wanted to see and did see, among them Harry with whom he'd first met Tamara. The first thing he asked Harry was: 'Can you organize a night at Ralph Curnow's, with plenty of booze, and get him to do his one-man drag act?'

Harry told Peter that Ralph was still alive but that his soirées of the pre-war days were long over. Instead, Harry organized a get-together of their old actor mates at a hall in Sydney's Oxford Street. Two five gallon kegs of beer were laid on for the occasion. One of the old friends who didn't attend was Buddy

Morley. 'Have you seen Buddy Morley?' Peter asked Harry, then added his own answer: 'I've seen him. He's become a derelict!'

On 17 August he arrived on location glad to be out of Sydney, and wrote off to his mother and Flavia:

My darlings,
Christ! and likewise phew! The official round I have been on here is killing: politicians, bazaars, balls, charities, dinners, civic receptions and two hours mail answering a day – so hence why I haven't written. Today, thank God, we arrived on location in Coonabarabran (believe it or not), the most picturesque town. The kid (*Dana Wilson who plays Buster, his daughter*) is wonderful – Hey! I have met a honey of a youngster here who lives in Rome and is (hold it), only 19. She looks like Gina Lollobrigida and is also a dear. She will be over to join the gang in October. If she arrives before, look after her – she is nice. Name of Spiffy Fairfax. I think I've gone a bit!!! Have got some Brubeck records up here.
I love and miss you all,
Peter.
Haven't heard from Aisha (*his current dark lady*). Has she gone?

The Shiralee had come about because Jack Rix, a production manager-cum-associate producer at Ealing, had come to Les Norman with the proofs of a new novel by the Australian writer, D'Arcy Niland. Norman read and immediately wanted to make it into a film. He sent it to Michael Balcon who read it at once and said: 'How dare you give me that filthy book with all that foul language!' Les said that the Aussies were sometimes inclined to call a spade a fuckin' shovel, but the strong language in the film could be excluded. He said to Balcon: 'Will you let me have the book for a few days and I'll write a screenplay for you that you won't find offensive, but that will retain the flavour of D'Arcy Niland's original.' It was agreed, and in ten days Norman wrote the screenplay of the novel, which he then sent Balcon who said: 'It's a different story.' Norman said: 'Not at all. I've just taken out the bad words and put it into cinematic form.'

Balcon then decided he wanted it rewritten by a professional screen writer, and sent it to Neil Paterson who, according to Les, generously sent it back and said: 'You've got a perfectly good script. Why send it to me?' Paterson said there was only one scene he'd alter so Ealing paid him a lot of money and he got a trip to Australia out of it. But Les had his own screenplay, less one scene, and the star of his choice, Peter, and the best child he could find in Australia to match him.

Les, who knew Peter well when they began the film and even better when they had finished it, completely understood Peter's inability to cope with his daughter, Anita, 'because I'd picked this little Australian kid, Dana, to play Buster. She was the best of the hundreds of kids I saw, and like any kid, once she knew she was going to star in the film, the little head started to swell alarmingly, and came the time I had to give her a good spanking. After that, no more trouble, good as gold and she and Peter were perfect together. When Peter met her it was a case of one child meeting another. He said to me: "Dana is a completely self-centred child, and she's like any good actress." I could see he was very jealous. I know his problem with Anita – she was a competitor, and for the same reason Peter absolutely refused to appear in public with Dana. He said: "Let her have the credit." But that was not the reason: the wily Finch understood the old adage, never act with children or animals.' Les Norman directed the whole film by ear, because he knew in Peter and Dana he had two instinctive imaginative childlike artists who could improvise the truth of the situation in an instant.

'In the scene where Macauley and Buster shelter from the rain under a bridge, I had them sitting side-by-side feeling the cold with the rain absolutely pissing down, and I said, "Peter what would that kid's reaction be at this moment?" He replied: "I think she'd be happy." "Why?" I asked. "Because she's ... close to me for the first time," and I said, "By Christ, Peter, you're right," and Finchie, cold and miserable and wet, sees the fun of it and then he starts to laugh. Then we had the sound of the truck and immediately Peter's back to reality. "Shut-up," he says to the kid and out they go to thumb a lift in the truck. All the way through the film we deliberately planned this hate-love relationship between Macauley and his child, Buster.'

In 1969 Peter told me that, of all his films, *The Shiralee* was the most autobiographical and the confrontation between Elizabeth Sellars (an actress well versed in law), playing his wife, and Peter, was a polemic battle off the set as well as on. Peter felt himself identifying with George Finch who had taken him away from his own mother because of her infidelity. He was trying to convince himself, as Macauley, that it was his wife's infidelity that had prompted him to take the child and suffer as an outcast in order to safeguard her, when he knew in his heart that he was taking her away to spite her mother for having had it off with Danny (George Rose), while he was away.

Both Peter and Elizabeth, according to Les, used to argue the finer points of who was right. She, from a legal point of view, and Peter from the experience of George Finch and his mother. For him it was simply a matter of drawing from his own background except, as he bitterly observed, George Finch was no Macauley: he couldn't have cared less and he showed it.

Les said he saw in an instant the moment when Peter became jealous of Dana, and friendship turned to resentment. 'We were working outside a little shop in Coonabarabran. It was a Saturday and people came for miles around in their cars, and we had to rope off the shooting area to hold them back. They all wanted Peter's autograph and after a while he got fed up. So little Dana, who had been sitting watching, said she'd give her autograph. "I'm a star, too," she said, and the look on Peter's face showed deep resentment. From then on he no longer liked Dana. He admired her and he'd help her, but he didn't like her. She had betrayed his inner code and he showed himself to be a complete child like her. Peter was seldom jealous of those he really considered better than him as an actor, but only of those around his own level or beneath him. In that respect he was like most actors, they don't admit it but they can't hide it.'

To Les Norman, Peter 'lived his work, but with a greater intelligence than most actors I've known. But Peter found it easier to talk to me when he'd had a glass or two. He was a man who through some terrible insecurity needed drink to release him. Peter could transcend his material, and a great deal of it was just crap, but he had the gift of total conviction.'

The last time Les Norman saw Finchie was in the Pickwick Club in London. 'He'd invited me to a party when he was married to Yolande. I took Bet, my wife. We were all drinking and suddenly Peter said: "You know what's wrong with you?" "What?" I asked. "You never get pissed. You can't enter my world." He felt I was judging him with a sober eye. "That's right, Peter," I said, "but I can appreciate those who do." '

Made by Ealing, taken over by Rank and released through MGM in 1957, *The Shiralee* didn't catch on in the States except among a small audience. Les Norman's scripting and Finchie's playing suggest to perfection the laconic and freedom-loving Aussie who respects nobody: Macauley the swagman, who tramps through the Australian inland country towns, carrying a cross of his own making in the lonely child with a cloth kangaroo. It gave Peter a character in a film of his own choosing and he couldn't fault the director, or the film's philosophy: Why should I put my saddle on one filly when I've got the pick of the Aussie paddocks? – which was Peter's too. It was Peter's favourite of all his films.

21 *A Town Like Alice*

Jack Lee, brother of the poet and writer Laurie Lee, directed
Finchie in three films, *The Wooden Horse*, *A Town Like Alice* and
Robbery Under Arms. Lee now lives in Sydney and is chairman
of the South Australian Film Corporation. Jack and Peter first
met in 1948 in an exclusive little London club, Le Petit Club
Français, in St James's Place. It was a great *rendezvous* for film
people and had been started for the Free French during the
war by Olwen Vaughan, a famous lady from the British Documentary Film School, who was half French and adored the
French and the French film makers. Olwen had arranged the
meeting and when Peter and Chips Rafferty entered, Jack Lee
recognized Chips at once from *The Overlanders* and *Eureka
Stockade*, but didn't recognize 'the burning romantic, slightly
swarthy character introduced as Peter Finch'. Jack Lee's impression of Peter was: 'A fascinating character whom women
obviously adored. He was a great raconteur, and what an
imagination!'

Jack's first professional contact with Peter was in 1950 when
he was directing *The Wooden Horse*, and there was a scene in the
film which, because they were over-budget and over-schedule,
the producer, Ian Dalrymple, had decided not to shoot. It took
place in the prisoner-of-war hospital with Leo Genn and Peter,
as an Australian prisoner-of-war, whispering to each other in
beds placed back to back, and Jack Lee felt it was a crucial
scene. 'We deleted it from the original shooting script, but
when the film was being cut and edited, I realized that it was
imperative we shoot it. So Peter was cast and the sequence shot
later. It was a simple two-handed scene and he was marvellous.'
When the British Film Institute ran the sequence for me recently,
I noticed that Peter didn't fall into the trap of putting on an
accent as most Aussies abroad do when asked to play an
Australian. Finchie once said: 'If you apply the tourniquet to
the Australian form of your expression when you come to
England, the blood will never flow again if you have to revert
back to playing a character of your own origins.'

Five years after *The Wooden Horse*, Jack Lee was preparing a film to be called *The Midnight Bell* when producer Joe Janni sent him a script of Nevil Shute's *A Town Like Alice*. He read it in an evening, decided to drop what he was doing and start on *Alice* at once.

'Who shall we get to play the part of the Australian Joe?' Janni said, but Jack Lee knew there was only one man in England he wanted for that role: Peter Finch. They got to work on the script. *A Town Like Alice* had been on various producers' desks for years and no one had actually got around to doing it. Once Olive Harding had made Peter see that the small part was a gem, Peter threw himself into it with tremendous enthusiasm. Lee and Janni went to Malaya to do the location reconnaissance and from Singapore one weekend they flew down to Alice Springs to find the right locations for the last ten minutes of the film.

Peter had just started his contract with Rank. The character of Joe Harman, the Australian soldier captured by the Japanese in Malaya, was made for him. 'We never considered anyone else for it,' Jack Lee recalls. 'He and Virginia McKenna both got on well together, but Peter was very put out when we told him the budget would not allow us to take him or Virginia to Malaya or Australia.'

There was a great respect and affection between Virginia McKenna and Finch. Peter had love affairs with many women but not with McKenna. They had a great rapport in every scene they played together, which Jack Lee still remembers when he thinks about the film: 'There was a scene we shot in Malaya when Peter has come across these struggling, starving, dying women and their children. He's a prisoner-of-war, driving a Jap truck and they are walking along the roads going from place to place, nobody wanting to have anything to do with them. He'd managed to get them little things like cigarettes, and he is so effective in one scene where he breaks his cigarette in two and Virginia and he smoke it together. In another scene they said they wanted meat of some sort. They couldn't get any meat and he said, "I'll steal some chickens," and he stole one from the Japanese officer. The scene was shot in the middle of a field outside Pinewood studios, an extraordinary scene it was, shot basically in three or four hours. A mist came down, an autumn mist, and we shot the scene using the mist.'

Virginia McKenna, remembering back over twenty years,

says: 'He made you feel happy in his presence. His charm and generosity to other actors was really heart-warming. With Peter, I always felt at ease and he was one of those actors who just seemed to draw the best out of you because in a scene his concentration was entirely on you, and he was the character he was playing. I remember too there was also a slightly shy quality about him which was unexpected, but then all those years ago we all were a little shy in our youth and lacked confidence (not that confidence necessarily comes with age!) *A Town Like Alice* was a very important film for both of us and our knowledge of each other was tied up with our characters.'

One of Finchie's best stories came out on location shooting *A Town Like Alice* during Jack Lee's and Joe Janni's first visit to Alice Springs. As Finchie wasn't on location its origin is obscure – and is probably grafted on to a similar situation when Finchie was present – but, like most of Finchie's stories, it probably has some basis in fact and, like all of them, was uproariously funny, especially when he himself recounted it.

One Saturday lunchtime Finchie and a few Pommy friends working on the film were driving in the outback in the vicinity of Alice Springs. 'We were very hungry, and through the dusty heat haze we spotted this weatherboard cafe, flywire doors and windows. We went in and ordered. The lady that owned the joint was fat, lethargic, and very sweaty. *Monsieur le Patron* could be seen through the other flywire door in the backyard in his braces and singlet chopping up the wood. The Englishmen ordered in their best Etonian accents.

'Two fillet steaks, one medium and one medium-rare, please.'

'Yea!' said the lady, scribbling down two steaks on a grubby piece of paper.

'What vegetables have you got?' asked one Pom.

'Might be able to rustle you up a few chips!'

The English faces expressed simply 'My God!' but the dialogue was: 'Well!...er...could we have salad?'

'SALAD!!!' It was about 110 degrees in the shade and not a blade of grass for thousands of miles. 'Nuh ... No salad,' said the lady.

'Oh well! Just the steaks, thank you!'

Half an hour later, back came two old black slabs of barbecued steak. Horrified amazement on the English faces. They now knew better than to argue.

'Excuse me, Madame,' said one as she was shuffling back, bedroom-slippered, to her chair in the corner. 'Have you any mustard?'

'What . . . ?'

'Mustard.'

'Oh, hang on a mo'. ' She went to the flywire door, opened it, and shouted to the wood chopper, 'Hey . . . there's two foreigners in 'ere an' they got some steak an' they're askin' for mustard!'

He straightened up with a look of utter disbelief! 'Mustard! What do they think it is! Fuckin' Christmas!'

Jack Lee wanted to do another film with Peter, and he and Janni approached him to play Captain Starlight, the bushranger, in Rolf Boldrewood's *Robbery Under Arms*. The idea appealed to Peter but not the script or the cinematic form that was finally shot. Peter knew that if the film was ever going to work on the broad sweeping lines that Jack Lee envisaged, they would have to scrub the episodic complicated Victorian novel with its plots and counterplots, and write it as an original screenplay with the dimension of a John Ford concept. Finchie had escaped and was living in Ibiza in 1957, and every time Jack Lee wanted to telephone him he had to call the village phone box – typical Finchie. The distraught Jack Lee and Joe Janni, sweating it out month after month trying to put *Robbery Under Arms* into some workable form, would frantically phone the local call box in Ibiza. When some Ibizan did lift the receiver, Jack and Joe had a list of Spanish words they had to shout into the mouthpiece: *'Señor Finch, llamada de teléfono de Londres. Por favor. Llama al Señor Finch, Don Pedro! Es muy muy importante.'*

But Finchie kept telling Jack he preferred living the simple life in Ibiza, and Jack assures me – and I need no convincing – that Finchie also liked those very comfortable expensive hotels. The luxury hotels and the patch of land up in the scrub country were all part of that game Peter Pan played all his life and played brilliantly. I've seen and known Finchie in both and he adored both according to his moods and/or his woman of the moment, and why not?

Jack got very fed up with Finchie and his Ibizan telephone box; the script was proving to be a disaster; John Davis was 'putting the heat on Olive Harding' to get Peter to do *Robbery*;

and Peter, back in Ibiza, kept reacting to the whole idea by playing hide-and-seek in his citrus orchard. Jack's solution was to shelve the project for nine months and start it in the Australian spring, by which time, with Finchie's help – which they eventually got when Jack finally met up with Peter in Rome at the Hotel Hassler – they could have knocked a workable script into shape. But Davis was adamant. The film had been budgeted, and was part of the Rank schedule. Finch and Lee had their instructions to get on with it and, as Finchie bitterly commented later: 'Off we all went at half-cock with a half-baked project rushed in and out of the oven because that was the chef's orders.'

He fought for a screenplay that would do justice to a neglected, misunderstood and often badly handled subject. Jack Lee, anxious to salvage as much as he could from his star, found him moody, sullen, evasive and devious. They started shooting for two weeks without him and had messages that he was on his way to join them in South Australia. The moment he arrived Jack knew he was in for trouble. Finchie was as pink-eyed as a rabbit with conjunctivitis, so they became involved with hospitals and doctors and a Finchie who was fretting bitterly for Yolande, whom he was to marry two years later. Jack remembers Peter putting a call through to London to his beloved but she had already gone to Paris with somebody else, so Captain Starlight began *Robbery Under Arms* in very bad shape, both physically and emotionally. For Finchie, in retrospect, it was his worst 'low' since *The Dark Avenger* with Errol Flynn in 1954.

They were riding round in the Flinders Ranges, 250 miles from Adelaide in blazing heat, and everyone slept at night in tiny cubicles for a bedroom. The situation was affecting Peter's work, his relations with Jack and the other actors. He started to try and rationalize his role of the bushranger. 'Jack,' he said. 'I think I'll play it as though it was the Risorgimento.' What a load of crap, thought Jack Lee, he thinks he's Garibaldi. But he felt that, during *Robbery Under Arms*, Finchie was at the height of his powers, and although he was unhappy on the film, there were compensations, and his mood, after hearing he and Virginia McKenna had won their first British Film Award for their performances, changed for the better, and he wrote to his half-sister:

Dearest Flavia,

Thank you and Mum for the congratulatory wire. Isn't it exciting? I won't be back for the presentation so I have asked Jimmy to collect it for me. 'Starlight' is becoming quite fun – lots of riding on the most wonderful horse in the world, Velox. He is so intelligent and good natured, it is going to break my heart to leave him. This is a hell of a location, 200 miles from the nearest town in a sort of camp. Just like the army again. Thirsty for mail – hot beer – no women. Don't mind really – get letters from Yolande regularly. Saving money like crazy, simply because I have nothing to spend it on. The suit is safe and the shirts intact. I miss you all. See you soon.

Peter.

To keep himself occupied while he waited between shots, Peter used to amuse himself with a challenge that was in keeping with his character as Starlight. He'd practise for hours on end with his long stockwhip against the trunk of a tree, at varying distances, until he could crack the whip at full length with the deft swing of an experienced drover. (Sometime later back in England at Pinewood, Peter, seeing an actor emerge from one of the sound stages, cracked his whip at a distance of fifteen feet, wrapping it round the waist of the unsuspecting and amazed actor in a neat coil without hurting him in the slightest.)

In shooting the death scene when Captain Starlight is besieged on a mountainside and eventually killed, Jack Lee decided to photograph the scene in extreme long shot. Instead of the actor wanting his big final moment in close-up, as is usual, Peter was delighted with the idea of dying away in the distance, but he had a great idea. He always used to carry lumps of sugar in his pocket so that Velox would always come when he wanted him. He decided to put plenty of sugar in his pocket so that, when he was lying dead, the horse would sniff the sugar and come and nuzzle him, making a very effective shot.

Jack Lee, talking of Peter as a friend of over twenty years, is detached, affectionate and understanding, especially about Finchie's womanizing. 'He had lots of women. They were chasing him all the time while we were making the damn film there. I must say he would always treat them with extraordinary respect and he was a very courteous man and a great drunkard, but only when he wanted to be.'

He was also sympathetic to Finchie's other problems, but as a director working in close proximity with him, Jack is sceptical about the persona of Peter as a hell raiser, and Finchie himself always maintained that his great 'hell-raising image' was wishful publicity by the press. I asked Trevor Howard about the Finchie he's supposed to have drunk and raised hell with. 'Hardly knew him, dear boy,' said Trevor. 'The whole thing is a fabrication. He used to ride past here on his bike when he lived up the road in Totteridge but never once did he come in to say "hello", nor did he frequent the local pubs.

'Yolande did ring me one day, the only time I had a 'phone call from Peter's house, and said she and Finchie had had a son and they wanted to call him Howard Charles Finch, and did I mind? I was flabbergasted as I hardly knew Peter really, and I was very touched. Why they thought I'd mind, I can't imagine. Originally I think I was to be a godfather, and then they thought better of it. The Peter Finch I vaguely knew was a man with a secret self that remained a secret to me. I'd have liked to have known him, because I admired him enormously. We made *The Heart of the Matter* together in the early 1950s, but all this Trevor Howard-Peter Finch drinking together as hell raisers is a load of press crap.'

Finchie and Jack Lee used to frequent the Spanish restaurants when Finchie was indulging his *afición* for flamenco. 'I've got to dance,' he'd say to Jack. 'I feel the *duende* inside me, the demon of inspiration,' and off he'd go on to the floor clicking his heels, stamping his feet and doing a very good Farruca, or a bit of Bulerías. To Jack, he was 'a most curious, irrational and maddening man, who, when he talked about his illegitimate birth or about being a Buddhist would suddenly become all mystical. He was a man of some erudition yet he'd assume roles and turn them on and off just to impress people. "My Buddhist night, it's going to be tonight", or "my political night", or "my night for deep esoteric conversation". I remember one night after work on *Robbery Under Arms*, as the cool of the evening came down, someone suggested we take a landrover out and go and shoot a couple of rabbits. We took two landrovers and went hunting these rabbits in the dark. Now we were not hunting kangaroos, but with Finchie as a passenger in my landrover, anyone would think we were brutal, bloodthirsty kangaroo killers! He'd had a few drinks and suddenly he'd obviously decided this was his evening for mystical Buddhism, and we had tears of mortification on perhaps a few bottles of South Australian wine. Next morning, of course, he'd forgotten all about it and that evening we tucked into a plate of rabbit, and he didn't even ask if they were the rabbits shot the previous night.'

After Jack Lee left for Australia in 1964 he tried many times to persuade Peter to go back on various film projects; but one by one Peter put them off or would not commit himself and Jack came to the conclusion that Finchie didn't really want to go back to Australia: 'I think he thought it was all part of his growing up. It may have been that he was afraid to come back, but I'm quite convinced he had no intention of ever going back. There was no lack of opportunities for him, no lack of stories or scripts, but he knew that all the offers were "oncers". He'd become used to the European way of life and he'd become in a strange way rather anti-Australian. He regarded it as a hedonistic and materialistic society, and became almost arrogant in his attitude towards the self-complacency which he said Australia was living in. He knew damn well that if he did come back the red carpet would be put out for a little while, and then he'd be a nobody again, and he realized he was going to stay where his work was.'

The last time Jack Lee saw Peter was in Rome around the mid-1960s. 'He had met Eletha and looked much happier then. He seemed to have gone through a very hard time financially and there had been a period when he wasn't getting quite so much work, but he always had great dignity. To me, curiously enough, Peter was always a very dignified character. He had many of the characteristics of the impecunious actor and yet he could take the hard times in his stride magnificently. It was when he was out of work that he was at his most charming because he was most relaxed. I believe now he is an object of affection in Australia to all the Aussies who knew him, but thirty years is a long time ago. I think he was afraid to go back. It's like going back to school years after. Fine, but you can't stay long. His friends were members of his old school which was Australia, so he liked to see them but not for too long, and it was a relief in fact when he'd shut the door on the past again and said, "Well, that's the end of that era".'

22 Flavia – and others

In the 1950s, between the break-up with Tamara and his marriage to Yolande, Peter's half-sister Flavia worked as his private secretary from home. (She is now married to half-brother Michael's best friend, Garth Magwood.) She looks back with great affection, humour and detachment on Finchie when they were closest, which was always when Peter was at his most lost, and when a marriage break-up was imminent or when there were no other women around. Flavia was devoted to Peter, but like his mother and Michael, because of Finchie's years as the lost son, there were never any possessive demands on either side and usually a great deal more laughter and tolerance than exists in many families. Betty, Peter, Flavia and Michael all told me the same story about the famous reunion at Carbis Bay in Cornwall in 1948: Finchie had gone to Somerset House, checked out his birth certificate, rung up his mother and made a date with her. Betty then rang Michael (Wing-Commander Michael Roscoe Ingle Finch, DFC and Bar, an ex-fighter Pilot in the 56th Squadron, at that time studying accountancy at Helford), to tell him that his brother was arriving from Australia – an actor with a Russian wife – and would he care to meet him.

'What? Didn't know I had a brother. You never told me. Christ! Yes, all right. I'll drop in. What's his name?'

On the appointed day, Flavia and Mother waited at the railway station to meet Peter, wondering whether the prodigal son would emerge from the train at St Erth with a large black beard and a parrot on his shoulder! Suddenly a very handsome, shy young man, with a beautiful dark girl at his side, appeared. Betty and Flavia were overcome. All Betty could think of to say was: 'Peter dear, you haven't cleaned your shoes.'

Tamara was horrified by what she considered to be Betty's lack of feeling but Peter understood exactly. 'What the hell else could she say? I'd been tramping through the rain and it was true.'

Back at the house, Peter and Michael soon tired of the polite conversation and they went down to the local pub and got thoroughly pissed. Finchie later told me about the opening scene with Roscoe: 'He described me as not a bad sort of bloke. Brother Roscoe had all the makings of a first-rate Aussie.'

With Flavia and Mama, Peter could come and go and do exactly as he pleased. Peter had no secrets from Flavia, and Flavia knew all about her half-brother's escapades. 'That Spanish dancer, Salud, from the Casa Pepe Restaurant?' She roared with laughter. 'Gorgeous and shrewd enough to see through Finchie and to realize she wasn't going to be caught. She had good, practical Spanish animal logic and kept him at a respectable distance, and let him wear himself out on the dance floor with his *farruca*.'

Tormenting him with her gorgeous provocative eyes, the *señorita* was able to enjoy Finchie's histrionic ravings with detached amusement. To Salud, a well brought up Andalusian girl waiting chastely for the right husband, Finchie's passionate advances were a hilarious game to be enjoyed over a glass of vino tinto at the Casa Pepe where she danced. She knew Finchie was definitely a man to be kept at a respectable distance, preferably at arm's length, or even in this case at a farther distance than Finchie's leg which could find its way to hers under a table. The outcome was that I had to give him a few basic lessons in *taconéo* (footwork), that endless and repetitive heel tapping that is generally accepted as flamenco dancing. Finchie, true to unpredictable and unique form, started off his initial lessons in flamenco far better able to move expressively with his hands than with his feet, which is the mark of a truly accomplished flamenco dancer. With his feet, he was heavy and uncoordinated, but with his hands he had a natural lyrical style. We used to have sessions down in what were once the cells of the Chelsea police station. By the mid-1950s, the old building was no longer used as a police station, but a community centre. We stamped away for hours on end at Finchie's *farruca*, which, if nothing else, exhausted him sufficiently to reduce his libido and get his mind off Salud. At least he was able, as a result of these brief lessons, to get nearer to her on the dance floor, with an army of observing chaperones to see he didn't overstep the mark. We had originally begun lessons at the Third Feathers Boys Club in Blantyre Street at the Worlds End, Chelsea. Neither the street as such, nor the Third Feathers exist any more, because the whole area came under the demolition hammer and is now a complex of red high-rise council flats. The long suffering lady who ran the club turned us out after two lessons because Finchie, very heavy on his heels dancing up on the second floor, was splitting all the walls. We came back one afternoon after cooling off with a couple of lagers at the local pub to find one of his shoes had had a protruding nail, which had peppered the floor with little holes and the walls and ceiling looked as though the building had been right in the path of an earth tremor. Cracks everywhere. We humbly apologized to the incensed lady and fled. I then realized why most of the great flamenco schools in Spain are usually to be found down in the musty nether regions of some Madrid basement.

Finchie's *farruca* was so lethal that Salud always insisted he dance shoeless and concentrate on the arms, but not around anywhere near her, as the moment he got near her he seemed to develop the tactile proclivities of an octopus.

As for Kay Kendall, Finchie adored her and she, along with Vivien Leigh, was the only one as mad as Finchie. 'We all loved Kay,' said Flavia. 'During *Simon and Laura*, she used to come to the house a lot. Yes, she was potty and, like a lot of people who know they are going to die (Kay had leukemia), she had this almost detached gaiety, her feet always slightly off the ground. She was really perfect for Peter but so wise not to get permanently involved with him.'

Finchie told Flavia that his affair with Vivien had not begun until they started filming in Ceylon. Vivien became very friendly with Flavia and Betty, who see her as one of the saddest people they ever knew, a person not responsible for her actions, once the depressive illness really took over. Betty told me that Vivien used to come and see her, very near the end of her life, and just sob in the old lady's arms. 'I used to hold her, sometimes for half an hour, and it was exactly like holding a taut spring that you felt at any moment might burst into pieces. She wanted a child by Larry and knew everything that had happened since the break up of her first marriage to Leigh Holman was of her own doing.' All three, Peter, Flavia and Betty, at different times, confirmed you could walk into a room packed with people, the most beautiful, intelligent and witty, and if Vivien was there, twenty years older than the prettiest woman, as Finchie said:

223

'the eye and the mind went to Vivien and stayed there. She had what it takes to hold you, and to draw you with her.'

The only time Peter ever threatened suicide, said Flavia, was over Vivien Leigh, a fact that I can vouch for as he'd told me he'd wanted to 'blot out the whole bloody business once and for all'.

'Give me something, anything,' he'd say to Flavia. 'I can't live without her. I want to go to her tonight, now!' 'No way,' Flavia would say, and she would sit it out with him through the night. 'Peter could never bear to be alone at night and I know that was why he used to get himself entangled with some unbelievably awful birds, and then off he'd go to bait Tamara whom, by this time, he'd left. When he got into that mood, he'd start to bite his lip and say: "I must go and see Tamara." That was it! Useless to argue, the steppenwolf was emerging from within him and was about to make its nocturnal prowl. "Leave her alone," I'd say. "Why torment her? It's finished."

'But Peter would get on the 'phone and open up the old wound. "I'm here with a black lady who is better in bed than you are" – even though Flavia would do what she could to stop him. He seemed to need to destroy Tamara, but Tamara was too strong for Peter and it was a case of the tyranny of the weak over the strong!'

Flavia knew that Peter wanted to get a rise out of Tamara, he wanted her to do something dreadful. Then he could have said: 'There you are. That's why I left her.' But Tamara never retaliated in the way Peter hoped. That was her power. Flavia believes that, after the marriage to Tamara, Vivien was certainly one of the most important women in his life, and certainly by his own admission, the greatest influence. 'I think after Vivien, Finchie went on a sort of zig-zag course. He just seemed to lose a lot of the stability he had in the early days here. Tamara had an amazing understanding of Peter, but the tragedy there, if you look at it superficially, is that she couldn't laugh in the same way Peter did. But the marriage, until the Vivien Leigh episode, held together because there was a spiritual element, shared interests and a basic sense of belonging which Peter needed but couldn't equate with his lack of self discipline in life, and thirst for liberty.'

Flavia confirms now that Finchie was indeed monstrous to Tamara. 'He had this awful habit, and he did it with all his women. He used to go round to Tamara's in the middle of the night when he was stoned and bring whatever woman he was shacking up with, stand on the door step and say: "Accept this woman, she's what I really need. You never were." And latterly he even took Eletha along. Tamara accepted this and put up with his nonsense, because she may not have been able to laugh at him, but she certainly loved him and showed it rather than said it.

'Peter had absolutely no trust in himself whatsoever. He'd lost his father though the irony of it was that both George and Jock were still alive, though George from the day he took Peter from my mother, just didn't want to know him.'

When Flavia married Garth, Peter became madly jealous. Garth spoilt all Peter's plans. He was possessive with Flavia but it only came out when she was with Garth, and no longer available as the adored sister. 'Peter had spent a long time when he was with us, building up the idea for the general public that he and I were living together. It was Peter's idea of a great joke and I used to let him play it and we used to kid everyone just for the hell of it, because we knew damn well if we were in a nightclub people would say: "Have you heard, he's living with his sister and his mother in Chelsea. He's chucked his wife out." So we used to play up this fantasy.'

Flavia described Peter's roster of 'birds' – on call after twelve o'clock at night and they all adored him. One used to give Betty and Flavia the giggles. They always knew when she was coming along Bury Walk because they'd hear her squeaking boots. Then there was the Belgian air hostess, whom he'd met in mid-air on the way to the Belgian Congo, and a dark girl who used to come and go like the Indian monsoons (except that she came from the Virgin Islands). He also got to know a German princess who had come over from Germany to be 'finished' in England.

One of Finchie's great loves during the carefree days between wives was a very beautiful coloured lady, the daughter of an African chieftain. One freezing Christmas they all set off for Dorset with this new love splendidly attired in a silver lamé suit. They all froze and 'we'd have died of an English winter if it weren't for a good supply of whisky to keep us warm', said Finchie. Another woman Peter truly adored was Shirley Bassey. Flavia felt that Peter was overshadowed by her, but she challenged him as an artist and fired him as a man. She was the only woman who threw Peter totally off balance by being every bit as good an artist as he was and by refusing to marry him and just leaving him. This was not a situation Peter was able to take in his stride but no sooner had Shirley Bassey gone out of his life than Eletha came in, and stayed the course.

I remember meeting the distraught Peter one day in Beauchamp Place, looking like a baby snatcher on the run about to be lynched.

'Peter,' I said. 'How are you?'

'Oh! Terrible!' he said. 'Things are really terrible.'

'Why? What's happened to you?'

'The publicity I got over Shirley. You wouldn't believe it in this day and age. I've been pushed into the gutter in Soho, I've been publicly called a nigger lover. They've disowned me in South Africa and the Southern States of America. I even got a bomb in the post that failed to explode – must have been an Irish one, luckily for me – and all because of my affair with Shirley. So I'm hiding out.'

'Whereabouts?' I asked, imagining him bricking himself up in that tunnel he'd once discovered beneath the crypt of St Mary's, Battersea.

'I'm up on the top floor of the Carlton Tower Hotel. Come up and see me,' and he was off back to his hideout in one of London's very smartest hotels. Finchie and Bassey were two people who liked to be free. Peter, cited as co-respondent in the divorce petition filed by her husband Kenneth Hume, was getting more critical public exposure than he'd ever known in his life. Finchie, himself in the situation into which he had placed so many of his women (of wanting to be loved and married to the love of one's life), was sending frequent SOS signals to Flavia and turning up very regularly at Bury Walk.

Whenever Peter went off on any of his film locations to Australia, Europe, Africa or America, he'd always say to secretary Flavia, 'Want to come with me?' Flavia loathed flying, and the idea of being big sister to Peter so he'd say, 'Keep the dollybirds under your thumb in London. Don't let them go off with anyone else.' So Flavia used to write and tell him where all his ladies were and what they were doing. Then a reply would come back from some remote outpost: 'Have stopped off at ―――――― and collected these measurements, so put her in the clan when she arrives in London. I've given her your number,' and all these women, unbeknown to each other, would all ring in and report to headquarters.

Peter was drinking more heavily during this period of his life, but it wasn't only the girls that drove him to the bottle. For instance, he absolutely detested film premières. He would start to go to pieces, and by three in the afternoon would be behaving like a frenzied *torero* with a corrida ahead of him at five. Flavia was his spare escort to quite a number. 'Sometimes he'd rush out in the afternoon and come back stoned. Several times he arrived with me at premières "grogged up". In the end, I locked the doors and windows and said, "Finchie you are not moving out of this house until the car comes. You've got a première tonight, it's a professional responsibility just as important to the makers of the film as your making it, so sit still, read a book and be quiet!" He'd burst out laughing at his own ridiculousness, then I'd see a stricken look and I'd put both the cigarettes and matches within his reach and would sit in an explosive atmosphere and wait for his next move. Twenty minutes later, he'd turn to his mother: "Oh! Do you want anything at the shops?" "No, nothing, thanks Peter." Another twenty minutes, and he'd suddenly stand up exasperated. "You're doing this on purpose aren't you?" and we'd say: "Yes, we are and you're going to attend this première dead sober and in your right mind and you are going to be yourself and you are not going to touch a single drop!" From five until seven he was angelic but those two hours would seem eternal. At seven he'd say: "Now can I have just a small glass?" "No," I'd say. "We've got another ten minutes," and then when I knew all was safe, I'd say: "Now you can have one whisky with me." Then the car would arrive and we'd get him into it. Never once did I drive with him to a première when he didn't say: "Please, please, let me out. I can't face them. I can't ... I just cannot go through with all this." That kind of public exposure was something he genuinely seemed unable to bear.'

But his heaviest drinking was during his marriage to Yolande, whom he married on 4 July 1959 after his divorce from Tamara became absolute on the 17 June. 'We had all tried to persuade him not to marry a second time,' said Flavia. 'We knew it was one of Finchie's blazing infatuations that couldn't last, but he'd got the bit between his teeth. He'd wanted her in the clan and was demented about those gorgeous legs. They married and, of course, they broke up and as is always the case, the two kids are the losers. She's a good mother, and the sad thing is Peter hardly ever knew them. He didn't seem able to adapt inwardly to the kind of life he was living in the early 1960s at all. During the marriage to Yolande he would keep returning to Tamara's house, until little by little he'd become a changed man. He had become increasingly self-centred and would never mention Anita or ask after her schooling.'

During the Yolande period, Peter went through the motions of living the grand life, but he never wanted Boundary House, with its three acres of land, swimming pool, private built-in bar, its garage block and staff flat – everything, in fact, he felt pretentious living could offer him. He found it inhuman and he hated it. His old friend Jack Lee said to me: 'What a mistake all that was with Finchie's planting elm trees, and oak trees, and beeches, and raising hens and cows and all that nonsense. Really a great waste of time. No actor should do that. So there was Finchie driving out from the studio in the limousine after work to his house in idiotic suburbia, and he knew damn well that was when things started to go really wrong for him, because he knew instinctively that what he was doing was wrong. I'm sure it wasn't the real Finchie who wanted this sort of life. Secretly that inner self of Peter's despised the mock Georgian house with big drawing rooms and a swimming pool and private bar installed, nannies and all that stuff. What he really liked doing of course was living in Chelsea and seeing his friends, writers, actors, artists. That is the life he loved. I know that very well. He loathed being the country squire and the clothes sat on him so badly. He was miscast and he could never come to terms with that role.' Jack Lee is right. Finchie loathed Mill Hill and the pretentious existence he knew he was living.

When my then wife, Bobo, and I went to dinner at Boundary House in 1963 the door was opened by a Spanish valet in a white jacket with sleeves that hung down practically to the tips of his fingers, and white gloves that were two sizes too large. Peter, very elegant in a grey polo-neck shirt, looking throughly miserable and out of place, greeted us and Yolande made a spectacular entrance down the staircase in a splendid creation from one of the Paris fashion houses. George and Hannah Pravda made up the party of six and, every time we needed a refill, Yolande would clap her hands and the wretched Spaniard would emerge from the shadows and refill the glasses. Finchie was trying desperately to be the perfect host and told us of his interest in finding out the fundamental truth in comparative religions. He ate nothing and drank steadily. The atmosphere was tense. The Spaniard's white gloves were deep in the large silver tureen he was holding from which his wife was ladling the tomato soup into plates for the 'guesties', as Finchie called us. The silver tureen was vast and obviously a dead weight, and the little Spaniard had to keep changing hands, and he managed to spray Bobo's white mini skirt, newly bought for the occasion, with polka dots of tomato soup. Finchie was superb. He leapt up, rushed to the kitchen and sponged off the offending spots with hot water. He told me in Rome some time later, that he had been so bored and fed up with 'family life' at that time that out of sheer devilment he'd bring home extra girls for a threesome to see if he could shock Yo. 'I think I went a bit too far even for Yo and yet I did love her, but I was having a surfeit of sex and grog because I had temporarily lost the power to feel. I was heading nowhere and it didn't seem to matter what I did because I had tied myself up in the wrong situation.'

Peter used to release some of what Freud would describe as his angst by painting his dreams at Boundary House around the walls. Rather weird surrealist *manqué* stuff, I saw some of it, but being no judge of painting can only say that Peter's work as an untutored painter expressing his fantasies was every bit as good as some of the canvases that seem to be acceptable as modern abstract art. What the experts will say remains to be seen if someone is enterprising enough to arrange a Finch exhibition in one of the London galleries.

Incidentally, Cyril Cusack, who worked with Peter on *I Thank A Fool* and *The Abdication*, says that what impresses him now almost more than anything of Peter's was his painting. 'I remember going to his house and seeing a fairly large canvas of a scene in the west of Ireland. A great deal of grey rock, but not a depressing picture by any means. I'd describe it as beautifully bleak and formidable. He had captured the essence of Ireland. You had the feeling of desolation, but of desolation with beauty. I'm sure his painting was instinctive, but I feel he had accomplished a work of art.'

Bill Constable was commissioned by Peter to do a mural on one wall at Boundary House and Finchie, according to Bill, used to have to ask Yolande for the money to keep him going. 'Finchie was so soft with people he really was, Yolande looked after the purse strings. She was a wealthy girl in her own right anyway and he'd say: "Can I have £30 to give Bill for the work so far," and she'd say: "Let's see how much he's done!" I never finished the mural; they never finished paying for it. Then the marriage just came apart and it was bound to. Finchie was playing the country squire and it didn't suit him.'

Peter said that English country life was getting him down and occasionally he wanted to 'break-out' and dance a bit of flamenco. So, shortly after the dinner Bobo and I went to, I found Peter one of the best flamenco records ever made. As I came down the hill one morning to give him the record I saw him emerging on his bike from the front gate of Boundary House. I pulled up by a drain with a large metal top, which was opposite his front gate, and gave him the record. He was like a kid, ecstatic, and wanted to go in there and then and play it right through. I had to get back to London so with the little time available he insisted I go through a few of the *farruca* steps. There was no denying him so out I got on the main road and we both stood on this metal sheet, like a couple of roosters strutting and stamping away. We ended up twenty minutes later with some thirty or forty cars parked along the curb while we danced to a group of bewildered but amused spectators with me humming the tune and Finchie in his element with an audience who obviously recognized him. He was totally uninhibited and determined to get the footwork correct, and the remarkable thing was he needn't have bothered about his feet because his arms and hands were just right. What he was trying to dance was not important. He had the feeling and was beginning to look the part.

Three Australian actors, very old friends of Peter's, also confirm he felt restricted and in the wrong environment. One night a London millionaire, throwing a champagne party in Mayfair, wanted a few actors around to liven up the proceedings, and had invited them along. They decided that to liven things up even more they would drive up to Mill Hill and Boundary House in Totteridge Lane, collect Peter and take him along. 'We arrived at the front door,' said one, 'and it was opened by this Spanish geezer with the white jacket, so we thought, this isn't Finchie's style, what's all this? This was in the early 1960s and Finchie was really playing the establishment ponce. Everytime I used to ring him up, Yo would say, "Pete's in the bath!" "Oh, come off it, Yo," I said one day. "That's bloody ridiculous. Finchie never had a bath in his life when I knew him. They had to cut his bloody socks off him to give him his first bath in the army at Ingleburn. I was f—ing there! Don't tell me he's rehearsing for a bubble bath commercial! Finchie's a one-take man on the screen and this bath scene's been going on for bloody months! He's going to be so damned clean the world won't recognize him."

'So I told the boys and they said: "Ah, the bastard's indulging himself in a new respectable image, is he?" Anyway we waited at the door, and this Spanish valet who had opened the door went in and spoke to Finch and a Finch we didn't recognize said: "No way! No way!" and he slammed the door in our faces, so we were about to leave when Billy said: "No, let's go round the back." So we crept round the back of the house, and found some French windows, and there was Finchie sitting in there, you know, in all the splendour of this bloody "Olde English Manor", all alone and looking bloody miserable so we knocked on the window and he said: "Piss off! Out of it! Don't want to know you! Get out!" We knocked on the window again, but he wasn't going to have anything to do with us. So Billy started peeing up against the French windows and then Finchie jumped up and roared, "Piss off you lot, and if you must pee, do it in the garden." So then Vincent and I started watering his window, and Finchie finally said: "All right, you mugs. One bloody drink and then finish." We said: "Want to come to the party?" He said: "No. You can come in for one bloody drink, and that's it!" So we went in. It was a very strange atmosphere, because he was sort of standing aloof, all the time, you know? I thought, Strewth! What's this? Anyway, a large scotch, and I was sitting tentatively on the edge of the chair and, after a time, after two or three drinks, all this façade sort of fell away, and from being the English gentleman, he was suddenly the full blooded Australian bloody hooligan, relaxed and laughing again. "Now listen, you bunch of bastards, you've got to go soon!" And there we were telling yarns about the war, and there were more dead Japs and Germans lying about the floor of that living room than had ever seen action in the Second World War! We had a bloody marvellous night because underneath of course, Finchie hadn't changed at all. He always liked me to sing a song called "You Got to Have

Heart" and that night I had to sing this over and over and over again. He said: "That's a great song, Backstop (his nickname for me over the years), a great song." Anyway, it got to about four o'clock in the morning. Everyone was well pissed and he buggered off into the dyke (Australian for the lavatory), and stayed there, and after half an hour, we just packed ourselves up and left!'

Knowing Peter, he'd had enough and had gone to the lavatory with an attack of remorse. Also, in fairness to him, it's more than likely, judging by his very angry reaction, he may well have been quietly trying to get under the skin of a very English character. He'd go along with the boys for a while like Prince Hal in Shakespeare's *Henry IV*, but then would just disappear to regain his balance.

At Boundary House, Peter's constant companion in his moments of solitude was Ginger the cat. The cat talked to Peter and he told me when Ginger and I were introduced that Ginger had been an Egyptian in a past incarnation. But, of course, in the end, when Finchie fled from Boundary House, Ginger was given to Flavia and had to be put down.

When his marriage broke up Peter went straight from Boundary House to Flavia and Mother, and then into a series of three-monthly-let flats. They'd prepare a flat, make it clean and tidy, put flowers in it and know he was there content for a little while with the lady of the moment. Then there'd be a telephone call. 'I can't stand that bitch another moment. I'm coming home!' He just wanted to sit and drink and talk and feel that he belonged somewhere. Sometimes, he'd be present in a room full of people: Spanish dancers, film people – a reception – and Flavia would get the look from Peter and over he'd come. 'I'm off! I'm off! I've got to go, got to go.' 'We'd get him a taxi,' said Flavia, 'phone the current lady and tell her Finchie was being delivered. When Finchie got the urge to go off into the wide blue yonder, nothing on earth would hold him.'

Flavia and Peter used to have flaming rows. Flavia would champion the establishment and the masters, and Peter would get himself into a towering rage defending the underdog. Peter started off one night about the poor, the underprivileged, and the persecuted, and they battled away on race, economics, politics and class distinction. 'It's all your bloody fault,' Peter suddenly yelled at Flavia. 'You're the ones who put them in the cattle trucks, you sent them to Belsen.' To which Flavia replied: 'Well, you're just a poor little well-to-do socialist *manqué*, perpetually on the run.'

Off went the affronted Peter, up the stairs like a hare, packed his small bag and said: 'I'll never enter this bloody house again,' and was gone, off to sleep the night in his dressing room at Pinewood studios. Next morning, Flavia was cooking breakfast when in walked Peter. 'Oh you're back! Breakfast's ready.' 'Yes,' said Peter. 'Wasn't that a gorgeous row we had last night. What are we eating?'

'It's true what many people say,' Flavia recalls, 'there wasn't any real malice in Peter. He used to sit at Mum's feet for hours, begging in a way, for something he'd missed and Mother wouldn't admit it, how could she?'

When Flavia was working for Peter she took on the day-to-day letters, while all the official letters went through Olive Harding, and an agency dealt with the fan mail. But it was Olive who, when Peter bought a potato farm on Ibiza and decided to convert it to lemons, had to clear with Inland Revenue the legality of Peter's rooting away to his heart's content in his Ibizan orchard. The tax inspector was informed that he had bought the farm because he needed relaxation and, thanks to Olive, he allowed the claim. A letter arrived from Peter saying: 'We've dug up all the spuds and we've decided to plant citrus, and we're keeping hens. Will you please buy me a pump!' He sent Olive a diagram of a large hole lined with bricks and gave her the rough dimensions of an engine. 'What the hell does he think I am,' she thought as she pored over Finchie's blue prints for hours, utterly flummoxed as to which was right side up. Finally, she took the problem to a friend who was an engineer and on his advice bought a pump, posted it off, and Peter put it together down his hole. A year later, Finchie had got fed up with the farm and given the place to a local farmer, quite forgetting to tell Olive anything about it.

23 Recognition – of a kind

With *Robbery Under Arms* completed Peter played Alec Windom, in *Windom's Way*. This has been classed as one of his good reliable performances in a film with no outstanding merit. He plays a normal decent Englishman, running a hospital on an island in the Far East. He tries to do his best to mediate between the exploited natives and the government in a communist infiltrated village. The value of the film for Peter is that it shows his sincerity, subtlety, feeling and technique when cast in the type of dull role he was so often castigated for accepting on both sides of the Atlantic. Windom's situation again reflects scenes from Peter's own domestic pattern – his marriage to Lee Windom (Mary Ure), who loves him, is finished and he is in love with an Asian girl, Ana Vidal (Natasha Parry). His sudden ruthless inflexibility with Mary Ure when she tries to assert some possession over her husband, and other aspects of Alec Windom, like his pacifism and his romantic susceptibility to the Asian Ana, were very much a part of Peter's own character.

At the end of 1957, with *Robbery Under Arms* and *Windom's Way* completed for Rank, and neither film doing anything to advance his career, Peter received an offer from Hollywood through Fred Zinnemann. As Peter wasn't always first choice for many parts for which he may be remembered, I asked Fred Zinnemann why he had decided on Peter as first choice for Dr Fortunati in *The Nun's Story*. Said Zinnemann: 'I had seen Peter in *A Town Like Alice* and *The Shiralee*. I was deeply impressed. There was no question in my mind that he would be ideal to play the agnostic doctor opposite Audrey Hepburn. All of us involved felt he was a star in the true sense. So many people said to me in those days, "Why doesn't he get bigger parts?"'

I asked Zinnemann why Finchie hadn't had bigger successes at that stage in his career, and he replied: 'I feel, being based in England rather than America in those days, he didn't have the choice of subjects. So many of his subjects were rather second-rate. Also, he was a character actor as well as a leading man. In *The Nun's Story*, I felt he was marvellous. But it was a comparatively small part and it didn't propel him to the top. I think the mistake he made in his career was that he didn't choose his material carefully enough. I think Peter was more interested in being the remarkable character actor that he was. His pictures weren't good enough, the material wasn't always up to his standard, so people didn't always see him and he wasn't well enough known to overcome this obstacle.'

I then asked him if Peter was easy to work with on *The Nun's Story*. 'Yes, of course. He understood at once the conflict between spiritual and medical dedication. His character, as we evolved it, was a fanatic in terms of medical dedication. Dr Fortunati, working fifteen to twenty hours a day, was totally out of patience with a church that could cause interruptions during the course of an operation by asking Audrey Hepburn's character, Sister Luke, to show her spiritual dedication in taking Holy Communion. Both artists understood all the unspoken undertones that they had to reveal to give the scene its requisite dimension. As a doctor working round the clock, he could also convey the irrelevance of any form of emotional attachment or involvement to a man single-mindedly absorbed in his realm of medicine and surgery. There would be flickers of emotion when he came to see her in the tree house. But it was never allowed to mature. That was the concept that Peter and I finally agreed on.'

Peter told me that after *Nun's Story* he had always wanted to make another picture with Zinnemann, because he admired the precision with which he dealt with the problems of our existence that are fundamental and perennial. Zinnemann used to the utmost the mental, physical and spiritual resources of his artists. Once Peter started to get involved with the character of Dr Fortunati under Zinnemann's direction he found that Zinnemann demanded everything he had in him as regards thought and feeling, but that, once the director had established a sound rational structure, the feeling automatically became predominant.

'Peter had intuition, great intelligence, and always the true feeling his scenes required,' Zinnemann continued. 'Had there been the opportunity, I would have certainly worked with Peter again, because his was a rare gift. I had the very greatest respect for his work. He had as a man the depth for the kind of subjects I film.'

I asked him what made Peter unique. 'It was a kind of magic, which emanated from the screen. It has nothing to do with good or bad acting. Gary Cooper wasn't really an actor in the sense Peter Finch was, but Cooper had the magic. In the profession, we usually say, "The camera loves him, the camera loves her." Do you know what I mean?' I said I felt exactly what he had just described when I was a kid, paid my sixpence and first went to the 'flicks' on a Saturday afternoon. I think this is something we all know instinctively. 'I know in my own experience as a director I have had the good fortune to direct any number of good actors,' said Zinnemann. 'But, why is it you only *see* Cooper or Tracy, Bogart, Garbo or Finch? You can take even a baby and place it on the screen and for no apparent reason everyone will watch the baby though the baby doesn't even act. But that's a very long discussion in itself: What is screen acting?'

When the company arrived in the Congo to do the location work on *The Nun's Story*, Fred Zinnemann had advertised for Congolese to participate in the film, and they turned up in their hundreds. He finally ended up working with two tribes. The whole unit befriended them all, loved them and the atmosphere was one of tremendous gaiety and friendship. Finch and Peggy Ashcroft like most artists, were racially colour-blind. Both told me that the Belgians, who were not supposed to be racist, didn't really like it when the British artists chatted and wanted to sit and eat with the African men, women and their children. Relations between the Belgians and the British became frigid. This incensed Peter. He claimed, having been married the second time to a South African girl, that although it was not the same as South Africa, blacks at that time in the Congo had to have identity cards, and a sort of apartheid existed. They could not, for instance, rise above the level of clerks in a hotel job. At the end of the location filming, Peter told me Fred Zinnemann was invited to the chief's hut for a drink, and the chief had said: 'We thank you. You have treated us with dignity and respect. You have never called us *sales cochons* (dirty pigs).' When the crew flew out from Stanleyville (as it was called then, for the massacre didn't take place until the following year), all the tribes rushed on to the airfield and danced and went completely wild, and Peter recalled, 'I felt somehow that I belonged there.'

Dorothy Alison, the Australian actress who played the nun clubbed to death on the verandah in *The Nun's Story*, remembers Finchie's infatuation with a Belgian air hostess, 'who, equally infatuated, was coming in to Stanleyville practically every week to visit Finchie, and ostensibly for dental treatment. The film unit were highly amused at Audrey Hepburn's remark that "if she keeps up appearances at the present rate she'll be giving her Finchie a very gummy smile!" '

Peter told me he nearly lost his life with her one day. In her old tank of a Rover he'd suddenly been seized with passion as they were speeding along the main highway just outside Stanleyville. 'Like a bloody fool I started to kiss her while she was driving.' The girl, mesmerized by Peter, took her eyes off the road and they hit a very chunky milestone. 'We were very lucky not to swap teeth,' said Finchie.

Peter had made *The Nun's Story* for Warner Brothers while still under contract with Rank and they now cast him in a war suspense film, *Operation Amsterdam*. By now Peter was so disgusted at the quality of films being offered him that he gave his friend Tony Britton one of the big surprises of his career. Tony was invited to Pinewood and offered a choice of two parts in the film. The parts on offer were the two male leads: Jan Smit, a Dutch diamond expert who becomes involved in snatching millions of pounds worth of industrial diamonds in Amsterdam in 1940 to help the Allied war effort; and Major Dillon, the British officer who leads the coup. Tony chose Major Dillon. When Tony asked why he'd been given a choice, the director told him that Peter Finch would play the other part. 'What?' said Tony. 'You're giving me first choice and Peter is to play what I turn down? It doesn't make sense.' Tony afterwards found out that Finchie was feeling so bogged down in the wastes of mediocrity, he had said to Rank when they told him about the film and the choice of parts, 'I'll take either part, it's all the same to me. Ask Tony what he wants to play. Get the bloody film over and let me off the hook.' He'd been turning down scripts by the dozen and had to do something, so Michael McCarthy, directing, was in a position to give Tony his pick.

They spent five weeks in the high summer of 1958 shooting in Amsterdam itself. One day during what Tony describes as 'a dreadful dreary bit of filming. I'm standing on the pavement, and Finchie's driving up in the car and that's all it was. He had to go round and round the block. We did endless bloody takes on this and the car seemed to have to go a hell of a long way off and return by the canal. Each time it took hours to line the shot up, and no one could understand why. Finchie was taking longer and longer each time to appear in his car. Finally, as he crawled past me for the umpteenth time, he said: "I've just seen a girl down there, sport!" Oh yes, I thought, so that's why we seem to be taking all day. "Yes," said Finchie. "I just stopped to have a little yarn with her, and I made a date for later on. She's down there in a bubble car. She's parked just around the corner." Off he went round the block for another take. Half an hour later he cruises up to me again. "She's a professor of Greek and mathematics, sport!" and he disappears again.' That lady became known as The Prof and was a passing but genuine love while Finchie was on the film.

To add insult to injury the Rank Organization, who had pencilled Finchie's name in for top billing for their proposed half a million pound film *Ferry to Hong Kong*, changed their minds and the producers were told that Rank policy was to use bigger star names as an insurance for their budget money on the international market. Finchie's name was the first to be crossed off the original casting list, and producer George Maynard signed Curt Jurgens instead of Peter, and he and Orson Welles topped the bill. This made press headlines in the show business columns everywhere, and Peter knew it was one of those axe blows that starts the sap running out of the tree, so he decided straight away to counter this move by the Rank Organization by returning to the theatre in his first play for six years, *Two For The See-Saw*.

Two For The See-Saw did a week at Brighton and then opened at the Theatre Royal Haymarket on 17 December 1958. A thirty-year-old American unknown, Gerry Jedd, played the character of Gittel, which Anne Bancroft had created in New York, but the Broadway success lasted only four months in London. The girl's role had given Anne Bancroft her rise to stardom in New York, but the romantic comedy didn't appeal to London audiences. According to Peter, he and Gerry 'just didn't match up as a couple'. He felt he was being outclassed and outplayed, and several of his more honest friends agreed with him.

Arthur Penn, who directed the play, is emphatic that Peter's performance was an authentic gem and an acting triumph. His great regret was that Anne Bancroft could not come to London, as she and Peter would have made the perfect chemical combination. Peter told me that the four months run at the Haymarket was a nightmare for him. Gerry, knowing no one in

London, wanted to go out with Peter after the show every night and Peter used to take his shoes off to try and get out of the theatre without Gerry hearing him. Unluckily for Peter, scrubbed and spotless as the stairs and corridors of the Haymarket .re, they creak. So, night after night, the voice would echo, 'Peter, wait for me!'

Early in 1959, Robert Stevenson directed Peter as Alan Breck Stewart in his own adaptation of Robert Louis Stevenson's *Kidnapped* for Walt Disney. They were anxious to have a very virile flamboyant actor in the part, and Peter apparently was the instant first choice. He emerges as attractive to women as Errol Flynn, and quite obviously could have played this kind of part for the rest of his life if he had wanted to. It is one of the rare occasions on screen when Peter acts in rhetorical style; with the villainous crew after the ramming of the ship he is silky and dangerous. During the course of the film Rob Roy MacGregor's son challenges Alan Breck to a duel, but, instead of swords, they use bagpipes. When Peter first read the script he said, 'There's only one actor I know who could play that part *and* the fucking bagpipes!' – that's how Peter O'Toole got to play in the film. In one of Peter's most robust extrovert performances on the screen as Alan Breck, he is well matched by Peter O'Toole as the flamboyant Rob Roy MacGregor, even in the bagpipe duel, where both actors play in sardonic, begrudging admiration of one another's prowess. But it is in the scene with John Laurie as the wicked Uncle Ebenezer where Alan Breck lures him on to declare his part in the kidnapping of David Balfour, that Peter's technique as a theatre and radio actor shows in the variety and vocal range how an actor at his best can handle a long speech on the screen. Made eight months or so after *Operation Amsterdam* this performance shows the difference in Peter playing a role that he felt challenged and interested him. As Alan Breck he really jumps in and plays the Scottish hero with all stops out.

Finchie gave the whole film extra dimension and quality through the range of his performance, and it was one occasion when his theatre training really stood him in good stead. *Kidnapped* was shot on location in Scotland, and immediately afterwards Peter went to Hollywood to make *The Sins of Rachel Cade*. He and Yolande had just married and the honeymoon was to be spent in Hollywood. Their daughter, Samantha, was born the following spring.

Warner Brothers, obviously impressed by Henry Blanke as producer and Finchie as the agnostic doctor in *The Nun's Story*, decided immediately to repeat the pattern with another Henry Blanke production, this time starring Peter and Angie Dickinson. But *The Sins of Rachel Cade*, based on Charles Mercer's popular novel, was demolished by the critics. It was another disastrous case of Hollywood imitating its own success, and an ill-advised choice for Finchie who was rated by the American press as a 'convincing, low-pressure performer'. One critic said it set both careers back years, but Peter recouped immediately with two of his best films, *The Trials of Oscar Wilde* and *No Love For Johnnie*, both made in 1960. But before he began either of these films, and immediately he had returned from Hollywood Peter wrote and directed his only film, a twenty-six minute documentary called *The Day*, shot in Ibiza, about a little Spanish boy who goes from his village with his donkey and cart to the city to bring news of the birth of a child. The film won him the Venice Festival of Children's Films Award for 1961 and he was also a prize winner in the section of films for adolescents at the 1961 Cork Film Festival.

The Day shows Peter's visual flair for capturing the essence of Spanish peasant life and the Spanish *ambiente*. Everything is suggested, nothing is ever stated. Shot in black and white it is full of beautiful, comic touches: the little boy filling his hat with water to give his donkey a drink; his attempts to reach the large door-knocker, just out of reach because he is too small. The humour is completely Spanish, ironical, satirical and reveals Peter as a director capable of identifying as a Spaniard to bring out the childlike quality of his visual narrative. *The Day* tells you more about Finchie than any of his forty-odd film performances, because it **is** Peter.

Through writing and directing his little film, *The Day*, which he'd made with Yolande, he'd wanted to go into the more creative side of filming; writing and directing his own feature film. He wanted to make his own mistakes as a director in films, instead of other people's, and he decided in 1962 to go into production and film Derek Monsey's novel *The Hero*, about a British officer who escapes from a POW camp in Italy during the Second World War and falls in love with one of the partisan girls up in the hills. Ralph Peterson went to Italy with John Von Kotze who had photographed *The Day*, and Peterson did a film treatment. When Peter saw what the prohibitive costs of making a film about the Eighth Army would entail, the whole venture was abandoned.

In April 1960 work began on *Oscar Wilde*, which was to win him his second British Film Academy Award for the Best Actor of 1960 and the Moscow Film Festival Award for the Best Actor of 1961. Yvonne Mitchell, who played Oscar's wife, Constance, in *The Trials of Oscar Wilde*, remembers the sudden change in Peter as the part took him over. 'On the first two days of filming there was this acquaintance I'd known for a number of years as Peter Finch. On the third day, there arrived a man I didn't know, with heavy eyelids, and a droopy sort of face who was Oscar Wilde, and he remained Oscar Wilde from then onwards.

'Apparently he used to sit on Yolande's bed at night, reading poetry and weeping. He turned into a totally different man. The most interesting thing for me was, just before the film finished I invited him to come the following week to dine with us and with some other people. He arrived as Peter Finch and I felt so shy with him because for six weeks I had known a man who was Peter Wilde/Oscar Finch and I couldn't reconcile him with this new man who was arriving at my dinner party.'

Oscar Wilde was an extremely difficult part to cast because the producers had to find a star of reasonable magnitude as a box office draw who could look graceful and aesthetic, but not overtly effeminate or remotely camp. Wilde had a beautiful voice and, according to those who remembered him, had the manner and presence of a theatrical actor of his time. When the film was made, the attitude to homosexuality was by no means as liberal or tolerant as it was to become in the late 1960s.

Ken Hughes and Peter Finch, as director and star of a film, would be a most unlikely choice unless you knew the capabilities of both men. Hughes, a voluble cockney, and Finchie took to one another like the Corsican Brothers. Ken Hughes is lucid, intuitive, a marvellous writer with absolutely no intellectual pretentions. 'Finchie and I were on the same non-intellectualizing vibe,' said Ken Hughes. 'What I felt about Finch was that he would level out any suggestion of the camp faggot because he was basically heterosexual. We do know that Wilde was poetic, a man of great sensitivity, but I must say Finchie surprised me. His performance was more thoughtful, delicate and considered and more Wildean than I ever believed Finchie was capable of producing.' As for the swollen hands Peter seemed to acquire during filming, Ken Hughes felt they were not caused by the power of thought, but by copious bottles of champagne and a surfeit of potatoes which Peter adored and never normally ate. He was becoming visibly more bloated in appearance as time went on. 'Peter did all he could to get under the skin of his role. He'd wear his Victorian suit around the house to get the feel of where the pockets were and that sort of thing. All he said to me was, "Look, I've been on a diet. Obviously now I can come off it – drinking was included," and he put on I don't know how many pounds in a short time.'

There was originally only one Oscar Wilde film to be made, but there were two producers: Robert Goldstein, who had been with 20th Century-Fox, and Irving Allen, at that time head of Warwick Films. Goldstein brought the subject to Irving Allen, with one writer, and Irving Allen brought in Ken Hughes. There were interminable delays over delivery of the screenplay, and Goldstein and Allen started a feud which resulted in Goldstein setting up a film with Robert Morley as Wilde, and John Neville as Bosie, Lord Alfred Douglas.

'Goldstein,' said Hughes, 'stormed out of the Irving Allen office with a final salvo: "I'm going to make this f . . . ing movie, and I'm going to put you in the f . . . ing toilet!" So I turned to Irving and said, "Well, that's just great. Now we haven't got a writer. Who's going to write our f . . . ing movie?" "You've got a f . . . ing typewriter," Irving snapped! "You write it!" ' The heat was on and Ken Hughes wrote the script in a week, with a shuttle service of cars picking up the pages as they came off the typewriter. Meanwhile Irving Allen cast the film. 'The 'phone rang. It was Irving to know if I could leave the typewriter for an hour to go round and meet Peter Finch. I sat opposite Finch, who was absolutely charming, but I thought, this Finchie Aussie bushranger to play Oscar Wilde? No way, I thought, who's kidding who? But as far as Irving was concerned it was a *fait accompli*. He had made up his mind. He had that marvellous native tough Hollywood cunning of the 1940s. Morley on the Goldstein film was probably closer in appearance and a much more obvious choice for the role than Finch, added to which Morley had already played Wilde in the theatre. I feel we were lucky in that the chemistry by a fluke was right with Finch, and with John Fraser as Bosie. It just seemed to work, and you can't analyse that process. We shot in colour, which helped.'

Finch, as Wilde, turned out to be one of the subtlest decisions any casting producer could have made.

With both Oscar Wilde films shooting in the studios, the producers were racing to beat the clock to the finishing post to be first out for distribution. Warwick Flms, with Peter as their golden hope, had four spies on the other picture, four crowd extras who were on the other Wilde film but in Warwick's pay. These four were picking up two pay cheques, one from Robert Goldstein and one from Irving Allen. They'd report to Peter's studio as soon as they could get from one studio to the other in a fast car, bringing copies of schedules and daily reports. Peter told a hilarious story about Goldstein having hell's own job getting hansom cabs of the period. Finchie's company hired every hansom cab in the country, parked them out on the Elstree lot and left them there. They just sat there during the whole picture and never moved. Hughes told me they also gave Goldstein trouble over costumes. 'Our deal with the London costumiers, Berman's, was that they did not deal with Goldstein. We went to Nathan's the other London theatrical costumiers, and set up the same deal. The opposition finally wound up advertising in *The Stage* with an ad, something like "Wanted, crowd artists with costumes, two guineas a day".'

From the day they started shooting *The Trials of Oscar Wilde*, to the end of the sixth week, they had a married print with the music score on it, as Ron Goodwin was actually writing the music for scenes they hadn't even shot. He would go to Ken Hughes' home each evening and Hughes would act out the scene as it would subsequently be shot. Goodwin would time it with a stop watch and then off he'd go and write the music. Next day, Ken Hughes would shoot the scene. It would be a few feet out here and there, but it was eventually happily 'wangled' for the final print. I asked Hughes if he thought the film had artistic merit. 'An artistic film? Balls! By the last day of shooting, it was like the last fifteen seconds of the Grand National. The competitive frenzy had made us hysterical. We had to strike a set, union rules went to buggery. Pandemonium broke out. The entire unit moved like people during a bomb scare. Finchie raced around like a fart in a hurricane, all dressed up in his Wildean best and moving plants, lamps, and humping furniture.

He looked just like some elegant removal man from another age who'd suddenly got snarled up timewise. The scene in itself would have been well worth shooting as a debunk. I said to one man, "You're a carpenter. What are you doing moving the camera?" "Don't fuck about," was the reply I got. "Do we finish this picture on time or don't we? We've got a winner here. Who wants to spoil it?"'

That was on the Friday night, the last day's shooting in the studios at Elstree. On the Saturday, Ken Hughes had one shot to do with Finch as Wilde walking along the beach at Brighton. That was the final shot scheduled for the picture. Friday lunch-time, the crew went to Ken and told him the camera gear and equipment were going off to Brighton. 'What do you need here to finish the interiors this afternoon?' they asked. 'Nothing,' said Ken Hughes. 'Take all the stuff to Brighton.' So they packed up the camera dolly, the mobile four-wheeled flat truck on which a camera is able to track, and away it went to Brighton. That afternoon they were scheduled to do a tracking shot in the studio.

'Right,' said Ken. 'While the lighting boys are working on this one, get the dolly!'

'Sir,' came a feeble voice. 'The dolly's gone to Brighton.'

'A-A-A-A-A-Ah! Christ!' An hour and a half to go and Oscar Wilde buggered for lack of a dolly!

'Well,' said Finchie, 'what price art?'

'I'm not trying to be arty, mate,' Hughes snapped. 'I've got to track on this shot, I've absolutely got to!'

Finchie, sitting on a piece of the set, suddenly looked down. 'Isn't this f . . . ing thing on wheels?'

'Got it,' said Ken, 'We'll track the bloody set.' And that is just what they did. Ken Hughes yelled for everyone to help and electricians, seldom seen during shooting, came crowding down off the grid and rails, sliding down poles. Fifty people altogether. 'This is my last great tracking shot. The whole thing wobbled a bit, and if Finchie hadn't moved you so much that you couldn't take a detached look, you'd notice it. When I gave the order to cut, Peter fell on the floor rolling with laughter, the tears pouring down his face.'

Immediately he'd finished *Oscar Wilde*, Peter started work, in August 1960, on *No Love For Johnnie*. It was one of the most successful British films Peter made and his portrayal of the shallow but brilliant Labour politician Johnnie Byrne won him the 1961 British Film Academy Award, in addition to the Silver Bear Award at the Berlin Festival that year for the best actor.

The film is based on the autobiographical novel by Wilfred Fienburgh an MP for one of the Leeds constituencies. He was killed in 1958, after his car hit a lamp post, leaving a widow and four children. The book ripped the lid off English politics in the 1950s and Ralph Thomas, who directed the film, knew in casting Finch he was giving him a very difficult challenge. 'Finchie,' he said, 'had to hit this dimension of shallowness as written in the screenplay of a vain, weak, verbose man caught up in the trimmings rather than the issues. By 1960 when we made the picture I found Finchie was a very ambivalent man politically, and the film itself hadn't got vast depth. Fienburgh was a marvellous man in his way but in no way like Peter basically. Yet I felt that Peter managed to get everything that existed in that man on to the screen, without ever having known him. People who knew Fienburgh really well identified Peter absolutely with the character.'

Ralph Thomas found Peter impeccably punctual, and although under great domestic stress at the time he was never difficult or in any way unreliable. 'He was marvellous with a lot of the young actors with little experience. He'd take them off and rehearse with them endlessly until they were perfect, and he was most unselfish in his performance. Unlike many actors he was genuinely interested in other people. Like Trevor Howard, Peter had a way in which he may have appeared to be a hell raiser, but he wasn't at all; that was simply an act, a part of his self defence. Peter, a man who lived completely in his imagination preferred to travel rather than to arrive.'

Billie Whitelaw who played the girl friend, adored Peter. The instant they met and began to film the chemical reaction was there. In this instance it was a case of both artists being in many ways tremendously alike: both physically very attractive, imaginative, sensitive, and Billie with the same ability as Peter to play a scene and get it right first time. But although there was an instant and dynamic physical attraction, Whitelaw realized that things had to remain very stable, and that it would be fatal if either of them started rocking the matrimonial boat. Peter found her irresistible but the relationship remained platonic. It had to, as Finchie, married one year with a three-month-old daughter, was already heading for stormy waters. Both Billie and Peter detested confrontations and rows. 'I think Finchie was one of the most compassionate men I ever met. Our intense friendship began the second we met and continued on the set of the picture. It was an absolutely exhilarating and shattering experience because, like so many of the truly great experiences of life and particularly of childhood, they remain in the mind and imagination. Peter and Samuel Beckett are for me the two men with more compassion than any I have met, and where does one go from there?

'Peter and I both worked in exactly the same way. When he had to cry, he really cried, but everything was controlled. He always used emotion, and never let it use him. He would say to Ralph Thomas, "I can't do that again, not like that," and there was never any need.'

'One morning,' Billie told me, 'we came onto the set to shoot a scene together in which Finchie had to break down. The bell clanged and the camera rolled on the first take. We had a quick run-through and Peter said "Come on, let's do it." I said okay. He did it and I remember it was perfection. He broke down and sobbed bitterly. It was our scene where the girl says, "I've had enough. I feel I'm being used," and he says, "Oh, for Christ's sake . . ." That was the gist of it. Finchie doing the splits between this girl and his career was just caught there! He turned to Ralph Thomas and said, "That's it! You won't get that again. It'll be a reproduction next time." Thomas returned, "We don't need the reproduction, Peter. We've got a perfectly acceptable original." When Billie saw *Network* she kept saying, 'I bet you only did that take once, Finchie.'

During the filming of *No Love for Johnnie* Peter would receive phone calls from home, at eight thirty in the morning, haranguing him for his 'impossible behaviour' and Peter would be desperate. 'I've got to go! I've got to go!' Billie could hear his anguish through the walls of her dressing room. 'Don't you understand I'm on the set in a few minutes?' Peter absolutely exasperated Yo with his drunkenness and infidelities and he claimed she wore him out with her materialistic shallowness. Theirs was a very physical relationship that both were trying to make work as a marriage.

Peter told me subsequently that after his marriage to Yolande had broken up and he was missing his kids, Samantha and Charles, he'd had one of his lunches that had been mainly 'grape' and plucked up Dutch courage to ignore all the hideous legal taboos on custody, had rushed off in a trance, banged on his door, rushed into the house and demanded to see the kids he was paying thousands of pounds to maintain, and never saw – tax, alimony and a demonic restlessness had sent him making films all over the world. He admitted he had behaved like a demented lunatic, and Yolande was disgusted that the only way he could cope with an impasse for which both were equally responsible was in a state of drunken hysteria.

Peter said he felt he couldn't cope with 'my own deeply primitive limitations as human being. A sense of freedom and liberty is necessary to me like some awful suffocating urge.' (Society understands that some are diabetic and must have insulin.) Peter in a moment of private domestic bitterness once called Yolande 'a professional divorcee'. Yolande was coping with Pete's reaction but getting trapped in her way to get the barb in his Achilles heel. If Pete had fought and fought, he could have had more access to his two children by Yolande.

Films, and the euphoric sense of the here and now the film ambience gives to those lucky enough to be on its trip, act as a palliative. Pete could for a while become remote from the agonies of reality and lose himself – in the way that money from films, if he was out of England, enabled him to do. Always, for a while, he could go footloose and fancy free.

Yet early on, when the marriage was young and his children were being born, Finchie was crazy about Yolande, as Ken Hughes testifies. 'When we were making *Oscar Wilde*, Yolande had become pregnant with Samantha. We'd all be talking and drinking and this besotted romantic would suddenly, with no warning at all, yell out: "Jesus, I love this woman. I've just got to tell you fellows, I love her!" He'd put his head down and listen to her stomach and say, "We're going to have the most beautiful baby in the world," and when the baby was born he was just bananas! He'd go peering into the cot like a mad witch-doctor; one look at the sleeping curled-up tiny creature and he went into a sort of performance somewhere between a whirling dervish and a baboon dancing a fandango, letting out mad primitive ecstatic cries! He was like a little boy gone crazy with delight over something Santa Claus had given him. We'd watch Yolande's face, just a smile that gave nothing away, she didn't seem to know how to handle this exuberant craving to express his pride and joy, or maybe in her own way she did know, but it certainly went dead later.'

Film director Andrew Stone, now living in retirement in Hollywood, knew Peter when he was making *In The Cool Of The Day* (1962) at MGM Elstree with Jane Fonda and Angela Lansbury, and remembers Finchie being equally anxious about his second child. Stone was a frequent visitor to Boundary House at Mill Hill when Yolande and Peter were entertaining in the style expected of Peter as one of Britain's best film actors. He recalls Yolande greeting him when he arrived at their dinner parties with a thick French accent. Expecting their second child she was well overdue but soon presented Peter with what turned out to be his only son Charles.

Stone recollects: 'I've never seen a man go so insane, because he was so worried about her. Unaware of anyone he'd hop round the place doing a sort of slow, agonized tango, arms lightly crossed over his belly like a man craving for the john! He loved Yolande and was worried sick that nature didn't seem to be responding to her plight in the natural way. Pete seemed to go off balance when the natural laws didn't go right. I could never ever figure Peter out because the rest of the time I'd be in his house he'd think nothing of sitting with another woman on his lap, loving her up in front of Yolande. What amazed me was that Yolande seemed to take it all in her stride. I never stayed very late so I don't know what went on after I left. But he'd be sitting there fondling some pretty girl, and the next day you'd see him beside himself with anxiety over what seemed to be the only woman ever possible in his life. I was very fond of them both but they were totally unpredictable. He certainly wasn't drunk on the set at MGM, at least I never saw him drunk, but we shared the same MGM hired chauffeur, Paddy, and he told me, six months later, he'd often drive Pete home dead drunk at four in the morning after he'd been having a wild flaming night with some beautiful coloured girl.'

Stone feels tremendous sympathy for Yolande who, night after night, would receive the recumbent Peter from the arms of Paddy the chauffeur, stoned out of his mind. 'He'd depart for filming at six o'clock one morning, and perhaps not return for several days. The big dinner parties, the elegance necessary to show status in the film business, the role of the English squire, were all a part of

Peter's existence at the time. Guests were always made to feel very welcome and they both seemed very free and easy.'

Ken Hughes recalls another night, when a party all went out to a London night club, the Don Juan. 'We were having a wonderfull evening. No one was drunk. We'd only been there a couple of hours. We'd just come back from Moscow where Peter had been given an award for the best actor in *Oscar Wilde* and we were talking about it, flushed with a feeling of triumph and a real sense of occasion. I watched Yolande feeling more and more uptight because nobody was talking to her. Suddenly she said: "Well, I am rather bored with hearing about Moscow, in fact I'm bored with the whole thing, and I think we're leaving." One or two people said, "Oh come on Yo, the night's young, only ten o'clock, the cabaret hasn't started yet." "I don't give a damn about that. I'm leaving." She got up and walked out, but Finch, instead of saying as you would expect, the hell with her, let her leave (which would be my attitude), then started the instant panic. He was beside himself to get out of the place and get to Yolande as fast as he could. "Must get the bill, pay the cheque." He'd have signed away all his money just to get out at once. Money was no object! He was picking up tabs all over the place, and before any of us could reach for our wallets, he said: "It's done! It's done!"'

That Peter wasn't just foolishly generous with money, but irresponsibly wasteful is borne out by Australian actress Gwen Plumb who knew Peter when he came out of the army and for many years afterwards. 'He had no conception of money,' she told me, 'never knew what he had in his pocket.'

In the autumn of 1960 came the longed for opportunity to acquire international status: 20th Century-Fox were setting up the multi-million-dollar *Cleopatra* with Elizabeth Taylor and the producer, Walter Wanger, contracted Peter to play Caesar with Stephen Boyd playing Antony. The film began shooting in England with Rouben Mamoulian as director, but he was soon replaced by Joseph L. Mankiewicz. Major rewrites were begun on the screenplay and then in October Elizabeth Taylor contracted a near fatal illness. She was given a tracheotomy which meant a rearrangement of the shooting schedule. Peter was called every day to walk up and down a gangplank with however many centurions there were. The film dragged on and on, then one day Olive Harding was summoned urgently to his house. When she arrived, the sitting room was absolutely bare except for one chair with wooden arms and a straight back. Peter was sitting in it, rigid. She walked over to him and said, 'Hullo, Pete,' and tried to kiss him. He wasn't even aware of her, he had become Julius Caesar. He had played the Roman emperor too long and was on the verge of a nervous breakdown. Olive got him into a nursing home for a fortnight, after which he took Yolande, Samantha and Nanny away on holiday and early in 1961, they went by boat to Jamaica, Finchie's first visit to the island.

When work on *Cleopatra* started again, Peter wasn't offered the part because 20th Century-Fox didn't consider him a big enough box office name and replaced him with Rex Harrison, while Richard Burton took over from Stephen Boyd. By that time Peter was glad to be out of it, but there quickly followed another setback when he failed to get the distributors' approval for the major role in *Cromwell*. The script for the film *Cromwell* was written seven months after *Oscar Wilde* was completed, and was then ready to shoot. 'We went to the major distributors at that time with the finished screenplay,' said Ken Hughes, 'and Peter Finch as a proposition to play Cromwell. But no distributor wanted to know about Peter, even though *Oscar Wilde* had received a British Motion Picture Award. But remember, we made *Wilde* for $350,000 and *Cromwell*, to begin with, was a $6,000,000 movie.'

Altogether, between the finish of *No Love For Johnnie* and the start of his next film, *Girl with Green Eyes*, in 1963, was a bad time for Peter with only a few radio interviews and a poetry reading, and it was impatience to work again that drove him into accepting two films which both proved unhappy choices. Both were made at MGM Elstree in England on location abroad: *I Thank A Fool* (1961), with Susan Hayward and Diane Cilento, shot mainly in southern Ireland, followed by *In The Cool Of The Day*, with Jane Fonda, in the summer of 1962 with its locations in Greece.

In *I Thank A Fool*, Finchie described the location period as, 'a term of purgatory in the anal wastes of Ireland,' and the studio shooting as 'an endless sequence of "OOPS, wrong side" whenever I tried to kiss Susan Hayward. I always seemed to land on the never-never side of her face. I had a scene with her on a bed. She said, "You can't kiss me there, you won't be seen." We had to move the door round to the other side of the set. When I read the reviews I realized we needn't have bothered.'

In *In The Cool Of The Day* (1962), Peter plays an English book publisher, Murray Logan, matrimonially manacled to, and tormented by, the scarred, embittered Sybil Logan (Angela Lansbury), who holds him responsible for her accidental disfigurement and the death of their child. Arthur Hill, as Finchie's New York colleague Sam Bonner, is married to Jane Fonda who is dying of a lung complaint. Angela, Jane and Peter go off to Greece (Hill can't get away). Angela runs off with a travelling salesman; Jane Fonda, who had been unable to make love with her publisher husband, succeeds with Murray Logan but expires a few days later in an oxygen tent. Peter's comment on *In The Cool Of The Day* was: 'Jane Fonda, looking like Cleopatra in modern dress, and I, in a situation that could have been Greek tragedy but turned out to be Greek travelogue, were photographed against practically every ancient Greek relic known to school kids: the Parthenon, Delphi, Mount Olympus, dancing the hassapiko (Greek flamenco) on a ferry, and unsuccessfully trying to find a secluded spot, like orphans in a storm, to embrace.'

Peter's American press left him in no doubt that the Hollywood-backed films he was making were giving him no opportunity to show his true quality and if you read through the list of films Peter did, you could well ask why he ever bothered to make many of them. As Olive Harding pointed out, 'no one ever forced him'. But the chaos of his domestic life plus divorce from Yolande which came in 1965 kept him on the move in every sense.

Olive also explained Peter's avoidance of television work: 'I remember the first time I had a television job for him, and I rang him up. It was a very good part, but he said: "No! No television!" and I said: "Peter, don't be silly. Everybody is doing television. It's wonderful! And they're paying good money now. I can get you really good money." He said: "I'm not doing it. I'm not doing it, Olive, because the moment I think about television I've got this dark thing inside me. A sort of dread, a foreboding." That was years ago. He appeared in the television version of a play he had done in the theatre, *Captain Carvallo*, but that was different.'

24 Peter! Peter! Pumpkin eater...

In the spring of 1963, producer Tony Richardson offered Peter the part of Eugene Gaillard, the observant, introverted philosophical middle-aged author, who allows himself to be drawn into a love affair with a very much younger Irish girl, played by Rita Tushingham, in the screen version of Edna O'Brien's *Girl With Green Eyes*. The modest film, superbly cast, produced, directed and acted, turned out to be a triumph for Peter. The American press liked it, too, and Judith Crist, reviewing it in New York, wrote: '*Girl With Green Eyes* is a gem, flawless, brilliant and beautiful. Finch plays Eugene Gaillard, a writer, a solitary sophisticate who is the stuff of schoolgirls' dreams. Peter Finch is excellent as Eugene, the glint of self-knowledge never absent from his eye, the air of adult detachment fading before the child's assault on his sensitivities, but never quite disappearing . . .'

Of all Finchie's leading ladies, he thought the most truly childlike was Rita Tushingham. While they were filming in Dublin, they used to go together to the zoo when they had time off. Both were fascinated by the balletic grace of the hippo, and they'd spend hours watching the monkeys. Finchie believed: 'You learn a great deal about yourself by watching the uninhibited behaviour of the monkeys doing many of the things human beings are too well behaved to do in public.' One day he'd be watching a monkey with a piece of glass in the Dublin Zoo and the next he'd be doing an improvisation of the monkey examining the piece of glass, and trying to see into its earhole and various orifices.

'During one scene we had together,' Rita recalls, 'he sensed I was nervous and inexperienced, and he was able somehow to envelop me in his own concentration. He gave me confidence; I think it was about my fourth film. Suddenly, at the end of a take, he'd break the tension and make me laugh. The story of the film is sad and genuinely romantic, and yet during the making of it with Peter, I was so full of laughter and did crazy antics. There was always laughter on the set of *Girl with Green Eyes*. In the scene where he says: "With this ring I thee bed and board," and we go into this hotel and ask for champagne and they had to do a closeup of Peter's hand holding the champagne glass, he started laughing so much he got the shakes and Desmond Davis asked Pete ever so politely if he couldn't keep his hand steady, but he just couldn't. He was so utterly different as a man to the withdrawn, sullen, rather selfish man that he was playing.

'You could be one of Peter's greatest friends for years and years, then suddenly, one morning, he'd be gone and you'd never hear from him. I mean we were the best and closest of friends, but he was as strange as he was wonderful, quite suddenly he'd be off and out of your life completely and then suddenly you'd meet him and he'd be just the same warm funny old Finchie, as though he'd never been off in that remote part of the world leading a totally different life with different people of different race. He had an amazingly compartmentalized life as a man in search of liberty.

'I remember a spine chilling sensation watching him, because when the camera turned the whole character of the man he was portraying was there. It all seemed to materialize and integrate into the instantly recognizable person Edna O'Brien had created. Peter as an actor reminds me of a writer in that he drew so much from a very close observation of all aspects of life. Peter had eyes everywhere and I could sense that experiences from his life welled up in him and he was suddenly able to hold them and use them.'

I knew what Rita meant because I'd seen Peter in action myself, assuming a role, changing before my eyes. On one memorable occasion it happened just after I'd decided to get married. As we tottered out of a bistro in the Kings Road, Finchie wanted to buy a paper. The news vendor on the corner turned out to be a friend from the Old Swan drinking and boating days at Battersea. 'Hey, Finchie, like to hold on to these?' he asked, thrusting a pile of *Evening Standards* under Peter's arm. 'I'm busting for a pee and a quick jar.' Peter very good-naturedly took the papers. I thought it was too good to miss and moved off to watch the fun. Off came Finchie's tie, his shirt was opened at the neck, and he cadged a cigarette off the amazed customer who bought his first paper. In a few seconds the face became loose and his expression just a shade moronic. He tousled his hair and he was a newspaper seller. Along came the customers and I wished I'd been armed with a camera for there were several classic double takes. One woman walked about fifteen yards before the penny dropped. She froze, and turned back to walk past Peter, ostensibly reading her paper but really to get a quick look.

Peter O'Toole recalls a truly Irish experience with Finchie which occurred while Peter was making *Girl with Green Eyes*. 'When Finchie was on location in Dublin, we were refused a drink at the bar one night, because they said it was too late. This bar was about seven or eight miles outside Dublin at Bray, and I think we both had our collars turned up at that time, whenever it was. Because it was too late to be served a drink, we decided the only way to get one was to buy the bar; so we wrote out a cheque for it on the spot. But the barman found Finchie and I so inept as bartenders that he was only too happy to give up his role as a customer, and serve us drinks. The following morning we realized what we'd done, went to the pub, and the barman very sweetly hadn't cashed the cheque. We became great friends from then on, but alas he died, and his wife invited Finchie and I to the funeral. Try to visualize this: Finchie and I kneeling at a graveside outside Dublin, the coffin being lowered gently down into its final resting place, both of us sobbing copiously and noisily. In the middle of this paroxysm of grief, Finchie turned away unable any longer to look at the box containing our departed friend. I caught his look of total amazement and followed his gaze. We were at the wrong funeral – our man was being buried a hundred yards away! The grief was there, but the object of our emotion had gone disastrously astray. I can't tell you why but that little memory will always symbolize Finchie for me. He was an extraordinarily eccentric gentleman in the true sense of the word, and I was very fond of him.'

In September Peter began work on *The Pumpkin Eater* for Paramount with Anne Bancroft. The director Jack Clayton had just seen him in *The Nun's Story* and felt that with his sensitivity he would be ideal casting in the Harold Pinter screenplay of Penelope Mortimer's novel. Peter had to register as the self-effacing husband, Jake, spending a good deal of his screen time conveying what he was thinking and feeling rather than what he was saying. Jack Clayton says that Finchie achieved the virtually impossible task of matching Anne Bancroft in both performance and 'size' on the screen: 'I don't believe that Peter by any means reached the extraordinary peak of his talent before his death. He had so much to give that was so diverse and I only wish that I could have worked with him again.' For Jack Clayton the variety and subtlety of the performances his two stars gave him were like a marvellous cocktail, and one of his most enjoyable experiences as a director.

While working on *The Pumpkin Eater*, Peter was asked to fill an impromptu role in another film. The producer of the film, *First Men In The Moon*, had cast William Rushton in the part of a process server, but Rushton was standing as a Labour candidate in some constituency in Scotland and was busy doing the hustings up north of the border. Rushton was due to arrive from Scotland that morning, play his scene and return to his politics as soon as he'd finished it. They lined up the shot but there was no sign of Rushton, so general panic set in. Lionel Jeffries, who had played the Marquis of Queensberry to Peter's Oscar Wilde and was also in the film, said: 'Finchie's next door shooting *The Pumpkin Eater* for Jack Clayton. Why don't we get him to come and play the scene? It will only take a minute or two and I'll direct it.'

Meanwhile, a telegram had arrived from Rushton to say he'd be delayed. The problem was to find Finchie. Though not actually called he was in the studios sleeping off the effects of a previous very heavy night's boozing. They eventually found him in an alcoholic slumber in one of the old houses at Shepperton Studios which were then being used as dressing rooms. Lionel told him they were in trouble and asked would he volunteer to help them out and play the process server. Finchie, still very high, said: 'Yes, I'll do it, and you can send me a crate of champagne – the rest of my fee can go to Oxfam,' and off he went with a night's growth of beard as he'd slept where he dropped the previous evening. They gave him the script, which, of course, he couldn't learn as, he said, 'I was in no state even to recite the Lord's Prayer.' Eventually, he tottered in front of the camera, played the scene, and Lionel took over from director Nathan Juran and did the necessary pick-up shot close-up and that was it! Finchie departed to resume his interrupted snooze, and a few minutes later Rushton arrived to be told his understudy had played the scene and he wouldn't be needed.

Peter in a bowler hat, bifocals, and with a loose denture that makes him very sibilant, gives one of the off-the-cuff characterizations at which he excelled. It's a cameo – a part obviously tailor-made for William Rushton, which Finchie just turned into his own. Luckily you never see his eyes! Like *The Wooden Horse* it's a one-take, one-shot sequence.

In February 1964, Peter was booked by the BBC Home Service to play Antony opposite Peggy Ashcroft, in Shakespeare's *Antony and Cleopatra*. R. D. Smith, who directed the play, remembers Peter's Antony as flat, unprepared and terribly rushed, as though he couldn't wait to be shot of a project he had not allowed himself enough time or thought to do. Peter felt he knew the character from his previous preparation, but when he started to work on it, he found he had left no time for the enormous work it needed. He said the experience of those four days was like trying to climb Everest with not enough equipment or oxygen.

His private life at the time was chaotic. He was drinking heavily, and admitted he was under dreadful strain. I heard the programme at home and knowing that Peter was capable of making Antony into something memorable, about half-way through I switched off. All the magic had gone.

Next, Tony Richardson cast him as Trigorin opposite Peggy Ashcroft as Madame Arkadina, in Chekhov's *The Seagull* – it was to be Peter's last stage appearance. The play opened at the Queen's Theatre in London on 12 March 1964. Rehearsals varied from days of argument and discord with Tony Richardson determined to weld together a cast of individual stars, to days when they all worked harmoniously together to try and capture the elusive spirit of Chekhov. 'The atmosphere,' said Peter, 'was barometric. Sometimes without any storm warning we'd be in the middle of a hurricane and the next moment, flat, dead calm, peace, harmony, and we'd move forward.'

Dame Peggy, and others I've spoken to, all agree that with Peter there was never any argument because he just seemed so immersed in what he was doing, and if the air needed clearing he'd make people laugh. The cast's impression of Peter was of an unshowy, unstarry, unselfish man, loving the play, the character he was playing, and giving himself completely to the performance and the atmosphere they were all creating. Dame Peggy said: 'If you had seen the performance on film, it would have been totally superb. But for some reason, I think that Peter had become so used to the camera that he didn't sense the need to project himself as he should. A lot of people raved about Peter as

Trigorin, but I would guess they were people who were sitting pretty near, and many others were disappointed, though there was nothing disappointing in his interpretation. It was only lacking in the amount of energy he used.' My impression watching from row K was: why is Peter's performance so insipid? He's like a painter working in water colours instead of oils.

Vanessa Redgrave, as Nina, found Peter very easy to work with. 'Peter was tremendously flexible. By that I mean he wasn't frightened to take any measures to keep his performance alive and true. He didn't believe that nothing must alter, even fractionally. Tony Richardson had said to us both, once we had rehearsed and set our scenes: "You can both do and move anywhere you like within the framework of what we've done. I don't care where you move." In fact, Peter and I virtually changed our moves every night in performance. Everything we did, we did in order not to get stuck, trying to produce some effect that we knew might work very well. What we were both after was the content of the scene. We always tried to keep the mood between Trigorin and Nina absolutely alive with that feeling of unpredictability. We were both in accord. I've never met another actor who was happy to take that risk. Peter knew exactly what he was doing. He left nothing to chance and I had to try and match him. I didn't know him very well but when you work with someone at that pitch of concentration, you get to know them instinctively, even if the friendship doesn't continue when the play is over. We used to alter the positions of where we would make our entrances. Peter would say: "Tonight I'll be coming on from such and such a place," and we'd play the famous scene between Trigorin and Nina not only using different inflections but from different sides of the stage, with different moves, and we always felt totally at ease with each other. For most actors it would be like working on a trapeze without a safety net, but he had such concentration and power of thought that he found it perfectly natural.'

Peter McEnery, who played Constantin, felt that drink and coming from working exclusively in front of a camera, had blunted Peter's judgment and timing and that he had lost the strength and stamina to sustain such a difficult role in the theatre.

Sir John Gielgud, who played Trigorin to Edith Evans' Arkadina with Peggy Ashcroft as Nina at the New Theatre in 1936 (in a production translated, directed and designed by

Komisarjevsky) describes Trigorin as, 'a thankless part. Very difficult to play because I found him like a chocolate éclair, rather soft and creamy inside. Poor Peter! I can imagine he had difficulties. Trigorin is also a bit of a gigolo and those weak, spongy characters are always impossibly difficult to play. I saw the performance, but I don't remember much about it. I think at the time I felt he had been in the cinema too long. The whole production seemed very hastily got together. It was a company that didn't know each other very well, which isn't good for Chekhov.'

Tony Richardson believes there was a reason for Peter's quiet, untheatrically projected characterization of Trigorin. 'He started off as a very extrovert character in the early 1950s. He was greatly influenced by Olivier and I feel Larry pushed him, perhaps unwittingly, into being a kind of very technical, showy actor, which was alien to Peter's nature. He used to come and watch Finch's Trigorin, and he told me it was the most fantastic acting, the kind of acting he would like to be able to do. They are perfect opposites: Olivier, who approaches his characters brilliantly from the exterior, and Finch who always worked from within. I think Peter in his wild days tried to be the Olivier style of actor with Mercutio, Iago and so on, and wasn't satisfied. That was principally why he gave up acting on the stage. Also there were very few opportunities for him, especially in the British situation, to play that kind of role. As an actor he got right into the heart of Chekhov's writing. He instinctively understood the background and had an empathy with Chekhov's world. He could play Chekhov much more truly than an English actor because of his natural European temperament. He was very like a Moscow Arts Theatre actor. Nothing was ever hit or miss during rehearsals. He was a perfect craftsman reminding me of a miniaturist – he worked with impeccable skill and he held his performance. It never fell away. He had no problems building the character of Trigorin; it was all there. He scarcely needed me as a director in rehearsal; he had it all perfectly thought out from the word go. I felt he was someone who paid a great price for acting, because by being so true, his kind of acting imposed an enormous strain.'

Tony Richardson never once saw Peter drunk. He was totally absorbed, thrilled to be playing Chekhov with such a distinguished cast and was completely dedicated. 'Peter was all of a piece. He had periods of great quietness as he had periods of flamboyant elation. Perhaps he was the kind of man one would call a manic depressive but in our professional association he was perfectly contained. The problem with the performance of the subtlety and style he gave as Eugene Gaillard in *Girl With Green Eyes* and again in *The Seagull* is that they don't really project and are better seen on film.'

By the time *The Seagull* closed in June, Peter's marriage to Yolande had become a nightmare, and he knew a break-up was inevitable. In the throes of his love affair with Shirley Bassey, he was now ready to shut the door on Boundary House and domesticity in London's suburbia. Yolande and the children were holidaying in Porto Santo Stefano in Italy and when Yo got wind of the Bassey affair, through a visit by press reporters, she challenged Peter who admitted the truth. Yolande took an overdose of sleeping pills. The Italian doctors had to give her heart injections and it was thanks to good nursing by the Italian nuns that her life was saved. Finchie himself admitted to me: 'Unbeknown to us we were followed by those gents in the bowler hats, and were actually caught in *flagrante delicto*.'

In the full frenzy of this double divorce, Peter began work on *Judith* that was to prove a very happy escape from all the adverse publicity his love life was bringing him. When the film began shooting Peter felt he had reached the nadir in his personal life. First of all he read in the papers that the break up of his marriage with Yolande was public knowledge, for that he was at least prepared. The following day he received a telegram saying that Shirley Bassey's husband Kenneth Hume had cited him as a co-respondent, along with John Patrick McAuliffe, in a divorce action. Then Shirley flew out to Israel to tell him the romance was over. He told me shortly after: 'I'm raw nerve ends, I feel like those bones you see in the desert or on tropical beaches, absolutely bleached. There's no protection, and it's all my own bloody fault. At forty-seven I seem to have learnt nothing.' The performance as Aaron Stein in *Judith* is one of the most emotionally contained he ever gave.

Although *Judith*, shot in Israel around Haifa, wasn't an American picture it was distributed by Paramount. Finchie played the character of Aaron Stein, Kibbutz leader active in the Haganah – the Jewish anti-British underground in 1947.

Finchie adored his leading lady Sophia Loren and respected

her. 'She is not a woman you ever make a pass at if you happen to be alone with her,' he once warned a colleague. 'She is one of those marvellous natural creations you feast your eyes on and leave it at that. One of the reasons she was so easy to work with is that her whole attitude is professional with no emotional undertow to drag you off course, and what a sense of humour!' (In Paris some time later, in an Italian restaurant, he saw a familiar face, secretive and alone, behind a mountain of spaghetti. 'Sophia,' gasped the amazed Finchie. 'All right,' she said, 'you caught me, but I'm eating out of 2,000 years of Neapolitan poverty.')

When I asked Sophia about the Peter she remembered, her answer was the briefest of all, but it came right from the heart. 'One of the gentlest, kindest and most talented partners it has ever been my luck to work with. I know these may be the conventional words you speak in such circumstances, but they are true . . .'

James Bacon's paper, the *Los Angeles Herald Examiner*, sent him to interview Peter, who was staying at the Blue Dolphin Hotel, right on the Mediterranean at Nahariya just north of Haifa. Bacon's driver, Paul, who had picked him up at Tel Aviv, told him that Mr Finch was waiting for him in the bar. They hadn't seen each other for ten years and James arrived at seven to be greeted by Peter: 'I'm on the wine wagon, only wine these days. Carmel wine, the local Israeli house wine, is marvellous. I can't handle spirits any more.' At four the next morning James threaded his way up to his room. Finchie was sound asleep in his favourite chair near the bar, having consumed an enormous quantity of wine. 'One thing I've learned from Errol, Chips Rafferty and Peter Finch,' James told me. 'Never have a night cap with an Aussie because you'll find you're still drinking when the sun comes up.'

When I spoke to Daniel Mann, who had directed *Judith*, I asked him why, of all available stars, he'd picked Finch as first choice. 'In terms of this Jewish story requiring a man of deep conviction, I felt Finch would convey the qualities of leadership. He had authority. I hadn't seen him in any particularly outstanding movies, and to be honest I don't even remember their names. I simply knew I wanted a man who could convey implacable will. But to me, casting is not only physical. I know in films we are involved in a medium that is visual, but as in music, there's a texture. People have a texture. If I'm thinking in terms of music and I need the sound of brass, the greatest string virtuoso wouldn't do. So, regarding ability, Peter had in his personality a texture of strength and vulnerability that was right for this character. Peter's vulnerability has very often been misunderstood as lack of strength. In this instance, it was meant to show by the way he was hurt by what he believed to be British injustice. I cast Peter because, although a non-Jew, he understood the Israeli struggle.'

I understood what Mann meant because though Peter wasn't Jewish, he often used to pretend that he was and he admitted to me in Rome that he often felt the need to belong somewhere, and that the Jews were a spectacularly gifted, persecuted marginal body with whom, like the Aborigines and the Negro people, he felt a tribal kinship. If you look at the great actors – Laurence Olivier, Marlon Brando, Jean-Louis Barrault, Eduardo de Filippo, Smoktunovsky, Nuria Espert, Wojciech Pszoniak – all are well rooted in nationality and project a tremendous national confidence and identity. It was the very lack of this which gave Peter such rare protean fluidity of characterization but it also worked equally against him.

I asked Mann whether, despite Finchie's personal problems, it had been a happy film. 'Very happy in the sense that we were involved with and working in a new country, and it was the story of people who were living witnesses of that 1948 conflict. Many of them were in our film, and were simply re-enacting their arrival on the beaches from the illegal ships. I had one woman in the film falling on her knees and kissing the sand. In real life she had originally come from a German concentration camp. She was my housekeeper while I was working on the film and she and Peter used to spend hours talking. Peter was absorbing all this background in thinking out his character and, having been hungry himself, he understood this woman who would never throw away even a potato peel.'

When he wasn't working, Peter was with Shirley Bassey in Haifa. Mann remembers that: 'She also came out on location and I remember things were very stormy one night when we were shooting some exteriors. There were great arguments, but it never affected his work in front of the camera.'

'Did you meet Mr Hyde, the hell raiser?' I asked Mann. 'I certainly did! The gentle, disciplined Dr Jekyll needed his release and after work, often, very often, he would get absolutely roaring pissed and when I say roaring, I don't mean he just wobbled about. He was mad and wild and, when he was really drunk, he really roared. He would rip off his shirt in public if things didn't please him. There was a latent rage there. Watching *Network*, I saw, without drink, that rage I'd seen at Acre, Nahariya, wherever he was drinking at the end of the day's work in Israel. The rage he had within him, I think, killed him. That hysteria passing out of his being in a fictional way, to me, was almost uncontrollable. When I saw that passion, I realized he'd held it down in *Judith* because that was the role. In *Network*, he was like an electric light just before it burns out; wild hot white light, you know; and then it blows and no longer functions. I couldn't believe that Peter's anger had to have that intensity. It obviously released so many things within him.'

'You felt he'd gone beyond art into reality?'

'Peter was using something that was now using him.'

During the making of *Judith*, the newspapers had been busy with Shirley Bassey's refusal to marry Peter. It was a case of a head-on collision between two people very occupied with their professions. Both publicly admitted they were selfish and, like Peter, Shirley wanted to be free. With two children of her own, and Peter with three, to whom he didn't seem capable of being a father properly, Finchie had to take no for an answer.

Peter's private life was in chaos with writs, divorce petitions, and all the entanglements and petty quarrels that were absolute anathema to him. Additionally, he had two lucky escapes, which must have shaken him. In Tel Aviv the lorry in which he was filming caught fire, and he was lucky to get clear with a few burns, and, when he returned to London in November, a bomb that failed to explode was put through his letterbox. This was probably the result of the publicity about his affair with Shirley Bassey, and they were again together when she saw him off at London Airport for America in April 1965. And it may have been connected with a record released in Britain, *Why I am Ready to Die*, by Nelson Mandela, on 5 November 1964, which also gave extracts from Mandela's speech at his trial. Peter felt very strongly about this issue and did the narration.

Peter's next Hollywood commitment was to play the British Army officer Captain Harris in *The Flight of The Phoenix* for Robert Aldrich at 20th Century-Fox. As a film, it didn't do much for Peter's Hollywood career, but as one of the pukka British military contingent, which included Richard Attenborough, Ronald Fraser and Ian Bannen, the respect and deference afforded the British actors by James Stewart and Ernest Borgnine turned to lasting friendship. Dickie (now Sir Richard) Attenborough, gave me his version of one of their parties. 'We were in the desert in a place called Yuma in Arizona. It was the hottest place on earth but we nicknamed it Buttercup Valley. With absolutely no entertainment whatsoever there was Finchie, Ronnie Fraser, Ian Bannen and I – what was known as "we English". Somehow or other, Finchie realized it was the Queen's birthday. We decided that we would have a dinner for the entire crew to celebrate. We phoned all over that part of America and finally got a Union Jack flown in from a consulate. At a particular point in the dinner, we all nipped out, and having borrowed black ties, marched back into the room, headed by Jimmy Stewart, with four pistols stuck in his belt. Finchie, Ronnie, Ian and I carried two dustbins – I can't remember who carried the flag, oh! yes, of course, it was Jimmy, the most English of us all.' Jimmy Stewart took up the tale: 'Peter had found a portrait of the Queen, secured an excellent bagpipe player from God knows where, and gave me the job of firing the twenty-one gun salute, which I did without losing count because of help from the audience. Naturally, we had no cannon, so I fired twenty-one blanks into an empty dustbin to get the proper effect. Peter was more than an actor's actor. He was a credit to his profession.'

But the autumn and winter of 1965–6 were to prove absolutely disastrous for Peter. On 11 November 1965, Yolande, still living at Boundary House, was granted a decree nisi against Peter on the grounds of his admitted adultery with Shirley Bassey. The courts allowed Peter reasonable access to his two children Samantha and Charles. And during that winter Peter, while filming *10·30 p.m. Summer* for Jules Dassin, caught hepatitis from the water in Spain. Peter had gone to dinner on the final day's dubbing of the film at Dassin's (and his then fiancée Melina Mercouri's) house in the Rue Weber in Paris. It was a case of 'the man who came to dinner' – Peter was taken very ill during the meal. The doctor was called and once he had diagnosed hepatitis, Peter was a guest of the Dassins, for forty days, and was acutely embarrassed by the situation. It had always been Peter's ambition to make a film with a good screenplay and a top European director. He'd seen Alain Robbe-Grillet's film *L'Immortelle* full of those bizarre unexplained incidents, and Marguerite Duras' *Une Aussi Longue Absence*, so when Dassin offered him the lead opposite Melina Mercouri and Romy Schneider in a film scripted by Duras he thought his long-cherished ambition had been achieved at last. But his comment on the film afterwards was that it was murky and confused, seemed to lack depth and substance, and for Finchie the only value of that picture was the friendship he formed with Dassin and Mercouri, who nursed him through the first stages of his very severe illness.

Peter was back in the papers at this time as having proposed marriage to a twenty-five-year-old girl who worked in a Chelsea fashion shop. She claimed he was going to take her to live in Italy. Then in Madrid a twenty-eight-year-old Hollywood writer called Florrie Christmas became his constant companion. She was writing a film script about America's deep south and Peter was toying with the idea of doing the film. Meanwhile the girl in London was given to understand that Peter had no intention whatsoever of marrying her. He took Florrie to Silver Seas in Jamaica where he got himself stoned day and night. His Jamaican friends, Ken and Ineth Ross, who were deeply concerned about him, remember him as absolutely lost. Florrie did what she could for him but he seemed to be well on the way to killing himself with drink. He could usually be found either at the Silver Seas Hotel or the Taj Mahal opposite, trying to blot out a situation for which he knew he had only himself to blame.

In 1966 he made his final break with his English way of life. When I spoke to him, he told me he was going to 'go it alone for a while. I've given away or chucked out most of my clothes, except for the odd sports jacket and what I need to get around in. Betty's got my old bike to give to some kid who'll find a good use for it.' He felt that without any material possessions he would be free of worry. He no longer gave a damn as to whether or not he was a popular film star, whether he'd be an international name or how he was even rated in the profession as an actor. 'I've got just enough to live on up in the Jamaican hills and I'm pulling out of the rat race,' he said. He had been through a period of introspection and he knew what he didn't want: secure domesticity. 'Jamaica suits me because I'm extremely selfish and very romantic.'

On a Rome-bound train, a short time before, he had realized just how romantic he was. He met a girl and chatted her up in Italian. Later he found out she was Irish and she discovered he was English. They had dinner together, laughed about the misunderstanding and the next morning she got off at Florence. Peter helped her with her luggage and they said good-bye. As the train drew out of the station, she rushed along the platform and threw him a red rose. 'I thought, as I watched her waving good-bye, that that was the way life should always be, and I was tempted to open the door and jump out, but there was another girl waiting at Rome station. Bastard I may be, but I don't think I'm unchivalrous. I threw the rose out of the window just as we came into Rome.'

By the end of 1966, Boundary House had been sold, for £34,000 according to Peter, with all his possessions. He told me at the time: 'I've made settlements on my wives and kids and I'm free of the curse of material things.'

Yo had been receiving an interim maintenance order of £4,500 a year, pending her claim for a lump sum, maintenance and secured provision. Finchie's counsel, Mr B. Holroyd Pearce, had sought an apology from Yo in court, describing her application to freeze his assets as 'irresponsible and mischievous' but Finchie did not get his apology though he wanted it on the grounds that it was never his intention to defeat his ex-wife's claim. Had Yo's solicitors approached Peter's, the assurance that he would not transfer his capital, Peter's argument ran, would certainly have been given. Finchie then gave the assurance but was ordered by the judge of the High Court, Mr Justice Rees, not to transfer any sum beyond £5,000 out of the jurisdiction until Yo's application for financial provision had been determined.

Peter's convalescence from hepatitis was extremely slow. He hadn't been really ill over a long period since the army days. He was deeply resentful of Spain 'and the bloody Spaniards', as he was convinced he'd picked up the illness from the water there. Forbidden alcohol, unable to work, vitiated physically, he was forced back on his inner resources. He had a lot of time to think, and I remember him telling me that, bad as 'the yellow jaundice' made him feel, illness, hunger, physical exhaustion, thirst, fever, stark terror were much less destructive to him than that indefinable, intuitively-felt presence of people. A door slamming, sudden hostile laughter, someone approaching him at the wrong time, all these threatened him with an extinction far worse than anything death could inflict, and charity, in its patronizing benevolent sense, could leave him feeling robbed of himself. At Stratford once, Peter, Vivien Leigh and I had a discussion about the breaking down of an inner compulsion to survive. Vivien had been reading Scott Fitzgerald's autobiographical fragments and observations, *The Crack Up*, and she had given Finchie and I a copy each. We were all struck by Fitzgerald's articulate way of describing those experiences that we probably create for ourselves, unconsciously perhaps as part of our personal evolvement, whereby we die a little while still young. Finchie believed the sudden great blows that life can inflict, that seem to come from circumstances beyond our control, seldom show their real effects at once. Like the axe blow in a great tree, the one that causes the tree to bleed its sap is struck long before the moment of actual death, and is often delivered by a human being where love or hate is the issue. The blow hits you in a deep centre and you never feel its true effect until it's too late to do anything about it, and you suddenly realize with an awful finality that, in some way, you'll never be the same again.

Once he'd recovered from his illness Peter was cast by Joe Janni and John Schlesinger in *Far From The Madding Crowd*, which began shooting in Dorset in the late summer of 1966. John Schlesinger didn't find Peter always amenable to his suggestions as a director. 'When I finally came to work with him as a director in *Far From The Madding Crowd*, he wasn't terribly happy, but I feel that he and Alan Bates gave absolutely wonderful performances. Some of the other performances in the film were uneven. But Peter, and Bates as well, were able to deal with that impossible kind of old fashioned sentiment and dialogue of Thomas Hardy, because of their extraordinary ability to imply much more than they ever spoke. In Peter and Alan I had two screen actors trained in the theatre with the dimension needed for Boldwood and Gabriel Oakes.'

Peter started to pit his intuitive knowledge, and experience as an actor, against Schlesinger's experience and objectivity as a director. They had a frightful row about one of the best scenes Peter played in *Far From The Madding Crowd*. It came about after he had seen the rushes of the previous day's filming. Peter had already directed his own film, *The Day*, and felt he was in a director's position of authority to judge the scene as far as he was concerned. Schlesinger was looking at the scene from all points of view and absolutely opposed him. Schlesinger had planned to do the shot in one take, but Peter wanted cover, and wanted John to cover the shot from another closer angle on him. John felt that an extra covering shot would break the rhythm of the film at that point, and also the mood of the scene. 'A covering shot on Peter was just not possible at that moment. He was supposed, as Boldwood, to be out at the destruction of his farm, the property he had just neglected. There was a terrible storm, and the idea was that he should stand helpless in the face of the devastation around him. The camera would shoot on Boldwood and then I'd cut to another shot of his farm being destroyed. Peter insisted I do a covering shot of the camera shot on him. Ridiculous! It was totally unnecessary. "Why can't you shoot it another way?" asked Peter. I said: "I feel the only way I can do it is to track in on you in one single take until we have you in an enormous close up". But at the rushes, he screamed and shouted, and ranted and raved. He was responsible for my never again showing rushes to actors, or allowing them to sit with me. He was wrong. I knew he was wrong, but he was marvellous as Boldwood. He never liked much rehearsal, and not too many takes. A marvellous actor! and you know one hardly had to say very much to him. Watch him when he's having lunch on his own, and he's playing the scene just looking at those clocks. He collected clocks, and he had his dogs, and he was just sitting quietly . . . an extraordinary scene that he played absolutely brilliantly in *Far From The Madding Crowd*. He understood exactly what was wanted of him. Being a lonely man, he understood perfectly how to play lonely people. This scene was a scene we shot very quickly, it was just suddenly thrown in, something added on the spur of the moment. It was a weather cover. He just improvised. It was raining so we had to do something quickly as an alternative, and he just did it like that!'

In 1967 Robert Aldrich made *The Legend of Lylah Clare* for MGM, and cast Peter as Lewis Zarkin, the arrogant egocentric old-time film producer, opposite Kim Novak. To generate the power he needed to play this movie monster Finchie would walk five miles from Beverly Hills to Culver City in a temperature of 100 degrees for the day's shooting. He used to watch each day's rushes as the film was being made and Kim Novak would ask

Peter how it was going: 'It's black mahogany gothic horror right on the edge of being too much,' he said. 'Bob's making monsters of all of us with a sense of parody.' The American public loathed the film and the English general public have never been allowed to see it on general release. Finch loved it and the critics loved Finchie, but very few liked the film.

A year later, during one of Peter's trips to Hollywood, before he and I dubbed *The Red Tent* in Rome in November 1969, Robert Aldrich and his company of associates decided to shoot a limited amount of footage on a film about Errol Flynn, Flo Aadland, and her daughter, Beverly – Flynn's fifteen-year-old mistress whose love affair made headlines at the time when Flynn died in the act of making love. Shelley Winters played Flo, and Finchie played Flynn. The completed project, as a full length feature, was never realized, but some of the footage still exists. The film is called *The Greatest Mother of Them All*, and according to James Bacon on the *Los Angeles Herald Examiner*, it was nothing short of a catastrophe that it was never completed. Ironically, some two months before Peter died, Bacon ran into him in the Polo Lounge of the Beverly Hills Hotel and suggested he should try to play Errol Flynn and make a big success with a money spinner. 'Tried it once in 1969 with Bob Aldrich,' Finchie replied. 'No one was interested and we just couldn't get the financial backing to make the goddam thing.'

Peter maintained that Flynn used to parody his own acting ability and intelligence, and was an infinitely better actor than he was ever given credit for. Errol Flynn, Humphrey Bogart, Spencer Tracy, Claude Rains and others of that era, said Peter, always took their work seriously but never themselves. 'Whenever Peter and I got together anywhere in the world we always got to talking about Errol,' said Bacon. 'He seemed to live his life by a principle that Peter could understand: that the whole world was three drinks behind. Errol was a deeply sensitive man, highly intelligent, who covered it up. He could charm the pants off anyone, especially women.'

Booze and women began Flynn's self destruction and drugs completed it. He told Finchie that he'd started on cocaine purely to kill the pain of his terrible hangovers. During the shooting of Romain Gary's *The Roots of Heaven* Errol actually conned some Belgian doctor in Africa into giving him cocaine for his hangovers, and when he found out that the black women in the region were ninety-six percent syphilitic, Errol persuaded the doctor to shoot him full of penicillin so that, for about four to five hours, he'd be immune from infection. If the Aldrich project had succeeded it would have been Peter's responsibility to convey all this by implication rather than by statement, a challenge he always regretted never materialized.

25 Russia and Rome, birth and marriage

The filming of the Italian Soviet epic *The Red Tent*, its Russian title was *Krasnaya Palatka*, in Russia and Rome, was spread over two years, 1968 and 1969, with Paul Maslansky in charge of production for the Italian producer Franco Cristaldi, who had put up forty percent of the £4 million deal. Peter first met Maslansky at Munich Airport in November 1967 when he, Claudia Cardinale, Eletha and Hardy Kruger all foregathered before going on to Moscow. The film had only a modest success in Europe, and didn't go at all well in America. According to Paul Maslansky, it was released at a time 'when anything Russian still had a tinge of "you shouldn't!", and people were afraid the cinema would be picketed.' He maintains Paramount, who had bought the rights, butchered the picture, and that the film as originally cut by Cristaldi and the Russians was a finer film than the version presented on the screen.

The role of General Umberto Nobile, marooned with the other survivors of his disastrous expedition until he was picked up some three weeks before the rest of his companions and flown out to Kings Bay at Spitzbergen by the Swedish pilot Lundborg, was too good to turn down. What appealed to him were the moral issues of the alleged mishandling of the dirigible, causing it to freeze up and crash; the accusation of cowardice against Nobile as leader of the expedition in leaving first in order, as he said, to bring back a rescue party as soon as possible; the subsidiary issues of blame and responsibility for the loss of the lives of several of his men. His friend Amundsen had lost his life in his plane searching for Nobile over the Pole. He had allowed three members of his expedition to attempt to walk out into the unknown, ninety miles across the ice by their reckoning, in attempts to find rescue at Kings Bay. One of the three, Dr. Malmgren had died on the way; as he lay dying he requested the other two to eat his flesh in order to survive once he had died. I dubbed the voice of one 'Zappi' into English (in Rome), but this whole issue has been deleted from the print available in London, and all that remains is an unintelligible exchange whispered between the two men watching Malmgren die. The problems of conscience still plagued Nobile, forty years after the event. His public condemnation as a coward and subsequent vindication, together with the style of the film which left the audience to judge whether the man was guilty or not, all fell admirably within the scope of Peter's art.

Peter was in Russia for eight months in 1968, flying intermittently to Rome to shoot interiors. He had a specific time booked to do the film but they were held up by good weather! They needed blinding snow but the sun shone! They wanted ice but the water refused to freeze. Sometimes they had to wait for days for the right backgrounds. Maslansky found Peter very understanding. He wasn't thinking about overtime but what it would be costing his friend Cristaldi in Rome. To Peter the picture was all important. The Russians understood his attitude and he became a popular figure. But the delays did irritate and he said to a visiting friend, Peter Thompson: 'We're not making a film, we're fighting a war to get the bloody thing made. The bureaucracy and the weather are getting me down.' And there came a time when the Italian unit felt they were not getting the cooperation they needed from the Russians, and they met privately in one of their hotel rooms to discuss what to do to get things moving. They decided to go above the heads of the go-betweens and deal directly with the fountain-head of power, the Minister of Culture himself. Having made the decision they'd just set off to make their appeal, when, from the opposite direction, a little sweating Russian came racing along the passage: 'Noh! Noh! Pliss comrades, you mustn't do that!' Now aware of the bugging devices in their rooms, they agreed to turn back!

During the film they had to shoot a sequence using a polar bear. The bear was supposed to amble across and investigate the buried body of one of the victims of the crash while the stranded crew stood terrified by the gondola of the dirigible. This bear had been hired from a gypsy circus somewhere in the Carpathians, and was extremely vicious, so everything was carefully rigged up so that they could all escape very rapidly if the bear suddenly got hungry. They were shooting towards the west with the now frozen Baltic immediately in front of them to make the bear appear to be advancing from the frozen wastes of the North

Pole. They put honey, rabbit flesh, blood, everything delectable to polar bears, on the ice to get the beast to come into close shot and paw the large propeller lying on the ice, which served as a burial cross for the dead victim. They were shooting over Peter's shoulder, and the bear's trainer, holding a pistol containing a blank cartridge, stood behind him. The director shouted 'action' and in came the bear, but the goggles Peter was wearing glinted in the sun and appeared to distract the bear, for it suddenly veered round and made for the paralysed Peter who, though he thought he was going to end his career then and there as Baltic mincemeat, manfully stood his ground. When the bear came to within ten feet the trainer fired and the bear made a sharp about-turn, and vanished out across the Baltic, never to be seen again, and it took them a week to find another.

When we worked together in Rome in 1969 it wasn't, of course, Peter's first visit to the Italian capital, a place over the years he had come to love. He first went in 1956 on holiday with Patricia Lewis Plummer, then working for the *News Chronicle*. At that time there were still currency problems with the British £50 allowance but they took the train for Rome as they were promised that a gentleman from the Rank Organization would be waiting for them with Peter's money. The weather had been foul, but as they approached Rome the skies cleared and Peter had his first sight of the dark apricot walls, cupolas and tiled roofs and towers among the Seven Hills. With his painter's eye, he was bewitched by Rome which was to become, like London, a second home for him. The gentleman from Rank met them and explained there had been some difficulty but that the money would be arriving at some stage. Luckily Pat had a few travellers' cheques, and at least the Rank Organization had installed Peter in luxurious splendour in a suite in the Parioli. Patricia then took him to meet Bertie and Lorri Whiting (sister of Prime Minister of Australia, Malcolm Fraser), two Australians who live in Trastevere. Bertie is a poet and Lorri a painter, and they became Peter's closest friends in Rome during his visits there over the next twenty years.

Diana Graves, who had what Peter called a '300-year-old voice', was also living in Rome at that time in a mini palazzo up five floors in what Pat described as a comfortable wheel house atop an old lift shaft. Peter suffered from vertigo, so he had to sit with his eyes closed and be led in and out like a blind man whenever he went to see her. Bertie and Lorri Whiting had some fascinating things to say about Peter during his various sojourns in Rome. On one occasion, apparently, they and Diana Graves, Peter and Pat decided to drive down to Positano. The weather was crisp and cold and they simply ate, drank and amused themselves. Positano was picturesque, quiet and un-eventful but on the day they left it started to pour with rain. They strapped all the luggage on Bertie's fast car, and then had lunch. During the meal Finchie told them about the nun who had haunted him since childhood. He had never actually seen her face, but when something was about to happen to him, she always knocked three times. After lunch, the five of them set out for Rome with Bertie driving. 'I suppose we must have gone about fifty miles when suddenly we heard Bang! Bang! Bang! on the side of the car. Finchie yelled: "It's my nun!" and I yelled: "It's our luggage coming off." But when I got out to check, none of the straps were loose, so it certainly wasn't the luggage, so we drove through the storm.' Night fell. They reached the hills above Rome. Bertie was driving very fast. The road was very narrow and, as he rounded a bend, two trucks, side by side, appeared, coming straight at them, and they only managed to make room for the car with fractions of a second to spare. Everyone was in a state of shocked silence. After a long time, Peter spoke: 'Well now, tell me! Was she trying to kill me or trying to save me?'

Bertie and Lorri remember Peter's hilarious description of his daughter, Diana's, birth in Rome in December 1969 which was attended by several genuine nuns. 'There was Finchie not married to Eletha, and Eletha with a son already, but not by Finchie; and Finchie, with two previous wives and children by them. The little Italian nuns were utterly amazed when Peter told them quite frankly what the situation was but seemed very happy to do their best for Eletha and the baby. Finchie then went to register the birth with the British authorities and en-countered what he described as: 'a particularly pinched wee lady with a very pinched Kelvinside accent, who took an instant dis-like to me! She took down the details and repeated them as though she was sucking a very sour lemon; and the way she told me what Eletha and I could or could not do as regards Diana, according to British Law, was as offensive as only a good Scots Presbyterian female could be. "Of course, Mister Finch, you

P.F.—13   273 realize, don't you, that your wee black child will have to be an Italian citizen!" "Thank God for that," was my instant reply!'

Peter was fascinated by Italian history and especially by the achievements and the life of the Emperor Hadrian; Bertie told Peter that Hadrian, just before he died in AD 138 had penned five lines of perfect poetry. One day they went out to Hadrian's villa at Tivoli and wandered among the ruined arches and into the vast amphitheatre, trying to visualize what it must have been like when the plays of Plautus and Seneca were performed there before the Emperor and his household. Now everything was a deserted ruin, covered with ivy and lichen. Bertie told Peter to stand centre stage and speak some verse while he and Lorri went up to the back of the circle to listen. Peter started to recite Hadrian's last words, and every syllable was distinctly audible in the eighteen hundred year old theatre. 'Peter's feeling for the rhythm and meaning of the verse was spellbinding,' said Bertie.

Animula Vagula Blandula
Hospes Comesque Corporis
Quae Nunc Abibis In Loca
Palidula Rigida Nudula
Nec, Ut Soles, Dabis Jocos?
Little Soul,
Host and Guest of my Body.
What will you do
Now that you go to inhabit
A pale cold bare place,
you, who were used
to be so playful?

Peter loved poetry and on one occasion he jotted down some lines on the back of an envelope and recited them at a party, and then promptly lost the envelope. 'It wasn't really a poem as such,' said Bertie. 'It was a feeling superbly expressed in verse, absolutely genuine, but Peter's trouble was that he would not take the trouble to polish and work on his verse. It wasn't so much laziness, as the fact that he was on holiday between jobs and he wasn't going to sit down and really work on his poems.' To the Whitings, Peter was the easiest man to quarrel with, very easy to offend, and Lorri, very detached about Peter, believes it was conceit that made him very touchy and tiresome. Both could only number a few among the hundreds of Finch's girlfriends to whom they had been introduced who had lasted more than three days. They remember there was one, a beautiful sensitive delicate girl, from a very good northern Italian family, who adored Peter. Peter had taken her off to Ischia and Bertie and Lorrie hoped that after a few months with her that he might settle for her, as he was sparking back on all cylinders and very much in love. To help things along Bertie and Lorri arranged a luncheon party one day in Trastevere for Peter and his madonna, feeling sure the Italian idyll would blossom into a proposal of marriage at any minute. Quite unexpectedly in the middle of lunch, in flew an old flame, the Belgian air hostess. As they were finishing the dessert, the air hostess's eyes flashed at Finchie, up rose Finchie's libido and with it Finchie, and he escorted her to the nearest bedroom forthwith. His Italian girl friend sat amazed and completely shattered, for there had been no indication on Ischia that there was a sexually rampant Mr Hyde lurking within the tender romantic Dr Jekyll. Bertie told her: 'Go back to Tuscany and forget the monster.'

One night in Rome, the Whitings had been having a particularly harrowing time with the ladies Peter had been treating badly; there had been considerable weeping and gnashing of teeth. They were just settling down quietly for the evening, glad to be rid of Peter and his domestic turmoil for a while, when the phone rang. It was Finchie: 'Do you want to come out to dinner with the two dames? I'll be at the Otello at eight.'

'Go to hell!' said Lorri. 'We've had more than enough of you and your bloody dames.' A few minutes later, Bertie suddenly twigged. Peter was taking Dame Edith Evans and Dame Peggy Ashcroft out to dinner! So they went along and Peter was superb. 'He was the Peter all of us who knew and loved him in Rome always hoped for. On that occasion he excelled himself. He was entertaining his "peers".'

One of the really revealing conversations between Bertie Whiting and Peter was over money. When Peter began to make a great deal of money Bertie said to him: 'Look Peter, you can be a rich man.' Peter looked at him and said: 'What exactly do you mean?' 'I told him,' said Bertie: 'Please Peter for God's sake, be sensible with your money, and be rich. I can put you on to a financier who can invest wisely and make enough for you never to have financial worries anymore.' He gave me such a look, as much as to say, here's another thief. So I just said to him: "Oh, go to hell, Peter, if you are going to think like that, go and do what you like with your bloody money!" The problem with Peter was that he often surrounded himself with doubtful people because they were the only ones who would put up with him most of the time, and then he was angry and on the defensive because they were pretty doubtful people.'

When Peter suddenly decided to marry Eletha, he asked Bertie to be best man. (Eletha, with Diana, now aged four, on whom he absolutely doted, wanted a proper wedding.) Bertie advised Peter strongly to make a fresh will providing for Diana (his first child by Eletha), and Eletha's son, Chris. He warned Peter that, by remarrying, he would invalidate any previous wills and that in the event of his death, there'd be legal complications with his previous wives.

'No! No! No! Bertie,' Peter protested. 'I've finished with women. They've had all they're getting out of me! That's the end of it with all women as far as I'm concerned. I'm an old work horse and I'm going my way!' And he added: 'I'm not going to live long.' That was late in October 1973, just at the end of filming *The Abdication*. Not long before they'd begun the picture, he had gone to the doctor with a repeated heart flutter. The doctor had told him: 'It's nothing to worry about, but you must not smoke, no wine, but you may have a few whiskies,' after which Bertie saw him smoking and drinking again just as before.

Peter and Eletha were married on Friday, 9 November 1973, with a civil ceremony at the Rome City Hall and a service at the Methodist Church in the Piazza di Sant Angelo. Peter was fifty-seven and Eletha thirty. They had been together for eight years. Burt Lancaster, the agent Jill St Amand, and Franco Nero were among the guests, and Prince Borghese, one of Peter's staunch old friends, opened his house to Peter. Their honeymoon was in Nigeria.

His Roman friends saw his marriage to Eletha with a more detached and sophisticated eye than some of his Hollywood friends. He loved her, no question. She was loyal, got him off the booze, tried to put his life in some sort of order and tried to make him save money. The Roman opinion is that, with her tremendous vitality, 'she was the one performing more and more in the centre of the stage and Peter was quite content to be the one standing by holding the curtains.'

26 A night at Otello's

Finchie was at his best as a raconteur, and as a companion, over a meal where wine flowed liberally, but as the carafe was gradually emptied, his mental equilibrium would move as imperceptibly as the needle on a barometer. The 'two pot screamer' would shift from some brilliant and lucid observation he was making on the character of Trigorin in *The Seagull*, to a fifteen minute monologue which was total gibberish. Finchie always maintained he was high on life, it was simply that alcohol made him higher. Food would always restore the balance and off we'd go on another excursion into the realm of self-analysis or even self-discovery. While Peter and I (as Captain Zappi) were dubbing *The Red Tent* in Rome, Peter told me with immense pride that baby Finch Number Four was about to emerge from the *toril* and enter the arena. He really wanted a child by Eletha. Finchita turned out to be a baby girl, Diana, the nut-brown apple of her daddy's eye.

'See you at the Otello in Santa Croce tomorrow for lunch at two,' he said. We began at two and ended – Finchie hated being alone without his woman at night – at dawn the following morning. A good deal of Peter's secret self emerged as a result of my reminding him that day of an afternoon some years before in the Old Swan in Battersea. I had met him there after an unsuccessful interview for a television commercial. I was feeling very depressed, and Peter had invited me to lunch. It proved to be a liquid lunch but I remember I had on a new Savile Row suit, a very expensive shirt, a Gucci tie and shoes, with a carnation in my buttonhole. We had been discussing the pros and cons of living on the Thames. He said he wanted to buy a house-boat and live on the river where I'd been living since December 1953, in the *Stella Maris* moored across the river alongside 106 Cheyne Walk, Chelsea. He asked if I'd ever fallen overboard. I told him, on my way out to a very smart dinner one evening, I'd stepped on to the gangway which parted unexpectedly from the boat, and had gone head first into two feet of stinking black Thames mud. I said I'd never actually swum in the Thames, and never wanted to as it was polluted, full of river traffic, and strong tides. The conversation turned to surfing in Australia, and we agreed that, if you could manage the long swim out through the heavy Australian surf, and make it back again to the beach, you could survive almost anything. I hadn't been to the Old Swan before and suddenly I felt the violent urge to pee.

'Where is it?' I asked Peter.

'Straight ahead through that door,' he said. 'Turn right, down the passage, then left, through the door and you'll find it!'

I did, and suddenly found myself going over a fourteen foot drop, into the swirling waters of the river Thames. A brisk swim, with a racing tide and an angry hooting tug dragging two cement barges, and I was on a direct diagonal course home to the *Stella Maris*. I broke all records, thanks to the fast outgoing tide, my anxiety to get out of the filthy water, and my rage at the loss of a very expensive pair of shoes and for taking Finchie's advice without looking where I was going. I turned back once to see Peter framed in the doorway, doubled up with laughter.

We next met in the dubbing theatre in Rome, but no allusion was made immediately to our last parting. We had both been pretty high but I was in little doubt as to who had sobered up quickest on that occasion. I had spent a gruelling day-and-a-half putting voice on film which included the part cut out by the Americans where the Scandinavian member of Nobile's Arctic expedition Dr Malmgren pleaded that Nobile's companions should eat his flesh once he was dead. By the time I reached Otello's, I was right off my food, but badly in need of a drink. Finchie, who had been released earlier, obviously felt the same way as he was half a carafe of wine ahead of me, and that barometer needle of insobriety had already risen perceptibly. He embraced me and suddenly removing the mask of politeness, inquired if I was keeping up my swimming. I asked him why the hell he hadn't warned me. He dismissed the episode lightheartedly. 'It wasn't until you disappeared through the door that I realized you might be taking your first dip in the Thames. I rushed out to warn you but when I got there you were already racing a tug half-way across and going like a champion. You didn't seem to have lost your Aussie stroke.'

This took us on to talking about the machismo cult among Australian kids; joining the surf club or the football club or any sporting organization and the need to prove manhood. Finchie admitted that the need to be accepted, which he had learned when he was young in Australia as one of the boys, had remained as a sort of ingrained need all his life. He reckoned his much publicized and exaggerated hell-raising image was part of what the press believed the public expected, and it was all so much balls when it came to what he was about as an actor. Peter knew perfectly well the truth of Harry Watt's assertion that one of the most pernicious influences on any actor is publicity. He agreed with Harry that publicity is worse for the soul than sex or drink, because it can work like an insidious poison, and an actor can begin to believe that he is much more talented and important than he really is. Even if he is reasonably intelligent, even if he tries to be objective, it is very difficult to retain a sense of reality. Peter despised the whole publicity bit, but he still subscribed to a press cutting agency.

I was curious to know why he seemed to have betrayed his own remarkable potential as a dedicated actor in the theatre. I reminded him of his persuasive eloquence in Repin's, nearly a quarter of a century before, when he had argued the need of every true actor to keep going back to the theatre in order to expand his creative talents to the full and try to gain the dimension and stature of people like Olivier, Laughton, Robert Donat, and the French actors Louis Jouvet and Gérard Philipe. He admitted he was deeply dissatisfied with being a product of the studios and with being caught up in the élite world of the star system, but he argued that the need to live intensely, to travel, and know more of the world was also part of being an actor. 'I'm ideal casting for Judas Iscariot. I can understand his kissing Christ out of sheer funk, knowing he was selling him down the line, and then thinking: "Oh shit, I'm a c—t," and rushing out in a fit of crazy despair, and stringing himself up on a tree! Haven't we all done that in our minds many times? Good acting should teach people to understand rather than judge.'

He agreed that he had changed, but felt the theatre had changed radically since the 1950s, and the more he worked in the cinema the more it suited his whole way of life. The theatre, like the cinema, had become a director's medium entirely, but he felt the theatre was also becoming stultified with too many inexperienced academics. The cinema to him was in a state of exciting change and no one could predict what might happen, but he admitted there were so many films and projects he either wanted to do, or was going to do and never did, because he was incapable of planning ahead and following through. I think now that Peter really lost his way, and his career became set on its ultimate course once he signed the contract for *Elephant Walk* in 1952.

He also talked a great deal about Tamara, Yo and his children. 'I behaved very badly to Yo, I was volatile and unpredictable. We had one thing in common, we enjoyed living it up, but that soon palls and doesn't hold a marriage together.' He told me a very Finchiesque story that he'd invented to shock, and amazingly, the story came back to me indirectly not long before I finished this book. 'I got so fed up with people crowing on about my penchant for black ladies that I told them I'd found a wild Nigerian girl who, every time she made love, crowed like a rooster, but that she'd had to go back to Nigeria. So I put it round for a joke that I'd found this marvellous woman who really performed like a black rooster and, within days, it was all round Soho: "Finchie's got to have a spade that crows like a cock when she's on the job," and the dark ladies were coming in from all over the place saying they could crow at a price. What a load of bull, but in those mad years it was all part of living the life I needed in order to escape from the basic dissatisfaction with myself and what I seemed to create. Yo was the victim just as much as I was.'

Anita, his daughter by Tamara, was another who was close to him whom he undoubtedly treated badly. On one occasion, to celebrate Anita's birthday, he promised to take her out to dinner, and Anita dressed up and waited. But he never arrived. He'd forgotten all about it. Yet, said Gwen Plumb, who maintains that Peter was a mixture of romantic feelings and excessive sentimentality, the next day when Gwen saw him Peter burst into tears because it was the anniversary of Mozart's death.

Anita herself, however, is amazingly detached and resilient about Peter, and speaks of him more as an unpredictable elder brother than a father. She remembers virtually nothing of him during her childhood: only that after he left the house which Tamara had insisted they buy as a guaranteed asset both for Peter and herself, he used to return intermittently around four in the morning, bang on the door, weave his way in, and there'd be rows. His current lady would invariably be left waiting in the car outside. Anita now feels that it was all a bit of a joke and that

Dad could be enchanting as a bar room companion, lady's man, actor in rehearsal, on stage, or in front of the camera; every pro's dream of what a professional should be. But to be involved with him – forget it!

I asked Anita if she'd ever discussed her ambitions with Peter, if he'd ever had a serious talk to her about anything. She had tried once to talk to him about acting. 'I was going off on my first professional job. I'd graduated from the Bristol Old Vic Drama School, and Peter and I had vaguely written to one another but I hadn't seen him for ages. He came round one night drunk, and we went out. I'd got my first professional job after drama school as an acting assistant stage manager, and he was filming as Nelson in *Bequest to the Nation* in 1972. He asked me out to dinner and I happened to be working in this play with Bill Kerr, and I thought what a good idea if Bill Kerr came along too. One of his old "mates". We ended up at the Buckstone (a popular actors drinking club), and he got absolutely pissed there. We went home and my mother said: "Isn't it marvellous! Anita's got her first job." He said: "Oh, I don't think I should help her. She should do it on her own. I don't believe in nepotism. I think it unprofessional and I don't want to know about it." My mother said: "But it's wonderful. She's the maid, and she's going off on tour, and the play's by Oscar Wilde." It was *Lord Arthur Savile's Crime*, and the maid is supposed to have a romance with the old butler, which in fact they cut out in the version I was in, because the guy playing the butler was so old and decrepit it would have been totally obscene. I remember Peter suddenly got up and started acting the old butler. "All right, come on," he said to me, "let's see what you can do. Let's do this scene!" Pissed out of his mind he played the doddering old butler. Very funny, he had us, his audience, falling about. But I wasn't going, at that moment, to attempt to play the little maid. I had no confidence. I just couldn't compete, and that was the last time I ever saw him.

'I only ever saw my father on locations or in film studios or with lots of people around. I remember one time I hadn't seen him for two years and he phoned up and said: 'Come to dinner with me and Eletha.' I said: 'All right. I've got this boyfriend.' It was my first boyfriend, an Australian actor. Peter hated the boyfriend, absolutely hated him. We all went to dinner at Prunier's; an evening of hideously stilted conversation. Then we all went back to Betty's (Peter's mother). The dinner and the whole evening had been absolutely stilted and ghastly. I know I was a bit of a thorn to Peter at this stage and the boyfriend obviously just set him off, and it was one of those smouldering interludes with father and estranged daughter, and boyfriend who was wishing he was back in Australia. Anyway when we arrived at Betty's, the whole family was there: Flavia, Michael, Eletha and that just seemed to be the spark that ignited the dynamite. My father was deeply disturbed by all those things that fester underneath and are unspoken, and then some other quite different irritant made him explode. Before anyone realized what was going on Peter and I were at it, like a couple of fighting cocks. What was so terribly funny, looking back on that God Almighty row now, was the three white faces and one black watching the verbal volleys hurtling across the room like the singles finals at Wimbledon. Suddenly, Pete threw down his racket, as it were, and said he was going to call a taxi. But both dogs by this time had the same bone, and neither would stop growling or let go. The next moment I remember we were in Bury Walk absolutely screaming the most unbelievable obscenities at each other. Windows opened. Lights went on. Curtains flew back. "You're just like all the other bloody Finchs," he raved. "Just a nest of vipers and I should have known!"

'The next day he took me to lunch at the White Elephant. Supposedly we were going to have lunch alone. And of course, lunch at the White Elephant meant fifty people queueing at the table saying: "Hello! What are you doing?" and all the rest! We never got a chance to talk.

'When I was sixteen, he did invite me for a week when he was filming *Far From The Madding Crowd* in Dorset. We were in a house miles away on a peninsular and he gave a lot of parties. I was on the set every day and we ate with everyone, but I don't remember ever sharing a moment of true solitude with him. Yet, he was such a solitary man.'

From the night Peter had given his last performance to Anita as the moribund old butler, no correspondence passed between them for over four years. But he always needed to keep the lines of communication open between Tamara, Anita and himself. He could never come to terms with his own nature over this. He paid a high price for the ruthlessness his weakness compelled him to use, and he knew perfectly well that the situation with

Tamara and Anita was not one he could or even wanted to resolve. But though he was often filming in London in those years between 1972 and 1977, he didn't get in touch. No phone call, nothing. Then, two weeks before he died, Anita got a Christmas card from him. The card didn't actually arrive until after Christmas and it said: 'Dearest Anita, as soon as we've finished the house, you must come over and visit us.'

She was working in the office of a friend who was an agent and she showed him the card and said: 'It's extraordinary. I haven't had a communication from him for four years and I suddenly get this card inviting me over.' The agent Anita worked for was a friend of Peter's agent so he suggested Anita should phone Barry Krost to see if she could get through to her father. It was six at night London time, so they knew by Los Angeles time they'd catch Krost at his office. The London agent made contact with Krost's secretary, explained the situation, and asked for Peter's private number. The secretary clicked them off, spoke on the direct line to Pete, and came back to the effect that if they waited Peter would call them directly but that was the last Anita heard. After he had died, Eletha phoned up and said: 'Why did you phone him? Did you know he was going to die?'

'No,' said Anita.

'But why did you get a friend to phone?' Eletha had asked. 'Why didn't you phone yourself? He wouldn't phone you back because he said: "If she can't phone herself, well bloody hell! What's she doing getting someone else to phone?"'

Apparently, Peter had been very upset, thinking she couldn't be bothered to phone herself.

Finchie was with Yo for six years and they were wild and extravagant years for him. He had a very high libido and a very healthy appetite for women of all shapes, sizes and colour. He spent wildly, 'and for a while', he told me, 'I went down among the stewpots and fleshpots but there were moments during that time that I loathed every second of it. I felt self disgust and I knew I was diminishing what powers I had as an actor.' But looking back, he believed it was a necessary part of his life and he had no regrets except that he was paying through the nose for it, and he was constantly out of pocket. He complained to me that day that he was lucky if, out of £50,000, he ever saw £5,000, but, then, in the early sixties he'd spent hundreds of pounds a night round Mayfair and Soho. The six years with Yo were what he called his lurid years of surrealist fantasy, the Salvador Dali period, 'where so much of what I did', he said, 'seemed to crumble and decay like those rich yellow and black Dali paintings.' He became debauched, which 'was a reaction from my marriage to Tamara, who was the antithesis of the jet set image'.

As I listened to Peter talking on into the early hours of the morning I realized again he was a man with an enormous level of inner tension, caused by the conflicting sides of his character. He would cover up a tremendous restlessness, at times, with an outward mental calm. He had a rich and inspired imagination which sometimes led him to overrate his ideas and his intuition, and this led him into wild extremes. But Peter was not, as I'd always thought, ruled so much by his heart as by his emotions. So much of what Finchie had given me over the years was an impression of himself. But the man, I realized, when the conversation turned to one of his very beautiful mistresses with whom he'd professed to being totally infatuated, was more superficial than I'd believed. 'Why did you go off her?' I asked, 'Or did she go off you?' 'No,' he said, 'she suddenly started tasting of nicotine.' I saw then that he had never loved in the deeper sense of giving or making great sacrifices. In love he was more the receiver than the giver. He didn't seem to have the feeling, as a man, that comes from the heart and soul, that is unchanging and that has depth, though he could convey it as an actor. His feelings were more reactions to life and what was happening to him at the moment. He could change himself and react to an environment because he had an abundance of emotional reactions. But he would never let the environment control him. He was versatile rather than adaptable. He couldn't and wouldn't adapt. I believed I saw in Peter, in that moment in the Otello, the perfect actor, and why. For anyone directing him he could bring out an abundance of nuances of character of his own accord. But he was more ideas and emotions than anything else. But he wasn't totally a chameleon, his personality was too strong. It was a question of whether he chose to adapt his personality, as an actor to the current situation, and only when he made the choice did he begin to use his versatility. The depth, truth, quality, was in the actor, and the man, though amusing and marvellous company at his best, was not at all what so many of us had thought. Sometimes the very unpredictability that could make him such a disappointing friend, made him attractive as a friend to both men and women. I met him once in the middle of Piccadilly Circus on my way to see a young actress who was very ill in St Bartholomew's Hospital. Peter had just bought a huge bunch of roses and a little glass cat for a very glamorous blonde he had on his arm. We collided and embraced. Where was I going? When I told him he seized the flowers from the girl, and the cat, and, saying he'd seen the sick girl in *The Living Room* and was mad about her, thrust them into my hands. 'Here!' he said; 'she's too young and too talented to be lying ill in a hospital. Give her these. You don't have to say they're from me.' The gorgeous girl who looked like Yo was open mouthed. 'Oh, you don't mind darling do you? I'll get you some more,' and off he rushed dragging the woman after him to buy her a few more roses. I can remember Dorothy Tutin's reaction when I gave her the roses and the cat from a true admirer, Mr Peter Finch!

Another chance meeting occurred in the summer of 1964 as Peter was about to go out to Israel to film *Judith*. I took my wife Bobo, and my mother to dinner at the White Elephant Club to which both Peter and I belonged. On entering we saw that the sad elegant figure immaculately dressed in grey on the far side of the room was Peter. He was absolutely sober and he rushed over and embraced my wife and mother. I was very moved to see him looking so well and invited him to join us for dinner. 'Nothing I'd like more,' he said, and I felt he meant it. We sat down and ordered, but just as the waiter brought the first course a few old Hollywood friends entered, and Peter very politely excused himself for a few minutes. We waited twenty minutes. No Peter. He returned on his knees two hours later stoned out of his mind and just collapsed under the table. With Peter you accepted him and admired him for the great actor he was, ignored the unpredictability, or just left him well alone.

Peter always needed a relationship with a woman, even if it was only a passing one. Success did inflate his ego for a while and it did have a corrupting influence. He admitted that, but, 'when I'm working everything is more in proportion,' he said. Very few women could have lived with Peter for a lifetime. He was a fickle, exhausting marriage partner and it was in any binding relationship that his worst faults were brought out. Many totally unexpected aspects of his character would erupt in marital rows and he was never capable, by his own admission, of being faithful to one woman. He had five women in his life who really meant a great deal to him – they included Tamara, Vivien, Kay Kendall and Eletha. He would have married Vivien or Kay. Vivien adored Peter but would never have crossed the Rubicon from Larry whom she adored and admired more than anyone. Kay wouldn't take Peter on. Peter always used to warn his girl friends: 'Don't try to collect twigs. I don't want a nest, kids or possessions. I simply want to be free to go my way,' and that probably didn't suit Kay. Eletha was the woman who knew how to go both his way and her own, and give him the child he was mature and responsible enough to really want.

Peter always had an obsessive fear of growing old, and he'd derived great comfort from Picasso's theory that you decide what age you want to be and stick to that. He told me during that all night session in the Otello that he'd been to see General Nobile then in his eighties and living in Paris. He said it was a strange experience to talk to the old man as 'he still lives intensely back in the time of his disgrace some forty years ago!' He found in playing Nobile a similarity with Oscar Wilde as both Wilde and Nobile had to face public trial and disgrace, albeit for entirely different reasons.

I decided at one point to try and crack the kernel of the nut as regards Peter, and I asked him bluntly why he had evaded the issues of responsibility as regards wives, children, women, and even platonic friends who had been kind and were genuinely fond of him. His reply was disarmingly frank. 'There are some things you cannot spare other people,' he told me, 'and the sudden lucid recognition of your destiny brings with it an almost buoyant ruthlessness. What no one knows is the price one pays oneself, and very often we really have no choice, as the necessity of the instant dominates all other needs and considerations by force of circumstances. You must act badly sooner or later in life. If deep down you are coward enough to lack the inner courage of your own ruthlessness, sooner or later the bile will run and begin to fester in a marriage or any close relationship. The only true purity,' he maintained, 'is the purity of absolute honest self-denial, and the priests and theologians, who are honest, are in no position to preach that one, because for them there is no acceptance of passion which the normal man or woman sooner or later undergoes.' By accepting the passion, according to Peter, you accept the tragedy and suffering that may ensue, and the pain you inflict on others is a recognition of your own destiny because it will surely boomerang back, often in the most unexpected and undesired way. 'Unkindness and insensitivity,' he said, 'are theoretical clichés used by bitter men and women indulging in self-pity. It's the great *cri de coeur* of the jilted and their sympathizers. Those outside the situation will argue that one hasn't the right to snatch at happiness with a woman, that has its only possibility in someone else's misfortune. But what rubbish to theorize. We're all a blending of good and evil and no situation is straightforward. What is to my advantage may be absolute poison to someone else. My actions may mean the emotional withering of someone with a far finer nature than mine. I'm prepared to shoulder the guilt. Everything has its price. It's a question of what you are capable of paying inwardly, once you've decided to 'opt' for momentary paradise.' He then put the question to me: 'Isn't it a form of hypocrisy to burn with desire, (and I'm talking aesthetically not in terms of lust,) and suffer the tormenting stagnation of inaction? We're all a little guilty, some of us even unwittingly: the genius of Einstein eventually led to Hiroshima.'

Peter claimed he often yearned for silence and solitude, but when the peace of silence and solitude suddenly turned to an emptiness which echoed, he would feel the inexplicable sense of spiritual loss and the need for complete glutted alcoholic oblivion. The sense of never having *belonged* in any sense, a hangover from early youth, had become magnified beyond reality. He had a compulsive urge to blot out an empty futile world; where days filled with cheap tarnished moments and restless sterile nights followed one another ad infinitum; where he was constantly pursued and confronted by the *self* he despised.

We began to discuss his films. He had loved *The Shiralee*: 'It may have its flaws, but like a woman I loved it because it was a completely natural piece of work. *Father Brown*, because it gave me a rare chance to do a bit of character work, and Wilde! Well, *Oscar Wilde* was a hell of a challenge, something as an actor I really had to reach for.'

His materialistic side; occasional deep melancholy; ambition; extravagance; self indulgence; indecisiveness; all these pulled him in different directions, and then he'd suddenly be overcome by the need to break the tension and escape, go off and make a clean start, like Gauguin did. The need to go in so many directions at once had a wonderful outlet in his acting. This was a perfect catharsis and his instinctive protection against what could have been negative and destructive traits. He also found the truth he aspired to as a man through his unique gifts as an actor. Peter was an interpretive artist, *deraciné*. He lived and belonged in other people, in a perpetual no man's land. Apart from his prodigious imagination, what family did he have in the formative years? What world in the material sense? None. At one moment, in vino veritas, he again dropped the protean mask. 'I feel such despair at times,' he said, 'I suppose it's the spiritual apathy of the religious who have become hermetically sealed off from the source of their religion, in my case the influence of Buddhism in Madras when I was nine, and then my subsequent western conditioning. How important to be free of the tyranny of self.' The egotist, the self-obsessed actor, the brilliant raconteur, and the other self aware man basically humble, unassuming and longing to be free of himself, were the two conflicting aspects of Peter, ineluctably intertwined within his personality. He was aware of his failure as a man.

I remember his last words at that time as we wandered along the deserted Via della Croce and turned into the Piazza di Spagna, with the twin cupolaed towers of Santa Trinita dei Monti just visible in the dawn of a grey November morning. 'I suppose part of the facility of being able to really act and reach the very top as an actor is that ability to become what those you *need* to impress, expect of you. It's a very personal intuitive process and they must never be aware of what you're doing, acting at its subtlest!' He laughed. 'I know I'm deteriorating at my centre and it's as though I the man am gradually assuming the characteristics of my tarnishing mirrored reflection, like Dorian Gray in reverse, if you know what I mean. But I feel I get nearest to the dark forces within me through painting and poetry and, of course, acting.'

27 *Sunday Bloody Sunday*

By the end of 1969, which Finchie described to me as his panic year, with *The Red Tent* virtually completed and on the verge of being a father for the fourth time, he was very elated at the prospect of starring with David Niven, Liv Ullmann and the Japanese actor (from Alain Resnais' *Hiroshima Mon Amour*) Eiji Okada, in *Man's Fate*. The director was to be Fred Zinnemann. MGM had made a deal with the Italian producer, Carlo Ponti, and everything was ready to begin shooting in London at the end of November. But then there was a shift of power at executive level at MGM, and, after years of preparation, the film of André Malraux's classic was cancelled, and Finchie started drinking heavily to release his feeling of violence, frustration and bitter disappointment. The birth of Diana took his mind off his troubles for a little while and then, one day, Olive Harding rang from London. 'You must fly to London at once, Peter. Joe Janni and John Schlesinger are in a mess. An actor has fallen ill and they want you to come over and play Daniel Hirsh in Penelope Gilliatt's *Sunday Bloody Sunday*.'

'I'm not a queer,' said Peter.

'No, dear,' said Olive, 'but I'd like to see you play one to prove you are an actor.'

So the casting of Peter Finch as the homosexual in *Sunday Bloody Sunday* happened by accident. Ian Bannen had originally been engaged but after about a month of shooting, he was not at all well, and John Schlesinger knew that they could not continue. 'We were in a dreadful dilemma. Time, as always in films, was a desperate priority. Our schedule had come to a halt, so we flew Peter, now available, over from Rome, very surreptitiously. We all met in the Hyde Park Hotel, and he read the script in an evening and then said: 'I think it's a fabulous script and a wonderful part, and I'd love to do it if you want me.'

'Then the real drama began. We had already cast the boy, Murray Head, and I had a terrible fear that the age difference would be too marked, but I was wrong, and it worked fine. Now, I can't think of anyone who could have done it better. For me, he was definitive. It was interesting, because I remember we'd had terrible difficulty with the opening scene of the picture. When Peter and I were on the set filming it, he said: "I'm sorry there's something wrong. I don't know what it is, but I resist. Can we go into your office for five minutes?" So I said: "All right," and I broke the set, and he said: "There's something wrong with the scene." We had already shot it with Ian Bannen and it hadn't worked. We started again with Peter. There was a kind of unspoken impasse, and I thought something was really wrong. Poor Richard Pearson, who was playing, said: "Is it my fault, is it my fault?" "No," I said, "it's not your fault. There's something wrong with the scene." We then realized that the scene had been written from the wrong point of view and needed reshaping. So we abandoned it, Penelope Gilliatt rewrote it and it worked perfectly later.'

I asked John Schlesinger what he felt made Peter a unique actor. 'I acted with him once, when he was playing Captain Langsdorff of the *Graf Spee*. I was his master-at-arms. I had very little to do in the film, but I remember being so impressed by Peter. There was an inner power and stillness, an intensity of concentration. You felt he **was** Langsdorff. One of the signs of great screen acting, in my opinion, is the ability to convey that there is a great deal more to come than is already evident. I think it's what makes the best screen actors, and Peter was certainly one of them. That's what *Sunday Bloody Sunday* was about, its sub-text. What wasn't said was as important as what was said, and we knew that when we were making the movie. But I think that's true of practically anything. It just so happened that Penelope Gilliatt gave us a very good script and Peter and Glenda Jackson were both superb performers.'

John Schlesinger is not in favour of analysing the process whereby the actor prepares, and achieves his characterization or the performance he aims to give. Like any good director, he approached Finch and Jackson individually and the scenes took shape, according to the response. Peter just did it, and there was never any nonsense or fuss. 'The interesting thing about Peter is that he didn't like rehearsing too much. He loathed the idea of analysing the scenes and discussing them. He didn't like the idea of rehearsing or improvising or anything like that. He was a deeply complex man. Film acting is not just acting, it's catching something about the essence of a personality very often, and I think that's what makes someone extraordinary in movies, and it was Peter's complexity that was inescapable. I remember sometimes he'd suddenly stop and say, "I've lost it! I've lost it! Please don't let's do any more!"'

Penelope Gilliatt, who wrote *Sunday Bloody Sunday*, saw in Peter an actor who could realize the potential she had envisaged when John Schlesinger and Joseph Janni were about to recast the part of Dr Daniel Hirsh. She had remembered Peter six years before as a definitive Chekhovian actor. 'Finch's Tregorin in *The Seagull* was the best I have ever seen, because he wasn't the traditional haunted figure. He was robust and looked as though he had a long future ahead of him. He looked like a real writer before anything was said to that effect. He seemed absorbed in his thoughts, as though he were gazing into a fire all the time, and seeing images. It was that performance which made me say: "Yes!" when John Schlesinger said: "Shall we try Peter out for Dr Daniel Hirsh in *Sunday Bloody Sunday*?" I shall always remember Peter saying, "Don't give me a line reading, I want to follow the text; so tell me why I'm doing something and then I can do it. In other words, don't give me an inflexion or anything that I can mimic. Give me the impulse, the spark from which I can create, the reason for which I am saying it."'

The conversation turned to that scene in *Sunday Bloody Sunday* which Peter had felt was wrong. 'I had rewritten the opening scene before Peter came in to play Dr Hirsh, and I agreed with Peter about the scene being written from the wrong point of view. I felt it lacked the sophisticated irony in keeping with the overall tone of the film. It was only about eight lines, but as they started the picture, until they were absolutely right, we were off to a wrong start. That is the difference between writing fiction for the printed page and fiction for the actor. As the film progresses you should see this doctor as very exposed, but at the beginning he must appear to be a very sophisticated and self-contained man. It's only much later that you see he is homosexual, Jewish, and has lots of trouble with both those backgrounds. But at first you have to see him as someone in command, and that was the essential thing that I'd missed. I'd written him as being sympathetic to a woman patient and it wasn't right; it had to be with someone who he could be slightly comic with and send up a little. The original concept I had, which instinctively worried Peter, was too serious. It is probably

291

only twelve to eighteen seconds of screen time but, like the first heartbeat of a child once it's born, it's vital! From then on Peter absolutely got the character. He saw that this was a man who was helping other people all the time and not exposing his own problems, and we see them only gradually. One realizes that he's in a state of devolution, that he's terribly in love with a boy whom he can't say he's in love with, to whom he doesn't want to say "Please come". He doesn't want to be grasping. In the end he has an affinity with the girl, which is why I found it absolutely essential to have a sort of apex where he and the girl meet and share the same sense of humour, and you have a curious feeling that these two are made for each other. These two older people have this meeting over the car when they share exactly the same, quick, soured, ironic sense of humour. The girl decides that her only way of coping with life, is to sweep the decks and say "No!" She's got to have nothing, and that nothing is better than something. The doctor thinks that something is better than nothing. He says, "Half a loaf is better than no bread." They both say precisely opposite things. They're so diverse that they're absolutely in communion. The polarity of opposites creating a real attraction.

'Peter was a technical actor, in the best sense, but he could rummage around in the attic of his subconscious to find what something or other connected with. He wanted to serve the text, which any good actor does, because I think any good actor has a literary sense and Pete being a writer, had a very good literary sense. He knew the structure, and he knew the problems of the writer as well as those of the actor. Very often, actors are blamed for not playing good parts, very often it's not their fault. They just don't get sent good scripts.'

Sunday freed Pete from tax worries and enabled him to remain financially stable, and it was Olive Harding who was responsible for that, for it was she who negotiated his contract for the film. After it, Peter asked her to work for him exclusively and she agreed. Then the next day she received an official letter asking her to send all his papers back to him as he was going to another agent, Barry Krost. Peter said he was riding the crest and this was his chance to go up into the big time. 'I had a letter from Peter terminating his contract. Then he kept trying to reach me on the 'phone. "Where's Olive? Is she on holiday?" One morning my secretary said: "Mr Finch is on the line," and I said: "I'm at Pinewood. Take a message." He wanted to have lunch with me. Luckily they had the sense to say they'd ring him back after they'd contacted me at Pinewood. A date was fixed. When I got to the restaurant, I was shaking like a jelly. While I was paying the taxi, the door opened and there was Peter. I was very calm. I gave him my hand to shake. He tried to kiss me and I just walked in and we went and sat down. The waiter came with the menu and I ordered something. Peter tried to talk and I wouldn't. Then we had something put in front of us and he said: "Did you get my letter?" and I said: "Yes, Peter, I got your letter," and he said, "And is it all right?" I said: "My dear boy, if you want to leave, leave. If I'm not good enough for you, try somewhere else. Off you go!" He said: "You don't mind?" I said: "I mind like crazy, Peter! I mind very much, but it's you we're talking about, not me," and he burst into tears. So did I. We had to get out of that restaurant very quickly, buying two bottles of champagne on the way. We went back and locked ourselves in my office while we both howled our eyes out. My secretary came up to the office and knocked on the door and asked if we'd like a cup of tea, but I said what we wanted were glasses for the champagne. He did funny things. People could make him change his mind, just like that. He'd come to me and say the most peculiar things about buying a house, here, there, or somewhere else, because everyone had told him it was a good idea and I used to say, "Oh well, Peter. We shall need a mortgage, we shall need this, we shall need that," and he'd say: "How many pictures would I have to make this year?" and I would say: "Oh, dozens I should think." "Okay," he would say: "Cancel the house!" '

Finchie, who by nature would have preferred to run barefoot with a knapsack on his back rather than live in a comfortable home with his slippers by the fire, always remained to Olive 'a little boy lost!' Finchie himself admitted: 'Olive was the only woman to whom I never actually lied. I never needed to! What was the point? Lying to Olive was like lying to myself. She could see through me every time!'

Olive's handling of Peter over his acceptance and contract for *Sunday Bloody Sunday* was an instance of her knowing how to guide him. Finchie knew this, and he also knew that Olive had the intelligence to give him his head and let him decide when she'd pushed him far enough. He reckoned he'd have lasted about half as long financially and professionally as he did up until *The Red Tent* in 1969, 'if Auntie Olive hadn't handled my affairs and thrown iced water over me from time to time'.

As the homosexual Dr Daniel Hirsh, Olive knew that Peter had to commit himself to one of the most taxing roles of his career without a lot of thought, 'without talking to all those ladies about playing the part, and listening to what each one said. He had to go into it on his own.'

Olive cannot bring herself to sit through either of his last two films, *Raid On Entebbe* and *Network*, because she is sure that in watching the films she will see exactly why he died. Ted Ardini, who had been really close to Peter at the beginning of his career in the George Sorlie days, feels the same way. Half-sister Flavia, on one of Peter's visits to England to film, had tried to persuade him to come back into the English theatre.

'I love being in London,' he said, 'to sit in a London theatre like the Haymarket or Wyndhams and see all the old gilt. There's an atmosphere and tradition which is unique. That's what I miss in Los Angeles and Jamaica. I'd love to work on the English stage again.'

'Why don't you?' asked Flavia.

'Oh come on, darling. They've forgotten me by now. It's too late.' She reminded him of what he'd done in his first years in London, and added: 'Your stage work has given your film work depth and subtlety. Why not concentrate on something that will really stretch all your faculties and potential in a season of classical plays ? For God's sake, come back!'

'Do you think I really could?' he said.

'I saw a look in Peter's eyes. We got terribly excited and then Eletha suddenly cut in. No way was Finchie going to stay in England. She felt they didn't need the English, and that was that! Peter had said that one aspect he disliked in the England he had returned to was the feeling of envy everywhere, boosted by advertising and the glossy magazines. The feeling of, "I'm as good as you and why should you have more than me ?" The whole socialist system he believed in had begun to breed a feeling of egalitarian discontent, everyone was richer and everyone was twice as miserable and very grey. But he loved London: London and Rome with all their faults were still home to him. Jamaica had been a wonderful escape, but he had been warned off there several times and as he had come to realize, "I'm a better actor than I am a banana planter." Hollywood provided ideal working conditions and he'd made some marvellous friends there. But the Hollywood sense of its own importance and status were still a joke to him. Just as long as he could work in an industry as efficiently run as Hollywood and enjoy life with his family wherever he wanted to live, that suited him perfectly.'

In 1971, Pete made what turned out to be an unsuccessful film, *Something To Hide*, based on the novel by Nicholas Monsarrat, shot on the Isle of Wight amid the buckets and spades, deck chairs and picnickers. Finchie played Harry, a middle-aged shy retiring Englishman, who takes pity on a pregnant hitch-hiking girl, played by Linda Hayden, who turns out to be ninety miles of bad road for Harry, whose wife, Shelley Winters, is absent. (The audience is left in some doubt as to whether he has done her in or whether she's on holiday.) Having cajoled and blackmailed Harry to let her stay at his place, the hitch-hiker has a baby and the spineless, weak-willed Harry becomes involved in its murder and subsequent disappearance. A pretty impossible melodramatic story, but one of the great underrated performances by Finchie, revealing brilliantly and touchingly so much of his own weakness, gentleness and vulnerability. His unspoken feelings of compassion and reluctance to give her a lift and the shots of Peter's reactions, after his prang when the aggressive girl leaps into his Morris 1000 Traveller, and later watching the incinerator smoke, are fine examples of a part permeating his whole physical being. Peter shows himself as an actor who never played for a cheap effect. He is, in this role, absolutely what Olive Harding describes as 'little boy lost'. But the film was yet another that added up to nothing for Peter at the time.

Peter Duffell, who directed Peter in the adaptation of Graham Greene's *England Made Me* in the winter of 1971–2, used to play flamenco guitar in the 1950s.

Duffell needed a box office draw to get financial backing for *England Made Me* and Krost suggested Peter Finch. Duffell asked Jack Levin, the producer, whether a definite offer could be made to Finch. Levin agreed Finch would be a good choice as an actor on whom they could raise sufficient money, so Peter was approached and, as an admirer of Graham Greene's work, accepted. He also accepted because he had not had the opportunity before to play what the character Erich Krogh, the millionaire industrialist, demanded of him: to dominate with self-imposed dignity, as a man who was ruthless, lonely, never able to let himself go, awkward socially. It was a role Peter knew Jean Gabin could play to perfection but for him it was a new adventure into the realms of characterization on the screen.

The character as conceived in the novel by Greene – to be realized on the screen with a change of locale from Sweden to pre-war Nazi Germany – meant that Peter had to portray German inflexibility and stolidness that was alien to his character. Desmond Cory and Peter Duffell omitted from their screenplay certain sympathetic characterizations Greene had included to balance Krogh's single-minded pursuit for personal survival, which Peter had to supplement in his performance. But Peter had a taut script by a master of characterization. He admired Greene enormously as 'an amusing Jacobite', and had enjoyed the challenge of playing Robert Louis Stevenson's (Greene's great-uncle) Jacobite, Alan Breck Stewart, in *Kidnapped*, eleven years before. Peter also had a healthy respect for Graham Greene's cool non-conformity; his curiosity to learn through travel; and what Finchie felt was Greene's 'commonsense Catholic atheism'.

As an occasional writer, Peter admired the exactness of Greene's prose, his understanding of true loyalty and the irony of love in both its comic and tragic aspects. He felt an affinity with Greene, a writer who really knew the sterile unbearable boredom of people like himself who lived through the imagination. Finchie always insisted that, like so many of Greene's characters, he knew good from evil but that he often didn't know right from wrong. Greene had a point of view with which he could identify and he respected Greene's total understanding of the ambivalent standards of morality. In Greene's writing, like chess, he always found an infinite variety of possibilities, but with a disciplined logical form on which his imagination could take wing, and he felt that Greene had the chameleon-like quality that he himself had as an actor.

He wasn't really concerned so much about whether he would be a success as Krogh, as he was about convincing himself that to suggest Teutonic, implacable efficiency and strength was well within his range. All through the shooting of the picture, in Yugoslavia, he was deep into William Manchester's *Life of*

Krupp, to find out the background and what the character was all about. He felt, on this project, he was in no way repeating other past work.

Peter received some very good discriminating notices in the press, as did Peter Duffell. When Graham Greene saw the film a second time, he felt able to see it less in terms of himself. On the first viewing he had felt that certain important points had been dropped, but Finchie does emerge as a rounded character – totally ruthless, but not unsympathetic – and Graham Greene was very impressed with what Peter had done with Krogh. He told me that, as Father Rank in *The Heart of the Matter*, Peter had left no impression on him at all. But, he added, that could have been the fault of the film.

Peter's performances in both Graham Greene films will probably be seen in a very different light when viewed retrospectively. Peter, faithful to Greene's concept of both characters, is very economic and subtle in two vastly differing roles.

It is also interesting to see the enormous contrast in his two German characterizations: the sensitive, introverted Imperial German Captain Langsdorff of the *Graf Spee*, driven by patriotism, and Erich Krogh, the less sensitive but also introverted pro-Nazi industrialist in *England Made Me*. As Krogh he suggests the heaviness of socially awkward people. Finch makes Krogh the phlegmatic businessman whose cold ruthlessness is masked by a stolid geniality. Peter Duffell summed up Peter's performance in *England Made Me* during the cutting of the film. 'The quality of any really good screen actor like Peter is that you can use any foot of film. In any scene he was in, you could almost play the whole scene on him. Those sort of artists never go dead. If an actor isn't used to film, very often in between his own lines, he can go dead behind the eyes. I've had producers say to me during rushes, "I'm a bit worried about so and so's performance," and I've replied, "Don't worry, wait until it's cut," meaning I'll cut out their dead seconds on the screen. I'll use part of my covering footage. That's part of a director's job; not to be on an artist when they've gone dead.'

Finchie, on location in Yugoslavia, told Duffell of an experience he'd had with John Kay when they were rehearsing *Le Malade Imaginaire* for the factory tours in Sydney. It was something he'd always remembered. 'I thought about my character of Argan at home. I worked everything out in detail. I left nothing to chance, even before we had the first read through with Kay. Then we got up on stage and began to plot the moves. He came to me and said, "Peter, this is going to be very good. You've thought about this, but at this stage you've thought too much. Leave a little something for *le bon Dieu . . .*" '

Immediately after shooting *England Made Me* in Yugoslavia, in 1972, Peter was cast to play Robert Conway, the idealized hero in the remake of the James Hilton novel, *Lost Horizon*. It was Hollywood producer, Ross Hunter (who had made such successes with Universal as *Airport*, *Thoroughly Modern Millie* and *The Magnificent Obsession* among others), who gave Pete – and Finchie was his first choice for the role – the opportunity to carry a major Hollywood multi-million dollar picture. But Peter had misgivings about it on two counts: firstly, Hollywood was imitating itself again as Ronald Colman, the original Conway, had been the perfect British romantic archetype in what had turned out to be a very successful movie; secondly, it was to be a musical version and Finchie had to sing. 'I couldn't carry a tune in a bucket and trying to sing when you are a non-singer is a bloody nightmare especially when there are millions of dollars at stake and you are supposed to be the romantic interest! I can't read music, I'm tone deaf. I had this lady who taught me for two months. She was a really brave woman. She had to literally drum the songs into my head, and she actually lasted out the eight weeks!'

Then, as though all that refined torture wasn't enough, there was the indescribable moment of truth when his songs had to be filmed which was done by recording each of the songs on a tape and then lip synchronizing to the tape while he acted in front of the cameras. An actor has to be spot on doing this, or he looks like a ventriloquist that's gone horribly wrong. 'I felt like a poor man's Charlie McCarthy on that movie,' Pete said. 'Christ! What an experience! It became my worst agony since I escaped from the army! I'd built up a psychological terror for this technical and, for me, impossible feat of singing.'

When I spoke to Arnold Weissberger, Rex Harrison's lawyer, about Pete's ability as a singer, he told me a client of his had been planning a musical based on Shaw's *Caesar and Cleopatra* called *Her First Roman*, and he wanted Weissberger to approach Finch about it. 'So I saw Peter and told him that, after *My Fair Lady*, when actors were asked whether they could sing, they would answer: "I can sing as well as Rex Harrison." I then said to Peter: "By the way, how well do **you** sing?" and he replied: "Oh, I sing as well as the people who say they sing as well as Rex Harrison"!'

Lost Horizon was unfortunately just another disaster. Ross Hunter, who had known Peter for many years, rang him in London after Peter had received the script for it, and said that at that time what appealed to Peter about it was the mystical aspect of the project, but he realized that as a theme it would need very adroit handling. The assembly of talent for *Lost Horizon* was prodigious and I asked Ross Hunter why the film was a failure. 'The true stories about the making of so many movies are never told. I can only say that when you're under contract to a studio, as I was with *Lost Horizon*, your hands are tied because you are forced to use certain people in certain categories who may be wrong for the movie, just to get rid of a studio's commitment. Nobody realizes that and they blame the producer. The producer, if he's any kind of a gentleman, will hold his head high and go along with the wrong chemistry and take the rap.'

But Ross Hunter has nothing but praise for Peter's loyalty and untiring efforts to make the film a success, and to promote it to the very best of his ability. Once he saw the rough cut he knew it was doomed and wrongly conceived. He and Bosley Crowther, the American film critic working as script advisor for Columbia, felt it would have been better to up-date the story into Vietnam.

What also endeared Peter to Ross Hunter, who took the responsibility for *Lost Horizon*, was that Peter would never let on professionally while working on the picture, what he really felt about it, yet he knew he was a glittering figurehead on a trivial empty structure. When I spoke to Sir John Gielgud about Peter and *Lost Horizon* (in which Gielgud played the Dalai-Lama), he said: 'Oh God! That film! It went on, and on, and on, in the endless deserts of California, or was it Arizona? I can't remember. Peter just used to vanish on Friday evening as soon as the blessed release bell went. He spent the weekend in the bar seeking his Shangri-La in forgetfulness of the eternal awful present. I adored Eletha. She was the only thing that made me laugh and restored my sanity. What a bore all that was!'

Lost Horizon was followed by a hardly more successful film, *Bequest to the Nation*. Peter and Eletha took a flat in what were once stables in De Vere Mews, Kensington, during the shooting of it at Shepperton Studios in the summer of 1972. It was rumoured that Richard Burton was very keen to play the role of Lord Nelson, but producer Hal Wallis wanted to make the picture with Peter Finch and with Glenda Jackson as Emma Hamilton. It was at this time, not long before his fifty-sixth birthday, that Peter hinted to me that he mightn't live as long as he hoped because his heart was beginning to find him out. It was something he'd sensed but he was quite determined to let nature take its course.

James Cellan Jones, who directed *Bequest to the Nation*, told me: 'There were no problems with Finchie's heart while we were shooting the picture. I wanted Peter, but I wanted Ava Gardner or Elizabeth Taylor for Lady Hamilton, because they would have been physically right, but Wallis insisted on having Glenda Jackson. Emma Hamilton was fourteen and a half stone. Glenda is about seven, but Hal Wallis' choice was final. What went wrong with the picture to my mind was that Glenda, who is a really fine actress, was woefully miscast and she knew it. She is too good an actress not to know it went sour on her. Finchie was absolutely furious with Glenda for putting out to the press before the film's release that it was a bad picture.'

But there were never any altercations on the set between Peter and Glenda, though there was great tension between the two stars. However, Peter and the director, James Cellan Jones, had one row during the shooting at Shepperton. James insisted that Finchie rehearse one long complicated wordy scene. Peter was fighting the scene. 'I insisted he learn it DLP (dead letter perfect), and that we rehearse it very carefully, and we did. He was an actor of enormous technical expertise as well as an intuitive actor, but he had a sort of superstitious quality about him which made him fear that if he played the thing too soon, and hit the right level of emotion at once, it would waste itself on the morning air and he'd never be able to recapture it, but he was an absolute joy to work with.'

Terence Rattigan did the scenario which, according to James, 'wasn't among Rattigan's best, as he was ill at the time. But Peter got deeply involved in the character of Nelson, though what he found difficult were his own religious feelings in relation to Nelson's. Peter found it difficult to identify with Nelson's point of view. But he did succeed in the end. When he had to do Nelson's (whose father had been a vicar) last prayer, they were

Nelson's own words, not Rattigan's, and Peter made it a very moving occasion. I feel, as its director, that bits of the battle came off and the very beginning and the very end of the film are good, but we used some library stuff in it and we shouldn't have.'

Peter was very disappointed that he was made to wear an eye patch as Nelson. 'Nelson never wore one and I didn't see why I should,' he said to Cellan Jones. It was a case of pandering to a public misconception, a sore point with Peter who was insistent they should be historically accurate. Finchie and Nelson had one thing in common, however; a complete disregard for convention and authority, and an obsessive love of their women. He was very down-to-earth about Nelson when I spoke to him in the flat in De Vere Mews. I remember we discussed his feelings about Nelson to the accompaniment of clipped English voices, the neighing of horses and the clip-clop of hooves on the cobbles below, as the flat was part of the Civil Service Riding Club.

Finchie showed me how he put his right arm down inside the back of his trousers, under his blue jacket with the gold epaulettes. I couldn't resist teasing him and asking him if he thought Nelson might have known 'the Indian flute player routine' which Pete had us splitting our sides over in the Chelsea pub. 'Nelson wasn't raised in vaudeville as I was. I doubt his brilliance in naval improvisation was ever below the navel like mine.'

Peter, who possessed one suit at his first wedding, one at his second and two at his third, was convinced 'Nelson didn't care a bugger at heart for the pretence of putting on his Sunday best. I'm sure the gilt and all those magnificent decorations from various European potentates were put on to dazzle those poor press-ganged sods who needed a one-eyed, one-armed god. What a part for an actor. He fucked up Napoleon's career, cocked a snook at Whitehall and they had to accept him. He broke the sacred British code and had such a loose upper lip he wasn't ashamed to weep. He had a smashing broad, and died in harness. Christ! They don't come better than that!'

A few days before writing this I went back to look at Finchie's horse-box where he'd flung his arms around me in greeting over the top half of the stable door like an excited child. 'G'day you fucking acrobatic flamenco-dancing bastard, wonderful to see you!' had been his first words as the bottom half of the stable door was unbolted, and I was swept in to meet 'Leta' and Diana, and we all watched Peter put the imaginary telescope to his blind eye while he told me he could see Villeneuve swinging hard to starboard off Copenhagen. He gave me gooseflesh because he made me really see the French man-o'-war so vividly – yet the film was such a disappointment on its release. When I arrived at De Vere Mews, Finchie's stables were boarded up, and the builders were transforming a hidden pocket of old London into smart modern luxury apartments for the new executive age.

After his success with *The Lion in Winter*, Anthony Harvey wanted Peter Finch as his first choice for the difficult role of Cardinal Azzolino, to play opposite Liv Ullmann in *The Abdication*, for Warner Brothers. Of all the films Peter made this was the one he was most reluctant to do because of the demands it made on his secret self. Judith Crist, writing for *New York* magazine said: 'Christina of Sweden, the seventeenth century patroness of culture and most powerful of Protestant monarchs who, claiming conversion to Catholicism, abdicated and journeyed to Rome to receive communion from the Pope. There, with a dying Pope and a College of Cardinals, sceptical of this "scandalous" woman's professions of faith, she was subjected to an inquisition at the hands of Cardinal Azzolino. And it was this scathing inquisition, which begins as a duel but slowly becomes a psychoanalysis and then a courtship, the developing relationship between the queen and the cardinal that provides the fascination of the film. Miss Ullmann probes to the heart of the problem, facing today's liberated woman as she subjects herself to the cold, intellectual scrutiny of Peter Finch's cardinal: a man of passion who has rationalized his own choice between the spiritual and the carnal . . .'

Tony Harvey first met Peter when he went to his home in Lugano, with the author, Ruth Wolff, and the blessing of Warner Brothers who felt Peter would be the ideal choice. Liv Ullmann had already agreed to play Christina. He phoned Peter to put the project to him and found that Peter was reluctant to tackle it. His last four films had drained him and now he was being approached to tackle a cardinal with a conscience, in a part that would demand more of him than any he had played hitherto. It took Tony Harvey three weeks to convince Peter, along with certain rewrites which he stipulated, that the role was worth his while, and that he and Liv Ullmann could create an unusual kind of screen magic.

On the first day's shooting at Pinewood Studios, Tony Harvey remembers: 'Peter had this incredible presence on the floor as Azzolino that you felt was a distillation of all those years as an actor. I'd seen him first as Iago in 1951, and from Peter came this quality of all the great screen actors of the old tradition. He just did it rather than trying to analyse it. I sometimes felt, watching him from behind the camera, that the performance wasn't coming across and when I saw the rushes on the following day, they were devastating because he brought to the character an inner quality which shone through.'

There was trouble with Peter's heart on *The Abdication*. 'The doctors say my heart misses one beat in every ten,' he told me. 'I told them it always had. "Well!" the doctors told me, "if you don't knock off the booze, cut the fags and live more simply, there'll be no more Peter Finch!" ' So, with pressure from Eletha, he tried to do just that for the next two years.

After Pinewood in May 1973, they shot in Italy, at the Palazzo Farnese at Caprarola, near Lago di Vico, outside Rome and down at Caserta. The difficult confrontation and battle of wills between Peter and his director came in Peter's key scene when Cardinal Azzolino falls to his knees just prior to the announcement that the Pope is dying, and bares his soul to the abdicator. Finchie, in that moment of filming, had to come to terms with himself and his own conscience. There were two ways he could play the scene: by holding back the bottled-up emotions of a lifetime; or by breaking down and showing total vulnerability, which very few actors have the courage to attempt. He chose the first. 'If I don't show emotion, if I play it with less than you want, it will be more moving.'

'No,' argued Tony. 'This is the moment when you can afford to show tears because you are being absolutely ripped apart. The need to be within a woman in perfect love is greater than the man's need for God who has been his mainstay through a lifetime of self discipline and genuine devotion. By letting yourself go, the chinks in the armour should start to open and we should see the rock-like Azzolino really come apart.'

They shot the scene and at the end Peter said to Tony: 'I'm not giving you what you want, am I?' They walked around for hours, then Tony said: 'Go on Peter, jump off the cliff. Be daring. Give yourself to the scene and just do it, as only you can.' 'All right,' Pete said. 'You win, but I can only possibly do it once.'

Tony said he did it in one take and that it was magic. In 1967, with John Schlesinger in *Far From The Madding Crowd*, he had wanted covering shots on himself. By 1973, he was saying to Tony Harvey: 'Do you really need that shot on me?'

Peter, conveying a man suddenly aware of his true nature, shows his maturity in playing Azzolino with a stricken sense of resignation at the inevitable act of renunciation he must make. Peter's honest cardinal is a man who has borne all the horrors of conscience with the awareness that free will is the supreme double-edged gift God had given to mankind. Many of the critics savaged the film, which opened in New York the night after Ingmar Bergman's *Scenes From A Marriage*, which also starred Liv Ullmann. But Bergman praised Liv's and Peter's performances, and Judith Crist rated Azzolino one of Peter's subtlest and greatest performances.

Finchie just laughed at the reaction to the film and decided to cool the film scene for a while and return to Jamaica. The bananas were calling. During 1974 and early 1975, Peter and Eletha together were to farm 107 acres of bananas, pimientos, citrus and timber on their north coast plantation, Brighton, not far from Ocho Rios. Peter's voluntary exile from the film industry lasted until early 1976 when he was offered the role of Howard Beale in *Network*.

28 Jamaica

Ali Dougal, who looks and sounds like an Irishman, with the added richness of the soft, Jamaican intonation, used to advise and look after Peter's property at Bamboo – seven acres of land in the parish of St Ann, on the north coast of Jamaica, on which Finchie subsequently built a house. He remembers Peter first arriving on one of the banana boats in 1961, with Yolande, a babe in arms, and a nurse. He stayed at the luxurious Shaw Park Hotel, and often did his drinking in the bar at Golden Head. He became fascinated with the idea of buying a small plantation which he would run himself.

Dougal is a white Jamaican. It was he whom I had tried unsuccessfully to find when I came to Bamboo looking for Peter in 1964, while I was working on the island a few miles up the coast at Runaway Bay. At that time, Finchie hadn't built his house. There was only this compact plot of land with a bamboo growing at the gate, and enough garden produce to make it completely self-contained.

Finchie told me, in April 1966 while building was under way, that Bamboo was 'the only house I ever really cared about, because I planned it; there was peace, freedom and those Jamaicans, and I loved them all!' But even Finchie with a bottomless well of love for his black brothers became highly frustrated by the lack of activity when it came to mixing the cement and digging the foundations and getting the 'bloody house up'. So off he went and bought them all the best tools and the equipment needed to build his earthly paradise, but when he returned later there they all were at eleven in the morning sitting under the trees, having done 'sweet f.a.'. So he thought, I'll show them, and he took off his shirt, lifted up the pick and began hacking away in the blazing heat. Having dug the trench he reeled down the chine, away to Ocho Rios, or wherever, to the tender ministrations of Eletha – and he left them to it. Now, he thought, they can't possibly go back on that and see a white man faze them. 'I managed to extricate myself from the sack and limp my way back up the hill thinking, well, the house will be halfway up by now. I got there and found these bludgers still sitting there, under the trees. "What the hell's going on?" I asked. "We're waiting for you, Petah. My God, you are a bloody good worker!" ' The house was eventually built in nine months and finished for Peter by Christmas 1966.

I went up into the little village of Bamboo with my driver, Blues Morris (who used to look after Richard Burton on the film *Seawife and Biscuit* and who drove Finchie everywhere until he met Eletha). About a mile and a half up the chalky road above the Bamboo property, there is a small rickety rum shop where you can get the real seventy percent proof white Appleton rum – a glass of that, and you can feel the cane-cutters quarrelling all along your colon. This was the fuel that gave Peter the added strength in a temperature of 100 to go hurrying down eight miles of road to St Ann's Bay. The little bar, more like a wooden shack, with its rows of rum and red-striped beer bottles, was full of Jamaicans. It was Sunday morning and the old juke box was beating out reggae. The old men, with deeply lined faces, sunken eyes like brown marbles blinking through linseed oil, were drinking and chatting away in Bamboo patois, while the knees and hips of the younger ones, moved to the reggae beat. I mentioned Finchie.

'Him talk to everyone. Him drink here, white rum, and then him go off with a little brown dog. Miles and miles he'd walk. Him love Jamaica. Not de posh Jamaica. Him no tourist. Him not like a foreigner. Flynch, him die sudden, but him well here.'

Having received an invitation while I was in Jamaica, I decided to go and see Eran Spiro, to whom Peter sold Bamboo in 1972. We sat on the verandah of the property and he told me how Finchie often used to go back and visit him, that he had never really wanted to leave it, as it served his needs as a contented bachelor. But never able to remain a bachelor for long, he found himself caught up with Eletha, and sought a new challenge farming 107 acres of bananas, allspice, citrus and timber on his next Jamaican estate, Brighton. When he came back to visit Eran Spiro he'd sit quite happily in the ingle-nook seat on the verandah at dusk, staring at the insects circling and looping about, just visible in the twilight. 'Look,' he'd say, 'imagine the ecstasy of being able to copulate in mid-air like those fire-flies.' One evening he and Eran were sitting silently over their drinks when a large 'John Crow' spread his wings and hovered motionless above them. Peter said: 'I can really imagine I am that bird hovering and I can see us down here from his position of flight. When I become that bird I realize more than ever that the world we live in is a global village, and that we've got to think and live internationally.' He told Eran (who was a kibbutz man from Israel) how he'd insisted they let him work on a kibbutz during the making of *Judith*, and how he'd been able, though not a Jew, to identify at once and become a part of the kibbutz community. Watch how in this, like all his films, Finch's skin tones and natural colouring always blend perfectly with any exterior landscape. He was very aware that the whole way of life in the modern world, where luxury has become a necessity, is a softening and vitiating process. He found the kibbutz environment like the life he was living in Jamaica – a way of recharging himself and living in greater harmony with the natural laws.

When Peter first met Eletha, he had already commissioned the Italian architect, Maffessanti, a Jamaican resident, to design and build him his house, and had probably decided then that he wanted a house there. Bamboo, now renamed, is a very simple but beautiful little fawn-coloured Jamaican villa with green jalousies and scarlet window frames. The cedar and pine doors and windows are treated to keep away the insects that would otherwise devour them in no time. Peter had insisted on one bedroom only, a central living room with a canopied fireplace and tiled surround in one corner, a cedar dining table and Welsh dresser, all specially built, a plain white kitchen with lots of cupboard space and plenty of surfaces to work on. A long verandah with two ingle-nook seats at right angles at one end; and he had a spectacular view from the high ridge where Bamboo stands looking down the mountainside across the Richmond Llandovery sugar plantation to the Caribbean coastline of St Ann's Bay. If Finchie had ever wanted to look through a telescope from his verandah at night, he could have seen the lights of Guantamano Bay in Cuba, ninety miles to the north. Everything at Bamboo is practical and designed for simple living. Peter's only home reveals the basic simplicity of his domestic needs. It is both natural and beautiful. He had two cedar desks made, one for the bedroom and the other for the little studio, a hundred yards away, across the garden, which Maffessanti designed as a place to live in while the house was being built. The surrounding garden, which is like a plateau above the countryside, consists of lawns interspersed with every kind of tropical tree, flower and vegetable imaginable: sweet sop, sour sop, pimiento, otahee ti, citrus, coconut, orchids, hibiscus, bougainvillea, yams, sweet potatoes, pumpkins, etc. It is not only an exquisite blaze of colour but a perfect little plantation, ideal for one man to live there productively.

To ensure Bamboo was productive in timber alone he planted cedar, mahogany and mahoe trees. The little property is characteristically Peter Finch and offers a benign welcome. Finchie had the Tolstoyan ideal that if you're going to work, share the sweat and effort with the Jamaicans, provided of course that you can induce them to work for and with you. He didn't believe in being a verandah planter.

The studio, a little rectangular building like a doll's house, consists of one room and a bathroom, with a window that looks down across lush, tropical vegetation to the town of St Ann's, four miles away. When Peter first met Maffessanti, he told him that he really loved Jamaica, that it was home to him, that he would come back to Jamaica whenever he could, and this is why he wanted his own house there. The agent, Ben Johnson, had found the land for him and had introduced him to the architect.

The conversation I had with Ernesto Maffessanti, on his verandah overlooking the bay at Ocho Rios, was on an evening punctuated by a gentle symphony of tropical night sounds, led by the Jamaican crickets, who seemed to tune up automatically the moment the sun went down. Peter had often sat on this verandah, sipping his rum, and commenting on the very same music.

'For goodness sake, why do you only want one bedroom?' the architect had argued when he and Peter were drawing up the plans.

'One bedroom . . . why more?' said Peter.

'What about your guests?'

'One bedroom – and the studio in the garden, as an escape for me.'

The pressure was really on to build the studio quickly so that he could have a private room. Meanwhile, he lived in a tent and used the makeshift bush lavatory that the builders had constructed for themselves.

During the building of the house, Finchie became a friend of the Maffessanti family, and was able to brush up his Italian. He came back intermittently to Jamaica in the 1960s, usually with a different woman, but eventually he met Eletha, twenty-seven years younger than himself, on the beach and Eletha really took him in hand.

Eletha was ambitious for Peter and was the driving force behind his easy-going temperament and attitude to life. She antagonized some Jamaicans, but others adored her. Peter certainly did. She gave him the single-minded devotion and care typical of a woman of her race, and at that period in his life she was exactly what he needed. By being close to Eletha, Peter was constantly in touch with the roots of Jamaica. But she was no passenger. She was financially independent when she met Peter, always drove her own car, which she paid for, has a very high IQ, and speaks French, Italian and German.

Finchie's relationship with Eletha was more than just an ideal. Everyone I spoke to concerning Eletha commented on her appearance: always a clean dress, a ribbon in the hair, perhaps a flower. It's generally agreed on the island that she is a very direct lady, with a passionate, completely uninhibited nature 'fiercely protective of her man'.

Eletha's fastidiousness about dress to please her Finchie, flattered and pleased him. He accepted from Eletha the ironed shirt, the clean handkerchief, the pressed trousers he was to wear for the interview or TV promotion because it was given for his sake, not for the sake of keeping up appearances. The image they presented to the world was inspired by the desire to please each other. It had its natural origins in love.

Eletha loved dancing, and through living there over the years Peter had become aware that the modern Jamaican music and song which is now such a tourist attraction evolved through a tradition which has its roots in slavery. 'Watch white people dancing the reggae,' he once told me, 'they're never contained.' He described the sort of relaxed euphoria which the Jamaicans seem to go into when they really get the reggae beat in their blood as 'a dread mood with contained anger'. He believed the lyrics and musical sound were a comment on the Jamaican social situation, and the ghetto suffering. For Finchie, Jamaican music had a creative tension built up between the despair and hope of the years and conditions of slavery: 'Their music and song absolutely get to me, because it is a cry from the heart, and it's a primitive compelling sound.'

Finchie had read a good deal about slavery over the years, and what fascinated him was the residue of evil it left in Jamaican folk lore. Along with the ashanti names and tribal religious customs, the slaves also brought that peculiar form of witchcraft known as 'obeah' which Finchie was able to use for his own purposes on one occasion. The first thing he did when Bamboo was finished, was build a shelf in the porch over his front door, where he installed a favourite object – his big black Buddha. A couple of weeks later, a local 'tiefed' it. The Buddha was about the only material possession that ever meant much to Peter, so up he went to the little bars and rum shops and noised it about that his black Buddha enabled him to work 'obeah' and if anybody tried to take possession of it, they were likely to die a very painful and lingering death. His Buddha had such powers of evil that death could also spread through the family. The following night, Finchie's Buddha was back in its niche where it remained undisturbed thereafter.

Finchie would think nothing of jogging the eight tortuous miles down from Bamboo into St Ann's Bay. Maffessanti would often stop his car and offer him a lift, but Finchie always refused.

'I need the exercise,' he told the architect. 'Keeps me from getting too soft. An actor has always got to be at his very best, like a racehorse, and like a racehorse, you're expected to win every time out. Also, I can really think and relax while I'm walking.'

Sometimes at night, having walked God knows how many miles, he'd appear unexpectedly at Casa Maffessanti. Or he might decide to cut across country over the mountains from Bamboo to Liberty Hill, to see his friend Leslie Nathan, who owns an old colonial plantation house with a long, shady vine-hung verandah with yet another breath-taking panoramic view of the coastline. When Finchie arrived, they'd sit down together with a large bottle of Scotch and discuss philosophy, comparative religion, music, literature, and then Leslie would drive him home.

Jamaica became very much 'home' to Peter. He'd met some Jamaicans once in Curacao. 'You goin' home, mahn?' they asked. 'Yes, I'm going home,' he replied. There were remote places near Negril and Savanna la Mar, at the south western end of Jamaica, with miles of white sand, where he and Eletha could find complete solitude, and if they wished, go down and help the fishermen bring in the nets. He'd wander for hours in the Blue Mountain ranges down in Portland, at the other end of the island, where the best means of travel is on the back of a mule. He'd sleep out under the stars and rise at three to watch the sun rise over Haiti just beyond the horizon. He seldom had any feelings of regret he wasn't acting.

When he first went to Jamaica, the locals used to ask him if he'd come there to retire. He was quite offended that they all seemed to think of him as an old man, until it was explained to him that as soon as any Jamaican made his pile, or just enough to get by on, he retired, even if he'd only just reached the age of consent. 'Why work if you've got bread?' was the attitude he found in Jamaica.

As a true Aussie bushman he was quite prepared to accept the Jamaican bush cures. Once he had a very bad bout of 'flu, and they immediately rubbed him from head to toe with that seventy percent proof Appletons white Jamaican rum. Finchie said he stank like a christmas pudding, but that the next day he was completely cured.

Before I first went to Jamaica in 1964, Peter told me about the Islanders' 'leaf of life' which does wonders for the nerves, and he also told me to be sure and sample 'strong back', the Jamaican aphrodisiac. But it is such a foul tasting root that Jamaican impotence might just be preferable.

Finchie also had a great rapport with the Rastafarians, a religious sect who swear allegiance to Haile Selassie, who wear their hair matted in locks and want to go back to Africa. They lived throughout the island of Jamaica and were not the most friendly people, but they always showed good will to Peter. I met a couple one morning this year in Ocho Rios. One was a very wild looking fellow with his hair in rats' tails as though he had been very busy with a pair of old curling tongs. He had known Finchie and used to chat to him sometimes when he went down to the local for a tot of rum at St Ann's Bay. He couldn't tell me why he remembered or liked Peter except that he was friendly and just seemed to fit in there.

Beyond Tower Isle, now called 'The Couples' (because the hotel refuses to take children), going east from Ocho Rios in the direction of Oracabessa, turn right by the river Nuevo, and some three miles inland, beyond Retreat in the Parish of St Mary, lies the property of Brighton, which Finchie bought after he sold Bamboo, and which was to occupy all his energies (and Eletha's) and planning as a planter for about two years. As you drive through the iron gates now, you realize Brighton has become a wilderness. The approach to the house, up a long winding drive, which Finchie had asphalted to make it manageable in wet weather, is a tangle of weeds and neglected banana palms, spreading over 107 acres of hills and gullies. To clear it now would be a daunting task for even the strongest and most experienced.

The water supply to the house had so little pressure that Finchie installed a ramp pump. The water from a spring above the property flowed down through a narrow trough and piping, which Peter installed himself, into a cool, wooded gully. The pump would then send the water up into a tank, fifty feet above the house so there was always a good head of water. He pulled down an old house near the back door and converted it into a concrete barbecue for drying pimientos which would then be put into bags and taken to St Ann's Bay for sale in the market. He needed three cutters and three or four women to head his bananas (carry them in bunches on their heads) from the fields, and two men for packing because the stems have to be packed in 'trash' (banana leaves) so they do not bruise the fruit. They would then be loaded into the Mercedes and Eletha would deliver them to the boxing plant, on a Monday or Tuesday. Bananas aren't seasonal, require tremendous capital outlay in land preparation, fertilizer and weeding, and are a full-time job. Every week, 100 to 150 bunches of bananas were probably carried out to the Mercedes and taken to the boxing plant, of which forty or so would be rejected through bruising, so they would be taken back and placed at the gates of Brighton. Finchie's bruised bananas would then be sold to the villagers, and Eletha would be the sales girl. Finchie used to maintain that of all his legal ties, his binding liaison with 107 acres of bananas at Brighton was the most demanding and gave the least in return. A bunch of bananas had to be treated far more delicately and with even more respect than Liv Ullmann, and then when they were got to market there was about a forty percent rejection – 'like being constantly turned down at auditions for parts you really wanted, only in this case it was because my bloody bananas had swamp spots.'

Finchie also grew limes and these were taken to the factory at Prospect, about six miles away, where the juice was extracted. He grew cedars, too, which were cut down and removed by an outside contractor. Near the house was a citrus grove, with every imaginable variety which Finchie nurtured and tended with great care and pride – he had always loved growing citrus from his days in Ibiza. The coconuts were stacked in the Mercedes and taken to the copra plant at Oracabessa, would be roasted and then sent off to Kingston to make oil and soap. When Norris Daly, a contractor at Ocho Rios, bought Brighton on 5 March 1975, Finchie had 36,000 coconuts locked up in his coconut house, waiting to go to market.

It seemed an ideal existence but Finchie had his troubles at Brighton. For one thing, his pimientos and limes would disappear, and once he had a fierce argument with a Jamaican he found stealing his bananas. In fact, he was being ripped off all round, but he was up against a great moral dilemma. Eletha had no sympathy with what she felt was laziness and dishonesty among her own people, but Peter had starved and knew what it was to have to steal in order to survive. He was well aware of the economic conditions in Jamaica that were causing such hardship among the very poor. How could he blame anyone for doing what he had himself condoned forty years before? Also, the last thing he wanted was to be involved in any Jamaican litigation over the cutting of his fences and the stealing from his land. Rows with the locals in that remote area were not advisable. To begin with, Peter had thought of raising cattle, stabling a few horses so he could ride round and oversee his estate. In the meantime he strode about every day in Wellingtons with his stick, and the Jamaicans who worked with him thought he was having a ball. But the truth is, he absolutely loathed Brighton. Although Maffessanti had restored the house at great expense, eventually Finchie took Eletha's advice and decided he had played the part of the Jamaican planter long enough. At the time he sold Brighton, it was feasible to make a profit, but had he remained, with the stringent current economic conditions, he could have ended up well out of pocket.

Norris Daly remembers Finchie, always smelling of banana

and fertilizer, walking along, his pockets stuffed with sweets. Occasionally he would meet a crowd of children on the dusty road. There would be a cry of delight from the kids, out would come the sweets and off he'd go to pick up his own two kids from Columbus Prep. When Peter sold Brighton to Norris Daly, there were two mules and a cow still there, and Daly arranged to buy them from Peter, so the last time he saw Peter was at Cardiff Hall, the third and last property Peter owned in Jamaica, which he bought in the spring of 1975. This Jamaican stately home had seemed the only workable solution to living in Jamaica, or at least to having a substantial *pied à-terre* there, and he had bought it on Eletha's advice. The house was built in 1789 for the Blagrove family and was originally on an estate of some five square miles. Now reduced to seven acres, the isolated house is just visible through the trees about a mile from the sea.

When Daly arrived at Cardiff Hall to see Peter about buying the livestock still remaining on the Brighton property, Peter was deeply engrossed in the script of *Network* which had just arrived in the post. He told Daly: 'We're going to make this old place a show-place, but at the moment I've got to get under the skin of this television character, Howard Beale.'

Peter, living in retirement, hadn't made a film for two years since *The Abdication* in the autumn of 1973, and he'd sweated his guts out playing the Jamaican planter at Brighton. Then there were those rows with the locals, and his produce being nicked every time he turned his back. 'Those bastards would never steal my allspice or my pimientos when they were dirty. They'd wait till I'd cleaned them all by hand.' He realized by the spring of 1975 it was high time he 'humped his bluey' from Brighton and moved on to the baronial ambience of Cardiff Hall.

Cardiff Hall lies isolated on a wild, thickly wooded hill over-looking Runaway Bay, about six miles up the coast from Bamboo. The approach is up a road eroded by heavy rain, landslides and overgrown with weeds. The huge black wrought-iron gates were padlocked the Sunday I arrived, and a little white gate at the side gave access to a long, curving drive. The ground was a carpet of soft pine needles and the only sound was the eerie soughing of the hot north wind through a canopy of pines. The whole place looked run down and no one seemed to be about. A beautiful, white Georgian house, with a palladian exterior and Adam-style interior decorations, it stands on a high rise with a lawn in front, now thick with weeds, and tall grass, and bordered by a perfect semi-circle of pines. It is recorded that no Jamaican property was handed down over so many generations by the same family as Cardiff Hall. The first Blagrove was a signatory of Charles I's death warrant, and first possession of the land by the Blagrove family was taken up there in 1665. Two large sandstone lions guard the front door, dark polished mahogany with two heavy brass lion head door-knockers. The elegant hall has wide mahogany floor-boards, four Renaissance-style columns, and an imposing staircase down which the ghost of a Miss Blagrove has been seen to glide in a white nightgown. Curving green and white sunblinds keep out the glare, and let in the light.

It is now sparsely but beautifully furnished with pieces of Chippendale and Sheraton, the hangings and draperies chosen by Eletha, but there are water stains on the ceilings and a general air of faded elegance. It is meticulously cared for by Miss Bertha, Eletha's mother, a little dignified old lady, in a straw hat and a blue dress with a white border, and cracked but elegant patent leather shoes. Eletha's brother, who informed me his name was Johnson, lives on the estate, and tries to keep the garden under control.

I was informed in London that the house would be surrounded by barbed wire, and occupied by Jamaican squatters with machine-guns, and that I would go there at the risk of my life. Both mother and son could not have been more friendly and hospitable. I was looking for some vestige of Peter.

At the corner of the house was his favourite coconut palm, from which he used to knock the coconuts. The tree now, like most on the island, has the tell-tale symptoms of 'lethal yellow', a disease carried by the birds that is killing off all the small palms on the island. An almost empty swimming pool, in a far corner of the garden – cracked tiles and a carpet surface of green slime – with a derelict summerhouse and four bleached, cracked flag-poles, gives the whole ruined garden a feeling of sad abandon. Along the coast they were burning off the cane fields, and the wind carried the smell of burnt cane in a haze of white smoke through the trees.

I wandered through the half-empty rooms of this once stately home which Peter and Eletha had planned to turn into a show-place for visitors. The one room that still retains a sense of life is the study. The bookcases were full of books, from Herodotus to modern geology, bound in fine Moroccan leather. A polished Moroccan leather-topped desk, with a photo of Eletha as a bride in Rome, dated November, 1973, and one of Diana, wearing Daddy's biretta from *The Abdication*, well down on her forehead like a large peaked cap, with the cardinal's crucifix round her neck. On the bookshelf a once very elegant but now dilapidated cinnamon felt hat with most of its silk lining hanging out, soaked in sweat, covered in dust, lay where Finchie the planter had thrown it after his last day's work.

29 *Network* and *Raid on Entebbe*

Charles Champlin, film critic of the *Los Angeles Times*, is another American who had been aware of Peter's talent for a very long time. But for him, as with so many Americans, it had only been fully revealed in *Sunday Bloody Sunday*. 'His acting in that,' says Champlin, 'was an exercise in sensitivity, and the ability to convey what's taking place inside a man's head and soul. It wasn't what Finch said, it's what he exuded. Peter had the art that conceals art. To me, he was the character, never Peter Finch. He was never conspicuous in the sense of the actor acting. I was also tremendously impressed by him as Boldwood in Thomas Hardy's *Far From The Madding Crowd*. Some actors can never be anything but contemporary. Julie Christie, whom I love as an actress, was indomitably contemporary as the Hardy heroine. Finch assumed the style, mannerisms and look of the Hardy character, but he never seemed to be acting. He was of that period, with strength, sensitivity, and every nuance realized.' Champlin feels that the irony of Peter's career is that people will remember him for the role which would have made him a superstar, rather than as a superlative actor.

According to Michael Maslansky, hired as Peter's publicist on *Network*, with whom he spent the last six months of his life promoting the film, Peter was fourth choice for the part: George C. Scott, Glenn Ford, and Henry Fonda, had all been offered the role and had turned it down ... Then Paddy Chayefsky thought Peter would be interesting casting and called him in Jamaica. There were to be certain stipulations. Peter had to pay his own fare to New York as they weren't sure he could do the accent, but his interview for the part would also be an audition. He had to convince producer, director and screenwriter that he could do it. If he really wanted to play Howard Beale those were the initial terms, and so he had to show he could deliver the goods. Finchie laughed. 'Bugger pride,' he said. 'Put the script in the mail.' The arrival of the screenplay absolutely galvanized him. His immediate fear was that someone else would be offered the part before he could stake his claim.

When he'd read the script he rushed to the telephone to try and get through to Paddy Chayefsky, but there'd been a hurricane in Jamaica and the telephone lines were down. He was frantic to let them know he was more than interested. When an actor really wants the part of a lifetime and the producers know it, the deal is never on the actor's terms. The money offered (according to press reports) was $100,000 up front and $150,000 on a deferred basis, but to Finchie this was a secondary consideration.

Howard Gottfried, the producer for MGM on *Network*, admitted Peter was a great break for them as the dazzling centre of an absolutely top Hollywood cast. He believes that Finch's presence on that film, with his aura of theatre experience and his dedicated professionalism, had its effect on Faye Dunaway and everyone in the cast.

Until the first meeting with Peter over lunch in New York, Gottfried hadn't realized the variety and amount of experience Peter had actually had in the theatre. The studio was apprehensive about using him, rather than an American, for obvious reasons. But when Gottfried heard the tapes Peter had made after listening to the various American television anchormen, he realized the meticulous preparation and intensive study Peter had put in before he even went for his first interview, and it was decided at once to cast this man who was obviously a formidable character actor. What impressed Gottfried was that Peter didn't want to give a perfect imitation of some American regional accent. He preferred to avoid sounding non-American rather than trying to sound American. 'As Peter described it to us,' Gottfried said, 'there was a very subtle distinction. It was the individual way he looked at it. He was as nervous as hell at that first meeting over lunch and just like a kid auditioning. Once we'd heard him, Sydney Lumet, Paddy and I were ecstatic, because we knew it was a hell of a part to cast. He worked his butt off. He didn't give a goddam what he did publicity-wise and work-wise. Nothing was spared to give of his very best.'

Howard K. Smith, Walter Cronkite and John Chancellor, America's top current television anchormen on ABC, CBS and NBC, all gave me their views on Peter as their cinematic counterpart: Howard K. Smith at ABC, who had admired Peter throughout his screen career, felt that he interpreted what was written with his usual excellence. 'But I am bound to say,' he adds, 'no anchorman would be allowed to behave in the manner of his character. Commercial networks are very conservative – though not in the political sense – and abhor any display of emotion beyond a certain limited level. I broke with CBS after being their chief foreign correspondent largely because I was a little too forceful for them in insisting that the winning of civil rights by blacks could not be halted – now a common-place thought. I could never have come near to approaching Peter's level of emotion without outraged opposition not only from my network, but from critics and the public . . .'

I told Walter Cronkite at CBS that Peter had spoken with tremendous admiration of people like himself and John Chancellor who were treated by the American public almost as philosophers and certainly as captains of opinion. 'Well, I'm damned, I had no idea,' laughed Cronkite. 'Watching *Network*, I felt that Peter was fine when he was playing it straight, up to the point where he goes mad, but after that it becomes a travesty. I'm never sure whether Paddy Chayefsky, who is a personal friend of mine, had his tongue in his cheek or not. I thought Finch was absolutely great, but it wasn't an honest representation of what we do in network television news.' I told him that Peter had repeatedly stated in public that he was playing satire, and Cronkite's view is that 'to many of us in the business, the worst thing was not what Paddy Chayefsky meant, but what people thought they saw in it. I imagine *Network* is a movie that will be looked at through the years as something of a classic in the sense that it was representative of a moment in time in our history, and as such I suppose that performance of Howard Beale will last.'

John Chancellor, the anchorman at NBC in New York, was the newscaster on whom Peter based his characterization of Howard Beale. Chayefsky, a friend of Chancellor's, told him he was going to write something involving television news and asked if he could come in and sit in on the NBC news meetings for a day or so. He then called again and asked if Peter Finch could also come in and look around. So it was arranged that Peter should go in to the NBC news department and watch them putting the programme together. Chancellor asked Peter if he wanted to sit in his chair on the set and read from the teleprompter just for fun, and he did. 'He had been speaking with what, I guess, was his normal, faintly Australian accent, and although I knew he was a terrific actor, I thought to myself, why an Australian if he's going to play an American anchorman? He said, "Thank you," in an Aussie accent and sat down, and in flawless American began to read from the teleprompter. His effortless transformation surprised me. I realized then he was more than just talented.'

Chancellor said that the night after he'd met Peter, he remembers going home and thinking, what a crackerjack anchorman that guy would make. 'I believe Peter Finch, in that one brief day I saw him, had in his own personality, without being over-bearing, great authority and sincerity. You felt that he believed very much in what he was doing. TV, in a sense, is a kind of lie detector over a long period of time, and people's flaws come out. If you try to dissemble, and you're on the screen a lot, that gets to the show. So when you think of people in my line of work, you think of people who are real, like Peter was. He was not only a magnificent actor, but I thought he had the qualities of presentation which would have made an ideal choice for our business.'

William Holden and Peter, merely acquaintances until they worked together for the first time on *Network*, belong to that community of actors who hold each other in the deepest respect. Holden was struck, as the film got under way, by Peter's unusual powers of concentration. 'Only an actor can understand the problems set by the prose that Paddy Chayefsky writes. Peter's effort and accomplishment on that character of Howard Beale was prodigious, although it seems effortless when you listen to his dialogue. It's much more difficult to work from Chayefsky's material than it is to interpret the words of any ordinary screenwriter. Chayefsky uses an entirely different pattern in approaching his subject matter. I'm not speaking of complicated words. I'm speaking of the structure of his writing. One day, while we were shooting, Peter had a very long and intricate speech ahead of him and the audience were all watching him, as you see on the film. And afterwards I congratulated him. I said, "God, Peter, that was just marvellous. It had such flow and such energy and it really went so beautifully." And I added: "You know, I'd hate to have been faced with your job." He said: "Well, I'll tell you something. The maids at the hotel think I'm absolutely insane." I asked him why and he said: "You see, it's the only place where I can rehearse and be near Eletha and my little Diana. I have to send them out of the room and then I lock myself in the bathroom. I run these lines in the bathroom. Then the maids come in to turn the beds down and they hear this man ranting and going berserk in the bathroom, they think I'm absolutely bananas!" So I said: "Well, don't do anything to change their minds and they'll leave you alone."

'For me, Finch's performance was brilliant and long before the award nominations, I wanted it put down for the records and stated I felt Peter really deserved an Oscar,' said Holden. Peter was very upset at his publicist's suggestion that he should try simply for 'the best supporting player'. He felt he'd rather go for the top award or be out of the competition altogether. The idea of the Oscar business amused him, but he did realize its importance and value for future choice of films and salary bargaining. 'After Peter died,' Holden said, 'I wandered around for days unable to believe what had happened. It's almost the measure of the importance of a human being if you feel they're still there. I felt that Finchie was still very much there somewhere.' I told Holden this was my reason for finally agreeing to write this book.

Network was the first and only time Peter was called upon to create a larger than life satirical caricature figure. He needed all his technique, and stamina, and more physical and nervous energy for the role of Howard Beale than he obviously had at his disposal. He was working from within, from the deepest centre of himself, and there were moments in his performance – as in the brief moment of hallucination when he's lying awake in his bed in the early hours of the morning – where the underlying strangeness of Peter is revealed for a second.

Finchie's own personal views about the power and influence of television, in America, were ambivalent. Like Beale's originator Chayefsky, he deplored the fact that television's only standard is the rating system, yet he saw the ironic paradox – that democratic governments survive on a mass rating system. It is the anaesthetizing process of TV, and the computerizing and vitiating of human individuality that he was against. It was the inroads television made into the minds of people over the age of six or seven that worried him. Up until that age he felt it was good for children who were at the stage of learning to read, as a preparation to learning and absorbing. He felt overall that television was dangerous – presenting capsulized history and capsulized news which dulls the ability to learn. Like Chayefsky, Peter was fearful that not yet, but in the future, TV could end up supplying only that social craving for entertainment and sensationalism, and could finish up without enough time to tell us all the news.

Peter appeared on television throughout America on the NBC Johnny Carson Show the night before he died, 13 January 1977, and on this show, probably the most important television show for Peter in the States, he spoke at length about *Network* and his nomination for the Oscar. He was very pleased about the nomination, but while he was making the picture, he had never thought about being nominated. 'You do the work because you love it, and if the prizes come that's an after-thought and the cream on top.' He then started to recall his childhood days at Vaucresson in Paris, and the avant garde life he led there, and his upbringing with all sorts of very weird people at an impressionable age. He spoke of his wonderful Bohemian grandmother who took her harp to parties, probably in a truck, Carson asked him if he got custody of the harp when Grannie passed on. 'No,' said Pete, 'because I was in Sydney and Granny died in Darjeeling writing pamphlets for Ghandi.' As he'd never been attracted to the harp and, as he didn't drive, the thought of the truck needed to take it to parties bothered him. With a roar of laughter and a burst of applause, Peter faded from the screen.

Carson is a man who has made a successful career of drawing out other people rather than being drawn. When I spoke to him about the last interview with Peter, he said he had noticed nothing wrong or out of the ordinary with his breathing. He'd interviewed him on his show some years before, but didn't know him personally. He agreed Peter certainly looked extremely tired and that the strain of constant promotion and public exposure which Peter was being subjected to was probably too demanding, and asking too much of any artist to be caught up at that pitch of mental and physical effort, month after month. But what was the answer?

On 4 July 1976, Israeli Prime Minister, Yitzhak Rabin, with the final democratic approval of his cabinet, launched Operation Thunderbolt and sent General Dan Shomron, the planner and military strategist, with his carefully rehearsed team on a 2,500 mile mission to Uganda to rescue the hundred or so hostages from the terrorists at Entebbe. On the day after the raid, Edgar J. Scherick put the 20th Century-Fox production of *Raid on Entebbe* into operation for less than $4 million. He contracted

Irwin Segelstein at NBC, the idea being to show the film on American TV as a Fox co-production with cinema distribution abroad, and then approached Irvin Kershner to direct. Barry Beckerman began on the screenplay and Daniel Blatt the producer and Edgar Scherick, as executive producer, started raising the money. Suddenly, they all realized they'd need a cast of thousands and had better start at once, casting from the top with Rabin.

Kershner had been to a party three weeks before, given by Barry Krost. The place was full of stars, the room crowded, and across the room Kershner spotted Peter, whom he'd never met. He'd admired his work and thought Schlesinger had used him brilliantly in both *Far From The Madding Crowd* and *Sunday Bloody Sunday*, and at once the only character that immediately locked into place for the casting of Yitzhak Rabin was Peter. 'The Israelis often have a British accent because they often go to school in England. Finch was a cultivated man and I'd studied all the pictures of all the cabinet ministers and generals, and I knew I wanted Finch. Interesting, they said, when I broached the subject, he's never done TV in America. So off they went to get Peter and found out he wanted an awful lot of money simply because he didn't want to do TV. We started working to try and get him, and finally he said he wanted a meeting. So I met Peter, told him about the project and he came back and said: "All right, I'll do it." '

'Was there trouble about his insurance?' I asked.

'Yes there was! They were very disturbed and came to me one day and said they were having problems with the doctor. The doctor said there definitely was a heart murmur and they felt they couldn't insure him. Peter got in a state and told them he'd always had a slight heart murmur; that he'd been going from one American city to another doing TV promotion for *Network* and that he'd been to a party the night before, had a few drinks and was just suffering from exhaustion, nothing more. The doctor kept arguing there was a problem and Peter kept trying to make light of it. In the end, they took a chance and insured him. I now had my first bit of casting and I built my cast from Peter.

'I met Peter several times beforehand and we discussed Rabin's character, and he started doing detailed research. He was a man who would get right into the part and care deeply. We talked about accent. "No accent," I said, "speak straight, perhaps sometimes a subtle inflexion change, or you have to search for a second in your mind to find the right word, because English isn't your first language – but just a suggestion."

'We shot the whole film in California and built Entebbe entirely from guesswork by blowing up one frame of 16 mm. film. That was all the research material we had but the hostages who were there told us we'd guessed exactly right, even down to the colour scheme.

'In one scene, Peter was sitting round a table with all the people and he suddenly stopped and said: "What does this line I have to say mean: 'the string has run out?' " I said: "It means time has run out. It means there's no turning back; that we must act."

' "It's a peculiar line," he said. "It doesn't work in the context. How do I justify it?"

' "I don't know," I said, and he kept thinking about it. He came back about an hour later and said: "I think I have it. This line is actually from Chekhov."

'I said, "Is it?"

' "Yes. He could have written that line in the context of this little story and so I'm doing it as if Chekhov wrote it." That's when he found the justification for it, and of course when we did the scene, suddenly he paused and said, "The string has run out." He said it simply, but with such truth. It was because it was internalized truth. At one point, he was working at the table with all the people around him, and he was playing with his glasses. He puts on the glasses and plays the scene through, and after the take was over I came to him and I said: "Pete, your glasses aren't quite ... There's a lot of stuff on them, finger prints. I don't think you can see through them. Can I clean them for you?" He said: "No, no, please don't." I said: "Why?" knowing it meant something, and he said: "Well, this is a very difficult scene. Everybody is looking at **me**. Everybody wants to know what I'm going to **do**. I can't be affected by them (he was talking as Rabin), I don't **want** to see them. When I put on my glasses I **know** they're dirty and I can't see the others. I can't see their expressions. I know they're there, I can acknowledge them but I can't see their expressions." That is inspiration; the true genius of an interpretive artist. You know, only occasionally does a director get let in on those secrets of an actor. Every actor has his own preparation and the director creates the situation, and then the actor must interpret and find his truth. These were just little instances. I mean, he did the most difficult things in that film and the only thing he came to me with as a problem was "the string has run out".

'If you look at the film carefully you will notice that all the scenes in that picture are divided up into sections. The cabinet and Rabin are all filmed inside, except for the end, in rooms and around tables. The camera flows; it never stops. It sees people between other people and Rabin is always in the middle of people. When you're with the hostages the camera is always hand-held. No flow and slightly tilted. In the war scenes, quick cutting so the visual rhythms of the film are always changing. I explained this total concept of the picture to Peter and he said: "Fine. I understand. Fine." So I said: "Therefore, we are going to do these five pages as one take. I am going to start on people, then I'm going to bring the camera in on you right on a certain line. But we've got to time it so that the speed of the camera and your line coincide. It will come as a surprise to the audience, because, first, they will hear your voice and then the camera will suddenly focus sharply on you in the middle of your speech, when the sudden realization hits you that it's already too late. In that second you must convince us as Rabin that you are going to take the bull by the horns. It is that terrible moment of dilemma! When you have to make a momentous decision – what to do? While that thought is in your mind, Peter, the camera will suddenly swing 180 degrees in the cabinet room and end up on you in medium shot." If you watch Finch on the screen at that moment, he speaks and then lifts up those hands and he hits the table. He says: "That's enough! That's enough! We can't delay any longer. We must act".'

Kershner continued: 'We never rehearsed it; just the mechanics, moves, positions, and then he did it. It was so astounding. One take. Most of his takes were one take and this was tied in with all these people. Peter was on it at the beginning. The film was shot over a period, October, November, December 1976 we shot thirty-two days in all and we started with him. Then he went off when we did all the hostages sequence or the war room – all that didn't concern him. Then, when he arrived back for the end scene, he was so elated, like a kid. "I'm so glad I'm back at work on it. I don't know what's happening." He was terribly excited to be there and in at the conclusion. Every single person felt something special was happening. It was a most amazing project. We all had this feeling. Finch kept asking me: "How accurate are you really?" And the only way I could tell him was to say: "Well, for instance, I just had a 'phone call from the brother of the young man who was killed, the soldier who was killed, the colonel. I was getting the costumes ready because we were going to shoot inside the aircraft and I got this call saying is there anything I can do to help? He'd just arrived in New York from Israel. Then I suddenly realized we didn't know what Israeli commandos had worn on their heads when they emerged from the planes on the Entebbe airstrip. I couldn't leave the set and I said: "Ask him did they wear helmets when they got off the planes or a sort of hat?" White caps, came the answer back, so they'd know each other in the dark, because the Ugandans could have been wearing helmets. So we took sheets, cut them up and put them on the fatigue caps.

'Acting was like breathing to Peter. It kept him alive and he had tremendous respect for himself as an actor. I was never able to tell Peter, because he died, that when I saw the real captain of the plane later in Paris, he had said it was uncanny how we'd got things absolutely right.

'The last time I saw Finchie was on the last day of shooting when we were filming his farewell shot on the screen as he stands on the tarmac, smiling as the hostages came in off the aircraft. His wife, Eletha, came everywhere with him. We all often used to have dinner together quietly after shooting at night, and we'd talk and talk. He adored her. She worshipped him, and they seemed to share every single thing in their lives, like soul mates. I think he was absolutely loyal to her.'

Peter was the second actor to die suddenly after playing one of the several film versions of the Entebbe affair. The American actor, Godfrey Cambridge, who played Amin in another version, also had a heart attack. President Amin said Finch's death was: 'a good example of punishment by God.'

30 Hollywood

Peter often told a joke against himself on his first visit to Hollywood. At one of the VIP functions he had to attend, there was a row of empty chairs in the front but Finchie preferred to find himself an anonymous place further back. The 'Hollywood Great' took their places in the chairs allocated, the lights were dimmed and as the president called out the name of each celebrity the spotlight flashed on them and there would be a round of applause. 'And now, Ladies and Gentlemen, that well-known English actor, Peter Finch,' and the spot stabbed chair after chair, vainly seeking him. So Peter stood up and a voice behind rasped angrily 'Siddown Schmuk'; and he did.

Ross Hunter and his associate producer on *Lost Horizon*, Jacques Mapes, were lunching one day at Paramount, and Peter decided quite unexpectedly to go and see them. He set off on his marathon constitutional: La Cienaga to Paramount. As neither Ross nor Jacques Mapes knew he was coming they hadn't left him a pass at the gates. The Paramount commissionaire didn't recognize him and wouldn't let him in, so, instead of throwing his weight about, Finchie went in to the little bar next door and sat there, didn't have a drink and waited until he saw someone he knew. Finally, their casting director, Billy Gussy, came in and he said: 'Bill, I want to have lunch with Ross and Jacques. Would you please call them and tell them I'm here.'

During the shooting of *Elephant Walk*, Peter was also witness to how Hollywood treated celebrities when he took a friend to a Hollywood party. When they arrived Finchie's host asked who his friend was and, when Peter explained, made it clear that the party was for him to meet other stars of his own status. The gentleman giving the party was extremely sorry, but his friend would not be accepted. Peter pointed out that the friend in question, Abraham Sofaer, was featured in the film, was a former member of the Old Vic, and was a highly esteemed actor of many years standing. But the party-giver was adamant. So Peter turned on his heel. 'If that's the Hollywood worship of status,' he said, 'they can stick it!'

Finchie liked walking and was often the lone walker on the deserted sidewalks of Los Angeles. Sometimes he had trouble with the police and always wished he'd had fellow loner Groucho Marx's quick wit and presence of mind, who was also often stopped by the police 'for walking'. One day, the patrol slowed down beside the ambling Groucho who gradually quickened his pace. The car did likewise. After about five minutes Groucho was fed up with his unwanted companions, and biting hard on his havana, barked: 'What's the matter, officer, am I moving too fast?'

Peter also had trouble with the cops once when, in Los Angeles, he and a friend were driving none too carefully down Santa Monica Boulevard and a patrol car cut in on them. The friend was very English, very well bred and excruciatingly embarrassed at being hauled out by the cops and handcuffed on the sidewalk. Finchie was taking the whole situation in his stride. The friend said: 'Oh, please don't handcuff Mr Finch, he's such a nice man,' in the most impeccable public school English. As the handcuffs clicked into place, his hands now pinioned firmly behind his back Finchie was heard to say: 'Barbarians! They don't even handcuff you in front so a man can pee if he needs to!'

Hermione Baddeley, who told me this story, is now living in Hollywood. She was devoted to Finchie. 'Always made you laugh darling, particularly at his own misfortunes. He was a naughty and very, very lovable man. Just before he died, I was going to the hairdresser's one afternoon and was waiting for the car. I thought I heard it, so I went out and leaned over the balustrade and there was this lean figure below with his little piccaninny on his shoulder. "Hermione! At last I've found you! I lost your address." He looked so touching with the little girl happily perched on his shoulder. God knows where he'd walked from . . .' Hermione remembers that once 'when Finchie was getting a rocket from one of the wives for drinking too much after a show, I tried to smooth things out. So he said, "Look, I don't want to cause any more trouble and set up friction between you and my domestic front, so if they think I've disappeared and I haven't, I'll always call on you and let you know exactly where I am and I know you'll put things right." This, of course, sometimes meant three in the morning. Bang! Bang! on the front door, and you'd hear Finchie's voice, "I'm all right, I'm all right," and off he'd go again into the night.'

I went to see Hermione in her beautiful long, low villa on an escarpment, on that vast dress circle of hills to the north that look down on the twinkling expanse of Los Angeles below. Hermione described an incident that had happened in Benedict Canyon where Peter was living the night before he died. Eletha had said that they were at the table. They had just had a light meal and suddenly there was a violent wind outside. Eletha had the most horrible feeling that something seemed to pervade the whole house. She tore to the back door and shouted: 'Go away! Depart, whoever you are,' and the children heard her call out. She felt there was a presence there she didn't want coming into the house. She closed the doors and went back to Peter. He was just getting up to go to bed and he said, 'Well, perhaps it's for me.' She said, 'What do you mean?' And he said, 'Well, you never know, perhaps it's for me.'

As early as 1972, Peter told me that his heart wasn't sound. The last time I danced flamenco with my Spanish group in Chelsea on a very hot August bank holiday in 1972, Finchie, filming *Bequest to the Nation*, was going to come. I'd invited Virginia McKenna, whom he hadn't seen for many years, and it was to be a surprise: Finchie, Eletha, Jimmy Cellan Jones (directing the film) and his wife, Maggie, and Virginia, were all to have met up. Only Ginny came, but Peter, at the last moment, sent me a telegram and when I met him a day or two later he told me they were having problems with the film and that the whole thing was just mistimed and not working. On top of that, 'My bloody heart has started to warn me I'm mortal!'

A great solace to Peter had always been his painting. He seldom talked about it, as he seldom, apart from the early days as a teacher at Mercury, talked about acting. He told me once that the water-colourist he most admired for sheer subtlety of tone and colour was Sir William Nicholson, the English painter, engraver, and illustrator who died just after Peter first arrived in England. For Peter, Nicholson was a water-colourist *par excellence* because like a great actor, never merely a technician, he also seemed to be able to put on canvas not only what one sees, but what is sometimes achieved by great directors in the cinema: a feeling of deep nostalgia through style, composition, a quality born of intuition and awareness, almost impossible to express. 'It either touches an immediate chord within you or it doesn't.'

Peter maintained as he got older that with painting as with acting, the process of expression is incommunicable: 'Let the performance or the painting or whatever speak for itself. If the critics and pundits in retrospect want to analyse, let them, but I don't want to be around.'

'I was criticized,' he said, 'in the early days when I started to paint, for putting too much make-up on my canvases, for hesitating, qualifying, and trying to polish everything I touched with a brush. Now I think perhaps you reveal more as Delacroix once said: "By not troubling so much about the language as in cultivating the soul and letting her show herself." '

Michael Maslansky told me that on the *Network* promotion trip to New York by train, because he refused to fly, he did three chalk drawings of the Grand Canyon on the way through. He had given up drinking due to pressure from Eletha, and was drawing or painting wherever he found the opportunity. He was doing quite a lot of pen and ink drawing again, working with water colours and had become absorbed in scratching around for Indian relics at Indo near Palm Springs.

On that last Friday morning he had an appointment with Sidney Lumet at the Beverly Hills Hotel. When I last spoke to Eletha, she told me she always drove Peter everywhere in the Mercedes, but there was a tacit agreement that if he wanted to go on his own, walking, she'd kiss him good-bye and off he'd go to walk and live in his own private world. On that particular morning she offered to drive him. 'I'd ironed Finchie a lovely shirt and he looked so smart in his jacket and tie, but he said: "No, darling. I might see a pretty girl I fancy and it'll do me good to walk, it'll clear my brain." '

Eletha said she had a strong feeling she should go with him, but dismissed it. He suggested they might have lunch and he'd see her at noon. She remembers him looking at the flowers and he kissed one, saying that that would make it grow. 'He gave that familiar wave and was gone.'

One afternoon, I decided to retrace Peter's last walk down to the Beverly Hills Hotel where I had an appointment with David Tebet, a senior vice-president of NBC TV, and look at a lot of what Pete may have seen on the mile and a half walk from Benedict Canyon to his favourite Polo Lounge at the hotel. He had only actually lived for thirteen days in the very modest little white cottage with its smart black, circular window, and grey-tiled roof, all screened from the road by flowering shrubs and camellia bushes. Eletha had worked hard to decorate and furnish it and make a home for the family in Hollywood. The various houses of the famous had been carefully pointed out to me, so on the way I took my time to gaze at the many beautiful Spanish-style, stuccoed, red-tiled villas and palatial homes. Finchie had lived in an oasis of the past near Pickfair, the Ronald Colman estate, with Fred Astaire up the road, and a very Scandinavian-looking timbered retreat, almost on stilts, where Ingrid Bergman had lived. John Barrymore's eyrie was way up beyond in the Tower Grove; Danny Kaye's elegant hide-out was virtually invisible from the road. Another house that, with its arches, wrought iron balcony, sun blinds and red-tiled roof, might have been part of a very secluded South American estancia, was where Olivier and Vivien Leigh rehearsed their Broadway production of *Romeo and Juliet* during the last shooting days of *Gone With the Wind*. 'The vastness and loneliness of Hollywood,' Vivien Leigh once told me, 'can be so horrible if you really do exchange your soul for fame and honour, and make your charm and personality the sum total of your investment.' As I walked down Benedict Canyon, with its long sidewalk lined with tall state-ly palms and gardens spilling over with eucalyptus trees, oleander, cyprus, magnolia, jacaranda, sycamore, bird-of-paradise, lilies, acacia, and hibiscus bushes, I thought of both Vivien and Peter who had lived so close to each other in such different eras. How differently each saw Hollywood. Peter was detached about it and enjoyed the good and the beautiful things it had to offer. He could take the synthetic, the false, the frivolous in his stride. He was old enough at sixty not to take anything too seriously. One remark of his did strike me as I walked along 'his' sidewalk where people never walk, with the Will Rogers Memorial Park away in the distance, and I certainly never saw a soul. 'It always amuses me how gardeners tend immaculate-looking billiard-table like lawns with silent lawn mowers, but you never see kids playing on them or a family sitting on the grass having lunch out. Leviathan Cadillacs glide past you with darkened windows and drawn venetian blinds, but you never hear that laughter you hear in Spanish or Italian villages, the raucous free sound of children and the distant echo of roosters, or the bark of a dog. The raucousness is there in Hollywood, but it's down there on Sunset Strip and around Grauman's Chinese Theatre, old fading fun-fair land.' But he used to feel that he was part of the living Hollywood legend of film. 'No history here, because it is all still happening.'

The entrance to the Beverly Hills Hotel must have made Finchie smile – a jungle of banana trees! The only vestige of Spain left there are two inscriptions on each pillar, '*Bien Venidos Amigos*' as you drive in, and '*Vaya Con Dios*' as you leave.

David Tebet, who had been staying at the hotel when Peter collapsed there told me: 'What actually happened was that, on the morning of 14 January 1977, I went down into the lobby and ran into Peter, who was waiting for Sidney Lumet. They were going over to the studios that morning for a talk show to plug *Network* on TV. When he saw me, he said: "Let's go get some coffee." He was very excited about a new idea he had had. "I want to play George Washington, with the wooden teeth on television, the real George Washington. Is that possible?" I told him, that in my opinion, it was more than possible and I felt that NBC would buy it without any question. He was very happy at the idea. We finished our coffee and then went upstairs for him to meet Sidney Lumet. When we got to the top of the stairs, a friend of mine, Cy Feuer, a Broadway producer, said: "Hello." I turned round, shook hands with him, kissed his wife on the cheek, turned back and Peter was on the ground. He just dropped, right there in the lobby.'

Dickie Attenborough was coming out of the Beverly Hills Hotel on 13 January 1977. 'It was the most extraordinary coincidence. I arrived in Los Angeles and I hadn't seen Finchie for God knows how long – years and years. I was coming down the steps and he flung his arms around me from behind. I didn't know who it was until I heard this voice: "Ah, yer pommy fuckin' bastard . . ." and of course I knew at once it could only be Peter. "Jesus Christ! How long is it since we've seen each other?" "Years and years," I said, so pleased to see him.

"Look," he said. "I'll call you tomorrow morning. I'll be coming into the hotel and when you give yourself time to settle, we'll get together."

'Next morning, when I came down from my room, there was a crowd clustered round a sofa and I thought, oh dear, somebody's not well, and I went on out. One of the porters came thundering after me and said: "I don't know whether you know, but the person in the hall is Mr Finch," so I rushed back in and he was

The Beverly Hills Hotel

AND BUNGALOWS

Room _____

Delivered by Bellman _____

The Beverly Hills Hotel

Dear Dicky,

I'm such a c----t. Forgot to congratulate you on your knighthood. Glad to see she forgave "Buttercup" valley; Lots of love

Archie

will call you.

obviously unconscious. He was being looked after. Sidney Lumet was there, having come to pick him up for a TV interview, and Sidney said: "Oh, Jesus God! The darling's passed out," or something to that effect, and he and I stayed, nothing one could do. One didn't know what to do. The paramedics had been sent for, and within a minute or two they were zooming up to the hotel, and they pumped his chest, gave him oxygen and spoke on the phone to the hospital. The hospital were telling them what to do. I had to go, because I had a studio of people waiting for me, so I said good-bye to Sidney and told him to give Finchie my love and tore out of the hotel. When I came back at lunch-time there was a note from Finchie. I kept it because it is the last thing he ever wrote.'

The United Press called Ross Hunter just after nine thirty and asked him for a statement about Peter Finch. 'I didn't know what they were talking about, because I had no idea anything was wrong. I was told he was ill in hospital, with a very slim chance of survival. I rang a friend, one of the heads at UCLA and he told me they could say nothing until Eletha was found. Jacques Mapes and I got in the car and combed Hollywood; the school, the shopping district where she shopped, everywhere. Finally, we decided to go as far as Sandra Dee's old house and as we came back she was driving up. She'd been to some gardener's place to get some plants and then collect the children. She jumped out of the car when she saw us, looked at my face, and knew at once something was wrong and then I told her . . .' Eletha started mumbling and talking very quickly about Finchie, obviously dazed with shock. Christopher stood absolutely silent and the little girl started to cry.

Epilogue

William Holden, David Tebet, Howard Gottfried and Paddy Chayefsky, all very close friends of Peter's, with their various ladies, decided to go to dinner the night of Finchie's funeral, as they felt Pete would have appreciated their mourning for him in merriment rather than sadness, by talking about the good times they'd had with him. They went to the Palm Restaurant, and the conversation immediately turned to their absent friend, the laughs he'd given them, his unusual quality as an actor, some of his loves, and his wife, Eletha.

'And before you knew it', said Tebet, 'our talk turned into a vicious tirade against the film business and how it could kill a man like Finchie. But Paddy Chayefsky said: "You can't blame the business. It's what we do to ourselves. We're all impulsive and neurotic about it." Paddy looked around at all of us and added: "But you know something, in spite of all that we've said here tonight, it's better than threading pipe." That got us back to Finchie and everything was fine.'

They discussed the coming Academy Awards and Paddy Chayefsky suggested that, if Peter won the Oscar for *Network*, his wife Eletha should, walk up and accept the award, but for some reason or other, when the time came, the director of the Oscar ceremony decided that Paddy should accept the award on Peter's behalf. He wanted a big name to accept the first posthumous Oscar and Chayefsky was the obvious choice. But one day, after that dinner Chayefsky called Tebet and said: 'Would you like to hear Peter's wife's acceptance?'

'You're putting me on!'

Paddy said: 'No, the producer doesn't know it, but when they call my name out, she's going up!'

'No one knew except Paddy, Howard Gottfried and me,' said Tebet. 'Chayefsky wrote her speech and rehearsed her at her home.'

Liv Ullmann, chosen to make a speech prepared for her as presenter of the 1977 Academy Awards, spoke very simply.

'One measure of an actor may be said to be his willingness not to conceal himself . . . but to show himself in all his humanity, and to expose both the light and darker sides of his nature . . . openly and truly. The nominees for performance by an actor in a leading role are:

Robert de Niro in *Taxi Driver*
Peter Finch in *Network*
Giancaro Giannini in *Seven Beauties*
William Holden in *Network*
Sylvester Stallone in *Rocky*

She opened the envelope. 'And the winner is Peter Finch in *Network*. Acceptor Paddy Chayefsky.'

Christopher and Diana were present with Eletha when this announcement was made and when Eletha went forward to accept Peter's award, the whole audience, to quote David Tebet, 'went out of their minds. I've never known a more gentle man, a sweeter man, a man without prejudice, a marvellous human being, and on top of that, one of the great actors. And you can't beat that. Finchie was probably one of the most popular actors in Hollywood. Without any question, had he lived, he would have become one of the Hollywood greats. He was on the threshold.'

Fifteen days after his death Peter Finch was voted the best actor in a dramatic film for his performance in *Network*, at Hollywood's Golden Globe Awards for 1976, and on 16 March 1978 he won his fifth British Film Award for the best actor for 1977, again for his performance as Howard Beale in *Network*.

Film and theatre chronology

Australian theatre chronology

Amateur

1934   Samuel Hackett, in *The Ringer* by Edgar Wallace, at
the Studio Theatre, Sydney
The Boot Black, in *Counsellor-at-law*, by Elmer Rice,
for Doris Fitton, at the Savoy Theatre, Sydney
A one-legged Pirate, in *Peter Pan*, by J. M. Barrie, for
Doris Fitton, at the Savoy Theatre, 1934 Christmas
Show. Transferred by Ben Fuller to the Majestic
Theatre, Newtown

1935   The fair Page Maudelyn, in *Richard of Bordeaux*, by
Gordon Daviot, for Doris Fitton, Savoy Theatre,
Sydney. With John Wyndham as Richard, Sumner
Locke Elliott as the dark Page

Professional

1934-5 Stooge to comedian Bert La Blance, (he sometimes spelt
his name Bert Le Blanc), and chorus song and dance
man, *Joe Coady's Vaudeville Show*, at the Maccabean
Hall, Darlinghurst, Sydney
Spruiker, for *Jimmy Sharman's Boxing Tent*, at the
Easter Show (Royal Agricultural Show), Sydney

1935   Douglas Helder, in *Interference*, by Roland Pertwee
and Harold Dearden, directed by Edward Howell, with
Edward Howell, Rosalind Kennerdale, Therese
Desmond, at the St James Hall, Sydney

1936   *For George Sorlie's Players, Under the Big Top*
The New English Comedy Company
Herbert Hughes, in *Laughter of Fools*, by H. F. Maltby
Smithers, in *Married by Proxy*, by Avery Hopwood
Pete, in *Fair and Warmer*, by Avery Hopwood
Hunter, in *Ten Minute Alibi*, by William Armstrong
All directed by William McGowan, with Murray
Matheson, Rosalind Kennerdale, Leslie Crane, Eva
Moss, Norman French, Julia Adair, George Douglas

1938	The juvenile in *So This is Hollywood*, presented by Ernest C. Rolls, with Robert Capron, Lou Vernon, Thelma Scott, at the Apollo Theatre, Melbourne Ashley, in *White Cargo*, by Leon Gordon, with Mary MacGregor, James Raglan, Frank Bradley, directed by Ben Lewin, at the Theatre Royal, Sydney Clyde Pelton, in *Personal Appearance*, by Laurence Riley directed by Peter Dearing, with Betty Balfour, Frank Bradley, Cecil Perry, at the Theatre Royal, Sydney, and the Comedy Theatre, Melbourne
1941–4	Army Concert Party work, producing and playing to the troops
1944	District Attorney Flint, in *Night of January 16th*, by Ayn Rand, directed by Frederick J. Blackman, with Lawrence H. Cecil, Thelma Grigg at the Minerva Theatre, Sydney The Earl of Harpenden, in *While the Sun Shines*, by Terence Rattigan, directed by Frederick J. Blackman, with Pat McDonald, Ron Randell, Roger Barry, at the Minerva Theatre, Sydney
1945	Appointed artistic director of Unit 12, the army theatre section of the Australian Army Amenities Services under Lieutenant Colonel Jim Davidson Played The Hon. Alan Howard, in *French Without Tears*, by Terence Rattigan Played The Earl of Harpenden, in *While the Sun Shines*, by Terence Rattigan, and directed both plays The plays with Peter Finch in the cast toured the hospitals and base areas, playing to the troops
1946	Co-founder and director of the Mercury Theatre Ikharev, in *Diamond Cuts Diamond*, by Nikolai Gogol, directed by Sydney John Kay, with Peter Bathurst, June Wimble, Frank Jarbo etc. Directed *The Pastry Baker*, by Lope de Vega, with Jerome Levy, Dennis Glenny, Frank Jarbo, Alan Poolman etc. Adam, the village judge, in *The Broken Pitcher*, by Heinrich von Kleist, directed by John Wiltshire, with Ethel Gabriel, Mitchell Hill, June Wimble, Hilda Dorrington etc.

All three plays were presented for two performances
on 16 and 17 July, at the Conservatorium of Music,
Sydney.

1947 Revived his army production of *French Without Tears*,
with members of the Mercury Theatre, and Mercury
Theatre students, for odd performances, at the Sydney
Radio Theatre, and the Killara Hall. The new cast
included: Leonard Thiele, Tom Lake, Alan White,
Adele Brown, Ron Patten etc.

1948 Argan, in *The Imaginary Invalid*, by Molière, directed
by Sydney John Kay, with June Wimble, Elsie Dane,
Al Thomas, John Faassen, Patricia Harrison, Allan
Ashbolt, Tom Lake, etc. The 50 minute lunchtime
version toured schools, factories, offices, and Peter
Finch's last performance in Australia was as Argan, at
the Sydney Town Hall on September 22nd 1948.
Directed the lunchtime productions of:
Lajos Biro's *Midsummer Night* and
Schnitzler's *Anatole's Wedding Morning* for the
Mercury Theatre.

British theatre chronology

1949 Ernest Piaste in *Daphne Laureola*, by James Bridie,
directed by Murray MacDonald for Laurence Olivier
Productions, at Wyndham's Theatre, with Dame Edith
Evans, Felix Aylmer

1950 Henry Adams in *The Damascus Blade*, by Bridget
Boland, directed by Laurence Olivier for LOP
provincial tour only, with John Mills and Beatrix
Lehmann
Professor Winke in *Captain Carvallo*, by Dennis
Cannan, directed by Laurence Olivier for LOP at the
St James's Theatre, with Diana Wynyard, James Donald,
and Richard Goolden

1951 Orpheus in *Point of Departure*, by Jean Anouilh, trans.
by Kitty Black, directed by Peter Ashmore for the
Company of Four at the Duke of York's Theatre, with
Mai Zetterling and Stephen Murray (took over from
Dirk Bogarde for six weeks on 12 March 1951)

Iago in *Othello*, by Shakespeare, directed by Orson Welles for LOP at the St James's Theatre, with Orson Welles, Gudrun Ure and Maxine Audley

1952   Papa in *The Happy Time*, by Samuel Taylor, directed by George Devine for LOP at the St James's Theatre, with Genevieve Page, Ronald Squire, George Devine, Rachel Kempson

Mercutio in *Romeo and Juliet*, by Shakespeare, directed by Hugh Hunt at the Old Vic Theatre, with Alan Badel, Claire Bloom, Athene Seyler, Lewis Casson

Mons. Beaujolais in *An Italian Straw Hat*, by Eugene Labiche and Marc-Michel, adapted by Thomas Walton, directed by Denis Carey at the Old Vic Theatre, with Jane Wenham, Gudrun Ure, Paul Rogers, Laurence Payne

1959   Jerry Ryan in *Two For The See-Saw*, by William Gibson, directed by Arthur Penn for H. M. Tennent at the Theatre Royal, Haymarket, with Gerry Jedd

1964   Trigorin in *The Seagull*, by Anton Chekhov, trans. by Ann Jellicoe, directed by Tony Richardson for the English Stage Company at the Queen's Theatre, with Dame Peggy Ashcroft, Vanessa Redgrave, Paul Rogers, Peter McEnery

As a theatre director

1950   Directed *The White Falcon*, starring Basil Radford and Sheila Burrel, which played: Grand Theatre, Blackpool; New Theatre, Hull; Kings Theatre, Southsea; Pavilion, Bournemouth; Theatre Royal, Brighton. The play closed on tour at the Theatre Royal, Nottingham

Was asked to direct *Pommie* (W. P. Lipscomb and John Watson), but was otherwise committed to play for Sir Laurence Olivier, and acted only as adviser

Film chronology

THE MAGIC SHOES
Australia 1935 (never released)
Director: Claude Fleming
Screenplay based on the *Cinderella* story by Peggy Graham
Cast: Helen Hughes, Norman French, Gloria Gotch, Peter Finch
Played: Prince Charming

DAD AND DAVE COME TO TOWN
Australia 1938 (UK title: *The Rudd Family Goes to Town*)
Director: Ken G. Hall
Screenplay by Frank Harvey and Bert Bailey
Cast: Bert Bailey, Fred MacDonald, Peter Finch, Shirley Ann Richards, Alec Kellaway
Played: Bill Ryan

MR CHEDWORTH STEPS OUT
Australia 1939. Made in 1938
Director: Ken G. Hall
Screenplay by Frank Harvey
Cast: Cecil Kellaway, Jean Hatton, Joan Deering, Peter Finch, James Raglan
Played: Arthur Chedworth

THE POWER AND THE GLORY
Australia 1941. Made in 1940
Director: Noel Monkman
Screenplay by Noel Monkman and Harry Lauder Junior
Cast: Katrin Rosselle, Eric Bush, Peter Finch
Played: Frank Miller

RATS OF TOBRUK
Australia 1944
Director: Charles Chauvel
Screenplay by Charles and Elsa Chauvel
Cast: Grant Taylor, Chips Rafferty, Peter Finch
Played: Peter Linton

RED SKY AT MORNING
Australia 1945. Made in 1943 (re-titled *Escape At Dawn*,1950)
Director: J. Hartney Arthur
Screenplay by Dymphna Cusack
Cast: Jean McAlister, John Alden, Peter Finch
Played: Michael

A SON IS BORN
Australia 1946
Director: Eric Porter
Screenplay from a story by Gloria Bouner
Cast: Peter Finch, Muriel Steinbeck, Ron Randell, John
McCallum, Kitty Bluett
Played: Paul Graham

EUREKA STOCKADE
UK 1949. Made in 1947–8 (US title *Massacre Hill*)
Director: Harry Watt
Screenplay by Harry Watt, Ralph Smart and Walter
Greenwood
Cast: Chips Rafferty, Jane Barrett, Peter Finch, Ralph Truman,
Gordon Jackson
Played: John Humffray

TRAIN OF EVENTS
UK 1949
Director: Basil Dearden (of Finch's episode)
Screenplay by Basil Dearden
Cast: Valerie Hobson, Mary Morris, Peter Finch, John
Clements
Played: Philip Mason

THE WOODEN HORSE
UK 1950
Director: Jack Lee
Script by Eric Williams from his own book
Cast: Leo Genn, David Tomlinson, Peter Finch
Played: RAAF Officer

THE MINIVER STORY
UK 1950
Director: H. C. Potter
Screenplay by George Froeschel and Ronald Millar based on characters created by Jan Struther.
Cast: Greer Garson, Walter Pidgeon, Peter Finch
Played: Polish officer

THE STORY OF ROBIN HOOD
AND HIS MERRIE MEN
UK 1952. Made in 1951
Director: Ken Annakin
Screenplay by Lawrence E. Watkin
Cast: Richard Todd, Peter Finch, Joan Rice, Hubert Gregg
Played: The Sheriff of Nottingham

THE STORY OF GILBERT AND SULLIVAN
UK 1953. Made in 1952 (US title *The Great Gilbert and Sullivan*)
Director: Sidney Gilliat
Screenplay by Leslie Bailey, Sidney Gilliat, Vincent Korda
Cast: Robert Morley, Maurice Evans, Peter Finch, Eileen Herlie, Dinah Sheridan, Isabel Dean
Played: Rupert D'Oyly Carte

THE HEART OF THE MATTER
UK 1953. Made in 1952–3
Director: George More O'Ferrall
Screenplay by Ian Dalrymple and Lesley Storm from Graham Greene's novel
Cast: Trevor Howard, Elizabeth Allan, Maria Schell, Peter Finch
Played: Father Rank

ELEPHANT WALK
US 1953–4
Director: William Dieterle
Screenplay by John Lee Mahin
Cast: Elizabeth Taylor, Peter Finch, Dana Andrews
Played: John Wiley

FATHER BROWN

UK 1954. Made in 1953 (US title *The Detective*)
Director: Robert Hamer
Screenplay by Thelma Schnee and Robert Hamer
Cast: Alec Guinness, Peter Finch, Joan Greenwood
Played: Flambeau

MAKE ME AN OFFER

UK 1954
Director: Cyril Frankel
Screenplay by Wolf Mankowitz and W. P. Lipscomb
Cast: Peter Finch, Adrienne Corri, Rosalie Crutchley
Played: Charlie

THE DARK AVENGER

UK 1955. Made in 1954 (US title *The Warriors*)
Director: Henry Levin
Screenplay by Daniel B. Ullman and Phil Park
Cast: Errol Flynn, Joanne Dru, Peter Finch
Played: Count De Ville

PASSAGE HOME

UK 1955. Made in 1954
Director: Roy Baker
Screenplay by William Fairchild
Cast: Peter Finch, Diane Cilento, Anthony Steel, Bryan
Forbes, Gordon Jackson
Played: Captain 'Lucky' Ryland

JOSEPHINE AND MEN

UK 1955
Director: Roy Boulting
Screenplay by Roy Boulting, Frank Harvey, Nigel Balchin
Cast: Peter Finch, Glynis Johns, Jack Buchanan,
Donald Sinden
Played: David Hewer

SIMON AND LAURA
UK 1955
Director: Muriel Box
Screenplay by Peter Blackmore, Frank Muir, Dennis Norden
Cast: Peter Finch, Kay Kendall, Ian Carmichael
Played: Simon Foster

A TOWN LIKE ALICE
UK 1956. Made in 1955-6
Director: Jack Lee
Screenplay by W. P. Lipscomb and Richard Mason
Cast: Peter Finch, Virginia McKenna
Played: Joe Harman
British Film Academy Award for the best actor, 1956

THE BATTLE OF THE RIVER PLATE
UK 1956. Made in 1955-6. (US title *The Pursuit of the Graf Spee*)
Director: Michael Powell and Emric Pressburger
Screenplay by Michael Powell and Emric Pressburger
Cast: Peter Finch, Anthony Quayle
Played: Captain Langsdorff
Royal Film Performance 1956

THE SHIRALEE
UK 1957. Made in 1956 (Ealing MGM made in Australia)
Director: Leslie Norman
Screenplay by Leslie Norman and Neil Paterson
Cast: Peter Finch, Dana Wilson, Elizabeth Sellars, Rosemary Harris
Played: Jim Macauley

ROBBERY UNDER ARMS
UK 1957. (Rank made in Australia)
Director: Jack Lee
Screenplay by W. P. Lipscomb and Alexander Baron
Cast: Peter Finch, Maureen Swanson, Ronald Lewis, David McCallum, Jill Ireland
Played: Captain Starlight

WINDOM'S WAY
UK 1957
Director: Ronald Neame
Screenplay by Jill Craigie
Cast: Peter Finch, Mary Ure, Michael Horden
Played: Alec Windom

THE NUN'S STORY
US 1959. Made in 1958
Director: Fred Zinnemann
Screenplay by Robert Anderson
Cast: Audrey Hepburn, Edith Evans, Peter Finch, Peggy
Ashcroft
Played: Dr Fortunati

OPERATION AMSTERDAM
UK 1958
Director: Michael McCarthy
Screenplay by Michael McCarthy and John Eldridge
Cast: Peter Finch, Eva Bartok, Tony Britton,
Alexander Knox
Played: Jan Smit

KIDNAPPED
UK 1959–60
Directed and written by Robert Stevens
Cast: Peter Finch, James MacArthur, Peter O'Toole
Played: Alan Breck Stewart

THE SINS OF RACHEL CADE
US 1960. Made in 1959
Director: Gordon Douglas
Screenplay by Edward Anhalt
Cast: Angie Dickinson, Peter Finch, Roger Moore
Played: Colonel Henry Derode

THE TRIALS OF OSCAR WILDE
UK 1960 (US title *The Man with the Green Carnation*)
Directed and written by Ken Hughes
Cast: Peter Finch, Yvonne Mitchell, John Fraser, James Mason
Played: Oscar Wilde
British Film Academy Award for the best British actor, 1960
Moscow Festival, Award for the best actor, 1961

NO LOVE FOR JOHNNIE
UK 1961. Made in 1960
Director: Ralph Thomas
Screenplay by Nicholas Phipps and Mordecai Richler
Cast: Peter Finch, Billie Whitelaw, Mary Peach, Stanley
Holloway, Donald Pleasance
Played: Johnnie Byrne
British Film Award for the best British actor, 1961
Berlin Festival Silver Bear Award for the best actor, 1961

I THANK A FOOL
UK 1962. Made in 1961
Director: Robert Stevens
Screenplay by John Mortimer
Cast: Susan Hayward, Diane Cilento, Peter Finch
Played: Stephen Dane

IN THE COOL OF THE DAY
UK 1962
Director: Robert Stevens
Screenplay by Meade Roberts
Cast: Peter Finch, Jane Fonda, Angela Lansbury
Played: Murray Logan

GIRL WITH GREEN EYES
UK 1963
Director: Desmond Davies
Screenplay by Edna O'Brien
Cast: Peter Finch, Rita Tushingham, Lynn Redgrave
Played: Eugene Gaillard

THE PUMPKIN EATER
UK 1964. Made in 1963
Director: Jack Clayton
Screenplay by Harold Pinter
Cast: Anne Bancroft, Peter Finch, James Mason
Played: Jake Armitage
British Film Award for the best screenplay, 1964

FIRST MEN IN THE MOON
UK 1964. Made in 1963
Director: Nathan Juran
Screenplay by Nigel Kneale and Jan Read from the novel by
H. G. Wells
Cast: Edward Judd, Martha Hyer
Played: Baliff's man

JUDITH
US 1965. Made in 1964
Director: Daniel Mann
Screenplay by John Michael Hayes
Cast: Peter Finch, Sophia Loren
Played: Aaron Stein

THE FLIGHT OF THE PHOENIX
US 1965
Director: Robert Aldrich
Screenplay by Lukas Heller
Cast: James Stewart, Richard Attenborough, Peter Finch,
Ronald Fraser, Hardy Kruger
Played: Captain Harris

10.30 p.m. SUMMER
US/Spain 1966. Made in 1965–6
Director: Jules Dassin
Screenplay by Jules Dassin and Marguerite Duras
Cast: Melina Mercouri, Peter Finch, Romy Schneider
Played: Paul

FAR FROM THE MADDING CROWD
UK 1967. Made in 1966
Director: John Schlesinger
Screenplay by Frederic Raphael
Cast: Julie Christie, Peter Finch, Terence Stamp, Alan Bates
Played: William Boldwood

THE LEGEND OF LYLAH CLARE
US 1968. Made 1967
Director: Robert Aldrich
Screenplay by Hugo Butler and Jean Rouverol
Cast: Kim Novak, Peter Finch, Ernest Borgnine
Played: Lewis Zarkin

THE GREATEST MOTHER OF THEM ALL
US 1969. Mini Film of 2 reels
Director: Robert Aldrich
Cast: Peter Finch, Shelley Winters, Alexandra Hay
Played: Errol Flynn

THE RED TENT
USSR/Italy 1969. Made in 1967–9
Director: Mikhail Kalatozov
Screenplay by Ennio De Concini and Richard Adam
Cast: Peter Finch, Sean Connery, Claudia Cardinale, Hardy
Kruger
Played: General Umberto Nobile

SUNDAY BLOODY SUNDAY
UK 1971. Made 1970
Director: John Schlesinger
Screenplay by Penelope Gilliatt
Cast: Peter Finch, Glenda Jackson, Murray Head
Played: Dr Daniel Hirsh
Society of Film and Television Awards for the best actor, 1971
Voted best actor by the National Society of Film Critics USA,
1971
Runner-up for American Academy Award, 1971

SOMETHING TO HIDE
UK 1971
Director: Alastair Reid
Screenplay by Alastair Reid, based on the novel by Nicholas Monsarrat.
Cast: Peter Finch, Linda Hayden, Shelley Winters, Colin Blakely
Played: Harry

ENGLAND MADE ME
UK 1972. Made in 1971–2
Director: Peter Duffell
Screenplay by Desmond Cory and Peter Duffell, based on the novel by Graham Greene
Cast: Peter Finch, Michael York, Hildegard Neil, Michael Horden
Played: Erich Krogh

LOST HORIZON
US 1972
Director: Charles Jarrott
Screenplay by Larry Kramer from James Hilton's novel
Cast: Peter Finch, Liv Ullmann, Sir John Gielgud, Charles Boyer, Michael York, etc.
Played: Robert Conway
Royal Film Performance, 1973

BEQUEST TO THE NATION
UK 1973. Made in 1972 (US title *The Nelson Affair*)
Director: James Cellan Jones
Screenplay: Terence Rattigan
Cast: Peter Finch, Glenda Jackson, Anthony Quayle
Played: Lord Nelson

THE ABDICATION
UK 1974. Made in 1973
Director: Anthony Harvey
Screenplay by Ruth Wolff
Cast: Liv Ullmann, Peter Finch, Cyril Cusack
Played: Cardinal Azzolino

NETWORK

US 1976
Director: Sidney Lumet
Screenplay by Paddy Chayefsky
Cast: Faye Dunaway, Peter Finch, William Holden, Robert Duvall, Beatrice Straight
Played: Howard Beale
American Academy Award for the best actor, 1976. Hollywood's Golden Globe Award for the best actor, 1976. British Academy of Film and Television Arts Award for the best actor, 1977

RAID ON ENTEBBE

US 1976 (Television in the US cinema abroad)
Screenplay by Barry Beckerman
Director: Irvin Kershner
Cast: Charles Bronson, Peter Finch, Horst Buchholz, Martin Balsam, Sylvia Sidney
Played: Yitzhak Rabin

Documentary films

ANOTHER THRESHOLD
Australia 1942 DOI (Department of Information)
Director: Ken G. Hall
Cast: Peter Finch, Muriel Steinbeck, Grant Taylor, Pat Firman
Played: Sergeant Pilot

WHILE THERE'S STILL TIME
Australia 1942 DOI
Director: Charles Chauvel
Cast: Peter Finch, Nola Warren
Played: The Young Soldier

SOUTH WEST PACIFIC
Australia 1943 DOI
Director: Ken G. Hall
Written by Tom Gurr
Played: RAAF Pilot

JUNGLE PATROL
Australia 1944 DOI
Directed and written by Tom Gurr
Narrator: Peter Finch
Chosen by British Ministry of Information for inclusion in a
special series of propaganda films shown in liberated European
countries.

PRIMITIVE PEOPLES
Australia 1947. Educational film for Rank Audio Visual
Director: George Heath
Peter Finch researched and narrated the film

THE DAY
Spain 1960. (Contemporary Films)
Director: Peter Finch
Screenplay by Peter Finch and Yolande Turner
Cast: Antonio Costa
Venice Festival of Children's Films, 1961
Prizewinner in section for adolescents, Cork Festival, 1961

Photographic acknowledgments

The author and publisher have made every effort to trace owners of copyright and apologize to any whom they have been unable to contact. They gratefully acknowledge the following for permission to reproduce the photographs specified:

George Ingle Finch: photograph from his book *The Making of a Mountaineer*

Betty Stavely-Hill: photograph of Major Edward Dallas 'Jock' Campbell; photograph of Peter Finch's mother and brother Michael

Sheila Smart: photograph of herself and Peter Finch, 1940

Mrs Elsa Chauvel: still from *Rats of Tobruk*

Paramount Pictures Corp. © 1953, and Irving Asher: stills from *Elephant Walk*

EMI Films Ltd © 1954: still from *Father Brown*

The Rank Organization Ltd © 1955, and Muriel Box: still from *Simon and Laura*

Flavia Magwood: photograph of Peter Finch aged forty; photograph of herself with Peter Finch

The Rank Organisation Ltd © 1960, and Irving Allen: still from *The Trials of Oscar Wilde*

Rex Features Ltd © 1962: photograph of Peter Finch with Yolande and children

Video Cinematografica S a S © 1969, Vides/Mosfilm, distributed by Paramount Pictures Corp.: still from *The Red Tent* ('*La Tenda Rossa*')

United Artists Corp. and Vecita © 1970, and John Schlesinger: still from *Sunday Bloody Sunday*

Warner Bros Inc © 1974: still from *The Abdication*

NBC television USA and Johnny Carson: photograph from the *Tonight Show*

Index

Note. More than 400 persons are mentioned in the book, and space does not permit the inclusion of all of them in the index. Entries have therefore been confined largely to those contributing personal reminiscences of Finch. Details of directors, scriptwriters, producers and supporting cast will be found in the chronologies under each film or play title. Figures in bold provide a quick finding reference to these chronologies.

363

Elspeth Huxley
Scott of the Antarctic £1.95

Through a close study of Scott's diaries and letters, those of his colleagues and reports of his expeditions, Elspeth Huxley has produced a splendid narrative that follows Scott's progress to his tragic end in the iceworld of Antarctica. A powerful portrait of the great doomed hero of polar endeavour.

'A story not only exciting but pathetic . . . direct and straightforward . . . totally absorbing' EVENING STANDARD

'By far the best account of Scott's life and death that has so far been written' SUNDAY TIMES

Robin Maugham
Conversations with Willie £1.25

Through the last years of his life, Maugham lived in the south of France. Bestselling author, renowned playwright, close friend of Churchill and Coward, he was wealthy, famous, embittered, gloomy, malevolent. Through the sunset decades at the Villa Mauresque, Maugham's nephew Robin recorded the charm, charisma and sardonic wit of 'the most famous author alive . . . and probably the saddest'.

'Brilliant, compassionate . . . a brutally stark portrait' DAILY EXPRESS

Richard Neville and Julie Clarke
Bad Blood £1.50
the life and crimes of Charles Sobhraj

Charles Sobhraj made friends easily. He was charming, witty, good-looking, intelligent. He was also a mass murderer. Born in Saigon, he turned to crime as a boy, his charisma and command of languages making him highly successful in the twilight underworld of smuggling. He lured tourists to his Bangkok flat then killed them off – horribly, by strangulation, burning, mutilation and drowning . . .

'Astonishing' SPECTATOR

'Fascinating in its evocation of dreams, drugs and poverty which characterize the Hippy Trail to the East' TIME OUT

Matthew Vaughan
Major Stepton's War £1.25

Gervase Stepton, a major in the Confederate army, has seen the brutality and experienced the agony that makes a soldier the killing machine he is. Serving under General Lee and the legendary Stonewall Jackson, he fights at the blood-soaked battle of Bull Run. Captured, Stepton suffers savage torture at Fort Delaware. Sure as hell he'll kill the Yankee bastards who slaughtered his family back home in Virginia. A tale of vengeance wreaked from the whorehouses of Richmond to the battlefields of Manassas and Malvern.

Somerset Maugham
The Explorer £1.25

This, Maugham's fourth novel, was first published in 1907 and reveals the hand of a storyteller of genius. Alec MacKenzie iron-willed stoic, vows never to reveal the reason behind the death of a subordinate in Africa. But the publication in the press of a letter accusing him of cowardice forces Alec to decide between keeping his word or forfeiting the love of Lucy – the dead man's sister.

Leslie Thomas
That Old Gang of Mine £1.25

Meet ODDS – the Ocean Drive Delinquent Society – a band of geriatric drop-outs chasing excitement and danger in their twilight years in the Florida sun. There's Ari the Greek, K-K-K-K-Katy the dancing queen, Molly Mandy who supplies the gang's arms cache (and one and only bullet), and ex-hood Sidewalk Joe.

Hot on their heels comes the baffled Salvatore, local police captain, and bumbling private eye Zaharran. Never was organized crime so disorganized.

'Hilarious' DAILY MIRROR

Robin Cook
Sphinx £1.25

Beautiful Egyptologist Erica Baron is mesmerized by a centuries-old statue in a Cairo antique shop, believing she has found the key to a dazzling hoard of untapped treasure. But there are others, more ruthless and corrupt than herself, determined to get there first, whatever the cost. Lost in a deadly web of intrigue and murder, Erica races to unlock the secrets of a pharaoh's tomb and plumb the curse that has kept it intact since time began . . .

Earl Thompson
Caldo Largo £1.50

Johnny Hand is in love with life, freedom and the unbridled pleasures of sex. In the brawling world of seagoing men, every woman in every bed in every port is a challenge – from Lupe, who shrugged off her marriage vows as easily as her dress, to Cehlo, the teenybopper temptress . . . A novel that swells with life and explodes with action – the deadly perils of Cuban gun-running, the scorching love nests of Mexico . . .

'Earl Thompson is an exceptional writer – full of power, able to expose a whole world, to create people who blaze off the page'
COSMOPOLITAN